SAP® Ariba® and SAP® Fieldglass™: Functionality and Implementation

Justin Ashlock

SAP® Ariba® and SAP® Fieldglass™: Functionality and Implementation

Bonn • Boston

Editor Meagan White
Acquisitions Editor Emily Nicholls
Copyeditor Eli Badra
Cover Design Graham Geary
Photo Credit Shutterstock.com/270492944/© pingvin121674
Layout Design Vera Brauner
Production Nicole Carpenter
Typesetting SatzPro, Krefeld (Germany)
Printed and bound in the United States of America, on paper from sustainable sources

ISBN 978-1-4932-1294-1

1st edition 2016

Library of Congress Cataloging in Publication Control Number: 2015034417

Contents at a Glance

Dear Reader,

The days of paper are waning.

While this may seem like a bizarre statement to start off a *book* (though I can picture our e-book readers nodding emphatically), it's clear that when it comes to integrating supply processes, an industry-wide shift is afoot. If the advent of on-premise solutions simplified the paper trail of invoices, purchase order, or records, then cloud solutions like SAP Ariba and SAP Fieldglass have steered it off the ground entirely.

Between these pages you will find all the information you need to get your supplier processes into the cloud with expert advice from author Justin Ashlock and his all-star contributors, Rachith Srinivas and Juan Barrera. They will guide you through your journey away from paper-based processes, answering your questions, large and small. How do I connect with supplier and buyers via SAP Ariba's business network? How do I give and receive discounts? How do catalogs work with SAP Ariba cloud solutions? How do I integrate SAP Ariba with my existing system? The answers are here.

As always, your comments and suggestions are the most useful tools to help us make our books the best they can be. Let us know what you thought about *SAP Ariba and SAP Fieldglass: Functionality and Implementation*! Please feel free to contact me and share any praise or criticism you may have.

Thank you for purchasing a book from SAP PRESS!

Meagan White
Editor, SAP PRESS

Rheinwerk Publishing
Boston, MA

meaganw@rheinwerk-publishing.com
www.sap-press.com

Contents

Preface

Procurement gets scant attention in some companies and great focus in others, but has always been a necessary function of just about every company and government. Corporate procurement departments focus on efficiencies, supplier optimization and partnerships, and, above all, cost savings. Government procurement departments focus on some of the same elements as corporations, but also spend much of their time trying to optimize their procurement practices to avoid the impression of impropriety. Up until the late 1900s, most procurement was conducted using paper.

One of the challenges in paper-based procurement, in addition to the unwieldy forms and drawn out procurement times, is understanding spend and financial positions. When computing began offering electronic means for supporting parts of the procurement process, the goal of having real-time financial postings and the ability to process reams of data for reporting became tangible. The generation of solutions available in the 1990s through the mid-2000s streamlined the paper-based, cumbersome procurement processes and focused on email correspondence and web interfaces, but still required installation, configuration, and maintenance at the customer's physical site. In the cross-company areas of exchanges and markets, locating these procurement systems and processes behind a corporate firewall limits collaboration with the supplier and restricts your ability to acquire up-to-date, internet-based product and pricing information. On-premise solutions are thus at a disadvantage for truly integrated procurement, even before you even look at the maintenance side of the equation. From a maintenance point of view, it is preferable to have all of the customers running on one platform in the cloud, versus having to support multiple versions at different customer sites, as SAP and other software vendors have to do for on-premise implementations.

The future for SAP's procurement solutions is in the cloud, an industry shorthand for internet-based, multi-tenanted solutions accessed via a customer's browser and internet connection. As the leading provider of software and solutions supporting business processes, SAP has defined a wide portfolio of procurement solutions in the cloud, which was enhanced with the acquisitions of Ariba and Fieldglass.

Ariba began as a focused solutions provider for internet-based procurement in 1996. Originally, Ariba offered many of its solutions as on-premise software, similar to SAP SRM and other on-premise SAP solutions. However, by the mid-2000s Ariba began charting a clear direction towards the cloud, buttressed immensely by what was then called the Ariba Supplier Network (now the SAP Ariba Network), along with a suite of cloud solutions.

In mid-2012, SAP announced the acquisition of Ariba. In March 2014, SAP also acquired Fieldglass, provider of the market-leading Cloud Vendor Management System, to further augment contingent and statement of work labor-lifecycle capabilities. SAP Fieldglass VMS has cross-functionality applications with both human resources and procurement, and is thus integrated with SAP Ariba for procurement and with SAP SuccessFactors and SAP Human Capital Management (HCM) for HR uses.

Like a reflecting pool mirroring a grand building, SAP continues to maintain a portfolio of on-premise procurement solutions that support similar procurement processes in the cloud portfolio, with one exception: the SAP Ariba Network. This network is the core collaboration engine for customers and suppliers and has a transaction run rate of three quarters of a trillion dollars with over two million suppliers currently. The SAP Ariba Network underpins SAP Ariba solutions and can be integrated with on-premise procurement projects.

Implementing a cloud procurement solution does not imply that no work is required to roll out this solution at your company. Rather, the focus, project participants, and project phases change. The focus shifts to the business and its business processes up front, rather than Information Technology (IT) landscape issues and software install. The project participants change, as IT's role shifts more to network and integration topics. The business engages earlier and drives the business case definition and resulting key performance indicators.

With systems readily available day one, you can leverage more iterative approaches for setting up parts of the system to the business user's requirements. Supplier collaboration and adoption rates are not an afterthought in these cloud solutions. Business models for SAP's procurement solutions in the cloud acknowledge the importance of supplier participation. This in turn influences the phases. Rather than traditional Kickoff, Blueprint, Realization, Test, and Go-Live phases, and variations thereof, for a cloud project, some of the design and realization phases are blended together. Not all of the requirements need to be defined before configuration in the system can occur. Nor can all of the configuration be done directly by the project team. As this is a cloud environment, core configuration is handled by the Ariba Shared Services organization, as this group is the sole group able to access certain configuration areas of the solution, in the solution.

This book covers SAP Ariba and SAP Fieldglass solutions in detail and lays out project implementation structures and guidelines for running successful implementations in each of the areas. Chapter 9 covers integration topics, when cross-system integration is required. This book provides you with the springboard for launching your SAP Ariba and SAP Fieldglass procurement projects.

Target Audience

This book should be of interest for anyone working with SAP Ariba or SAP Fieldglass, or looking at rolling out procurement solutions in a cloud environment. Business users, procurement managers, and consultants are the primary beneficiaries of this type of book. This book assumes a familiarity with and interest in procurement solutions and terminology, as well as project management and delivery topics around these solutions. For the integration topics outlined in Chapter 9, a more advanced understanding of middleware and technical configuration skills is helpful. Finally, critical reasoning skills in understanding just where these solutions will provide your organization the most value individually and in concert will serve you good stead in this journey.

Objective

This book's focus is on implementing the cloud half of SAP's procurement portfolio, principally SAP Ariba and SAP Fieldglass solutions. These solutions cover a vast area of collaboration and processes between your company and its suppliers. While it is not possible to cover every permutation of configuration in these solutions, this book will provide an in-depth look at each of the solution areas and furnish project-specific guidelines, methodologies, required roles, and timelines.

Structure of this Book

This book is organized into ten chapters. The first half will cover what SAP Ariba calls "upstream" procurement solutions—solutions used to identify, vet, and onboard suppliers, create and manage sourcing events, and award orders and contracts. Beginning with Chapter 4, this book will turn its focus on to the "downstream" parts of the procurement process. By chapter, this book covers the following:

- **Chapter 1: Introduction**
  SAP has made sizeable investments in its procurement solution portfolio. The primary cloud solution offerings in this area are SAP Ariba and SAP Fieldglass. This chapter introduces the various solutions offered by SAP Ariba and SAP Fieldglass in the context of the shift from on-premise procurement solutions to procurement in a cloud-based environment.
- **Chapter 2: Sourcing**
  SAP Ariba Sourcing enables you to develop a sourcing strategy and negotiate, source, and manage the resulting contracts and supplier data. An augmenting solution is SAP Ariba Discovery, which suppliers across the SAP Ariba Network can register with in order to access any new requests for information (RFIs), requests for proposals (RFPs), and requests for quotes (RFQs), collectively known as RFx. This chapter outlines SAP Ariba Sourcing and SAP Ariba Discovery as solutions, and highlights their key functionalities and how to implement them.
- **Chapter 3: Contract Management**
  SAP Ariba's Contract Management provides a powerful platform to efficiently and effectively manage procurement and sales contracts, license agreements, internal agreements and various other kinds of contracts. SAP Ariba Contract Management also automates and accelerates the entire contract lifecycle process, including the contract signature process by enabling digital signatures. Standardize the contract creation, authoring and maintenance process. Strengthen operational, contractual, and regulatory compliance. This chapter reviews the SAP Ariba Contract Management solution and how to implement these features.
- **Chapter 4: Operational Procurement**
  Once a source of supply has been identified and an agreement, such as a contract, has been put in place, it is time to go shopping. This chapter outlines SAP Ariba Procure-to-Pay, SAP Ariba Services Procurement, SAP Ariba Procurement Content, and SAP Fieldglass VMS. It connects the dots between the solutions' functionalities, and shows how to implement them.

- **Chapter 5: Invoice Management**
This chapter covers Ariba's solutions in the area of accounts payable. This includes SAP Ariba Invoice Automation, SAP Ariba Invoice Professional, SAP AribaPay, SAP Ariba Payment Automation, and SAP Ariba Discount Professional. This chapter will outline the solutions' functionalities, business benefits, and implementation approaches.
- **Chapter 6: Supplier Information and Performance Management**
This chapter outlines the SAP Ariba solutions for understanding and managing supplier relationships, with a focus on SAP Ariba Supplier Information and Performance Management (SIPM) functionality and implementation of the various components.
- **Chapter 7: Supplier Collaboration**
The Supplier Collaboration chapter provides an overview of the SAP Ariba Network and discusses the processes for onboarding suppliers using the Ariba Network, the enablement process, and how to become a supplier on the sales side of the Ariba Network.
- **Chapter 8: Spend Analysis**
This chapter outlines SAP Ariba Spend Visibility as a solution and shows how to implement it to get a closer look at procurement operations at large and learn where to make changes. Depending on the SAP Ariba solutions you have implemented, you may also run reports on other areas of procurement, such as sourcing events, contracts, purchase orders, requisitions, and suppliers. However, SAP Spend Visibility, as well SAP Ariba Supplier Information and Performance Management (discussed in Chapter 6 of this book) are the main reporting areas that feature their own focused solution.
- **Chapter 9: Integrating SAP Ariba and SAP Fieldglass with SAP ERP**
SAP Ariba can integrate with SAP ERP via the SAP Business Suite Add-On for PO/IV integration, SAP Process Integration (SAP PI) for the SAP Ariba adapter, and cloud integration toolkits (CI-5 or CI-6) for solutions such as P2P and sourcing. SAP Fieldglass can integrate with both SAP HCM and procurement functionality in SAP ERP, leveraging the same CI route as SAP Ariba. This chapter provides an overview of the integration options, as well as a roadmap for planned integrations to newer products such as SAP S/4HANA.
- **Chapter 10: Conclusion**
This chapter provides a synopsis of the preceding chapters, procurement in general, and makes some predictions for the future of procurement solutions.

References and Resources

The following resources were used as references by the authors in the course of writing of this book and should be referred to for continued learning:

- **SAP Ariba Connect**
  http://connect.ariba.com
- **SAP Product Documentation, Downloads, Service, and RDS Content (Integration)**
  http://service.sap.com
- **SAP Fieldglass**
  https://www.fieldglass.com

Acknowledgments

Many colleagues and friends made significant contributions to this book. In particular, I would like to thank our editors, Meagan White and Emily Nicholls of SAP PRESS, the contributors, Juan Barrera, Director Americas, Western Region, Procurement Line of Business Global Services, and Rachith Srinivas, Platinum Consultant at SAP Ariba. My mentor for all things IT and career—Professor John Leslie King, William Warner Bishop Collegiate Professor of Information and Professor of Information, School of Information, University of Michigan. Craig B. Myers, Global Head of Procurement Services for SAP's Ariba Customer Organization, Balaji Vankadara, VP of North American Ariba Delivery Services, Sahiba Nagpaul, Ariba Consultant, Jason Jablecki, Global Vice President, Ariba Network Integration, Andrea Weinfurt, Fieldglass Content Marketing Manager, Jim McCormack, Global Head of LoB Customer/Procurement SAP GCD, Marko Navala and Raj Alluri, SAP Product Managers for Collaborative Supply Chain, the SRM LoB Practice colleagues Paul Bibb, Matthew Cauthen, Jonathan Chung, John Corcoran, Kim Glaze, Bob Gotschall, Lora Holst, Liliya Kalyenich, Jeff Kurowski, Workman Meeks, Amar Neburi, Tuan Pham, Scott Reagan, Randy Roberts, Alan Salgado, Mary Lane Seigenfeld, Rachith Srinivas, Ramesh Vasudevan, Joe Wolff, and Sasirekha Yuganandhan, and my wonderful wife and son for putting up with the long weekends and writing sessions.

Justin Ashlock
Chicago, IL—November, 2015

This chapter provides an overview of the SAP cloud solutions, as well as SAP-recommended implementation methods.

1 Introduction to SAP Cloud Solutions for Procurement

Procurement solutions have taken a long journey in a short period of time. While there has always been a need for an organization, no matter how small or large, to procure the materials and services needed to fulfill its goals and purpose, in the last 50 years, things have changed immensely. Increased computing power, internet-based trading networks, and algorithmic agility (i.e. software) is driving a revolution in the speed, scale, and efficiency of the procurement process heretofore unimaginable. Since 1972, SAP has been a leader and key driver of many of the changes in business computing for procurement, and with today's shift to cloud-based solutions, SAP continues to play a leading and growing role in the transformation.

At the forefront of cloud procurement are two cloud solution offerings from SAP Ariba and SAP Fieldglass. This chapter will introduce the various solutions offered by SAP Ariba and SAP Fieldglass in the context of the shift from on-premise procurement solutions to procurement in a cloud-based environment. We will walk you through the main considerations in the procurement solutions space in Section 1.1, SAP Ariba and SAP Fieldglass solutions in Section 1.2, cloud, on-premise, and hybrid models in Section 1.3 and Section 1.4, and implementation methodologies for SAP's cloud-based services and solutions in Section 1.5. In the following chapters, you will gain focused insight into the individual solution areas, as well as accelerated project management approaches for each solution, highlighting key objectives and considerations for successful implementation.

1.1 Procurement: From On-Premise Solutions to the Cloud

Starting with paper-based processes, procurement has always been about the buyer understanding the organization's needs and interacting with suppliers to obtain the required materials and services. As with any process, its complexity arises in the steps and details. The main considerations and challenges for the procurement process are:

- **The principal-agent problem**
  How can the organization be sure that the buyer is acting on its behalf, and not the agent's own interests? This is known as the agency problem, or the "principal-agent" problem. At its worst, this conflict of interest can lead to ethical breaches, whereby the agent colludes with the supplier, overcharges the organization for shoddy equipment or services, and pockets the difference with the supplier. An organization merely relying on a buyer's word to act on its behalf only lasts until this trust is violated, at which point the organization seeks to establish the systems of checks and balances.
- **Demand planning**
  Reacting to needs that have already arisen and which the organization needs filled yesterday puts the organization in a tougher negotiating position, vis-à-vis the suppliers, and creates inefficiencies, as divisions and actors for the organization wait for supplies and services to arrive. Some form of demand planning, based on known targets, goals, historical needs, and external factors, is required to alleviate the last-minute, reactive nature of tactical procurement.
- **Suppliers**
  Once the demand has been defined and/or raised, suitable suppliers need to be identified, and a procurement plan put in place. How do you define the group of eligible suppliers, create urgency and competition around your requirements, and arrive at the best price, product, and supplier?
- **Purchase agreements**
  After negotiating with the suppliers and selecting the most suitable one, a contract or purchase order needs to be defined for the particular item/service being procured. This agreement needs to clearly define payment terms and other items, while being usable at an operations level to allow for consumption of the contract.

- **Consumption of goods**
  With the order/contract is in place, the item or service is ready for consumption/deployment by the organization. How do employees find and consume this item with the proper approvals and process? The key is to make the "finding" portion of the process intuitive for the employee, while still conforming to company approval processes and financial regulations
- **Invoicing**
  As a company consumes items following the aforementioned steps, the supplier begins to submit bills for the items, unless the items required payment up front. Either way, a company requires an approach to processing invoices: one that matches the invoices up to actual requests, ensuring that payments made to suppliers reflect the agreement's terms and the amounts actually ordered and delivered by the supplier.
- **Analysis**
  Once payment is verified, this process can start again—ideally smarter this time, leveraging the knowledge gleaned from the preceding procurement cycle. Here, organized data and analytics, as well as the processing power to perform timely analysis on large swaths of transactions and other data, are needed.

Core business processes, such as procurement, are moving to cloud-based solutions at an increasing rate. Procurement lends itself nicely to a cloud model, as continuous interaction between suppliers and customers is required for successful procurement operations. On-premise software could address much of the process requirements from behind a customer's firewall, but when it comes time to interact with the supplier at a system level, phone calls and emails often supplement the lack of capabilities for real-time interaction with the supplier.

From the very beginning of procurement, processes and systems were needed to optimize efficiencies and address the agency problem. Early computer-based systems relied on what was available to address the steps and issues described earlier. Early on, this meant using an on-premise model for the system, as information technology (IT) was largely managed on servers and mainframes within the four walls of the company. SAP R/3 and follow-on versions of SAP ERP brought this approach into real time, allowing finance and buying organizations to understand where orders were and what the financial liabilities would be.

Procurement, at its core, involves tight interaction with entities outside the four walls of an organization, namely with suppliers. As on-premise procurement systems became more integrated with other key SAP ERP modules, such as finance, equal demand grew for integration with outside suppliers. This demand was less simple to address on the on-premise side. Security concerns about opening up high risk areas of the IT infrastructure behind the firewall typically trump supplier access needs. Even upon navigating security concerns, cost-saving pressures on IT departments tasked with building what are essentially standard processes in their in-house environments on an individual basis grow. In these cases, all of the servers, installation, configuration, customization, and administration is carried by the customer. Connecting to a supplier for document exchange is equally cumbersome in electronic data interchange (EDI), as establishing EDI linkages requires individual, point-to-point mapping of the transmission for each supplier, and can take several iterations to set up a single linkage. While the procurement efficiencies offered by on-premise approaches, as well as the integration advantages with the rest of the internal IT landscape, are much better than paper-based transactions, there is also pronounced room for improvements.

1.2 SAP Ariba and SAP Fieldglass

From a process standpoint, the basic areas covered by SAP Ariba and SAP Fieldglass are depicted in Figure 1.1.

The process areas span the full source to procure-to-pay (P2P) process in SAP Ariba and SAP Fieldglass. The main process areas include:

- Find a deal (sourcing): SAP Ariba solutions for this include SAP Ariba Sourcing, SAP Ariba Discovery, SAP Ariba Spend Visibility, and SAP Ariba Supplier Information and Performance Management (SIPM).
- Sign the deal: SAP Ariba Contract Management supports this area.
- Broadcast the deal: SAP Ariba catalogs and SAP Ariba Procurement Content allow for broadcast and selection for consumption of sourced items.
- Buy it: SAP Ariba P2X and SAP Fieldglass support the end-to-end, procure-to-order/pay process for items/services and contingent labor, respectively.
- Be invoiced: SAP Ariba Invoice Automation (part of P2P) and Invoice Professional support this process.

- Pay invoice: SAP Ariba Payment Automation, SAP AribaPay, and SAP Ariba Discount Professional all cover different aspects of this area.
- Network: All of these SAP Ariba and SAP Fieldglass processes and solutions leverage their respective business networks, to varying degrees. At each step, the business network can underpin and augment numerous areas, creating richer and more efficient transactions between buyers and sellers.

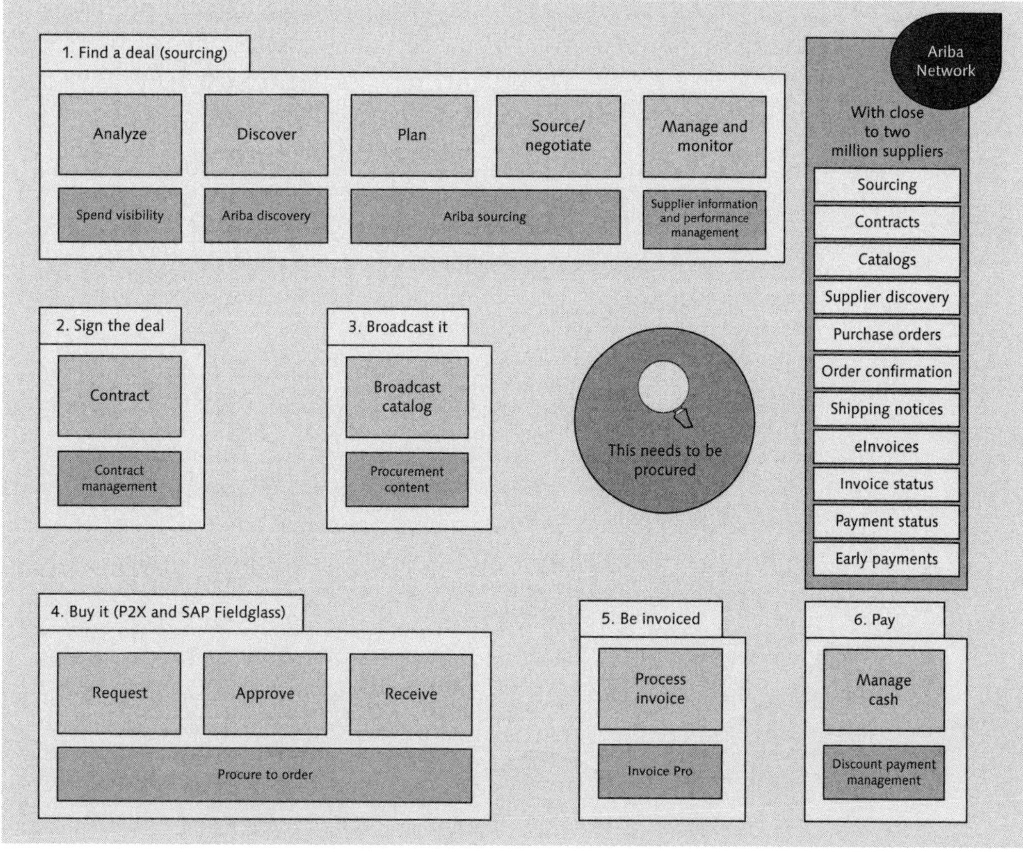

Figure 1.1 SAP Ariba/SAP Fieldglass Solutions Overview

Mobility and intuitive user interfaces also deserve mention. SAP Ariba released two major updates in this area in 2015. The first was a mobile application supporting approvals and basic look ups for SAP Ariba. The SAP Ariba mobile app supports requisition approval, tracking, requisition, and previous approvals viewing.

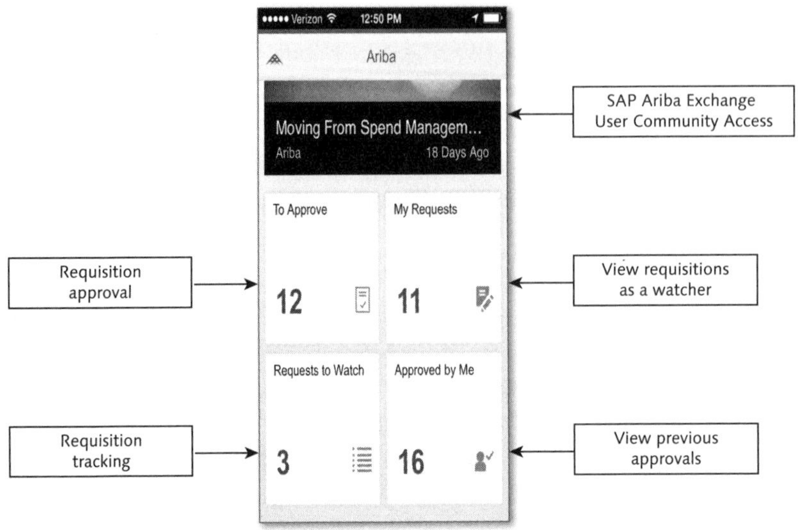

Figure 1.2 SAP Ariba Mobile: Features

The second, now in 14s solutions, was a complete renewal of the user interface. In July 2015, SAP Ariba announced the availability of SAP Ariba Mobile 1.5 for iOS (shown in Figure 1.2) and the renewal of the UI, under an initiative called the SAP Ariba Total User Experience. The SAP Ariba Total User Experience represents a complete paradigm shift in what user experience means—not just for SAP Ariba customers, but also for the industry as a whole, and SAP is delivering that shift through three fundamental tenets:

1. **Work anywhere**
   The user should be able to access SAP Ariba applications anytime and anywhere.
2. **Learn in-context**
   The user can access in-context guides and community expertise from the application.
3. **Modern user experience principles**
   Adoption of SAP Fiori-based user interaction paradigms.

With the this initiative, SAP Ariba incorporates modern user experience principles utilizing SAP Fiori-based user interaction paradigms for a new and improved visual design for all SAP Ariba on-demand solutions. Figure 1.3 provides a glimpse into the new UI.

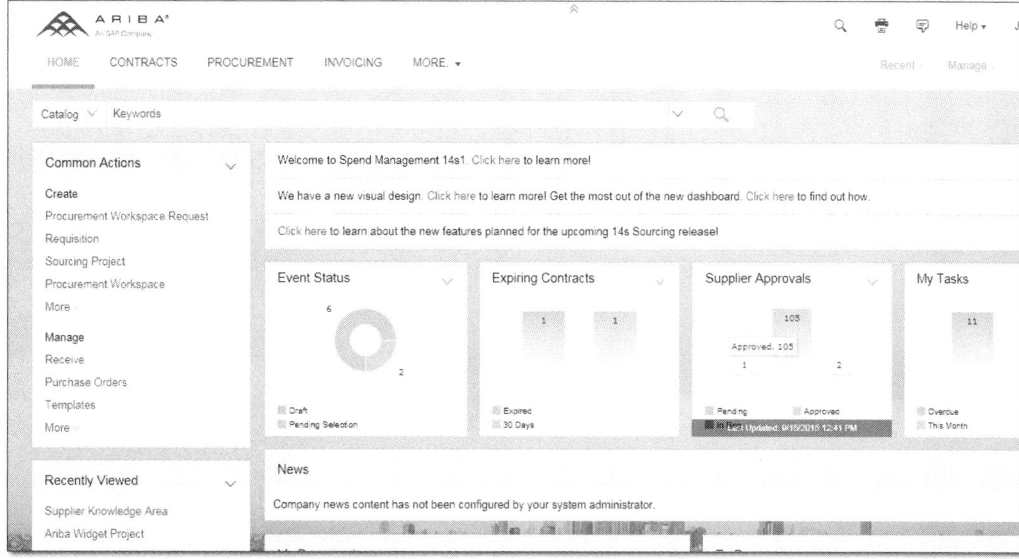

Figure 1.3 SAP Ariba Updated UI Screenshot

1.3 Cloud Solutions at a Glance

For cloud computing and services, an internet connection and a subscription are all that is required. With the advent of cloud computing, both sides of the equation, integration with corporate environments and supplier interaction, are simplified. In addition, the expensive infrastructure supporting a company-specific instance of the software is no longer needed. Procurement also benefits from the network effect: the more suppliers you can access and understand, the better the competition around your purchasing becomes, which leads to finding better suppliers, relationships, and pricing. The more activity and potential customers that suppliers see in a particular network, the more likely they are to join the network, leading to a virtuous cycle. The most obvious example of an offline supplier network of this type is a traditional marketplace, where buyers and sellers come to exchange goods.

Point-to-point networks, a contradiction in terms, were often the only option for on-premise solutions. Here, a customer laboriously sets up each relationship and linkage by supplier, and then broadcasts requirements to individual connections and conducts purchasing transactions with the winning supplier. Networks and online marketplaces are a key argument for cloud solutions in procurement, as you reap the benefits of supplier interaction and competition and avoid the lengthy setup and maintenance requirements of an EDI or other on-premise approach. The SAP Ariba Network is a powerful example of a transaction platform in the cloud, and one of the largest of its kind, with over $500 billion USD in transactions already flowing through this network on an annual basis. Suppliers set up their transmission methods with the network, and new customers transmitting purchasing documents to the supplier do not need to worry about additional setup for transmission methods—it is already all set up and maintained in the network.

Support also is less burdensome in a cloud solution. If something fails to transmit, a supplier needs to register, or an auction needs focused support, the network host can support and resolve any issues not on the internal IT department. If you only use the supplier monthly, or even annually, a supplier record can quickly become out-of-date. When a new order is finally placed, the supplier record may first require updating via phone or email. At worst, the purchase order is issued to an outdated address and the order is not fulfilled in a timely manner. These manual interventions and updating cycles are minimized on the customer-side with a network model. When the supplier updates its record on the SAP Ariba Network, the supplier records for buyers on the network also receive the update.

1.4 Pure Cloud, Pure On-Premise, and Hybrid Models

SAP, with the acquisitions of Ariba and Fieldglass, offers cloud procurement solution counterparts to all of its on-premise solutions, covering all spend types and stages of the procure-to-pay process, as you can see in Table 1.1.

Stage	On-Premise Solutions	Cloud Solutions
Spend Analysis	SAP Spend Performance Management	SAP Ariba Spend Visibility
Sourcing	SAP Sourcing and SAP SRM	SAP Ariba Sourcing and SAP Ariba Discovery
Contract Management	SAP Contract Lifecycle Management and SAP SRM	SAP Ariba Contract Management

Table 1.1 Cloud and On-Premise Solutions Addressing All Spend Types

Stage	On-Premise Solutions	Cloud Solutions
Operational Procurement	Materials Management in SAP ERP and SAP SRM; SAP Commodity Procurement	SAP Ariba Procure-to-Pay, Sap Ariba Services Procurement, SAP Ariba Procurement Content, and SAP Fieldglass Vendor Management System
Invoice Management	SAP Invoice Management by OpenText	SAP Ariba Invoice Management, SAP AribaPay, and Discount Management
Supplier Information and Performance Management	SAP Supplier Lifecycle Management	SAP Ariba Supplier Information Performance Management
Mobile Procurement	SAP Fiori	SAP Ariba Mobile
Supplier Collaboration	N/A	SAP Ariba Network

Table 1.1 Cloud and On-Premise Solutions Addressing All Spend Types (Cont.)

The main solution covering supplier collaboration for both on-premise and cloud, however, is the SAP Ariba Network. While there is an on-premise solution for collaboration, supplier self-services (SUS), SUS is not able to provide the same level of collaboration as the SAP Ariba Network. There are several integration options for connecting your on-premise SAP ERP and/or SAP SRM solutions to the SAP Ariba Network, and interacting with suppliers via the network, while still leveraging your investments on-premise.

Per Figure 1.4, there are numerous ways to integrate SAP ERP with different SAP Ariba and SAP Fieldglass solutions. First, regarding the models available, most companies have existing SAP ERP implementations in place, which house core processes and functions connected to procurement. However, if you are starting fresh, you could house all of your procurement operations and processes in the SAP Ariba and SAP Fieldglass cloud solutions. This would be a pure cloud model. Reasons for going this route, and for leveraging the cloud in general, center on the areas outlined in Figure 1.5: automatic upgrades, standardized processes, accelerated innovation, and technology foundation advantages. As a cloud user, not only are you able to upgrade to the latest release much more easily, the innovation in a cloud solution is also more robust and continuous. In the cloud, if the system shows issues with certain navigation areas, those issues can be identified and addressed for all of the system's users much faster than in the on-premise world.

On-Premise
SAP ERP
SAP Ariba P2P/P2O
The SAP Ariba Network
SAP Fieldglass

Integration technologies:
PI: SAP Process Orchestration
ITK: SAP Ariba Integration Toolkit
HCI: SAP HANA Cloud Integration
D: Direct connectivity via SAP Business Suite Add-On for Ariba Network Integration

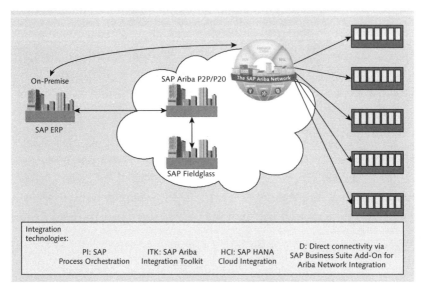

Figure 1.4 SAP Cloud Solutions with SAP ERP Integration Points

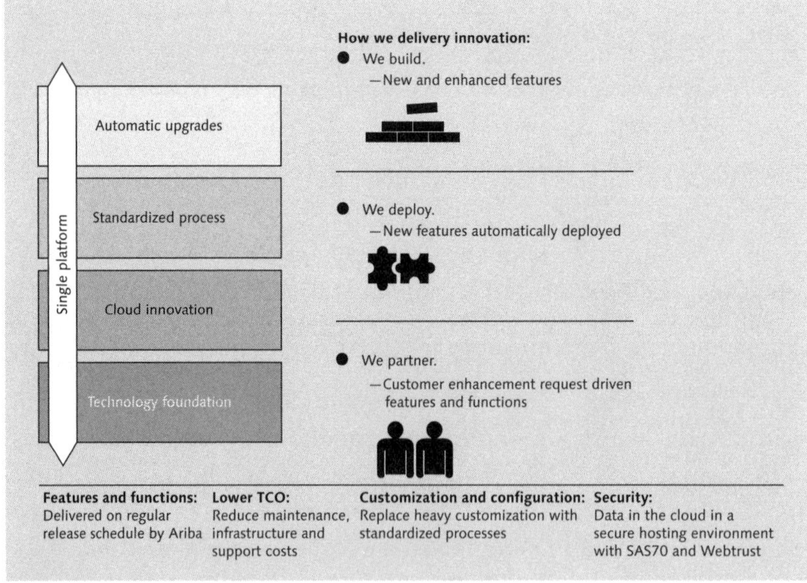

Figure 1.5 Benefits of Moving to On-Demand

However, most companies quickly face the realities of their existing investments and infrastructure when evaluating a pure cloud model. Some public sector enterprises or large corporate customers simply cannot move to a pure cloud model in one, or even multiple, steps, given the complexity of their operations and the expense of moving off of existing investments in IT. These companies may even be inclined to stick with a pure on-premise approach, especially if regulations, high levels of customization, complexity, and/or heavy existing investments in on-premise preclude them from moving to the cloud at this point. By and large, you can mix and match solutions from both of SAP's procurement solution portfolios, based on requirements, landscape/existing environments, as well as regulatory requirements.

In this case, there are still several possible ways to leverage cloud solutions, and doing so typically centers on a "hybrid" approach to cloud solutions. Areas, such as contingent workforce management/vendor management systems with SAP Fieldglass, SAP Ariba Procurement Content, SAP Ariba Network, and SAP Ariba P2X, all provide ample integration options with SAP ERP and SAP SRM to augment existing investments. Chapter 9 of this book discusses integration approaches in more detail.

1.5 Cloud Implementation Model

Managing a cloud implementation project is different from on-premise projects. With less hardware, process permutations, and architecting to consider, more focus can be placed on solving business requirements and issues. In the following sections, we will cover different implementation models for cloud projects.

1.5.1 SAP Activate

The overall implementation methodology for SAP cloud projects is SAP Activate. SAP Activate is a prescriptive and predictable methodology that is lean and fast, while at the same time incorporating the iterative and agile approach where it makes sense, as with configuration and testing. This allows consultants and project team members to lead with best practices and simultaneously involve experts on the business' subject matter in the configuration and testing cycles to ensure that the solution suits their needs.

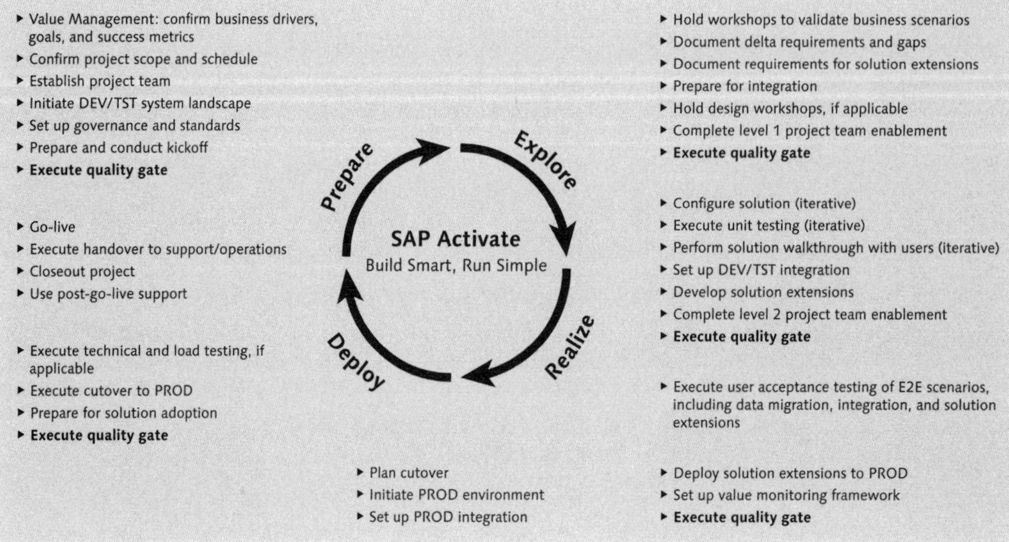

Figure 1.6 SAP Activate Workstreams

Per Figure 1.6, SAP Activate leverages four phases: explore, realize, deploy, and prepare. The main components of the methodology are streams. Streams are collections of tasks required to achieve one or many deliverables, and can span many phases, as in Table 1.2.

Work Stream	Description
Project management	Covers planning, scheduling, governance, controlling, and monitoring the execution of the project.
Solution design	Covers the validation of scope, identification of detailed business process requirements, fit-gap analysis, and functional design of the solution.
Solution configuration	Covers the configuration, setup, and unit testing of the system (without custom development) to fulfill the customer's requirements per solution design. Items that can be configured include, but are not limited to: forms, workflows, user permission/security, screen layout, reports, master data setup, notifications, etc.

Table 1.2 SAP Activate Workstreams

Work Stream	Description
Solution walkthrough	Covers the demonstration of the configured/developed solution to the customer project team, after each iteration cycle, for customer acceptance and identification of adjustments needed for the next iteration.
Integration preparation	Covers identification of integration requirements, integration points, integration approach, and integration solution design.
Customer team enablement	Covers the enablement of the customer project team to work on the project effectively. This includes standard product orientation to prepare the customer for product requirements and design discussions, as well as key user and admin training to prepare the customer for test case development and test execution.
Data migration	Covers the discovery, planning, and execution of moving legacy data to the new system and the archiving of legacy data.
Integration setup	Covers the setup of the integration environment and middleware between the solution and any external systems.
Solution testing	Covers test strategy, planning, test case development, and execution of user acceptance test, integration test, performance test, system test.
Solution adoption	Covers value management, organization change management, and end user training.
Support readiness	Covers the establishment of the helpdesk process, incident management process, post go-live change management process, and user-related operations standards and processes.
System management (N/A to public cloud)	Covers the solution landscape, deployment concept, system architecture, technical system design, environment (development, testing, production, failover) setup, technology operations standards and process.

Table 1.2 SAP Activate Workstreams (Cont.)

Work Stream	Description
Custom extensions management	Covers the design, development, and deployment of system functionality that the standard product cannot provide, and which therefore needs to be custom-developed.
Cutover management	Covers planning and execution of activities to cutover the system into production including the hyper-care support period shortly after cutover.

Table 1.2 SAP Activate Workstreams (Cont.)

SAP ASAP methodology was previously the go-to methodology for SAP project delivery, and SAP Activate maps very accurately to this methodology, as shown in Table 1.3.

SAP Activate Workstream	SAP ASAP Equivalent
Project management	PM: Project Management ALM: Application Lifecycle Management (project standards)
Solution design	BPM: Business Process Management
Solution configuration	
Solution walkthrough	
Integration preparation	TSM: Technical Solution Management (integration design)
Customer team enablement	TRN: Training (project team)
Data migration	DM: Data Migration DA: Data Archiving
Integration setup	TSM: Technical Solution Management (environment setup)
Solution testing	ISM: Test Management
Solution adoption	VM: Value Management
	OCM: Organization Change Management TRN: Training (end user)
Support readiness	TSM: Technical Solution Management (helpdesk process, incident management, change control management) ALM: Application Lifecycle Management (operational standards for process and people)

Table 1.3 Workstreams Alignment—SAP Activate and ASAP

SAP Activate Workstream	SAP ASAP Equivalent
System management (N/A to public cloud)	TSM: Technical Solution Management (solution landscape/ deployment concept, dev/Q, failover environment setup) ALM: Application Lifecycle Management (operational standards for technology)
Custom extensions management	BPM: Business Process Management (custom enhancements)
Cutover management	COM: Cutover Management

Table 1.3 Workstreams Alignment—SAP Activate and ASAP (Cont.)

The streams are grouped into milestones called quality gates (also known as Q-Gates). Examples are the project verification and solution acceptance Q-Gates. Quality gates confirm that all stakeholders of the implementation project agree that specific deliverables meet their requirements, and consequently that the project can continue. The streams that show an ellipsis indicate that other services/streams can be connected, depending on the customer's business requirements. The phases, streams, and Q-Gates establish the sequence of activities as in Figure 1.7.

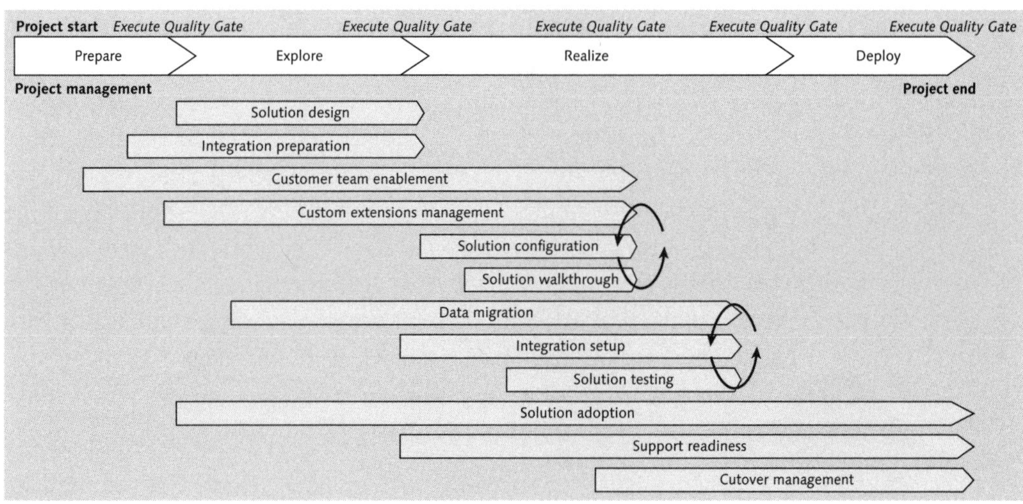

Figure 1.7 SAP Activate Implmentation Methodology

Depending on the solution, SAP Ariba leverages some aspects of this SAP Activate approach, but currently the phases and streams can be somewhat different. This difference is due in part to variable project requirements by solution. For example, in order for the project to be successful, SAP Ariba P2X implementations require significant supplier onboarding, along with supplier and internal user adoption. Typically, supplier enablement is an afterthought for an on-premise project, and the sole responsibility of the customer. In the procurement cloud, where subscription users and supplier participation are paramount and part of the payment model, these streams are fundamental to a project's success. So, in overall comparison to SAP Activate, you will see more emphasis and separate streams set up for supplier and internal knowledge transfer in a focused SAP Ariba project methodology for SAP Ariba P2X. As some phases blend together in this SAP Ariba approach, especially the design and configuration phases, Q-Gate approaches become less frequent, as opposed to with on-premise projects, which have defined, separate phases.

1.5.2 Time-to-Value Acceleration

Combining phases is one of the many ways that cloud solutions seek to quickly deliver value after the decision to implement is made. As cloud solutions do not depend on the installation of software, architecting, and designing of the customer's landscape, nor the baseline configuration setup of the system (the realm arrives ready to go at a baseline level of configuration), this phase of the project is condensed vis-à-vis an on-premise project. As with all projects, and with cloud projects in particular, implementation can move very quickly if both customer and cloud solution provider are in agreement on the urgency of getting the system into production. SAP Fieldglass's subscription model only applies once the suppliers begin submitting invoices via their network, while SAP Ariba begins assessing subscription fees upon signature. In either instance, the customer can elect to exit the subscription at a later date, so there is a strong emphasis on customer satisfaction and providing value from day one, not to mention going live in a timely manner in order to realize these objectives and key performance indicators (KPIs).

Another big difference is the nature of a multi-tenanted cloud environment vs. on-premise software deployments. The customer and consulting resources cannot access all of the areas of the SAP Ariba realm or SAP Fieldglass without going through authorized shared services resources with access to these sensitive areas of the overall systems. Certain changes and modifications to the system could upset the other customer systems running in the cloud, and as such must be carefully shepherded by shared services during the project and in production. This has two main impacts on a project:

1. **Realization phase**
   The realization phase of a traditional on-premise project comprises a significant portion of that project's resources, time, and, ultimately, costs. Tight harmonization of technology deployment, landscape architecting, configuration, and development to simply realize the requirements and business processes defined during blueprint are required during this phase. In a cloud deployment project, much of these areas are either already in place (technology and landscape), or partially in place (configuration and development). In addition, you are more limited in what can be configured and developed in a cloud environment, and thus the decision trees and design process is simplified. In a multi-tenant cloud environment, a customer/project cannot completely subvert a business process, such as procurement, which would be possible when using an off-the-shelf piece of software and changing core code. (Not that this has ever been recommended by on-premise software vendors if you want to maintain your warranty/support). The realization phase in a cloud deployment is thus focused more on business process, asking "what do you want this system to support in your business processes?" It focuses less on the technical minutia of enabling the environment and code. All of this translates into a different type of realization phase.
2. **Larger emphasis on and coordination with SAP Ariba's shared services**
   In an on-premise project, while the resources can be onsite or offsite, you generally have the option to co-locate at the customer site with hardware, software, and the team. In an SAP Ariba OnDemand project, the SAP Ariba shared services team is a core part of the overall delivery and, ultimately, the gatekeeper to the multi-tenant cloud environment hosting the solution. For a basic project, no onsite consulting resources are even required—SAP Ariba shared services can work with the customer on design and deliver the entire project remotely. Table 1.4 outlines the differences in role responsibilities between SAP Ariba Shared Services and onsite consulting.

SAP Ariba Shared Services	SAP Ariba/Partner Consulting Services
Only works on tactical activities directly related to setting up the SAP Ariba applications.	Performs strategic planning and management, as well as activities related to holistic business solution and change management.
Primarily guides and supports customer activities. Only executes activities that the customer can't perform, such as documenting and building certain configurations into the SAP Ariba applications.	Can execute any project activities, including high-bandwidth heavy lifting.
Provides expert information on the configuration and functionality of SAP Ariba applications and generic best practices.	Analyzes customer's specific business challenges and provides expert advice on both holistic business solutions and how the SAP Ariba applications can advance them.
Works 95% remotely.	Works mostly on-site.
Shared across multiple clients.	Usually dedicated to one client at a time.

Table 1.4 SAP Ariba Shared Services and SAP Ariba or Partner Consulting Services

1.5.3 Enhancement and Modification Limitations

As a multi-tenant solution in the cloud, SAP Ariba on-demand and SAP Fieldglass solutions do not offer the flexibility for modification or process-changing customizations to the same degree as on-premise. In an on-premise environment, a customer can reach directly into the code of the application, either via user exits or modifications. The latter has never been a preferred approach, or recommended on projects, as modifications essentially void the warranty on that area of your software, or the entire piece of software altogether. If you call a software provider with a support issue, and you are running heavily modified software, the provision of support received from your software provider may be severely restricted, as the software provider did not build these modifications and is not obligated in standard contracts to support code that the provider did not write. When it comes time to upgrade the release version of your on-premise software, if you have heavily modified the software, a simple upgrade may become intensely complex, requiring significant in-house development, testing, and revising to bring your system into the next release. Given the complexity of upgrading for some customers with modified systems, older releases of software are kept in production well beyond their end-of-lifecycle date on extended maintenance or no maintenance at all; if the customer experiences a system down issue, they have to address the issue with limited support from the provider, which is not usually a preferred risk scenario for the IT department, executives, or otherwise. In general, cloud updates and upgrades roll out on a quarterly basis, whereas an on-premise software customer base typically upgrades every two to three years. Some customers go well beyond that average, running decade-old legacy systems and re-implementing, rather than upgrading, when supporting the legacy system finally becomes unbearable.

For customizations, user exits in the software permit a developer to take action and add functionality to the software that was not in the standard version. These types of customizations can be quite complex and drive significant behavior changes at runtime. If a customer logs a support ticket, they still can obtain software on the rest of the package, as the software provider has created this user exit as an area in the software for additional customizations, and can quickly determine whether the behavior/error is a bug in the provider's code, or due to the user exit code. If the customer's user exit code proves to be the source of the error, the onus is on the customer to address the error. If the code issue is found to be in the software itself, SAP typically fixes the code and issues a note to address the discrepancy, which the customer applies to their system. During a software upgrade, adjustments and testing may be required for the user exits in order to migrate your customizations to the new version or release, but an upgrade is less arduous in this case than with modified software.

In an on-demand environment, there is one code base to a degree, so you cannot modify the software (which is typically a good thing), nor can you customize to the same degree via user exits. However, you do have significant customization latitude via the configuration, and some limited user exit-type code access points for interplay with the main codebase of the solution. Not all customization is switch- and table-driven in SAP Ariba and SAP Fieldglass, but the nature of the cloud model restricts the options for customization and modification. This is a trade-off, it but also instills discipline in following best practices and standards driven by the centralization of the system. In exchange for significantly reduced upfront investment, ease of exit, no capitalization/assetization of investment, maintenance requirements, accelerated implementation times, ease of updates/upgrades, and general peace of mind that you will not be stuck in a system dead end and have to re-implement, you do not have the same ability as in on-premise to completely change the solution.

1.6 Summary

Solutions for procurement have evolved dramatically since the early days of computing. We are now at another inflection point, where whole procurement process areas are moving to cloud-based solutions, and real-time analysis is possible in the transaction system via in-memory database solutions like SAP HANA. Business networks, mobile, big data, and the Internet of Things are also core themes and trends for procurement. With SAP Ariba and SAP Fieldglass solutions for cloud, as well as its rich background and install base for SAP ERP environments and supplier relationship management (SRM) procurement suites, SAP covers both on-premise and cloud with end-to-end solution portfolios. This book outlines SAP's procurement cloud products, implementation approaches, and integration strategies for deploying these SAP solutions optimally for your company.

SAP Ariba Sourcing includes an array of augmenting solutions, from SAP Ariba Spot Buy to SAP Ariba Discovery. These solutions, in addition to the SAP Ariba Network, form the sourcing platform described in this chapter.

2 Sourcing

With SAP Ariba Sourcing, you develop a sourcing strategy and negotiate, source, and manage the resulting contracts and supplier data. Its sister solution is SAP Ariba Discovery, which suppliers across the SAP Ariba Network can register with in order to access any new requests for information (RFIs), requests for proposals (RFPs), and requests for quotes (RFQs), collectively known as RFx, that you issue in their areas of coverage. This chapter outlines SAP Ariba Sourcing and SAP Ariba Discovery as solutions, and highlights their key functionalities and how to implement them.

A strategic approach to sourcing is essential for achieving immediate needs, as well as for sustaining enterprise-wide cost reductions. Locating a supplier and pricing an item is simply not enough: sustainable savings come from identifying cost-cutting opportunities, defining and executing a supplier selection process, and creating contracts that convert these facets into actual savings. This requires being able to evaluate the total cost impact of sourcing decisions while shortening the amount of time and effort spent on administrative tasks.

Effective supplier discovery and supplier information management are critical for the sourcing process to generate sustainable results, yet many organizations struggle to keep their supplier information current. Strategic sourcing provides the single greatest opportunity to impact the cost, quality, and performance of the supply chain, and is among the quickest paths to lowering costs and increasing revenues. But increased globalization, soaring energy and commodity costs, and tightening supply markets have kept many companies from achieving their full sourcing potential.

2.1 SAP Ariba Sourcing

SAP Ariba Sourcing is designed to help companies overcome challenges in supplier information management. A unique software-as-a-service (SaaS) solution, SAP Ariba Sourcing is the most-widely adopted and complete strategic sourcing offering in the marketplace, and is used by thousands of companies to create and implement competitive best-value agreements.

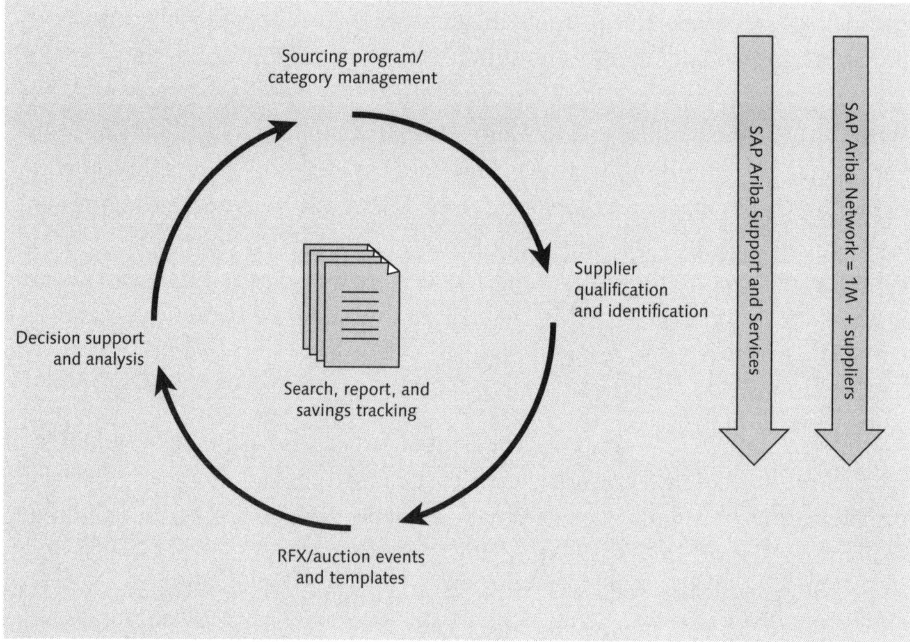

Figure 2.1 SAP Ariba Sourcing

Per Figure 2.1, by combining best-in-class sourcing and negotiation technology with access to a global network of suppliers and unparalleled strategy and category expertise, SAP Ariba Sourcing enables companies of any industry, size, or geography to drive fast, sustainable results by automating and streamlining critical tasks across the sourcing lifecycle. These tasks include:

1. **Strategy development**
   Identify savings opportunities, assess market dynamics, and develop an informed sourcing strategy.

2. **Sourcing and negotiating**
   Identify and qualify suppliers, negotiate best-value agreements, derive optimal award allocations, drive project collaboration, standardize processes, and manage knowledge.
3. **Monitoring and managing suppliers and agreements**
   Quickly implement supplier agreements, track and realize savings, and manage supplier performance.

SAP Ariba Sourcing delivers frequent innovation to ensure speed, consistency, and repeatability, and its use is not limited by organization size or industry. SAP Ariba customers have leveraged this solution to connect with suppliers in over 500 categories, reduce their costs, and cut process and cycle time.

In the following sections we will cover the two versions of SAP Ariba Sourcing, SAP Ariba StartSourcing and SAP Ariba Sourcing Professional, how indirect procurement works as a sourcing strategy in SAP Ariba, and three sources of supply assignments: manual, RFx, and auctions.

2.1.1 SAP Ariba StartSourcing and SAP Ariba Sourcing Professional

There are two versions of SAP Ariba Sourcing available: SAP Ariba StartSourcing and SAP Ariba Sourcing Professional. In this section we will cover the features of both versions individually, and then transition into coverage of the features available in both version, the RFx creation and management process within SAP Ariba Sourcing, and the community and support options for this solution.

SAP Ariba StartSourcing

SAP Ariba StartSourcing is the basic version of SAP Ariba Sourcing, and has the following features:

1. **Dashboard**
   The dashboard surfaces significant, actionable, and relevant user content to role-based user dashboards.
2. **Basic event management**
   This feature includes:

- A wizard with templates for creating standard events of various types, including requests for information (RFIs), requests for proposals (RFPs), and reverse and forward auctions
- A sourcing library that stores documents and customer-created standard event content such as questionnaires, lots, line items, and past event content
- Event content uploads in Microsoft Excel files
- HTML text formatting in event content, including bold, italics, underlining, bulleted lists, and active URLs to allow users to clearly convey event information to suppliers
- Flexible, competitive event rules and features such as starting gates, forced bid decrements, bid buffers, ceiling, floor, and initial prices, and tie bid control
- Multi-stage event process
- Event monitoring interface
- Events published to SAP Ariba Discovery, where new suppliers can find them
- Supplier participation through one-click bidding and uploading bids in Microsoft Excel files at line or lot level
- Supplier profile information storage and event invitation capabilities
- Suppliers who participate in events register with the SAP Ariba Commerce Cloud

Note

Users must create SAP Ariba Discovery postings for all events for which they wish to receive responses—postings are not created automatically during the RFx process.

3. **Communications**
   This feature includes:
   - Event messages: the MESSAGE tab in the event monitoring interface stores all event messages. Suppliers and buyers can communicate using event messages; buyers can provide event-related information and suppliers can ask questions and receive answers
   - Private messages: users can send messages to all suppliers or to other buyers on the event team

- Notifications: customer sites generate a number of automatic notifications related to invitations, changes to events, event closings, awards, and so forth

4. **Reporting**

   Reporting capabilities include:

   - Reporting on individual events during event monitoring
   - Supplier activity reporting
   - Audit log reporting
   - RFI reporting
   - Standardizing sourcing processes using templates

SAP Ariba Sourcing Professional

The SAP Ariba Sourcing Professional solution includes process management features that allow organizations to control sourcing projects from the planning stage to the awarding of individual events.

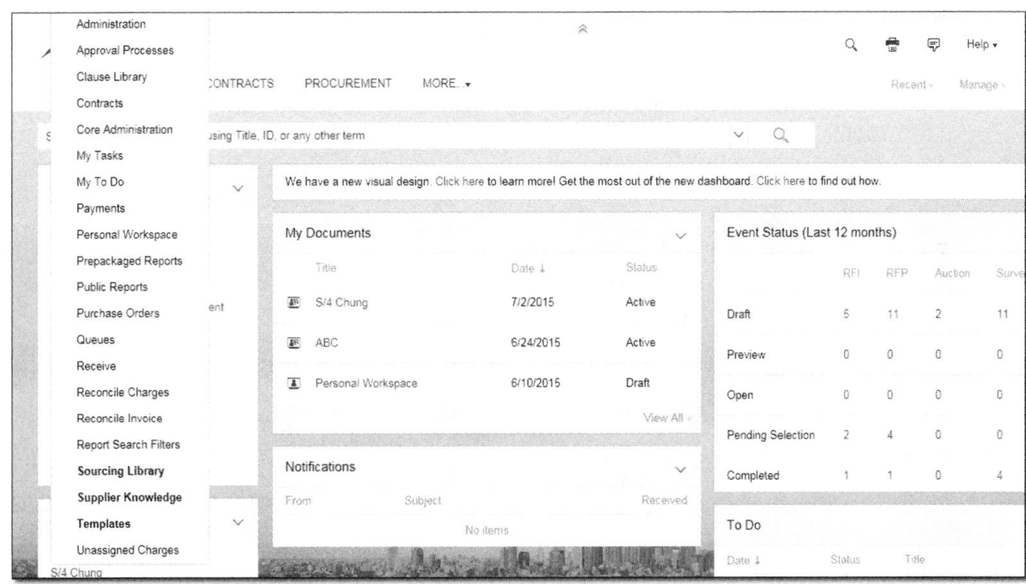

Figure 2.2 Sourcing Main Menu Screen

Per Figure 2.2, SAP Ariba Sourcing Professional goes beyond the SAP Ariba Start-Sourcing capabilities with more robust, customizable functionality for complex sourcing activities, while including the core features of Sap Ariba StartSourcing, such as:

1. **Dashboard**
   The dashboard surfaces significant, actionable, and relevant user content to role-based user dashboards. Users can personalize content by dragging and dropping that content on their active dashboards.

   Dashboards can include:

   - A personal calendar for each user.
   - SAP Ariba data, such as watched sourcing projects, event status, announcements, to do lists, and document folders that users can add to their dashboards.
   - Company news content that displays important information to users. This content can show data from RSS feeds, and customers can configure this news content for their sites.
   - Users can create multiple dashboards that cover different strategic areas.

2. **Basic event management**
   Basic event management drives off of a wizard with templates for creating standard events of various types, including RFI, RFP, reverse and forward auctions, total cost auctions, index auctions, and bid transformation auctions. It also contains the following:

   - A sourcing library that stores documents and customer-created standard event content, such as questionnaires, lots, line items, and past event content
   - Event content uploads in Microsoft Excel files
   - HTML text formatting in event content, including bold, italics, underlining, bulleted lists, and active URLs allows users to clearly convey event information to suppliers
   - Flexible, competitive event rules and features such as starting gates, forced bid decrements, bid buffers, ceiling, floor, and initial prices, and tie bid control
   - Multi-stage event process
   - Event monitoring interface
   - Events can be published to SAP Ariba Discovery to find new suppliers

Note

SAP Ariba Discovery is a service that allows buyers to find new suppliers, read profile information and feedback about suppliers, and access other supplier information. SAP Ariba Discovery is not a part of the sourcing solution to which you subscribed, but rather a separate service. In some circumstances, you can access SAP Ariba Discovery from different SAP Ariba solutions. SAP Ariba Discovery is currently free for buyers. Before you first access SAP Ariba Discovery, you will be asked to accept the online Terms of Use applicable to SAP Ariba Discovery, and those terms will apply if you choose to proceed and use SAP Ariba Discovery.

- Supplier participation through one-click bidding and uploading bids in Microsoft Excel files at line or lot level
- Automatic or manual scoring and team grading of events
- Supplier profile information storage and event invitation capabilities
- Suppliers who participate in events register with the SAP Ariba Commerce Cloud

3. **Advanced event management**
   This feature includes:
   - Custom event templates with custom formulas, item definitions, event rules, and item rules
   - Advanced event types, such as Dutch auctions, which allow buyers to specify an initial lot price and then incrementally raise it until the supplier accepts
   - Matrix pricing for more advanced pricing negotiations
   - Serial and parallel lot timing rules
   - Post-event decision support with constraint-based optimization scenarios
4. **Project management and workflow**
   This feature includes:
   - Sourcing process management using projects with tasks and phases, project teams, documents, milestones, dependencies, review and approval flows, sub-projects, and predecessor and follow-on projects
   - Custom project templates to capture and enforce best practices. Figure 2.3 can be configured to show different data fields and customer-specific processes
   - Automatic project configuration based on project attributes and conditional question responses

- Detailed tasks with descriptions at each step of a process support consistency, learning, and self-sufficiency, and enforce company policies; review and approval workflows provide visual status indicators

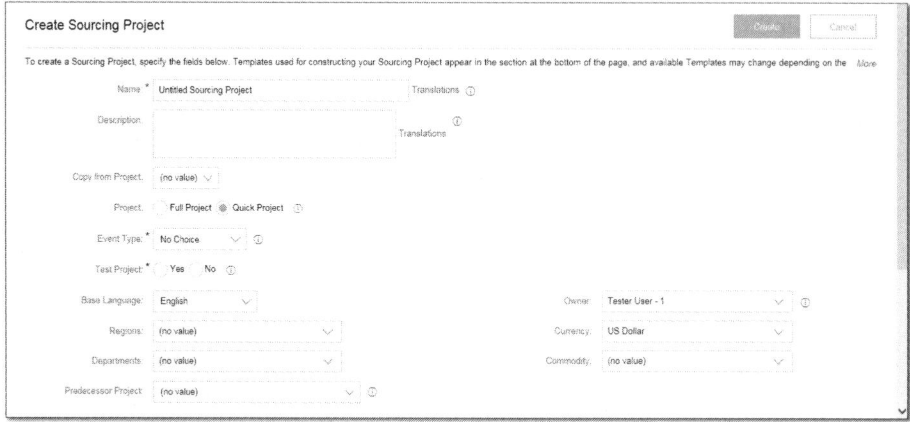

Figure 2.3 Sourcing Project Request

5. **Document management**
   This feature includes:
   - A repository for all documents related to projects or category knowledge areas
   - Both individual projects and the sourcing library enable easy document collaboration, sharing, and management with version control, commenting, and an audit trail
   - Knowledge and resource management
   - Both the sourcing library and project templates capture organizational and category knowledge for re-use
   - Projects and project reporting show user priorities and staff availability, and provide team management tools for deploying users across multiple projects
6. **Communications**
   This feature includes:
   - Event messages: the MESSAGE tab in the event monitoring interface stores all event messages. Suppliers and buyers can communicate using event messages: buyers can provide event-related information, and suppliers can ask questions and receive answers

- Private messages: users can send messages to suppliers or to other buyers on the event team
- Project messages: project message boards facilitate communication between project team members
- Notifications: customer sites generate a number of automatic notifications related to invitations, changes to events, event closings, awards, project tasks, and so forth

7. **Reporting**
   Reporting capabilities include:
   - Reporting on individual events during event monitoring
   - Cross-event reporting
   - RFI reporting
   - Supplier activity reporting
   - Audit log reporting
   - Project and project task reporting
   - Custom analytical reporting, including reporting across multiple fact tables
8. **Third-party integration**
   SAP Ariba Sourcing Professional also provides a way for customers to integrate their SAP Ariba solutions with third-party systems either through web services or file-over-HTTPS transfers so that event owners can quickly create and update their events based on item masters and send or report results back to third-party systems. Third-party integration can:
   - Automatically update department, commodity, user, supplier, exchange rate, and other master data.
   - Provide single sign-on to SAP Ariba solutions and third-party systems.
   - Update third-party contract systems with SAP Ariba data.
   - Copy documents between third-party document systems and SAP Ariba solutions.
   - In addition to document copy, URL documents in SAP Ariba solutions can point to objects in third-party systems, and you can create hyperlinks ("web-jumpers") to connect third-party systems to documents and projects in SAP Ariba solutions. SAP Ariba Sourcing Professional also includes standard integration with SAP ERP.

Sourcing Events: Features and Navigation

Sourcing events typically start by leveraging previously used templates, suppliers and processes. SAP Ariba Sourcing follows this approach for both versions with numerous features that allow for reuse and further refinement of knowledge and approaches gleaned from previous sourcing events. These features include the following:

- **Sourcing templates**
  A template, such as the one in Figure 2.4, serves as a starting point for a project. Users must select a template to create a full or quick sourcing project. Templates are pre-populated with documents, tasks, and team members. Template authors can also set conditions in templates to automatically display or hide content according to information such as location, commodity, or other project attributes.
- **Create and manage project documents**
  Sourcing projects provide centralized storage locations where users can store and manage multiple versions of project documents. Sourcing managers can also pre-populate sourcing project templates with documents to standardize their use across multiple projects.

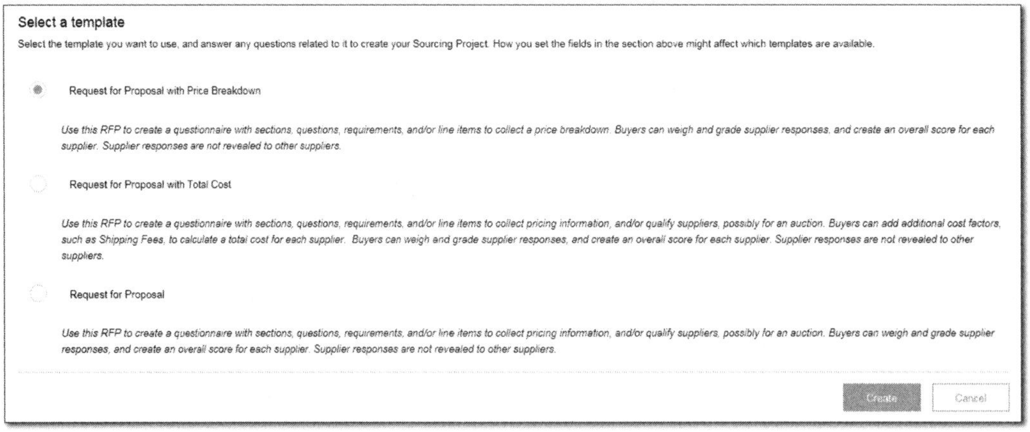

Figure 2.4 Sourcing Templates

- **Setup and launch sourcing events**
  Allows you to create and run sourcing events in which sourcing users can exchange business information with other companies. Some types of sourcing

events that can be created using SAP Ariba Sourcing are request for information (RFI), request for proposal (RFP), auction events, etc.

- **Send email notifications**
  The system can be configured to send an email to notify users when projects are started, completed, or modified, as well as when users are assigned to tasks.
- **Organize and standardize workflow**
  The system can be configured to setup milestones tasks, predecessor tasks, and follow-on tasks to standardize workflow and make sure that parts of the project are completed before others start.
- **Automatically track savings**
  Integration between SAP Ariba Sourcing and SAP Ariba Contract Management can help organizations create savings tracking forms to automatically track savings for procurement contracts that are, or which will be, associated with sourcing projects.
- **Create reports**
  Users can create reports about contract projects using data from multiple contract fields that is filtered, sorted, and compared in multiple formats.

As discussed earlier in the chapter, you are not limited to reporting solely off SAP Ariba data. With SAP Ariba Sourcing, you can integrate not only with other SAP Ariba solutions, but also with third party systems that use Web services and file channels.

RFx Creation and Management

SAP Ariba Sourcing includes a broad set of RFx types, including RFI, RFP, reverse auctions, and forward auctions. There are a number of features supporting and accelerating these core request processes in SAP Ariba Sourcing, including:

- **Integrated supplier discovery**
  SAP Ariba Sourcing enables searching on suppliers based on commodity codes, geography, and numerous other data points. SAP Ariba Discovery allows for expanding RFx postings to suppliers in the SAP Ariba Network.
- **Rapid RFx creation**
  Templates can be converted immediately into official RFxs.

- **Competitive bidding and timing options**
  SAP Ariba Sourcing allows competing suppliers to see current winning bids, countdowns, and timing.
- **Sealed envelope bidding, Dutch auctions, and total cost events**
  Sealed envelope bidding allows for bids to be opened all at once, so as not influence the bid process—commonly used in public sector RFx processes. In a Dutch auction, the price is increased until a willing supplier steps forward. In a total cost event, a supplier can define and edit the line item costs, which are then summed for the total cost of the bid. A transformation event only allows for bidding on the total price, so suppliers and the RFx owner only see the total price and not line-by-line items.
- **Matrix and tiered pricing**
  With matrix pricing, suppliers define pricing for an item to customers, based on customer attributes, such as customer size, geography, purchasing volumes. Tiered pricing typically turns on volumes, where at certain volume thresholds, the price for the item changes.
- **Bid optimization and decision support**
  Unlike many on-premise solutions, SAP Ariba Sourcing has live support to assist in complex bidding events and processes as seen in Figure 2.5.

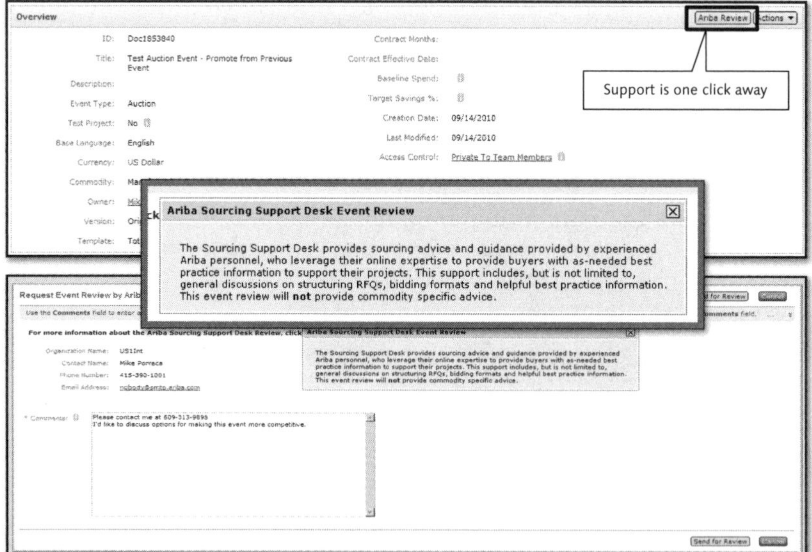

Figure 2.5 SAP Ariba Sourcing Live Support

- **Flexible supplier bidding options including buyer and supplier bundles**
  This allows supplier to bid on parts of the RFx, if enabled as an option, and propose bundles of items in response to a single request.
- **Supplier response management**
  There are numerous options in SAP Ariba Sourcing for communicating with suppliers and processing responses.
- **Team grading and collaborative scoring**
  Many RFxs require collaboration between diverse business units to create and manage. For example, purchasing, engineering, and finance may work together at various times of the RFx, in order to procure a complex item in the most cost efficient way possible.
- **Conditional content, table questions, and event prerequisites**
  Conditions can be created in SAP Ariba Sourcing to manage RFx content, questions, and event qualification.
- **Communications and messaging**
  Communications options and messaging are available pre-, post-, and day-of RFx event management. This includes general message posting and email.
- **Global, multi-lingual, and multi-currency capabilities**
  Suppliers can log into bidding events globally, in multiple languages, and submit bids in multiple currencies.
- **Category management**
  Managing by category allows for a particular category of material or service to trigger activities in sourcing. For example, all IT purchasing needs to go to RFx.
- **Project management**
  SAP Ariba Sourcing includes sourcing project management with the ability to embed best practice sourcing processes, include collaborators, and integrate follow-on activities such as further RFxs and contracts.
- **Workflow and approval**
  Approvers can be brought in during all the main steps of the process.
- **Document and knowledge management**
  Managing RFxs in SAP Ariba Sourcing allows for document management, including attachments and supporting documentation, as well as the building of a knowledge base, as each RFx conducted enriches your repository of possible templates and playbooks for future sourcing activities.

- **Resource management**
- **Sourcing analysis and reporting**
  Using analysis and reporting in SAP Ariba Sourcing, one customer was able to quantify the value of having additional bidders participate in sourcing events Figure 2.6.

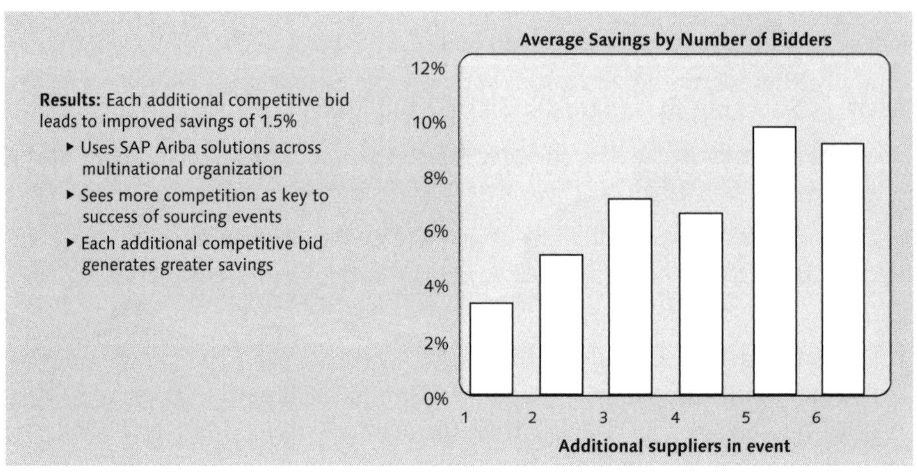

Figure 2.6 SAP Ariba Sourcing Customer Analysis—Adding a Bidder

- **Integration to third-party systems using web services and file channels**
- **Savings pipeline and tracking**
  Includes reporting data access control for savings forms, dForms, surveys, scorecards and sourcing events.
- **Category playbooks integrating SAP Ariba expertise**

Community and Support

The toolsets and resources surrounding SAP Ariba Sourcing from a network and community perspective include:

- Integrated access to the SAP Ariba Network for supplier discovery, qualification, risk assessment, and competitive negotiations
- A peer benchmarking program with dedicated customer success teams
- Access to SAP Ariba Exchange, a community designed to drive networking and best practice sharing and accelerate adoption

In the event that you require additional support, SAP Ariba offers further services as part of its delivery portfolio. These services include:

- Expertise and best practices delivered via a flexible delivery model ranging from onsite consulting to web-based templates
- Bundled empowerment support services, including basic product support, event day management, and a sourcing support desk

2.1.2 Sourcing Strategies in SAP Ariba: Indirect Procurement

Indirect procurement differs from direct procurement in that the items are not used directly in a product produced by the company. Rather, indirect procurement items are used to support and enable the business processes a company uses to deliver their products to market. Indirect procurement is one of the primary focuses of SAP Ariba solutions. Recently, with the introduction of SAP Ariba Collaborative Supply Chain, direct procurement is being further integrated and expanded into the SAP Ariba Network.

Sourcing in SAP Ariba, whether indirect or directly materials-related, leverages the same toolset. SAP Ariba Sourcing uses specific vocabulary for sourcing activities and functionality in the system. The key terms are:

1. **Project**
   A *project* is a specific plan/design that accomplishes a defined set of goals and objectives in a given timeframe, usually with defined stages, and with designated deliverables. This term is usually referenced in sourcing and knowledge projects.
2. **Workspace**
   A *workspace* is a specific plan/design that accomplishes a defined set of goals and objectives in a given timeframe, usually with defined stages, and with designated deliverables. This term relates primarily to contract workspaces or supplier workspace.
3. **Header attributes**
   Header attributes are the key data elements that a user enters when creating a project. These data elements drive content within the project through the use of conditions, provide information to project stakeholders, and provide key data from which to report in the analysis module.

Header attributes are the data elements captured on the CREATE PROJECT screen and are also editable within the project's OVERVIEW tab. These fields are used for informational purposes, reporting, and searchability within a project via conditions.

4. **Custom header attributes**
   Custom header attributes are the custom fields that you are able to add to the HEADER ATTRIBUTES section. You are typically allowed a defined number of flex fields based on your statement of work with SAP Ariba for each sourcing, contracts management, and supplier performance management project.
5. **Flex fields**
   Flex fields are the custom fields that you are able to add to the HEADER ATTRIBUTES section.
6. **Project overview**
   The OVERVIEW tab displays the project's header-level information. There are also sections of the OVERVIEW tab that display project announcements, shortcuts to frequently used documents, and a high-level summary of the project schedule.
7. **Sourcing library**
   The *sourcing library* serves as a repository for RFx content and documentation. Users can access the library during RFx events in order to add content, or they can access it outside of an event in order to view any local policies, practices, etc. Each region will have its own folder in the sourcing library, which can be used to store localized content and documentation.
8. **Tasks**
   Phases, sub-phases, milestones, and tasks are presented to a user in an expandable/collapsible format (e.g. Microsoft Explorer). Phases, sub-phases, milestones and tasks are clearly distinguishable via icons and text.

   Some tasks are identified by the template as required tasks. The project owner may not cancel (hide) these tasks. Any tasks not identified by the template owner as required tasks may be cancelled (hidden) from the project task list by the project owner.

   Default tasks are never deleted from a project, but rather cancelled (hidden) by the project owner. If the project owner needs to later add any cancelled (hidden) tasks back to the project, he may un-cancel (un-hide) them. By default, all tasks are assigned to the project owner. However, the project owner will be able to re-assign tasks to specific team members.

Any team member with write access to the project may add additional tasks to the project. The descriptions of these tasks are input as freeform text by the creator. Only the project owner may hide (cancel) tasks within the project.

When viewing the details of a task, the DESCRIPTION field provides further details about the task.

9. **Task dates**
   Tasks can be assigned a specific due date, or can initiate based on the completion of a previous task or milestone. For example, if you designed a task called "File Tax Return," you would assign it a fixed due date of April 15th.

10. **Project teams**
    The TEAM tab of a project displays the project's team members and the associated group(s) of each member. The project owner may add team members to a project by searching and selecting users from this list. If the status of a project is either cancelled or complete, then no new team members can be added to the project. Only the project owner has the ability to add or remove team members from a project.

11. **Project/workspace documents**
    The DOCUMENTS tab of a project is where all documents related to the project are stored. Via the project's selected template, unpopulated documents (RFxs, spreadsheets, etc.) will be automatically placed into the project's DOCUMENTS tab when the project is created.

    The DOCUMENTS tab is broken into two sections—a listing of all documents on the bottom half of the screen, and a QUICK LINKS section on the top half. The QUICK LINKS section simply provides shortcuts to commonly used documents on the bottom half of the screen. The QUICK LINKS section gives users the flexibility to avoid repetitive searching through a multi-level folder structure for a common document (e.g. commodity strategy documentation). The project's template also defines an initial folder structure for the bottom half of the screen, and dictates which documents are placed into the QUICK LINKS section.

12. **Knowledge projects**
    Knowledge projects are separate projects that run outside of the sourcing process with the sole intent of serving as a document repository for important supplemental content for the sourcing, contract, or supplier performance management (SPM) processes. Knowledge project owners can set up the documents to display within a sourcing, contract, or SPM project, depending on

the commodity, department, and/or region associated with the project. These documents can show at a project, phase, and/or task level.

13. **Project groups**
    A role is a set of specific system permissions which can be assigned to groups and users. Users gain system permissions through their role assignments, either directly as users or indirectly through their membership in a group. Certain roles are required in order to perform certain tasks in SAP Ariba Sourcing Professional. These roles can be assigned to groups and users that are added to the system.
14. **Conditions**
    Conditions are logical constructs that trigger whether or not a particular field, document, or task is included in a project created from a template. Conditions have no use on their own—they only control field, document, task, or team inclusion in created projects when they are linked to questions or fields.
15. **Template questions**
    Questions in the template can be customized and/or added to drive your specific task-based processes and scenarios.
16. **Questions and answers**
    Questions in SAP Ariba Sourcing Professional help define specific project content for a given template during project creation. Questions, when used in combination with conditions, make the definition of project conditions for a specific project more user friendly. Answers are predefined responses to questions in templates. Answers may be used to trigger conditions; whether an answer is visible is controlled by its visibility condition.
17. **Access control**
    Access controls can be set for a project, document, or RFx content in order to control visibility to the appropriate internal parties. For a project, this is set on the OVERVIEW tab; for a document, it is set in the ATTRIBUTES section; and for RFx, content is controlled at the individual section or item (question, requirement, etc.) level.

    There are the different access controls available for a sourcing project, or a document within a sourcing project. However, sourcing agents can set any project to PRIVATE TO TEAM MEMBERS by changing the ACCESS CONTROL of the sourcing project. Figure 2.7 shows the various tabs, including the TEAM tab, which form the structure of the sourcing event.

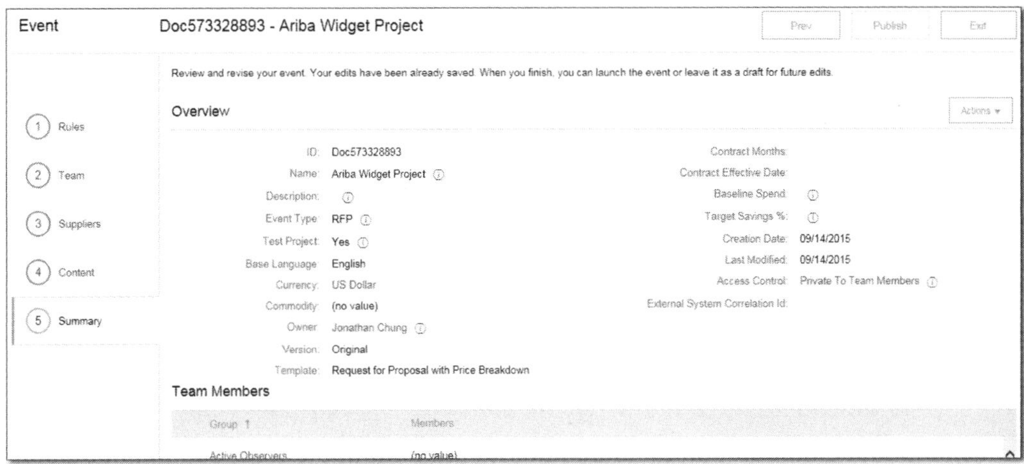

Figure 2.7 Sourcing Event Summary

18. **On-demand sourcing (OnD)**
    The SaaS model of SAP Ariba Sourcing Professional is the main deployment option for SAP Ariba Sourcing at this time. SAP also offers several on-premise options in SAP Supplier Relationship Management (SRM) and SAP Sourcing, which are outside the scope of this book.

Overall, indirect procurement is more difficult to plan at a micro level than direct. You will know, based on your demand forecasts, roughly how much product is needed to be manufactured when. In fact, most companies have their direct procurement and production planning/demand forecasting down to a science. It is more difficult to predict when someone will need to reorder pens and paper in a particular office. At a macro level, however, the indirect procurement picture becomes clearer. Although you may not know exactly when an order will need to occur, you do know that the office will typically consume a certain amount of office supplies during a given period. Moreover, you will know your suppliers and potential suppliers based on this information. With these two areas covered, you are ready to begin putting together a sourcing strategy.

A good sourcing strategy involves understanding both your needs and the market in which these items will need to be procured. If you have a monopoly situation with your supplier-base for this particular item, you can argue until blue in the face over discounts and likely not obtain the desired results. With a monopsony, where your company is the sole buyer of a particular product, negotiations may be much easier. Since both of ends of the spectrum occur rarely, looking for commodity categories with lots of aggressive suppliers is the second best place to land if you are dictating prices as a monopsony. Analytics bear this out—adding more suppliers to a sourcing event typically equals more savings. This should color how you source your items as well, whether manually assigning a supplier, going to RFx, or running an auction.

2.1.3 Source of Supply Assignment: Manual, RFx, and Auctions

The main ways SAP Ariba Sourcing allows for assignment of suppliers to orders is through manual/contract entries, RFx, and auctions. Manual is typically used for one-off items with a low dollar value where you have a provider identified, whereas RFx and auctions are typically used for larger items or in competitive supplier markets where your price is inversely related to the number of competitive offerings you solicit. It should be noted that both of the latter options for assigning source of supply involve effort on both your side and that of the suppliers, and these efforts add costs and friction to the buying process. Even if facilitated by SAP Ariba, greatly reducing the costs and frictions, sourcing via RFx and auction requires a higher degree of participation, effort, and time than manual assignment.

Identifying when it makes sense to go to RFx or auction is thus a key process in sourcing and defining business rules for thresholds. Most companies define dollar thresholds, where larger purchases require a bidding process of some sort. Other companies identify specific categories with sole source providers, to achieve volume discounts and having a sole vendor relationship to worry about. These rules sometimes fail to address a unique situation, however.

Auctions are difficult to run, but can be very effective at reducing prices. If you have a large purchase and the suppliers will drop prices further if they are faced with lower bids, running an auction can make sense. Oftentimes the most difficult part of running an auction is getting suppliers to participate and making the auction itself smooth from a technical and support standpoint. No supplier or participant in an auction likes to feel like a technology glitch or format of the auction prevented them from getting a fair shake. SAP Ariba, with its real-time support and robust auction capabilities, seeks to address this. Pulling in more suppliers to these bidding processes and auction events is made easier with tools like SAP Ariba Discovery, as discussed in the next section.

2.2 SAP Ariba Discovery

SAP Ariba Discovery is a service that allows buyers to find new suppliers and read profile information, feedback, and other information about them. SAP Ariba Discovery is not a part of the solution to which you subscribed, but it is rather a separate service. In some circumstances, you can access SAP Ariba Discovery from your solution. SAP Ariba Discovery is currently free for buyers. Before you first access SAP Ariba Discovery, you must accept the online Terms of Use applicable to SAP Ariba Discovery, and those terms will apply if you choose to proceed and use SAP Ariba Discovery.

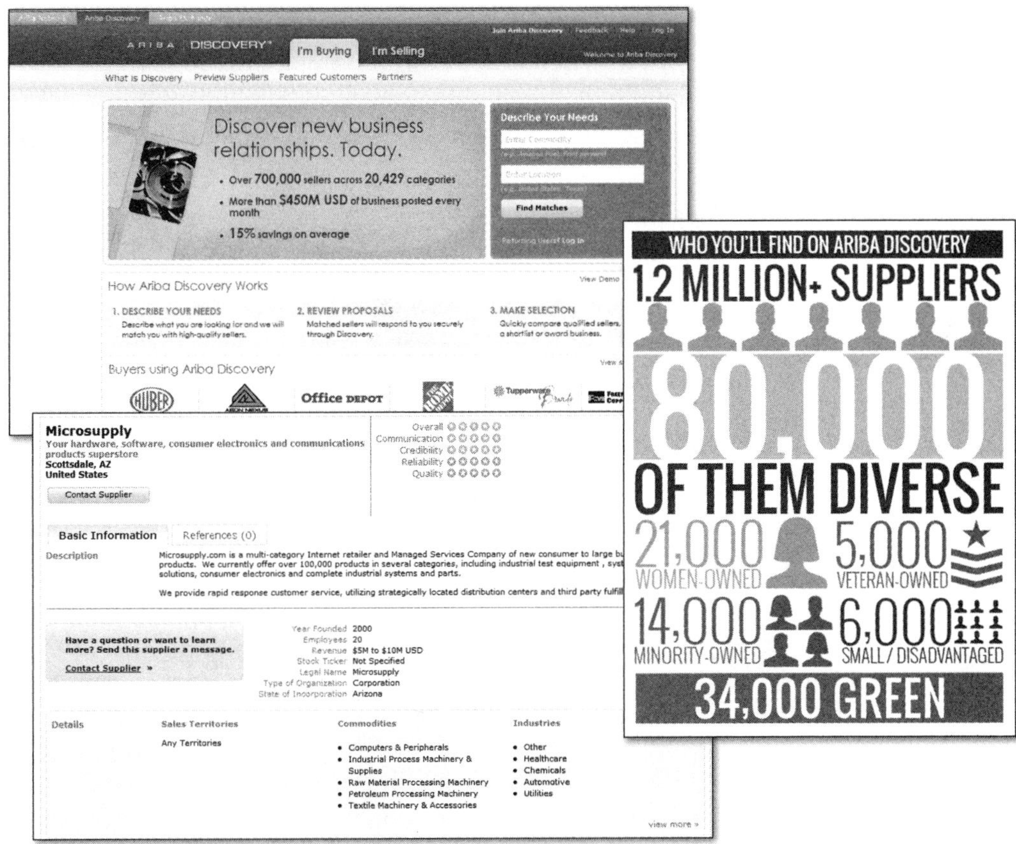

Figure 2.8 SAP Ariba Discovery

SAP Ariba Discovery, as seen in Figure 2.8, augments SAP Ariba Sourcing for suppliers with the following functionality:

1. **Searching for suppliers**
   An intelligent matching tool to identify suppliers that meet specific buyer needs in a category and pulled from a global database of more than one million suppliers in 140 countries. Supplier profiles contains enriched information with community insights.
2. **Engaging with suppliers**
   The ability to invite newly identified suppliers to qualification events or RFx. Once the supplier has responded to a posting and has passed the initial qualification rules set, you can move the supplier further along in the qualification process or directly into an RFx or auction.
3. **Onboarding suppliers**
   If awarded business, you have the ability to onboard a supplier quite easily. The tool includes ongoing self-maintenance of a supplier's profile information with a unified Supplier Dashboard—a one-stop shop for suppliers to update their information and collaborate on RFx, contracts, etc.

In the following sections we will cover how to incorporate SAP Ariba Discovery into your sourcing process and provide some recommended sourcing scenarios for SAP Ariba Discovery. As with sourcing in general, there are scenarios that benefit from SAP Ariba Discovery, such as a fragmented market where you are not familiar with all the suppliers, but are looking to invite as many as possible to your RFx or auction to achieve further price reduction. Conversely, in a situation where the supplier enjoys a monopoly for a particular good or service, SAP Ariba Discovery may not be able to provide many more options.

2.2.1 Incorporating SAP Ariba Discovery into Sourcing Processes and Solutions

SAP Ariba Discovery allows you to quickly and easily find new suppliers, conduct market research, and retrieve quotes. You can access SAP Ariba Discovery at different points in your SAP Ariba Sourcing solution. There are four primary use cases for SAP Ariba Discovery:

1. **Supplier research posting**
   This allows you to find and evaluate new suppliers before a sourcing event.

One of the most common ways to access SAP Ariba Discovery is by using the supplier research posting link to find new suppliers and conduct market research prior to a sourcing event. You do not need to own or create a sourcing event to conduct a supplier research posting.

2. **Quick quote posting**
   Use this to obtain a quick quote for your spot buys. The quick quote feature to also retrieve fast responses for spot buys and non-contract items.
3. **Posting as part of a sourcing event**
   After you have selected one of the links in SAP Ariba Sourcing, you will be taken to SAP Ariba Discovery to begin your posting. Clicking on Post Now! will launch a three-step process for creating a posting on SAP Ariba Discovery. Figure 2.9 outlines some of the popular categories for posting.

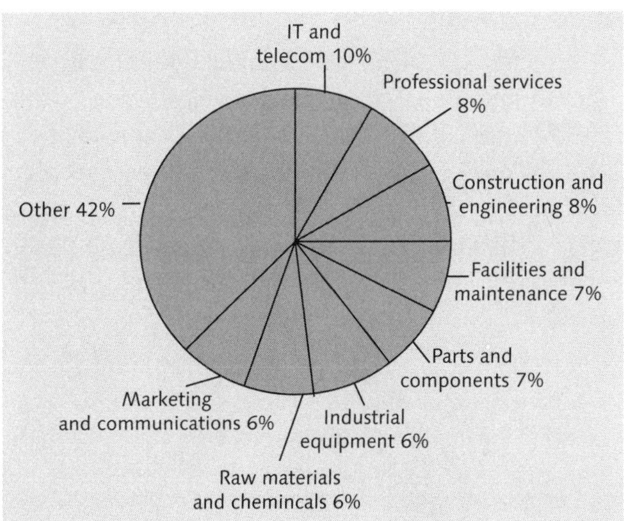

Figure 2.9 Leading Buyer Posting Categories on SAP Ariba Discovery

4. **Inviting additional suppliers**
   You can also invite additional suppliers in SAP Ariba Sourcing by adding suppliers from your database to those automatically matched to your posting by SAP Ariba Discovery.

Once you are satisfied with the posting content, click Publish. Your posting will go live on SAP Ariba Discovery within 12 hours, and an email notification will be automatically sent to suppliers matching your posting.

Once you have created a posting, you will want to review responses, answer questions, or edit your postings. SAP Ariba Discovery allows you to do so from multiple locations for added convenience. You can manage postings from the following areas:

1. Within an SAP Ariba Sourcing event
2. From the SAP Ariba Sourcing dashboard
3. From SAP Ariba Discovery

You can then award the posting and import suppliers into SAP Ariba Sourcing. Close the project by awarding the project, saving newly discovered suppliers on SAP Ariba Discovery, or importing them into your sourcing database.

2.2.2 Recommended Sourcing Scenarios for SAP Ariba Discovery

Finding the right balance of suppliers for each event in sourcing is challenging. Inviting too few suppliers leads to suboptimal outcomes in savings, while inviting too many can quickly degenerate into confusion, as unqualified suppliers overshadow and underbid potentially qualified ones. SAP Ariba Discovery enables you to add additional qualified suppliers to sourcing events that otherwise would lack a sufficient number. Figure 2.10 shows in graph format where having more suppliers adds the most savings, and where the marginal utility of having an additional supplier starts to taper off.

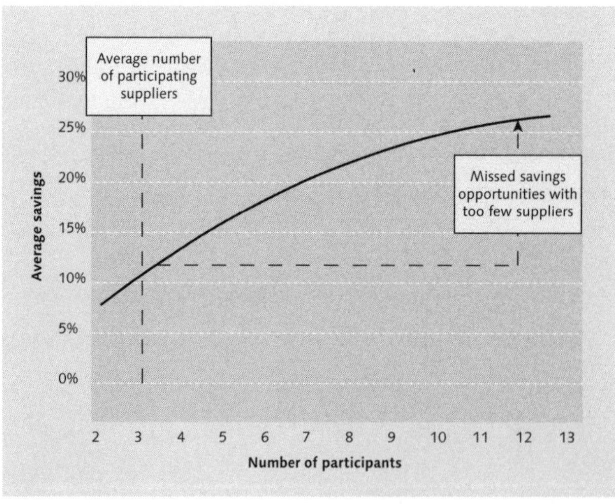

Figure 2.10 Additional Savings with More Suppliers

Managing quote solicitation and processing entails real effort, and thus expense, on the part of your purchasing organization, so there is a point where further suppliers can actually detract from the savings realized.

The optimal number of suppliers in a sourcing event can vary by material or service being procured. Market constraints can be geographic and/or due to the consolidation of suppliers (market share), or the complexity and strategic significance of the item or service. In a market where there are few providers, having a couple of suppliers participate in a bidding exercise may be all that is possible. For more commoditized markets with many suppliers and a wide variance of pricing and quality, having a large number of suppliers participate may provide significant cost savings.

Project	Complex Sourcing	Strategic Sourcing	Spot Buying
Description	The roles: Sourcing Event Manager Supply Material Research Main uses: ▸ Large spend of $3–50M ▸ Multiple teams and event	The roles: Strategic Sourcing Manager Main uses: ▸ Large spend of $100K–5M ▸ Single strategy owner and event	The roles: MRO Buyer, Plant Manager, Procurement Agent Main uses: ▸ Competitive bidding for $5K–100K ▸ Quick spot-buy, no sourcing event
SAP Ariba products	**SAP Ariba Sourcing:** ▸ Use full projects ▸ Launch postings in RFI template ▸ Link RFI to RFP or auction event	**SAP Ariba Sourcing:** ▸ Launch postings early in sourcing process with independent supplier market ▸ Research posting	**SAP Ariba Sourcing:** ▸ Create quick quote posting from the CREATE menu **SAP Ariba Procure-to-Pay/Procure-to-Order:** ▸ Without a requisition: create a quick quote posting from the CREATE menu ▸ With a requisition: create a non-catalog item first, then create a posting

Table 2.1 How to Use SAP Ariba Discovery

Per Table 2.1, you can use SAP Ariba Discovery for complex sourcing, strategic sourcing, and spot buying. The timing of when to create postings in SAP Ariba Discovery varies by scenario. For complex sourcing, you would leverage Discovery during the RFI-template process, whereas during a complex sourcing event, Discovery would be best used early, in order to identify additions to the supply base targeted via research. The supplier profile can reveal a lot as to the applicability of the supplier for a sourcing event. A supplier profile in SAP Ariba Discovery contains:

- Company information
- Product and service categories, ship-to and service locations, and industries
- Diversity, quality, green classifications
- Transacting relationships
- SAP Ariba Ready certification
- Customer references and ratings
- D&B credit scores

For tactical spot buys, posting at the time of purchase, as soon as the need surfaces, is still preferable to not activating SAP Ariba Discovery at all.

2.3 Implementing SAP Ariba Sourcing and SAP Ariba Discovery

SAP Ariba Discovery is a service requiring little configuration. Per Figure 2.11, SAP Ariba Discovery is already integrated with SAP Ariba Sourcing, SAP Ariba P2P, P2O, and SAP Ariba Spot Quote on the buyer-side, and proposals, contracts, and orders and invoices on the SAP Ariba Network for the supply side.

The majority of an implementation of SAP Ariba Discovery resides on the change management end of the project (i.e., educating your internal users when and how to leverage SAP Ariba Discovery to realize savings). As with any change management exercise, there will be a learning curve and different groups of adopters at different points of the curve within your organization. As per Table 2.2, building awareness and identifying key scenarios for the usage and benefit of SAP Ariba

Discovery will allow you to realize quick wins and savings. Once you establish the benefits of the tool with a pilot organization or group, you can expand to other parts of the organization and processes. Complex sourcing processes typically rely on a limited number of suppliers. Over time, this reliance becomes a routine, and then a rut. Suppliers can begin taking advantage of the routine and reduce their quality and/or raise price. Providing these complex sourcing activities with new, qualified suppliers during the RFI phase thus can generate a quick win.

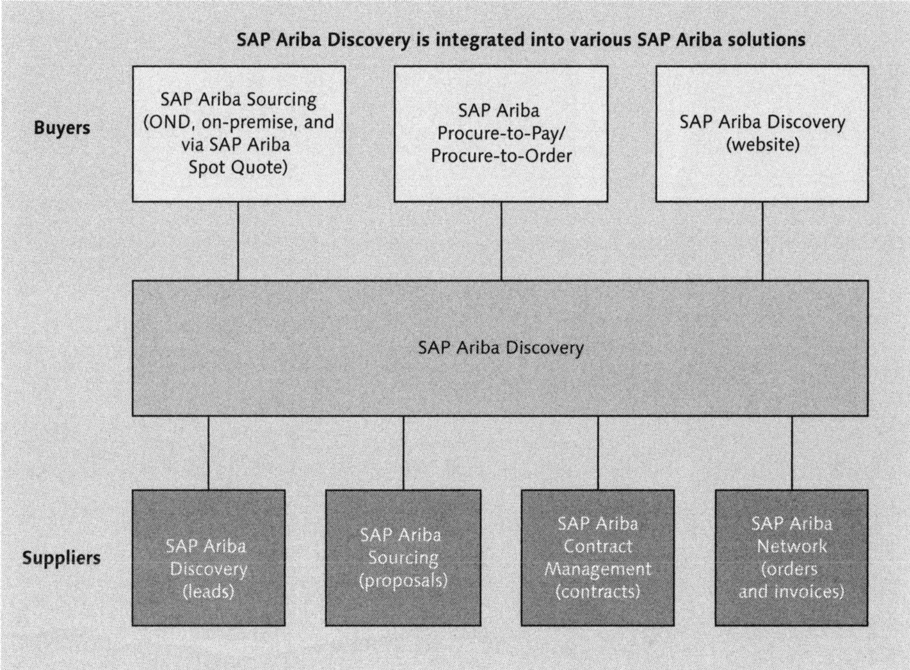

Figure 2.11 SAP Ariba Discovery's Integration with Other SAP Ariba Solutions

Groups conducting strategic sourcing, as they purchase significant volumes, are also good opportunities for wins with SAP Ariba Discovery. All it takes is identifying a supplier in SAP Ariba Discovery who delivers a lower price in a big sourcing activity to show the group and the rest of the organization, not to mention executives and project sponsors, just how valuable SAP Ariba Discovery can be.

	Non-Users	Early Adopters	Converted	Evangelists
Percentage of SAP Ariba Discovery adoption in your organization	0%	1–10%	10–50%	50–100%
Key tasks	▸ Build awareness ▸ Identify business process owners ▸ Identify any core blockers ▸ Schedule in-depth demo for power users/account owner	▸ Identify internal evangelists ▸ Build on early wins as proofs points from postings ▸ Dive to train entire sourcing team (expand usage)	▸ Identify additional expansion points ▸ Drive inclusion in documented company processes and business metrics, make it a key step in documents sourcing model ▸ Make it the primary resource for all spot buys	▸ Partner with SAP Ariba to align strategic objectives ▸ Drive to expand beyond strategic sourcing (e.g., spot quotes/RFQs)
Note: Penetration defined as a percentage of SAP Ariba Discover postings as compared to sourcing events (RFI, RFP, auctions).				

Table 2.2 Roadmap to Success—SAP Ariba Discovery

The targets for change management and driving adoption of SAP Ariba Discovery should thus center on strategic and complex sourcing. Once these groups are won over, users can begin integrating SAP Ariba Discovery in their everyday processes and spot buying. Rolling out SAP Ariba Discovery is typically done after SAP Ariba Sourcing is in place, at the tail end of a sourcing project, as you would train users on a complex feature of the solution after training the basics.

The next sections of this chapter will cover process and implementation aspects of SAP Ariba Sourcing, beginning with the definition of sourcing processes.

2.3.1 Defining Sourcing Processes

Defining the various sourcing processes your organization uses and would like to use after deploying SAP Ariba Sourcing is a key part of SAP Ariba Sourcing implementation. Per Figure 2.12, a high level sourcing process consists of identifying a need, identifying a supplier or group of suppliers, agreeing on a non-disclosure agreement (if required), engaging in dialogue around the item or service required, and then initiating the RFx process best suited for the supplier group and item or service requested. Less complex items allow you to skip straight to a quote request (RFQ), whereas more complex items may require several rounds of information gathering and supplier analysis/evaluation.

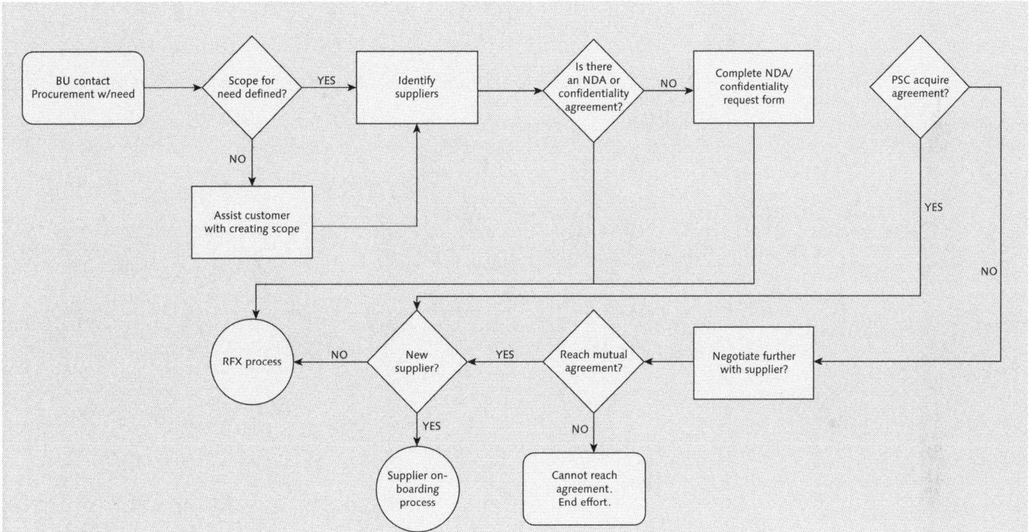

Figure 2.12 Sourcing Process

Best practices for setting up SAP Ariba Sourcing processes are as follows:

1. **Identify opportunities/analysis (offline activity)**
   - Gather available spend data and identify sourcing opportunities
   - Identify opportunities that have multiple suppliers, large spend amounts, no current contracts and/or a large volume that may have been identified via spend data
   - Perform opportunity risk assessment and analytical support

- Perform analytical support activates, including consideration of the following:
  - Spend analysis: current baseline spend and volume
  - Published literature and research: price/market conditions, industry leaders, business impact, and price drivers
  - Conversion analysis: cost to change suppliers and return on investment (ROI)
  - Business analysis and impact: validate value potential (cost/benefit)
- Identify historical data by:
  - Reviewing historical spend volume via purchase order history, accounts payable system, current suppliers, end users, and/or budgets
  - Reviewing previous spend initiatives (date of last initiative, type of sourcing initiative, product/service sourced, suppliers involved, stakeholders involved, results)
- Assign project team and kickoff project
  - Identify project team members
  - Schedule initial project meeting
  - Review roles and responsibilities
  - Review project goals
  - Develop project charter/scope
  - Develop project time line/milestones

2. **Develop strategy (offline activity)**
   Complete stakeholder analysis by:
   - Performing interviews with stakeholder representatives to:
     - Discuss business requirements/specifications
     - Discuss current and future demand
     - Discuss current supply base and service/quality performance/needs
     - Discuss total cost components
     - Discuss how the commodity works for the stakeholder
     - Discuss market trends
     - Discuss delivery locations
     - Discuss implementation issues (people, process, technology)

  - Discuss commodity strategy
  - Discuss sustainability
  - Prioritize opportunities
- Performing gap analysis (desired state vs. actual performance)
- Highlighting critical gaps
- Developing and rank key performance indicators
- Obtaining approval/participation

Identify suppliers and conduct supplier profile analysis so that you may:

- Identify potential supply strategies
- Identify new sources of supply
- Research market supply and trends
- Identify initial list of potential suppliers
- Identify additional suppliers
- Identify supplier selection criteria
- Discuss incumbent talking points
- Set a supplier outreach timeline

Finalize your optimal sourcing strategy and determine the type of sourcing events you wish to use.

3. **Source and negotiate (online activity)**
   - Define and create requests for information (RFIs)
     - Add a title according to naming conventions
     - Make appropriate selections for required and optional fields
     - Select appropriate RFI template(s)
     - Determine timing rules, bidding rules and market feedback
     - Add already identified suppliers, if any
     - Add content—review best practice sourcing content document in the sourcing library and include multi-stage information if applicable
   - Create an SAP Ariba Discovery posting to identify additional potential suppliers
     From the Supplier tab of your event, create an SAP Ariba Discovery posting

to match potential suppliers and for suppliers to communicate their intent to submit a response. It is recommend to allow at minimum one week between posting closing and the publishing of the event.

- Import qualified suppliers from SAP Ariba Discovery
  Import qualified suppliers from the SAP Ariba Discovery Network that have indicated an intent to bid.
- Send the RFI to SAP Ariba Sourcing support for review
  On the SUMMARY tab of your RFx, click the SAP ARIBA REVIEW button, enter comments for the reviewer, and submit. The SAP Ariba Sourcing support desk will use all reasonable efforts to provide feedback within one business day.
- Publish RFI
  Release RFI for supplier review and response.
- Monitor RFI
  Respond to Q&A board and address any issues that may arise with event.
- RFI event review by team graders
  Team Graders will access the event to review and score supplier responses. Email reviewers may be added as required. To adjust graders' weights, access the SUMMARY page of your event and edit the OVERVIEW by clicking ACTIONS • EDIT GRADERS' WEIGHTS.
- Export and Analyze RFI Responses
  Export and analyze RFI results. Promote/disqualify suppliers based on predetermined criteria; move to next stage (i.e. RFP, auction).
- Award the RFP by:
  - Creating award scenarios and selecting the best possible outcome.
  - Submitting the chosen scenario and notifying awarded and/or non-awarded supplier(s)

4. **Auction**
   - Define and create auction
     - Add a title according to naming convention
     - Make appropriate selections for required and optional fields
     - Select appropriate auction template
     - Determine timing rules, bidding rules and market feedback

  - Add already identified suppliers, if any
  - Add content—review best practice sourcing content document in the library, and include multi-stage information if applicable
- Create SAP Ariba Discovery posting to identify additional potential suppliers
  From the SUPPLIER tab of your event, create an SAP Ariba Discovery Posting to match potential suppliers and for suppliers to communicate their intent to submit a response. It is recommended to allow at minimum one week between posting closing and the publishing of the event.
- Import qualified suppliers from SAP Ariba Discovery/finalize supplier list
  Import qualified suppliers from the SAP Ariba Discovery Network that have indicated an intent to bid. Determine a final list of suppliers who will be participating in the auction.
- Conduct internal practice auction with stakeholders
  Determine lotting strategy and conduct a mock auction including test suppliers. Make modifications/additions as needed.
- Conduct practice auction with suppliers
  After lotting strategy has been determined, conduct a practice auction with your suppliers including fictitious information. Monitor and answer questions from suppliers. It is recommended that you do so 1-3 days prior to live auction.
- Send LIVE auction to SAP Ariba Sourcing Support for review
  After auction has been finalized, on the SUMMARY tab of your RFx, click the ARIBA REVIEW button, enter comments for the reviewer, and submit. SAP Ariba Sourcing support desk will use all reasonable efforts to provide feedback within one business day.
- Publish auction
  - Release auction for supplier review and response. The auction must be published at least 24 hours ahead of time so that SAP Ariba Auction Administrators can monitor the auction. Recommended two weeks prior to open time.
  - Respond to Q&A board and address any issues that may arise with event.
- Export and analyze auction responses
  Export and analyze auction results. If applicable, analyze RFP results in conjunction with auction results

- Award auction
  - Create award scenarios and select the best possible outcome.
  - Submit the chosen scenario and notify awarded and/or non-awarded supplier(s)

5. **Project closeout**
   - Document any lessons learned
   - Update project state

2.3.2 Defining Project Resources, Phases, and Timelines

A typical SAP Ariba Sourcing Professional project can take six to seven weeks, depending on its size and scope. If combining with SAP Ariba Discovery, the project adds one to two weeks in change management training. The phases of an SAP Ariba Sourcing project are as follows:

1. **Pre-kickoff**
   The customer secures the resources needed for the project team, identifies roles in deployment, and documents the in-scope sourcing processes.
2. **Kickoff**
   Hold the project kickoff: call and confirm the schedule and resources for weekly meetings. The customer then registers on SAP Ariba Connect, a resource portal for projects and SAP Ariba solutions.
3. **Data collection**
   Data collection can include supplier data, commodity code data, as well as template definitions and workflows. The following key areas are included in data collection:
   - Enablement workbook: SAP Ariba consulting and/or partners provide the customer with a training code and schedule, data collection guidelines, and a Sourcing enablement workbook. SAP Ariba reviews the enablement workbook with you, and you then complete it. Once the workbook is confirmed and submitted, SAP Ariba loads the enablement workbook data into a test site.
   - Custom header fields: SAP Ariba reviews the custom header field data collection template with the customer, and the customer then completes the template. Once submitted, SAP Ariba configures custom header fields in the test site. SAP Ariba then reviews the custom header field configuration in the test

site with the customer (including its layout). Finally, SAP Ariba updates the field configuration according to customer feedback.

4. **Site configuration**
   Based on the workbook definitions and design sessions, a test realm is set up covering the following areas:
   - Sourcing process: SAP Ariba reviews the documented process with the customer, and the customer provides the documents to be associated with the process. The process is then built in the test site and reviewed with the customer. Lastly, the process is updated per customer feedback.
   - Form development (if applicable): SAP Ariba reviews the form data collection template with the customer, who then completes the template. SAP Ariba then configures the form template in the test site and reviews the form template configuration with the customer (including layout). As with the other areas, the form template configuration updates per customer feedback.
5. **Configuration freeze**
   This phase includes testing, production site configuration, and wrap-up, where the customer conducts configuration testing on the test site. SAP Ariba makes changes based upon configuration testing and the customer validates those changes and approves the test site configuration.
6. **Configuration of production site**
   SAP Ariba moves all configurations to the production site, and configuration testing takes place on the production site. The customer conducts configuration testing on the production site, and SAP Ariba makes changes based upon that testing. The customer then validates these changes and approves the production site configuration.
7. **Wrap-up**
   The customer is introduced and transitioned to the customer support team. From an organizational change management (OCM) standpoint, key subject matter experts and training needs to occur throughout the project and during wrap up. Key demonstrations to schedule during the project, or at least prior to gating out of wrap up, include:
   - Dashboard and project overview
   - Supplier self-registration
   - Supplier profile questionnaire
   - Supplier administration

- SAP Ariba Discovery (including company aliasing)
- Sourcing library and content creation
- Template creation
- Post-bid optimization
- Reporting
- Users, groups, and access control

During the project, and shortly before go-live, focused change management is crucial for a successful implementation of SAP Ariba Sourcing, as well as SAP Ariba Discovery. Many of the sourcing activities have a defined, limited group of users who can be integrated into the project for feedback during design and configuration phases, and who can also act as multipliers once the project is live. Successful change management efforts start with an analysis and a plan/strategy, prior to bringing in the various users for instruction. Steps include identifying core stakeholders, defining key groups and their needs for the transition to the solution, communication and training plan definition, and, finally, execution. For SAP Ariba Discovery, a parallel or integrated plan should be crafted.

Ideally, SAP Ariba Discovery should be included with every SAP Ariba Sourcing project. This allows for increasing the participation rates of qualified suppliers in sourcing events, which invariably drives down your price. However, some projects may not include SAP Ariba Discovery for a variety of reasons. If the supplier group from which sourcing events is limited to the supplier list provided by the customer, then further suppliers may not be necessary/possible for sourcing events. Sometimes SAP Ariba Discovery roll out occurs after SAP Ariba Sourcing has been implemented in a pilot event, testing with a defined group of suppliers before buyers expand their supplier base of participation.

2.4 Summary

Defining a competitive source of supply during requisitioning is a key area that drives saving and further volume and relationship savings for future procurement. SAP Ariba StartSourcing and SAP Ariba Sourcing Professional, along with supporting tools such as SAP Ariba Discovery, provide the platform from which to manage this part of the process in a holistic manner. From an implementation standpoint, defining the process and the templates are the twin pillars for supporting a successful implementation for SAP Ariba Sourcing solutions.

Say goodbye to misled and mismanaged paper contracts, and to the risks associated with them. This chapter describes the SAP Ariba Contract Management solution that helps you better manage your procurement, sales, and internal contracts—resulting in greater efficiency, lower costs, and improved relationships.

3 Contract Management

Contract management, or contract lifecycle management, is the process of managing the complete lifecycle of a contract from creation, to execution, to maintenance. Effective and systematic management of a contract minimizes the risks associated with the contract while maximizing its operational and financial performance. Contract management is a process that enables parties to a contract to meet their obligations in order to deliver the objectives required from the contract.

Contracts are vital documents that contain important (and, in most cases, legally binding) information on the relationship of an organization with its partners—suppliers, customers and employees. Contracts can also contain important cost-saving incentives, such as early payment discounts. Mismanagement and noncompliance of contracts is quite costly for organizations in terms of lost savings and/or regulatory arraignments. In larger organizations, or as an organization grows, and an increasing number of contracts are executed, maintenance and compliance enforcement of contracts can become a nightmare.

The strategic direction that many customers take is moving their procurement processes to the cloud to achieve faster ROI and improved innovation cycles. SAP's answer to cloud procurement is the SAP Ariba suite and SAP Fieldglass. SAP Ariba Contract Management is an integral part of the SAP Ariba procurement suite and has tight integration to SAP Ariba solutions for strategic souring and supplier information management, as well as other SAP Ariba solutions, SAP ERP, and third-party solutions, as shown in Figure 3.1.

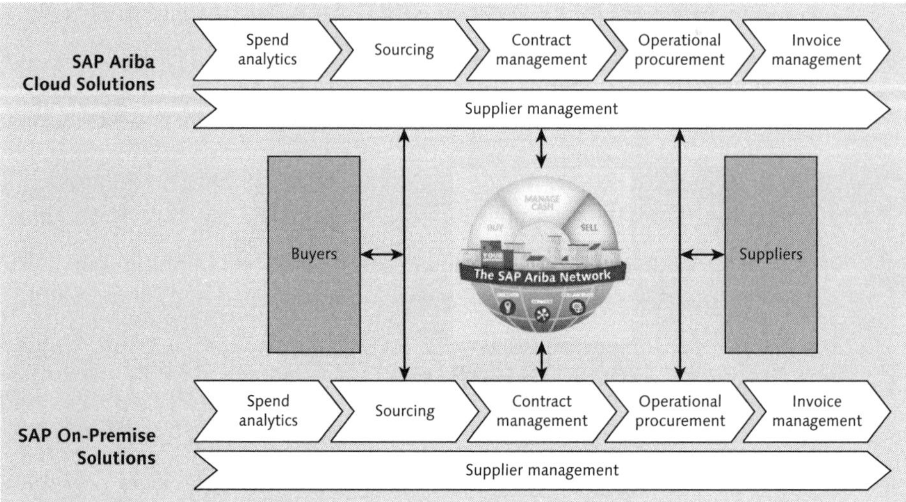

Figure 3.1 SAP Ariba Spend Management

SAP Ariba Contract Management reduces the cost of managing and updating contracts by eliminating the need for paper and ink from the creation, execution, and management of any type of contractual agreement. SAP Ariba Contract Management is a leading SaaS (software as a service) solution that is accessible anywhere and anytime.

Furthermore, in today's digital economy SAP Ariba Contract Management provides a powerful platform to:

- Manage procurement and sales contracts, license agreements, internal agreements and various other kinds of contracts
- Automate and accelerate the entire contract lifecycle process, including the contract signature process by enabling digital signatures
- Standardize the contract creation, authoring and maintenance process
- Collaborate with both internal and external stakeholders with a complete audit trail of changes made to the contract though out the process
- Strengthen operational, contractual, and regulatory compliance

Some additional benefits of using SAP Ariba Contract Management include:

- Fast time-to-value: Get underway quickly in the cloud, enjoying lower total cost of ownership (TCO) and always current versions with minimal demand on IT.

- Easy-to-use: Create contracts quickly and easily using Microsoft Word and pre-approved templates and legal clauses.
- Controlled processes: You'll be alerted if pre-approved format or language is modified, helping you control non-standard agreements.
- Efficient collaboration: Work quickly and effectively with all stakeholders via a shared workspace on a multitenant, web-based platform.
- Complete visibility: Stay informed throughout the contract lifecycle with automatic alerts, handy dashboards, and configurable reports.
- Central repository: Never lose track of a contract with secure electronic storage and powerful search tools for access on demand.
- On-time renewals: Receive notifications well in advance of key milestone dates, and make the most of your business opportunities.
- E-signature savings: Eliminate time and expense of shipping and signing of multiple contracts by adding e-signature capabilities.
- Stronger compliance: Stay informed about any off-contract activity with controlled processes, automated tracking, and a full audit trail.
- End-to-end commerce: Integrate your contract processes with additional SAP Ariba Solutions, your SAP ERP system, or other third party systems for unrivaled compliance and control.

This chapter outlines the SAP Ariba solution for understanding and managing contracts within SAP Ariba, with a focus on the SAP Ariba Contract Management Professional package, and its implementation.

3.1 SAP Ariba Contract Management

SAP Ariba Contract Management combines the contract creation, negotiation and amendment process with the authoring process into a comprehensive contract management solution. With SAP Ariba Contract Management, companies can develop best-value agreements by addressing the two major components of contract lifecycle:

- **Contract management**
  This stage goes from contract request, to contract authoring, to negotiation and approval of contacts using electronic signatures, to contract execution.

- **Commitment management**
  This stage includes all ongoing compliance and performance management through task-driven reminders and search and reporting capabilities, as well as contract renewal activities.

In this section, let us look at some of the pain points in the contracting process for indirect procurement, and how SAP Ariba Contract Management helps alleviates some of that pain. We will also look at how contracts are created and handled within SAP Ariba Contract Management.

3.1.1 Contract Strategies for Indirect Procurement

Indirect procurement relates to the procurement of goods and services that are not directly used in the product or service provided by the organization. For instance, for a financial institution, office supplies are an indirect procurement.

While indirect procurement may share common business and legal issues/risks, drafting and executing contracts for indirect procurement has some unique and critical differences as compared to direct procurement or other kinds of contracts.

The following are some of the risks and issues observed in the contract management for indirect procurement, and the contract strategies that can be enforced in SAP Ariba Contract Management:

- **Terms and conditions management**
  Terms and conditions (T&Cs) management proved to be an area of weakness in a large number of indirect contracts. Most contracts lack consistency in terms of the usage of standard language. In addition, as the language used in each contract is different, the language is usually not pre-approved by legal, thus considerably increasing the risk associated with the contract. Implementing standard contract templates with approved mandatory, optional and alternate T&Cs clauses for various types of indirect goods and services is a key step required to mitigate contract management risks.

  SAP Ariba Contract Management provides comprehensive contract authoring and clause library functionality, which enables the creation of standard required/optional clauses and contract boiler templates. Additionally, the feature allows for defining alternate clauses and provides an outline view of sections and clauses in the contract document. End users can review and replace standard optional clauses with alternate clauses found in the clause library.

Certain contract terms and conditions will need to be negotiated based on the nature of purchase, and/or the supplier's relative power. SAP Ariba Contract Management provides negotiation functionality with a comprehensive auditing and version control feature. SAP Ariba Contract Management also provides standard prepackaged reports, in order to identify standard clauses that contract creators constantly change. This allows legal or contract template administrators to revise the clause or create approved alternate clauses.

Using SAP Ariba Contract Management and enforcing the usage of standardized contract templates and approved or alternate clauses reduces the contracting risks considerably, and accelerates the contract creation and negotiation process.

- **Contract planning and negotiation planning**
  Many contracts lack proper planning and consistent process for negotiation and execution of the contract. An efficient contract management process requires proper contract planning and negotiation planning processes that involve scoping requirements, contract negotiation planning, and planning for post-award contract administration. The negotiation plan should leverage the analysis performed during the strategic sourcing process.

  SAP Ariba Contract Management, with standard integration to SAP Ariba Sourcing, provides improved strategic sourcing and contracting process design. The SAP Ariba Contract Management solution helps improve the contract planning and negotiation process considerably, by enabling faster, paperless contract creation, authoring, and back and forth collaboration/red lining of the contract with external contracting parties, such as the supplier. SAP Ariba Contract Management also provides tasks for internal reviews and highly configurable workflows, and can be customized for each contract template based on the customer's internal processes for handling contractual risks.

- **Post award contract management and control**
  Contract compliance is a major area in need of improvement for a large number of organizations. Most contract management solutions lack integration to operational procurement where transactions are executed based on contracts, thus ensuring contract compliance.

  SAP Ariba Contract Management provides seamless integration with SAP Ariba P2P solutions, thus enabling contract compliance and reducing maverick spending by ensuring the negotiated terms are used during the execution and release of contracts. SAP Ariba Contract Management also provides a set of prepackaged reports for monitoring contracts. Task-driven reminders and renewal reminders notify contract authors (owners) of expiring contracts well in advance, so that they can re-negotiate those contracts and terms and thus realize further savings. In addition, SAP Ariba Contract Management fully supports the contract amendment process, whether it's an administrative amendment, renewal, or termination of a contract. All changes to a contract are recorded for audit purposes. Standard amendment templates can also be maintained with standard clauses to standardize and accelerate the amendment process for all contracts maintained within SAP Ariba Contract Management.

In the following section, we will discuss the processes for creating contracts.

3.1.2 Creating, Consuming, and Amending Contracts

SAP Ariba Contract Management helps resolve a number of challenges in the contract process, including standardizing and controlling contract creation, automating the approval process, and enabling electronic signatures. It also allows you to manage procurement and sales, internal agreements, and IP licenses. Its overall effect is to automate and accelerate the entire contract creation and execution process.

In this section, we will cover contract creation, execution, and consumption and how to use electronic signatures in SAP Ariba Contract Management; we will conclude with an overview of amending contracts.

Contract Creation

SAP Ariba's spend management solutions, which include SAP Ariba Contract Management, SAP Ariba Sourcing, SAP Ariba SIPM, SAP Ariba P2P, SAP Ariba Discount Professional, etc., have multiple dashboards. Upon logging into, the user sees the Home dashboard. The particular information displayed on the dashboards, and access to specific features and other dashboards, depends on that user's permissions and roles. User with access to the SAP Ariba Contracts Management will be able to click the Contracts dashboard to access information on contracts.

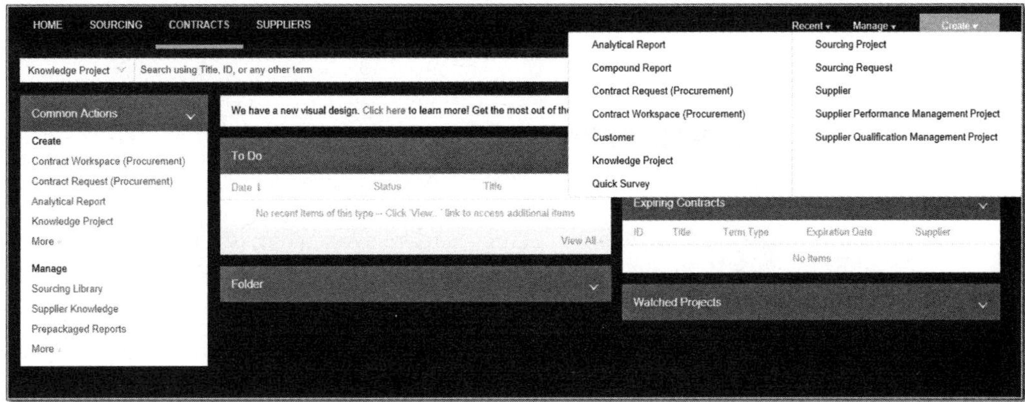

Figure 3.2 SAP Ariba Contract Management—Contracts Dashboard

Per Figure 3.2, the following kinds of contracts can be created in SAP Ariba Contracts: procurement, sales and internal contracts. There are four ways to create a contract within SAP Ariba Contract Management, which can be accessed using the following file paths:

- Common Actions Create
  - Common Actions Create • Contract Workspace (Procurement)
  - Common Actions Create • Contract Workspace (Sales)
  - Common Actions Create • Contract Workspace (Internal)
- Contracts (Dashboard) • Create
  - Contracts (Dashboard) • Create • Contract Workspace (Procurement)
  - Contracts (Dashboard) • Create • Contract Workspace (Sales)
  - Contracts (Dashboard) • Create • Contract Workspace (Internal)
- Sourcing Event • Award • Contract • Create New Contract • Select Participant
- Contract Request • Documents Tab • Contract • Open
  - From a Contract Request (Procurement) • Documents Tab • Contract • Open
  - From a Contract Request (Sales) • Documents Tab • Contract • Open
  - From a Contract Request (Internal) • Documents Tab • Contract • Open

Note

Each contract type (procurement, sales and internal) requires a separate subscription. Depending on the contract type(s) that a customer chooses to subscribe to, the relevant CREATE menu options will appear. In Figure 3.2, only procurement contracts are enabled for this realm.

A CREATE CONTRACT WORKSPACE screen is displayed when a user clicks CREATE • CONTRACT WORKSPACE, irrespective of the type of contract workspace (procurement, sales or internal) that the user choses. For simplicity, this book shows screens for creating CONTRACT WORKSPACE (PROCUREMENT), but the process and screens are similar for all type of contracts, except for some differences in standard fields such as:

- Contract Workspace (Sales)
  - CUSTOMER
  - PRODUCT
- Contract Workspace (Procurement)
  - SUPPLIER
  - AFFILIATED SUPPLIER
  - BUSINESS SEGMENT

The contract workspace creation screen in Figure 3.3 is configurable, for the most part, based on customer requirements. The screen is made up of standard and customer-defined fields. The fields for procurement, sales and internal contract types vary slightly.

Customer-defined and standard fields can be made optional or required. Required fields must be completed before creating the contract workspace.

In order to create a contract in SAP Ariba Contract Management, contract templates must be created and published by contract template administrators (see Section 3.2.1 for more details). Visibility of the contract template for selection in the contract workspace creation screen can be controlled by the entries in the standard fields, and/or custom fields (conditions).

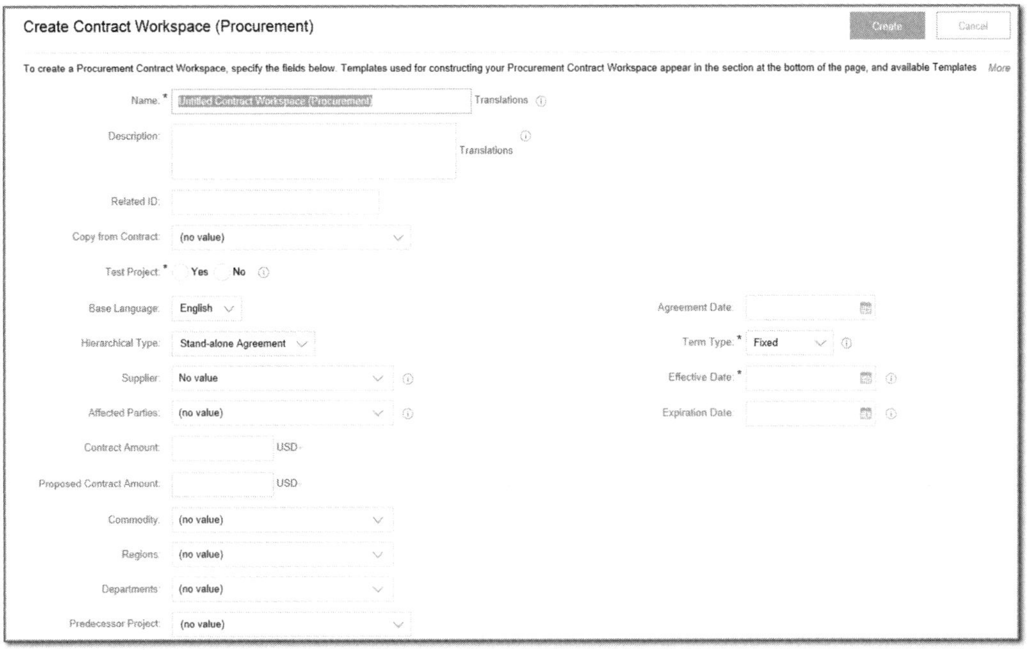

Figure 3.3 Contract Workspace Creation Screen

Contract Execution and Consumption

The contract template selected during the creation of the contract workspace drives the contracting process. The process to take the contract from draft to execution and the standard contract document templates (if any) will be inherited from the contract template. In this section, we will cover the various tabs you will use during contract execution.

Overview Tab

Figure 3.4 displays basic information about the contract, such as the CONTRACT STATUS, VERSION, LANGUAGE, OWNER, ACCESS CONTROL, and other standard fields, such as DESCRIPTION, COMMODITY and REGIONS. The CONTRACT ID is a contract number generated by the system.

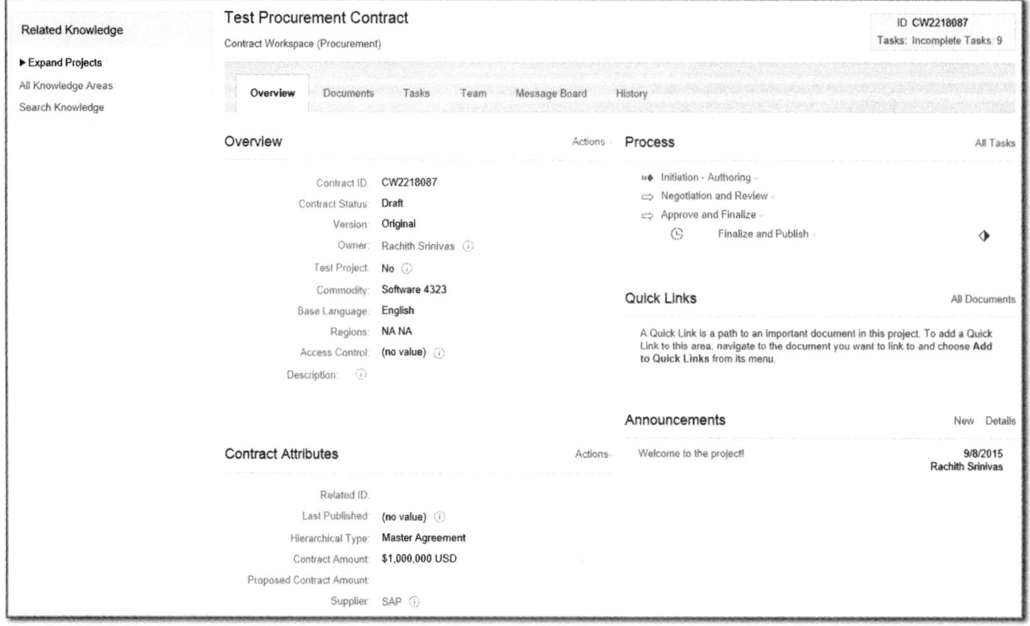

Figure 3.4 Contract Workspace Overview Page

Other sections under the overview are:

- **Contract Attributes**
  Displays standard fields such as HIERARCHY TYPE (Master Agreement/Sub Agreement/Standalone), CONTRACT AMOUNT, SUPPLIER and SUB AGREEMENTS, and all of the customer-defined fields.
- **Contract Terms Attributes**
  Displays standard fields such as TERM TYPE (Fixed/Auto Renew Type/Perpetual), EFFECTIVE DATE, EXPIRATION DATE, and other fields related to renewal reminder notifications.
- **Process**
  Displays the contract process phases and any milestones defined in the contract process. The status for each process and milestone is displayed via images to denote phase status and milestone status. (For instance, a green check is displayed next to a completed milestone).

- **Quick Links**
  Displays any quick links created to important documents within the workspace.
- **Announcements**
  Displays any announcements created within the workspace for members to view.

Documents Tab

Per Figure 3.5 the Documents tab in the contract workspace is used to create the master agreement and contract addendum from standard approved clause templates, or to upload a supplier paper or non-standard contract document. Contract template administrators can choose to include the standard contract document (with approved clauses) as a default document in the contract template. When a contract workspace is created from this contract template, the standard document automatically builds, and will appear in the Documents tab.

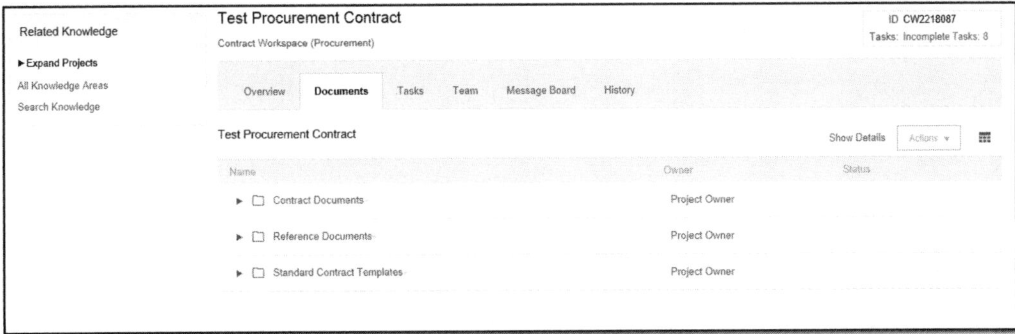

Figure 3.5 Contract Workspace Documents Page

Documents created or uploaded can be edited and modified from the Documents tab. All changes to the contract documents are saved as versions. Editing contract documents in SAP Ariba Contract Management required that DFS (document file synchronization) is enabled.

> **Note**
> DFS will only work with Internet Explorer.

Folders can be created in the DOCUMENTS tab, as well. The complete folder or individual documents within the folder can be associated to to-do or workflow tasks. If a whole folder is associated to a workflow task, then upon its submission for approval, all documents within the folder will be included in the workflow approval process.

Tasks Tab

Figure 3.6 outlines the TASKS tab in the contract workspace, which is used to define the contract phases, and the tasks and milestones within each phase.

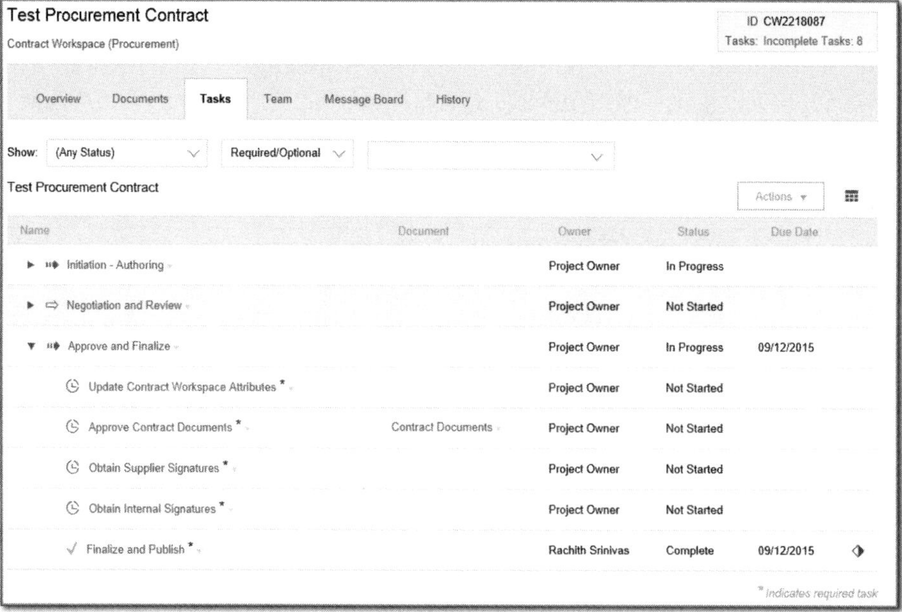

Figure 3.6 Contract Tasks Screen

Due to increased regulatory pressure to reduce costs and standardize the contracting process, organizations are looking for ways to enforce standard processes for creating and managing contracts internally.

SAP Ariba Contract Management allows contract administrators to define a standard contract process with phases, tasks and milestones. The task could be a to-do task, or a workflow approval task. The following are the types of tasks that can be created:

- **To-do task**
  Requires the task owner to perform some activity. Document folder can be linked to a to-do task.
- **Review and approval task**
  Routes documents associated to these tasks to the reviewer or approver. Reviewers can leave comments upon reviewing the document. Approvers will need to approve/deny the document. Document folder can be linked to a review or approval task. All documents within the document folder will be part of the review or approval process.
- **Negotiation task**
  Captures the negotiations between two or more parties concerning a contract, or any other type of document. Comments from negotiating parties are captured, as well as any changes made to the document.
- **Notification task**
  Sends email reminders to recipients. It is used primarily after the contract's publication to remind users to take some sort of action, such as periodically checking contract activity or market pricing periodically. These reminders can be set up to be sent once, on a repeating scheduled basis.

Tasks and milestones based on the standard process can be created at the contract template level. These tasks can be required or optional.

Contract workspaces created from the contract template will automatically inherit the template's tasks and milestones. Contract creators can choose to add additional tasks to the contract process, and/or delete optional tasks that have been pulled from the contract template.

Teams Tab

Collaboration throughout the contracting process is key for ensuring a faster and less error-prone execution of contracts.

SAP Ariba Contract Management allows collaborators or team members to be added manually or automatically to the contract workspace within the TEAMS tab, as shown in Figure 3.7. Project team groups, such as contract managers or contract observers should be created first, before adding team members to these project team groups. Team members can be individual users or groups of users. Each project team group is defined a role: VIEW ONLY or VIEW/EDIT.

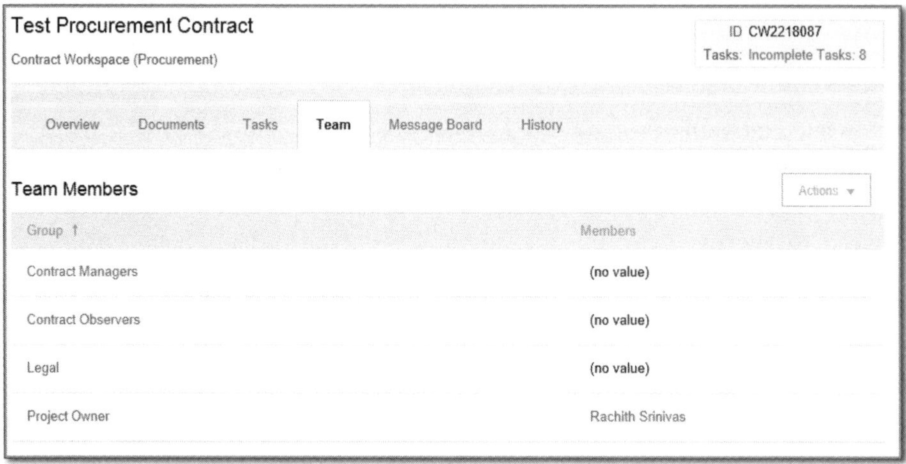

Figure 3.7 Contract Teams Screen

Similar to tasks, project team groups and team members can be set up by the contract administrator in the contract template level. Contract workspaces created from the contract template will automatically inherit the project team groups and team members, ensuring certain team members will always be added to any contract workspace created.

Project team groups can be added to the review and approval tasks.

Message Board Tab

Shown in Figure 3.8, the MESSAGE BOARD is another medium for communicating with the team members, as well as with stakeholders outside of SAP Ariba.

Within a contract workspace, the MESSAGE BOARD tab allows contract authors or team members with edit access to create new message topics, or to initiate a message via email. New topics created within the contract workspace's message board will be visible and accessible to all team members of that workspace.

New messages posted via email triggers the email application (e.g. Outlook). The mail generated will be automatically CCed to the auto generated contract workspace email address. Additional recipients can be added as required. Emails will be sent to each recipient. When REPLY ALL is selected, responses are automatically forwarded and recorded in the MESSAGE BOARD tab within the contract workspace.

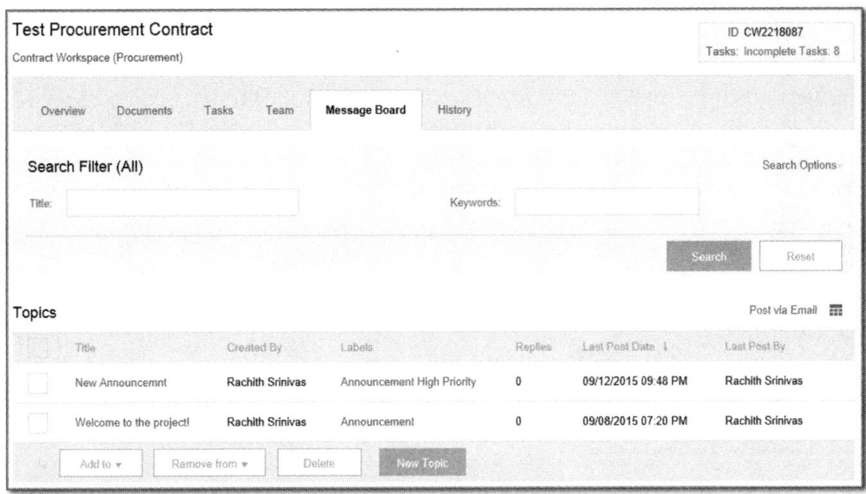

Figure 3.8 Message Board Screen

History Tab

Figure 3.9 outlines the History tab within the contract workspace. The History tab captures in chronological order all changes that were made to the contract workspace. It also includes a filter-based search report to display and narrow searches on changes made to the contract workspace.

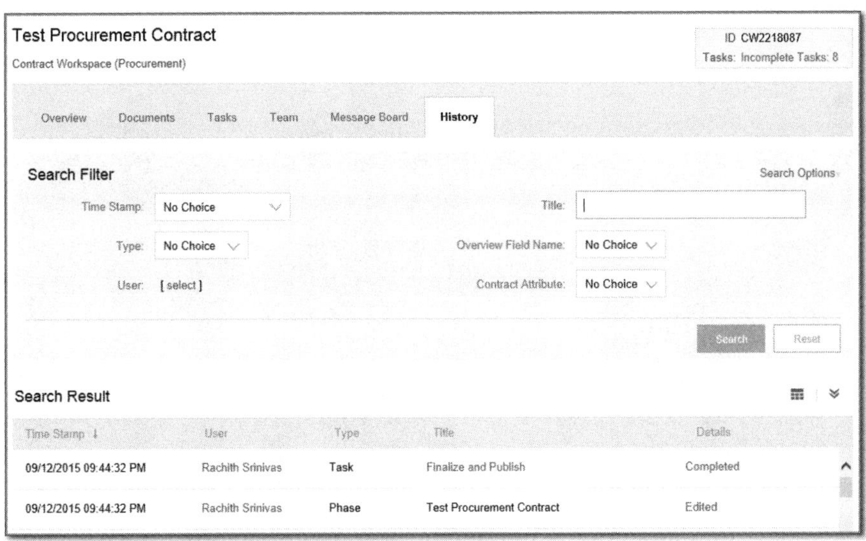

Figure 3.9 History Screen

Contract Amendment

SAP Ariba Contract Management provides features for different types of contract amendment, though the most common contract amendment type is *renewals*. Contracts that have the status of published or expired can be renewed.

SAP Ariba Contract Management provides timely reminders for contract renewals. By default, renewal reminders are sent to the contract author, but additional recipients can be added to receive the renewal reminders.

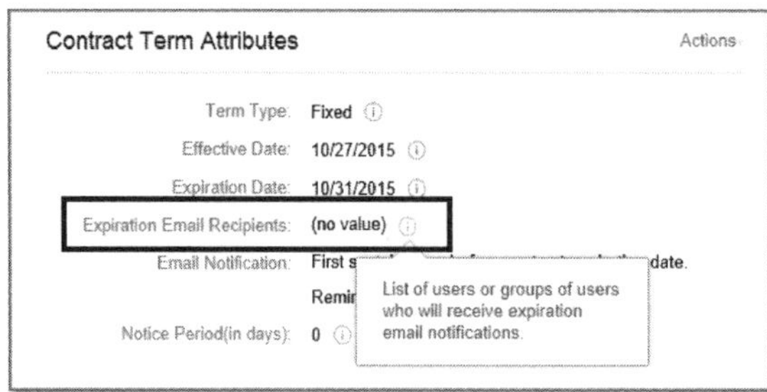

Figure 3.10 Contract Expiration Email Recipients

SAP Ariba Contracts Management provides a standard Expiring Contracts report that is included in the SAP Ariba Contracts Dashboard. On logging into SAP Ariba Contracts Management and navigating to the Contracts Dashboard, the user sees all contracts that he/she owns and that will expire within the next 90 days. You may alter this time period to fit your own business needs.

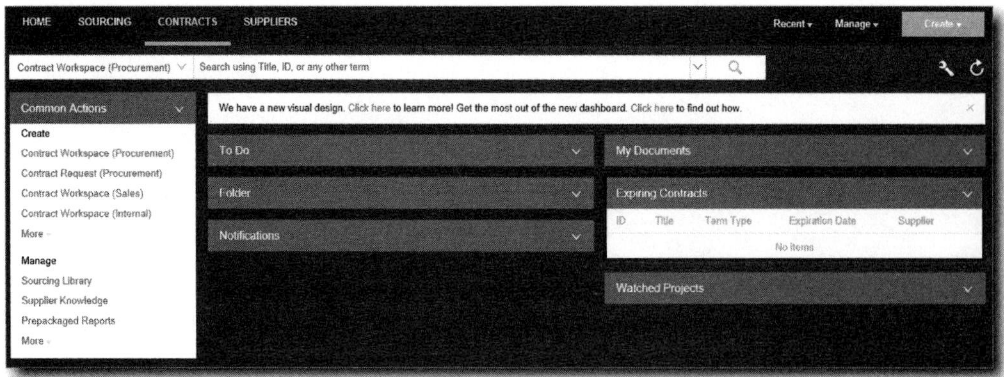

Figure 3.11 Expiring Contracts Report Channel on Contracts Dashboard

Expired or published contracts can be renewed by amending the contract and choosing RENEWAL as the amendment type.

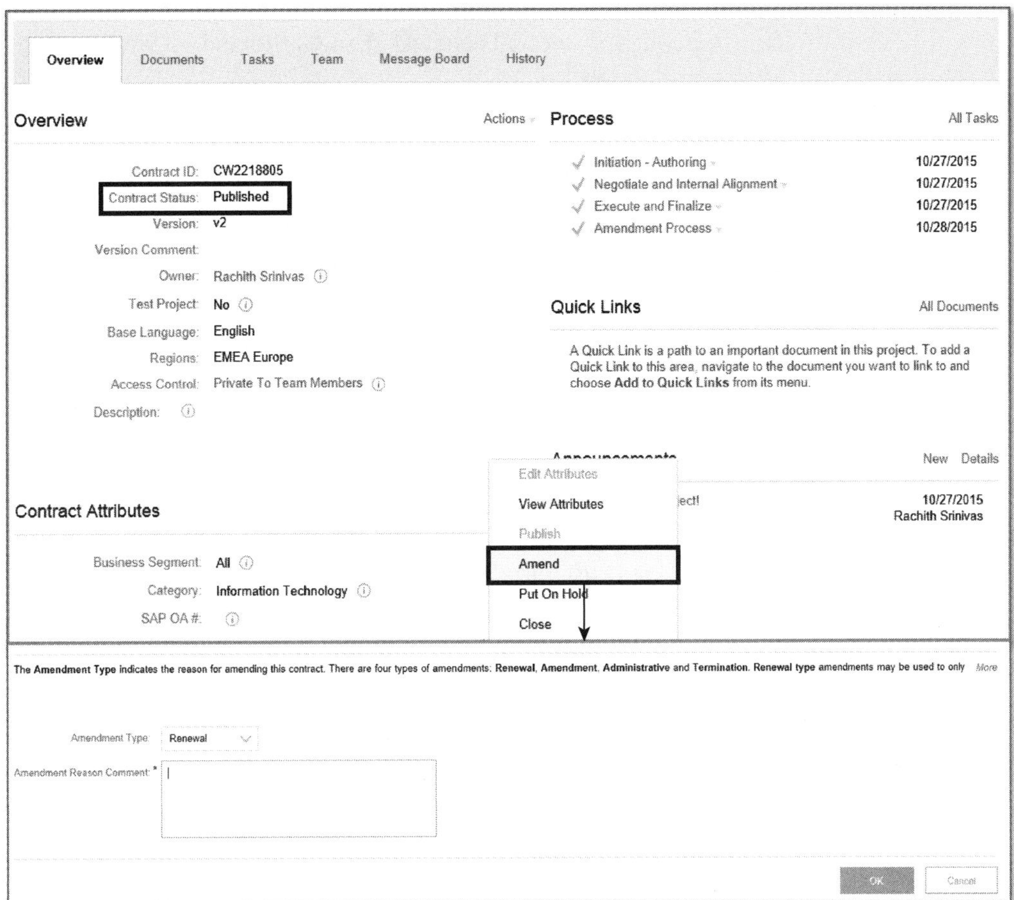

Figure 3.12 Amend a Published Contract

The following changes can be made during renewals:

- **Contract term attributes**
  Effective date and expiration date can be changed.
- **Tasks**
  Certain tasks including approval tasks can be enabled during contract renewals. Required tasks must be completed in order to publish the contract.

- **Documents**
  Documents in the DOCUMENTS tab can be amended. Additional documents can be added as needed.

The contract is re-published once all renewal changes—including any associated approval tasks—are completed.

Other amendment types include:

- **Amendment/full amendment**
  This amendment type is used when the complete contract workspace needs to be changed. The contract is republished once the changes are completed.
- **Termination**
  This amendment type is only available for published contracts. Closed or expired contracts cannot be terminated. The expiration date and email notification settings can be changed during this amendment process. This process is used to close the contract before the expiration date due to adverse conditions or disagreements. The contract is closed once the changes are completed.
- **Administrative**
  This amendment type is used to change non-contract details, such as adding a team member or uploading a supplemental document. The status of the contract does not change when performing an administrative amend. Republishing the contract is not required once this amendment process is complete.

Electronic Signatures in SAP Ariba Contract Management

SAP Ariba provides electronic signature capabilities in SAP Ariba Contract Management through integration to third party digital signature services, such as DocuSign and Adobe eSign. A signature task within a contract workspace routes the document electronically and securely via the internet to the document signee, in order to complete the signature electronically using one of the two services enabled in the landscape.

Note

While detailed configuration of eSign and DocuSign services is not within the scope of this book, please see SAP Ariba help documentation ARIBA • ADMINISTRATION • ADMINISTRATION AND INTEGRATION DOCUMENTATION • CONTRACT ADMINISTRATION for more information.

All SAP Ariba users who will be submitting eSign Service/DocuSign tasks must have an email associated with their user that matches the email of a valid and active eSign Service/DocuSign account (or have the auto-account creation option turned on for DocuSign). Those users that will need to work with signature tasks must also have the "Document Signer" group assigned to them.

Per Figure 3.13 and Figure 3.14, signature provider services can be enabled by administrators.

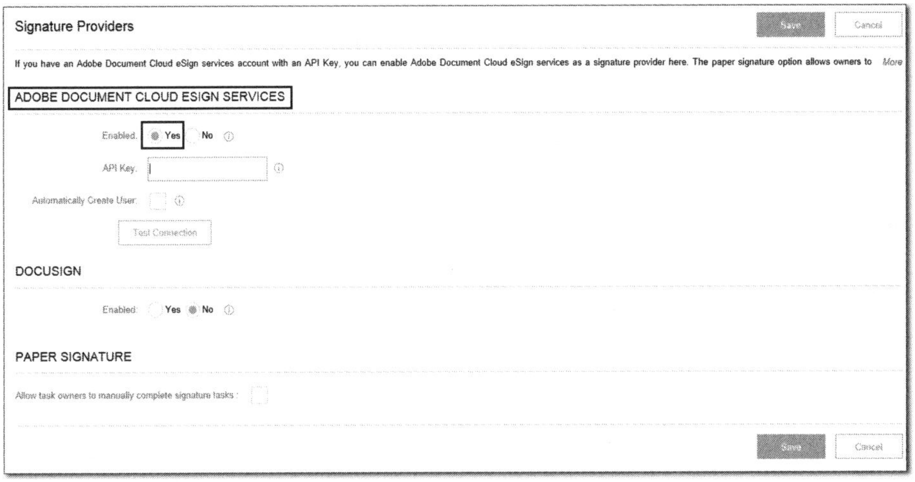

Figure 3.13 Enabling Signature Providers

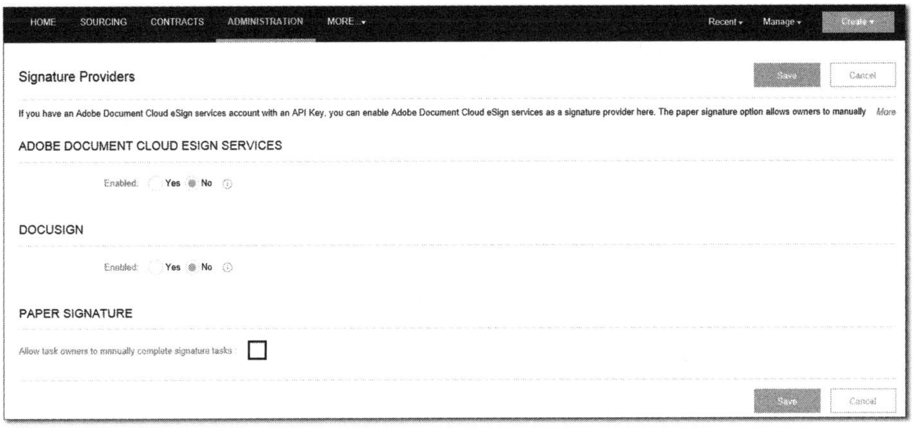

Figure 3.14 Enabling Paper Signature

The paper signature option allows signature task owners to manually complete a signature task by uploading an image of the signed document. To complete a paper signature task, users can submit a file with an electronic image of a "wet" signature (an image of a signature originally stroked on a paper document, using wet or pen ink). To enable paper signatures simply navigate to the SIGNATURE PROVIDERS option under MANAGE • ADMINISTRATION • SIGNATURE PROVIDERS, and check the box seen in Figure 3.14.

Creating a Signature Task

Signature tasks can be created off of individual documents or folders by clicking on the relevant document/folder within a contract workspace (CW) or contract request (CR) and selecting SIGNATURE under the CREATE NEW TASK options, as demonstrated in Figure 3.15. If you only have one signature solution enabled, the task will simply be created. If you have multiple signature solutions enabled, you will be able to select the desired solution per Figure 3.15. You can create multiple signature tasks within a single CR or CW, but you can only have one signature task associated with a single document or folder. Note that you can create signature tasks within an individual workspace, or at the process level.

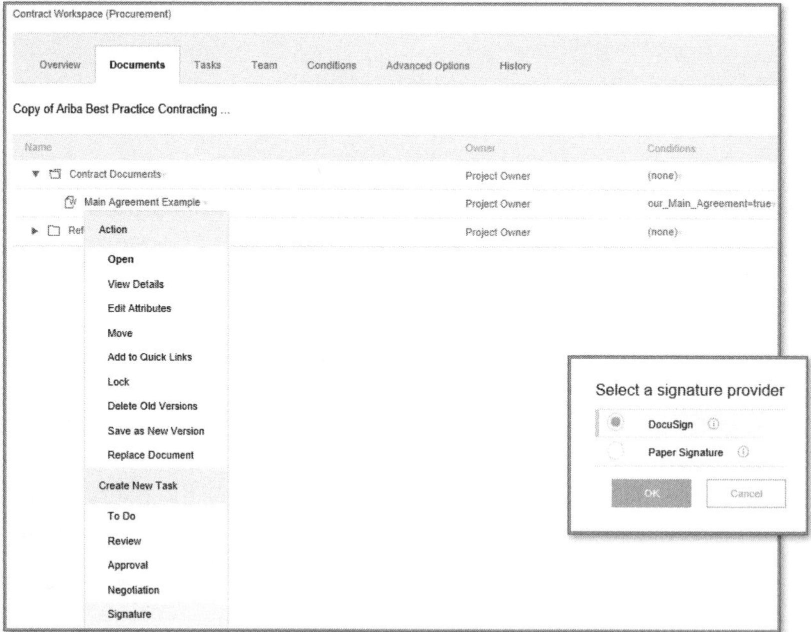

Figure 3.15 Creating a Signature Task

You can also assign any project group the "document signer" role, which will allow anyone placed in that role to sign a document. A combination of this project group/role setup and team member rules can be used to automate signers in line with the customer's workflow (delegation of authority), similar to approvals.

Submitting eSign/DocuSign Signature Task

To submit a signature task as in Figure 3.16, you must edit the NOT STARTED task created in the previous step. Here, you can add both internal and external signers of the document. You can also create new contacts to identify for signing, like in a review task.

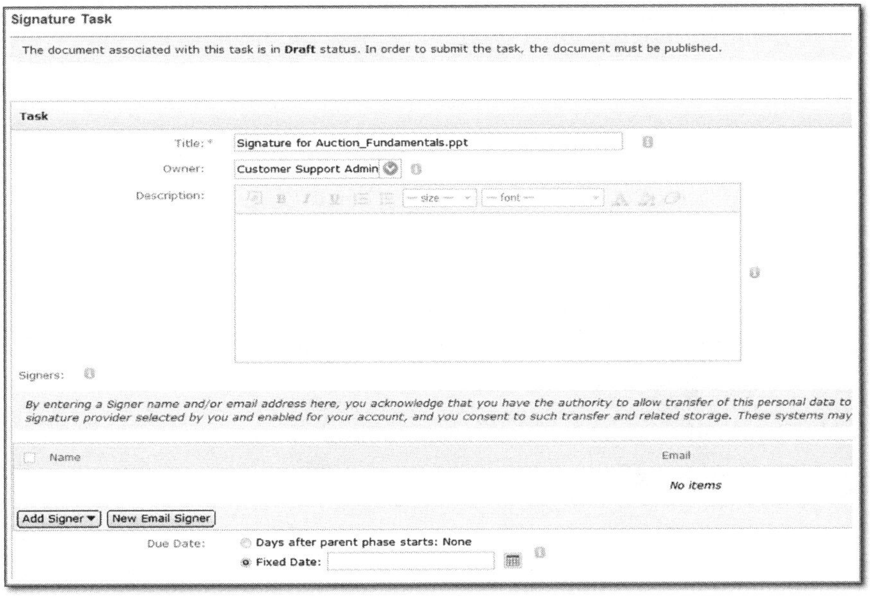

Figure 3.16 Submitting a Signature Task

Upon submitting the task, the user is directed to the eSign or DocuSign interface, where additional signature tags can be added. If a single document is associated with the task, then that document is routed for signatures. If a folder is associated with the task, all published documents within the folder are routed for signatures.

After submitting the task for e-signature, the task's status changes to SIGNING. Depending on the signatories' actions, the status will then change to SIGNED or DENIED (see Figure 3.17). The system checks for returned document every two hours.

Signature for 737836_Upstream_Integration_Work_Instructions[1].doc*	737836_Upstream_Integration_Work_Instructions[1]	Ariba Signature	Signing
Signature for contract.pdf*	contract	Ariba Signature	Signed
Signature for GroupDescriptions.xls*	GroupDescriptions (v2/2)	Ariba Signature	Denied

Figure 3.17 Signature Task Status

Receiving a Signature Request

Signers for both eSign and DocuSign tasks receive an email, as shown in Figure 3.18, requesting them to complete the signature of a document, or a set of documents if the task is associated to a folder. The title of the email will contain the SAP Ariba Contract ID (contract workspace ID) and the name of the document (or first document) to be signed.

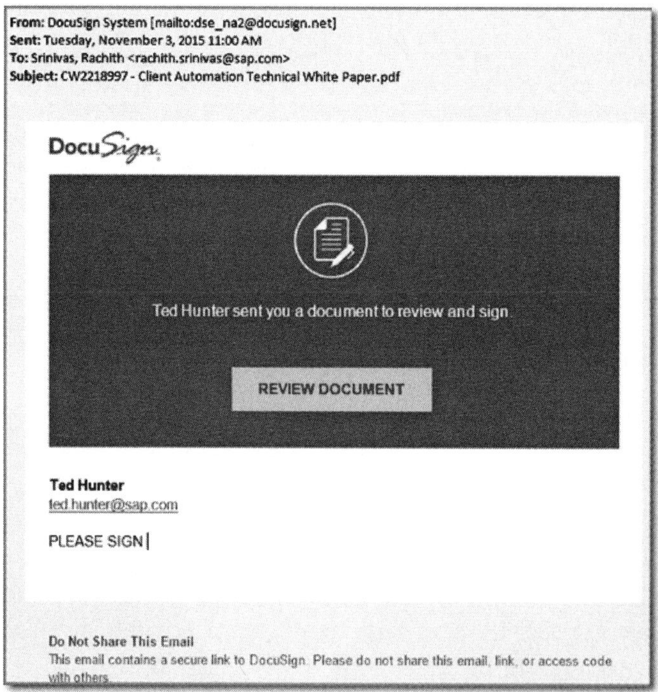

Figure 3.18 DocuSign Email Request

The signer can open the email and follow the instructions to complete the signature task, or forward the email to someone else who is able to complete the signature. The status of the task—as shown in earlier—changes based on the action taken by the signer.

Completing the eSign/DocuSign Signature Task

Once the signer returns the document (which moves the task to a status of SIGNED or DENIED, as shown in Figure 3.19), the task is officially complete. You can start a new round, or withdraw a signature task (in any status) by viewing the details of the task and selecting the correct options.

If the document is signed, it will be returned automatically to the contract workspace (CW) with a new title of the format shown in Figure 3.19. This signed document will return to the workspace or a specific folder, based on our task setup.

Signed_Ariba - On-Demand Solutions Technical Information_1	Ariba Signature	Signed

Figure 3.19 Signed Document

3.2 Implementing SAP Ariba Contract Management

SAP Ariba Contract Management provides a flexible solution to create, execute and manage enterprise-wide contracts such as procurement, sales, and general agreements with business partners. In the following sections, we will cover the implementation of SAP Ariba Contract Management, from setting up contract templates to defining your workflows, project resources, phases, and timelines. We will conclude by discussing the steps needed to configure and enable DocuSign electronic signatures, and some best practices for the SAP Ariba Contract Management implementation process.

3.2.1 Contract Authoring Process

The SAP Ariba Contract Management solution provides the ability for contract template administrators and legal departments to create and maintain standardized, enterprise-wide contract templates (or master agreement templates). These templates function as the starting point for contract creation by end users. The contract template is comprised of sections and clauses. Clauses are created, approved, and maintained in the clause library. Standardized clauses can be used in multiple contract templates, as shown in the Figure 3.20.

Per Figure 3.20, a clause corresponds to one major point or piece of information, and often corresponds to one paragraph within the document. Similar clauses can be organized into sections. It is a common practice to start with a current contract and create a master agreement template. Then, the clauses from this template are published to the clause library so that they can be reused in other master agreement templates. Thus, it is important for your clauses to be succinct, and for them to use standard language.

How to handle clauses that are similar

Major section		Clause	Similarities to be...	Main Agreement Masters: Services	Engineering	Consulting	Construction
Recitals	A	Recitals	Standard	✓	✓	✓	✓
Definitions	1	Definitions	All different				
Services	2.1	Descripton of services	All different				
	2.2	Change order	Standard in 3	✓	✓	✓	
	2.3	Work orders	Standard in 3	✓	✓	✓	
	2.4	C/O, W/O Authorizations			✓	✓	
	2.5	Limitations	Standard	✓	✓	✓	✓

Clause name

Whenever possible, reword similar clauses to create a standard clause which can be used in multiple agreements.

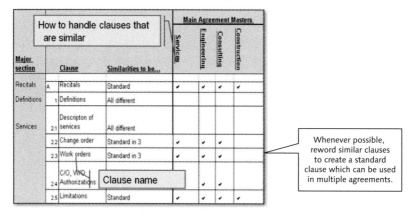

Figure 3.20 Contract Document Structure

The best practice is to reword similar clauses to create a standardized clause, thus reducing the number of clauses in the library.

In the following sections, we will cover the six major steps in preparing the main agreement template: document cleansing, style mapping, bookmarking, uploading the template to SAP Ariba, creating document properties, and adding conditions to the template. You can see an overview of this process in Figure 3.21.

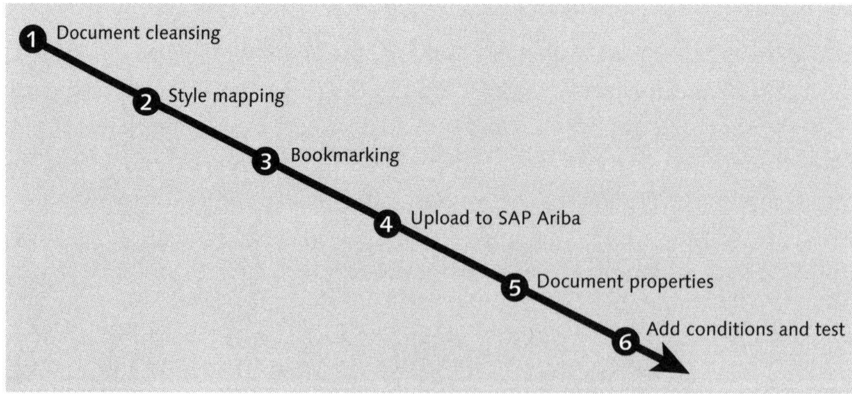

Figure 3.21 Process Steps to Create a Master Agreement Template

Document Cleansing

SAP Ariba Contract Management extensively uses Microsoft Word's built-in features for contract authoring. Note that Microsoft Word features are not always backward compatible, because all Microsoft Word documents contain embedded code that affects things such as formatting within the document. As it is impossible to know what version of Word was used to create the original document, in order to avoid potential problems within SAP Ariba Contract Management, it is imperative to cleanse the document. This can be done by simply copying and pasting the original document's content into a notepad editor before copying the content over to a new word document.

The following should be kept in mind while creating master agreement templates, in addition to the steps outlined in Figure 3.21:

- Do not overcomplicate
- Group clauses that should stay together
- Put each section title on its own line
- Make each clause its own paragraph when possible
- Remove hard-coded numbering

Style Mapping

The style mapping feature enables you to define the styles in Microsoft Word that the system will use to format sections and clauses when it generates contract documents. Style mapping is specific to each master agreement. Therefore, multiple master agreements use the same clause, that clause will be formatted differently, depending on the style mapping defined for each template.

Style mapping is done in SAP Ariba Contract Management, where you apply your styles to specific levels of your main agreement or contract addendum.

Bookmarking

In SAP Ariba Contract Management, bookmarks tell the system how to organize your main agreement or contract addendum into clauses and sections. They also determine where the document begins and ends as shown in Figure 3.22. Bookmarks are not considered text, and so do not appear in the printed version of the document. When the Microsoft Word document is uploaded into the template, the system uses the bookmarks to identify sections and clauses. With bookmarks, you can specify exactly how you want the system to parse the document. If any content within the document is not bookmarked, the system will interpret each paragraph as a clause.

Use the bookmarking format seen in Table 3.1.

Bookmark Type	Name in Microsoft Word
Section	`sectionSAP Ariba_<UniqueID>`
Clause	`clauseSAP Ariba_<UniqueID>`
Entire Contract Document	`sectionGlobalContract`

Table 3.1 Bookmarking Format

Some important notes to keep in mind while creating bookmarks to separate the template into sections and clauses are:

- No special characters in the unique ID in bookmarks.
- For clauses, always insert the ending bookmark before the paragraph marker.
- For sections, always insert the ending bookmark after the paragraph marker for the last line of the section.
- For `sectionGlobalContract`, the bookmark should be on a line by itself and not beside the document title.

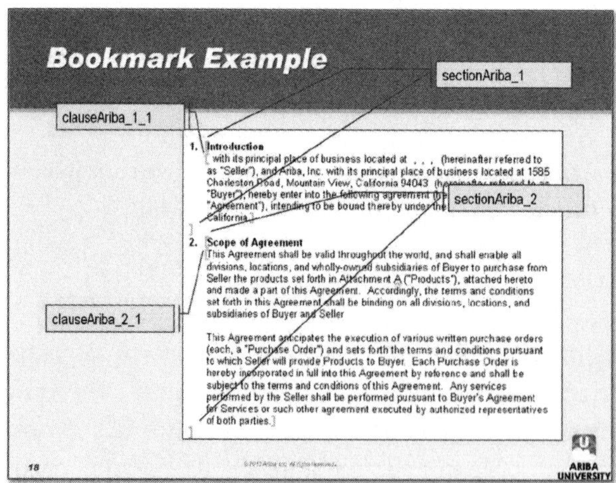

Figure 3.22 Bookmark Example

The following notes provides information on partial bookmarks and how SAP Ariba contracts handle partial bookmarking:

- All properly entered bookmarks are respected.
- If a particular paragraph is not explicitly bookmarked, it is treated as a clause. SAP Ariba Contract Management interprets all ad hoc and unmarked paragraphs as clauses.
- If a manual section bookmark is used, the first paragraph of the section serves as that section's title. The rest of the content within the section is handled based on the bookmarking rules.
- Every word document in SAP Ariba Contract Management should only have one `sectionGlobalContract` bookmark.
- If the `sectionGlobalContract` bookmark has not been added, the system adds one, which spans the entire document.

Uploading Main Agreement

Once formatting is complete, the document must be closed and uploaded to the SAP Ariba Contract Management template as a master agreement or contract addendum document. The system will read everything within the `sectionGlobalContract` marker and ignore the rest. The system parses the documents and builds the sections and clauses. Once the document loads, you can review the sections and clauses in the outline view.

> **Note**
>
> DFS (document file synchronization) must be enabled to leverage the complete contract authoring feature in SAP Ariba Contract Management.

Document Properties

Document properties can to define placeholder tokens within the clause content of the contract management templates. Those tokens will eventually be replaced by content defined in the OVERVIEW section of the contract workspace during the creation of the contract workspace.

Note

Document properties can be created in the contract management templates (master agreement/contract addendum documents) or directly in the contract workspace. However, this is usually done at the template level.

The two main document property types are:

- **Read-only document properties**
  These are only updated in the contract document when the corresponding field is changed in the contract workspace. Changing these in the contract document will not update the contract workspace. Read-only document properties may be used multiple times in a contract document.
- **Editable document properties**
  These are similar to read-only properties, except they also update the contract workspace if changed in the contract document.

  Editable document properties may only be used once in any given contract document, and they MUST appear in any document for which they are enabled.

Conditions on Clauses

Conditions are logical constructs that can be used within SAP Ariba Contract Management to control the visibility of a contract management template or documents, tasks or team members within a template that will appear in the contract workspace.

Conditions can also be used on sections and clauses within a master agreement template that define when a section or clause should be made visible when a master agreement document is created from the template. This allows a single main agreement template to create workspaces with different main agreement content, based on information entered by the workspace's creator. This can greatly reduce the number of main agreement templates required. The same is true of contract addendum templates.

3.2.2 Defining Workflows and Expiration Reports

In this section we will discuss the standard workflow capabilities and prepackaged reports that are essential components of SAP Ariba Contract Management.

Workflows

SAP Ariba Contract Management provides an approval workflow process task for enforcing strong compliance and oversight, and for reducing contracting risks within the organization. The workflow task, along with the electronic signature task, provides a seamless process for internal and external signatories to quickly and efficiently review, approve and sign contracts within SAP Ariba Contract Management, without the need for paper and ink. This considerably speeds up the contracting process, while simultaneously reducing the associated risks and non-compliance of contracts.

The workflow task can be defined in each contract template and is highly customizable. You may also set it as a required task, and it can be associated to a specific document or to a folder within the DOCUMENTS tab. When assigned to a folder, all documents within the folder will be included in the approval workflow process.

Per Figure 3.23, upon triggering the workflow task, all documents within the folder will be routed for approval, and an email with all documents attached will be generated and sent out to the approvers in the approval flow.

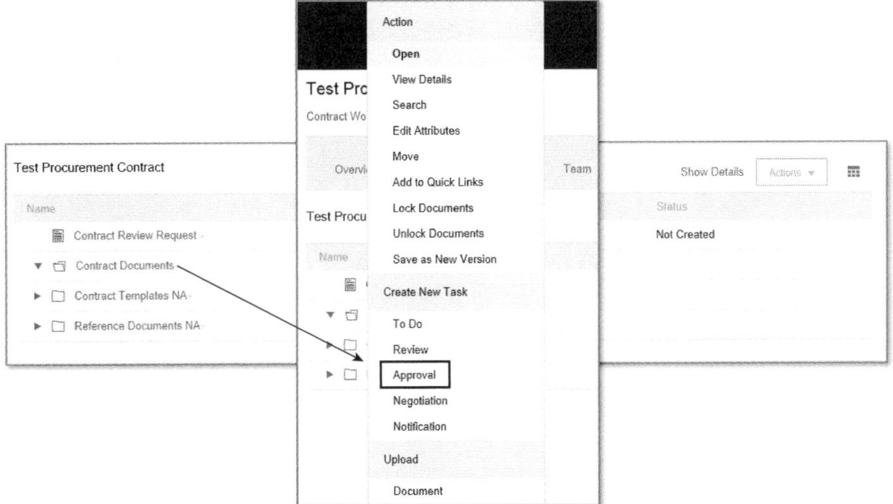

Figure 3.23 Create Workflow Task in Document Folder

SAP Ariba Contract Management provides a flexible approval workflow task that can be customized based on the customers approval process. The following approval flows are allowed:

- **Parallel**
  Multiple approvers/groups of approvers will receive the approval email simultaneously, allowing approvers to take action on the task simultaneously.
- **Serial**
  Each approver/group within the approval flow will receive an approval email in a serial order. An approver/group will receive an approval request email only after the previous approver/group has approved the document(s).
- **Custom**
  Customers can define a more complex workflow with a combination of parallel and serial approvals. Customers with a more complex approval flow can use this feature to design their approval process.

Figure 3.24 Approval Workflow Task

You can add approvers to the parallel and serial approval flow by clicking on the APPROVERS field and adding multiple users/groups within SAP Ariba Contract Management, as per Figure 3.24. Approvers must review and approve the document(s) within the folder associated with the approval task. You may add observers to the approval workflow, as well. Observers do not have to take any action throughout the process, but they will have access to review the status of the approval, in addition to the documents within the approval task.

Custom approval flow is a flexible option that SAP Ariba Contract Management provides to define a customized and complex approval process. On selecting CUSTOM as the flow, parallel and serial approval steps can be added to the approval process as shown in Figure 3.25.

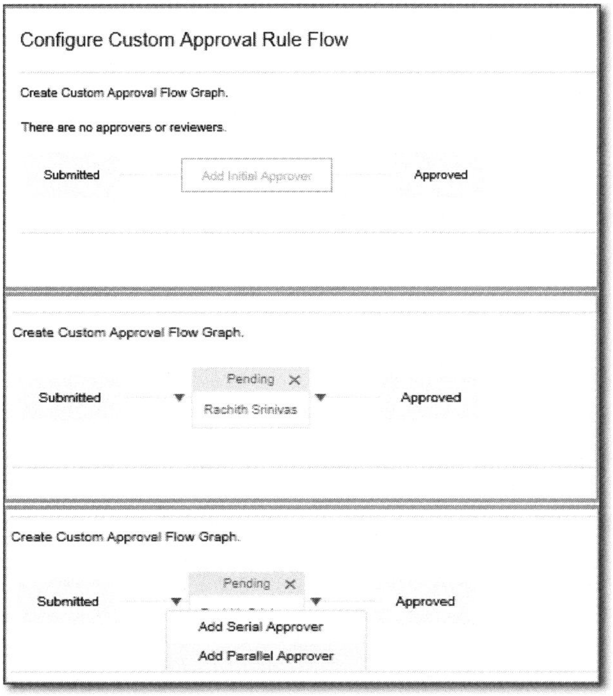

Figure 3.25 Creating Custom Approval Process

As in Figure 3.26, SAP Ariba Contract Management allows contract template administrators to define approval workflow tasks at the template level and setting the task as a required task. This allows organization to standardize the contracting process and thereby alleviating risks in the process.

When the workflow task is defined at the template level, the approvers in each step can be set to a project team member. When a contract workspace is created and a user/group is added as a project team member in the TEAM MEMBER tab, the user/group automatically becomes an approver of the document.

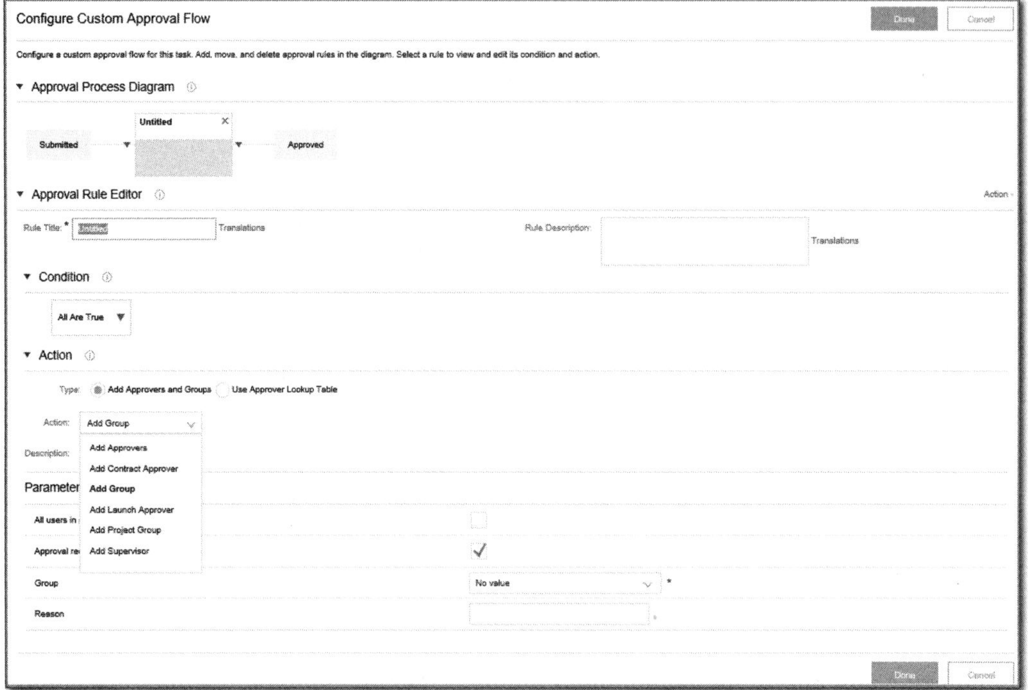

Figure 3.26 Defining Custom Approval Tasks in Contract Template

Reports

SAP Ariba Contract Management solution comes with prepackaged reports that users with sufficient permissions can access, which usually means having senior analyst system permission.

To run a prepackaged report, follow these steps:

1. Click on MANAGE • PREPACKAGED REPORTS.
2. Select a REPORTING AREA by clicking on the area and selecting OPEN. Which prepackaged reports will be visible to the user depends on the solutions enabled on the SAP Ariba realm (system).

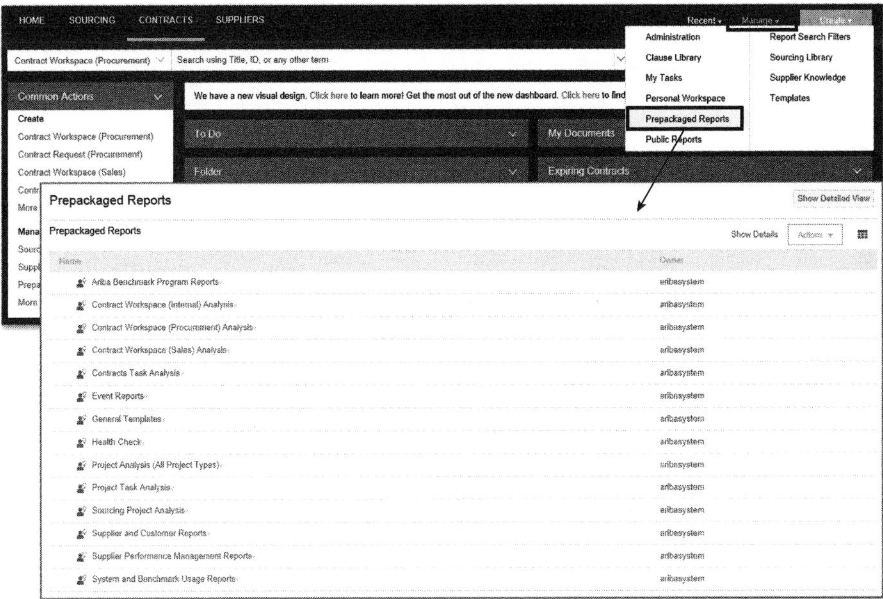

Figure 3.27 Prepackaged Reports

Reports can be added as pivot tables or charts. These reports will run dynamically to reflect current information, as shown in Figure 3.27. The contract expiration report can be added to the contracts dashboard by the system administrator and set as required content.

Three major contract management prepacked reports that you will likely want to make use of are:

- **Contracts expiring in the next three months**
  Lists all contracts expiring within a certain time period. A contract manager might use this report to identify the contracts that must be reviewed within the next month/quarter/year, prior to their expiration.
- **Active contract workspaces by owner**
  Lists all active contract workspaces by user. Contract managers and administrators might use this report to see all workspaces for which they have ownership.
- **Contract workspaces to start in the next three months**
  Lists all contracts with effective dates within the next three months. A contract manager might use this report to judge their upcoming workload or a manager may use to determine resource loading.

Note

There are several prepackaged reports which involve clause usage. These reports are only available in SAP Ariba Contract Management Professional, as clause library is not a feature for SAP Ariba Contract Management Basic.

3.2.3 Defining Project Resources, Phases and Timelines

The SAP Ariba Contract Management implementation approach leverages the SAP Ariba on-demand deployment methodology. The SAP Ariba on-demand deployment methodology consists of five key phases: kickoff, solution planning, data collection and site configuration, testing, and wrap up. Figure 3.28 contains further detail on these phases.

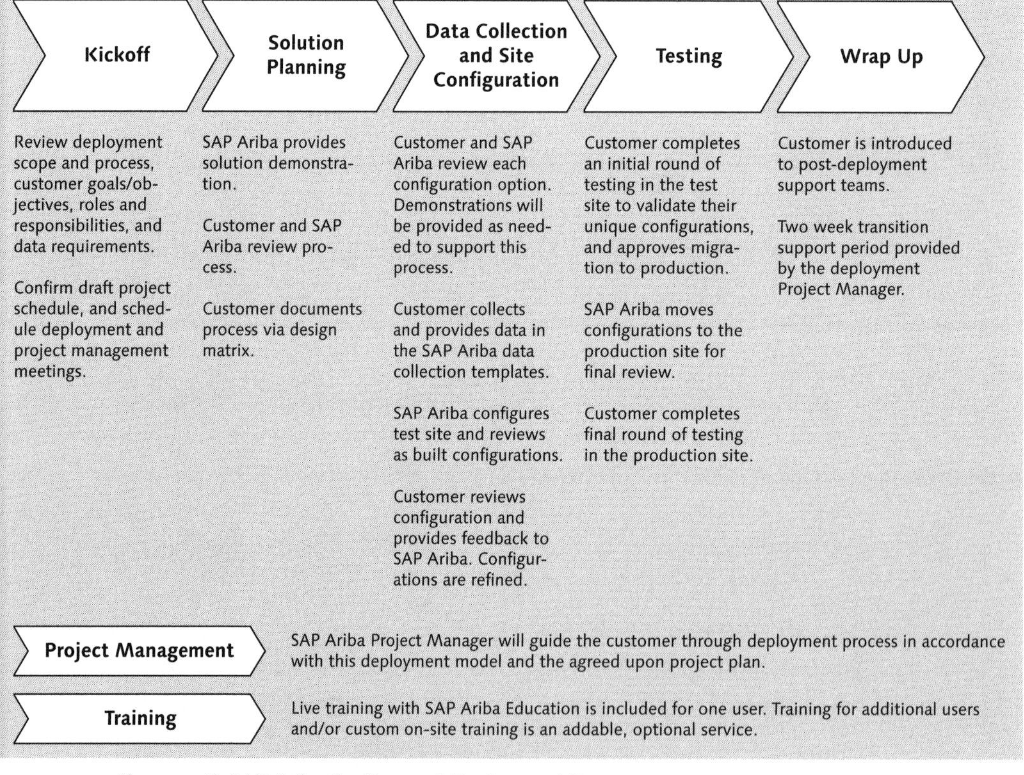

Figure 3.28 SAP Ariba On-Demand Deployment Process

Kickoff Phase

The kickoff phase is the first phase of the SAP Ariba Contract Management deployment project. During kickoff, the following tasks have to be completed:

- **Lead kickoff meeting**
  The purpose of this meeting is to introduce the SAP Ariba on-demand deployment methodology and the SAP Ariba project team to the customer, and to gain final alignment on scope and objectives. The audience for this meeting is the customer deployment team (including the project sponsor, project manager and core deployment team members), and the SAP Ariba team (including the SAP Ariba project manager, SAP Ariba configuration lead, consulting resources, customer engagement, executive, and account team). The SAP Ariba project manager is responsible for leading this meeting, and the team members' roles are outlined in Table 3.2.

Team Member	Title	Phone	Email	Team Member Role
	SAP Ariba Project Manager			▸ Responsible for day-to-day project management including managing scope, project plan, and SAP Ariba resources ▸ Provides functional knowledge of SAP Ariba software capabilities ▸ Facilitates configuration sessions and conducts functionality demonstrations ▸ Distributes project documentation at the conclusion of the project
	SAP Ariba Configuration Lead			▸ Responsible for technical aspects of the deployment, including data loading and functionality configuration ▸ Facilitates testing by providing a test script and responding testing related issues ▸ Provides administrative demonstrations

Table 3.2 SAP Ariba Resources

Team Member	Title	Phone	Email	Team Member Role
	Manager, Upstream Deployment			▸ Escalation point of contact
	Customer Engagement Executive			▸ Acts as the day-to-day operational advocate ▸ Assists / manages issues escalation ▸ Assists in coordinating with SAP Ariba teams throughout the length of your contract ▸ Contact to discuss events or changes within your organization that would impact your use of SAP Ariba products/services ▸ Offers on-going adoption support during the length of your contract ▸ Point of contact to manage contract extension
	Account Executive			▸ Commercial point of contact

Table 3.2 SAP Ariba Resources (Cont.)

Table 3.3 lists roles and responsibilities on the customer side.

Team Member	Team Member Role	Team Member
Customer Project Sponsor	▸ Act as champion for the project and provide overall project vision ▸ Escalation contact for deployment issue resolution ▸ Drive change management and high level communication in support of the project	

Table 3.3 Customer Resources

Team Member	Team Member Role	Team Member
Customer Project Manager	▸ Primary point of contact for overall deployment ▸ Partners with SAP Ariba Project Manager to manage project timeline and on time deliverables ▸ Manages all customer resource activities including internal meetings and decision making ▸ Resolve issues and escalate as necessary to ensure the deployment remains on track	
Functional Lead	▸ Define business process and participate in data collection and configuration efforts ▸ Complete unit testing throughout deployment ▸ Responsible for customer testing ▸ Lead roll out and training efforts post deployment	
Process Experts/Pilot Users	▸ Provide input to configuration decision ▸ Participate in testing as needed	

Table 3.3 Customer Resources (Cont.)

- **Finalize project plan with customer**
  A project plan containing the standard project timelines and resources must be presented to the customer deployment team, as in Table 3.3, during the kickoff meeting. The customer is usually presented with two timelines:
  - Aggressive/accelerated schedule: Assumes dedicated customer resources and/or limited scope
  - Relaxed schedule: Assumes part time customer resources, complex scope, enhanced testing phase, and/or complicated customer internal approvals.

While schedules can be tweaked based on the customers need, the project manager must use the standard project plans as a starting point. Sample timelines can be found in Figure 3.29 and Figure 3.30.

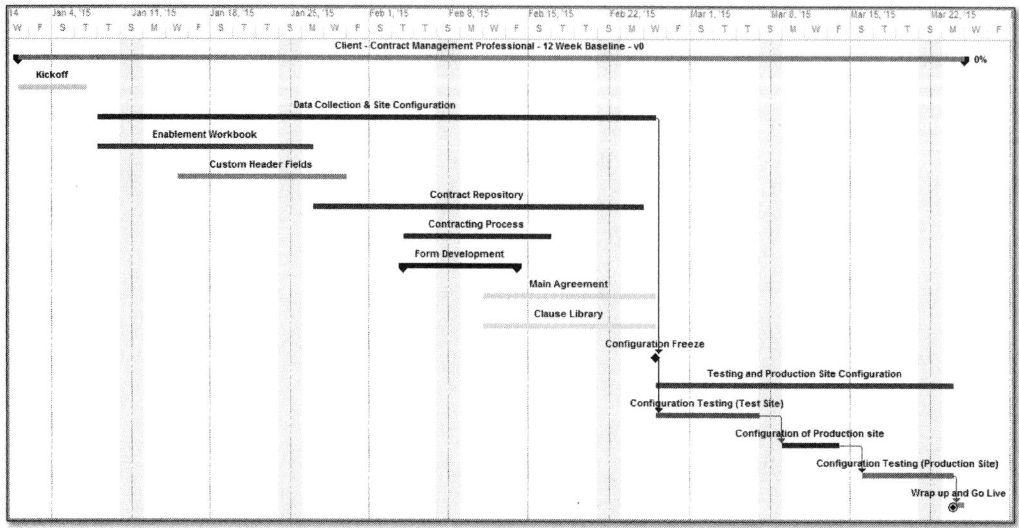

Figure 3.29 Contract Management Deployment—12 Weeks

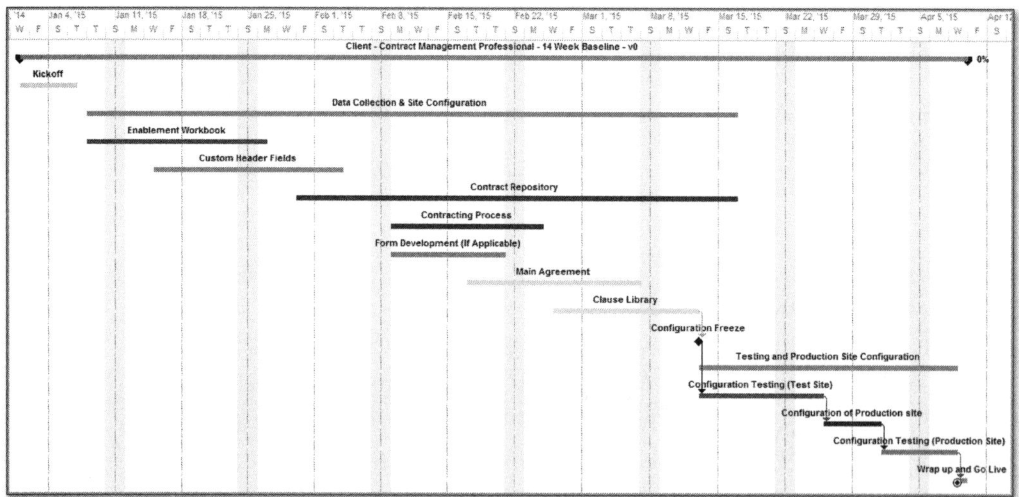

Figure 3.30 Contract Management Deployment—14 Weeks

Solution Planning Phase

The purpose of the solution planning phase is to review the customer's requirements and define the key gaps. During this phase, the SAP Ariba project manager and lead consultant, along with the SAP Ariba shared service lead, will hold process design review sessions to document AS-IS processes for the contract management. The standard SAP Ariba processes will be demoed and the AS-IS process will be documented in the contract process design document that will act as the reference document during the site configuration phase. Custom fields specific to a customer are defined in a custom header fields workbook.

Data Collection and Site Configuration Phase

This is the deployment phase of the project. The first part of this phase is to review and define the master data, such as suppliers/customers, departments, regions, currency etc., required for contract creation. The lead consultant will work with the customer deployment team to finalize the master data in an enablement workbook. The workbook will then be used as the basis for loading master data in the SAP Ariba Contract Management solution.

The master data is loaded to the test system, and the contract processes and related configurations—including contract templates, master agreement and clause library setup, and build of custom fields—will be completed in this phase.

Table 3.4 shows the deployment configurations in a typical SAP Ariba Contract Management deployment.

Configuration	Deployment Description
Master data	▸ Loading of master data via enablement workbook
Custom header fields	▸ 10 custom header fields
D-Form (1)	▸ Up to 50 fields/line items ▸ Up to 10 conditions
Custom report	▸ 1 custom report to be reviewed during deployment
Contracting process (1)	▸ Up to 30 tasks ▸ Up to 20 process configuration conditions ▸ Up to 10 process related documents
Main agreement (1)	▸ Up to 50 clauses ▸ Up to 10 conditions ▸ Up to 5 document properties for syncing from header field information

Table 3.4 Deployment Configurations

Configuration	Deployment Description
Clause library	▸ Up to 20 preferred clauses may be loaded into the clause library ▸ An alternate (or fallback) clause may be loaded for each Preferred clause
Contract repository load	▸ Up to 250 legacy contracts can be loaded during the deployment, with up to 2 documents average in each

Table 3.4 Deployment Configurations (Cont.)

Following are the data collection items required during the deployment of SAP Ariba Contract Management, and any sub-items within each category:

- Master data
  - Enablement workbook
- Customer logo
- Custom header fields
  - Customer header field data collection template
- Form development
  - Form data collection template
- Contracting process and document attachments
  - Contracting process design matrix
- Contract repository
  - Repository data collection template
  - Contract documents (OCR format preferred) submitted via encrypted disk
- Main agreement
  - Contract document
  - Identification of any conditional clauses
- Clause library
  - Clause library template
  - Clause language in MS Work format
  - Approvals on use/modification
- Customer analytical report

Testing Phase

On completing the site configurations and reaching the configuration freeze milestone, the lead consultant and customer deployment team will plan the UAT (user acceptance testing). The customer deployment team is responsible for defining the test scripts for UAT. During this phase, the UAT test scripts are executed, and the lead consultant and shared service resources in SAP Ariba immediately fix any issues that arise from this testing. On completion of the UAT, and upon receiving a sign off on configurations, the shared services resources in SAP Ariba will migrate all the configuration changes to production environment.

Wrap-Up Phase

This is the final phase where a wrap-up call is held by the SAP Ariba Project Manager who will introduce the post deployment support team to the customer's deployment team. On completing the wrap-up call, the SAP Ariba Contract Management solution is deemed Live. The SAP Ariba project team gives the reigns of the system are transferred to the customer and the post deployment support team.

3.2.4 E-Signature Configuration

The following two steps are required to enable electronic signatures in DocuSign:

1. Contact DocuSign and set up an account for the customer.
2. Add user accounts for the DocuSign account for task owners.

After you complete these steps, the users in your organization can begin creating signature tasks on documents with extensions of PDF, XLS, XLSX, TXT, RTF, DOC, DOCX, PPT, PPTX, PNG, JPG, GIF, and TIF.

You will also need to set up two types of DocuSign accounts:

- A single DocuSign administrator account
- A DocuSign user account for each task owner who will be creating signature tasks

The customer is responsible for creating the single DocuSign administrator account. Users on the customer side who have access to this administrator account can see all documents submitted for publishing. In order for task owners of the signature task to send the documents for signature, a DocuSign user account must be created for each task owner. This user account must be associated to the DocuSign administrator account.

Document signers do not need to have a DocuSign account in order to sign. DocuSign will send an email the first time they are invited to sign a contract electronically.

Once the DocuSign administrator account is setup, the following steps need to be taken to activate the electronic signature service using DocuSign:

1. Go to Manage • Administration • Project Management • Signature Providers.
2. As shown in Figure 3.31. and Figure 3.32, navigate to DocuSign area of the page and select Yes for the Enabled radio button.
3. Check the Automatically Create User box, Figure 3.33 if and only if customer has provided written confirmation.

> **Note**
>
> Checking the Automatically Create User box will create a user automatically under the customer's corporate eSign account. Creating users can lead to licensing fees.

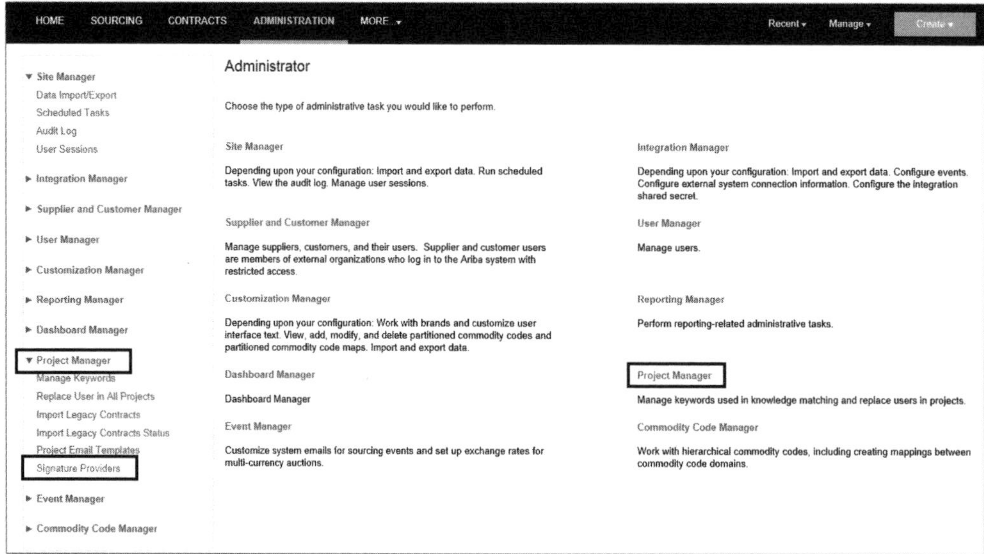

Figure 3.31 Signature Provider Settings

Figure 3.32 Enabling DocuSign

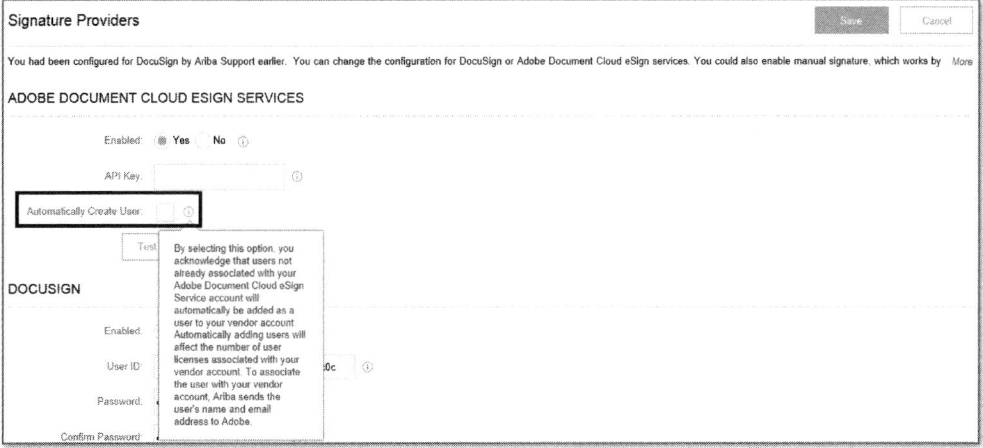

Figure 3.33 Enabling Automatic DocuSign User Account Creation

4. Enter username and password for the DocuSign administration account created previously. Select Demo Account to set up and test the connection.
5. Click Save to save your configurations.

All users creating contracts will be added to the SAP Ariba document signer global user group.

DocuSign also enables you to view an audit trail for documents in the DocuSign system, and to create and view reports for documents submitted for signing.

Some of the functionality available to you to monitor documents in DocuSign include:

- The DocuSign administrator can view an audit trail for documents in DocuSign system. SAP Ariba polls DocuSign recursively for updates on this information.
- The DocuSign administrator can create and review a report of documents that have been submitted for signing. This is referred to as *envelope report* and includes the sender (task owner) and recepient's (signer) email addresses and statuses.
- DocuSign administrators, senders and signers (optionally with DocuSign accounts) can view DocuSign documents in multiple ways, from within the DocuSign interface (outside of SAP Ariba).
- DocuSign's interface includes:
  - Envelopes: Inbox, Sent, Draft, Deleted, and Client Information
  - Search: Awaiting my Signature, Expiring Soon, Out for Signature, Completed, and Last Search
  - Admins ONLY: Templates, Shared Templates, All Account Templates, and PowerForms
- The availability of DocuSign's reporting tools are based upon set permssions, and include twelve other reports which can be customized and scheduled.
- DocuSign also includes a dashboard with charts and graphs on envelope status, out for signature and other factors.

The other major option for electronic signatures is eSign. All eSign Service (formerly EchoSign) settings are customer-facing, allowing a true self-service setup model. eSign Service users must make Adobe aware that they will be using their account with SAP Ariba so that additional configurations can take place on the eSign Service side. If the customer does not take this step, they will not be able to submit signature tasks. In order to enable eSign in SAP Ariba you must have the account API key.

To activating eSign in SAP Ariba, you must:

1. Go to MANAGE • ADMINISTRATION • PROJECT MANAGEMENT • SIGNATURE PROVIDERS.
2. As seen in Figure 3.34 and Figure 3.35, once on the SIGNATURE PROVIDERS page, navigate to ADOBE DOCUMENT CLOUD ESIGN SERVICES area of the page and select YES for the ENABLED radio button.

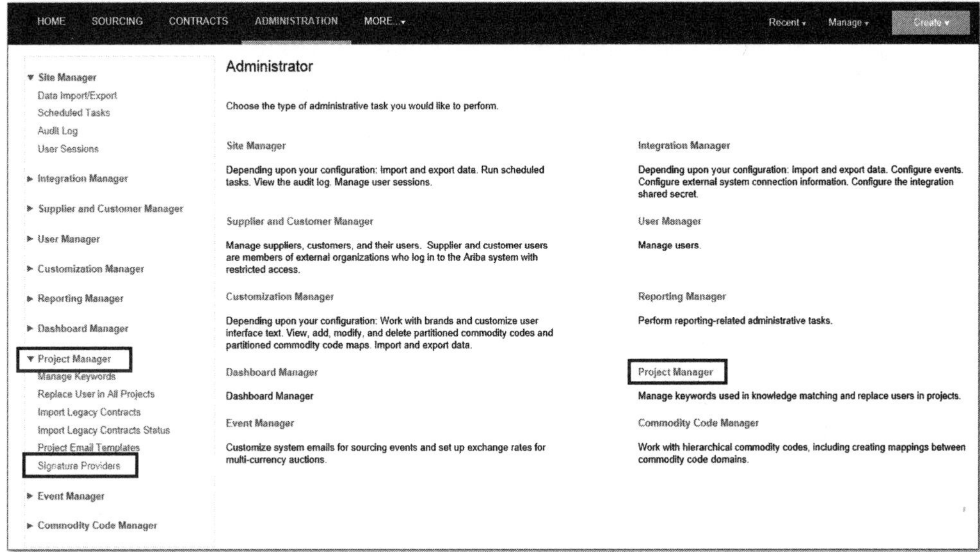

Figure 3.34 Signature Provider Settings

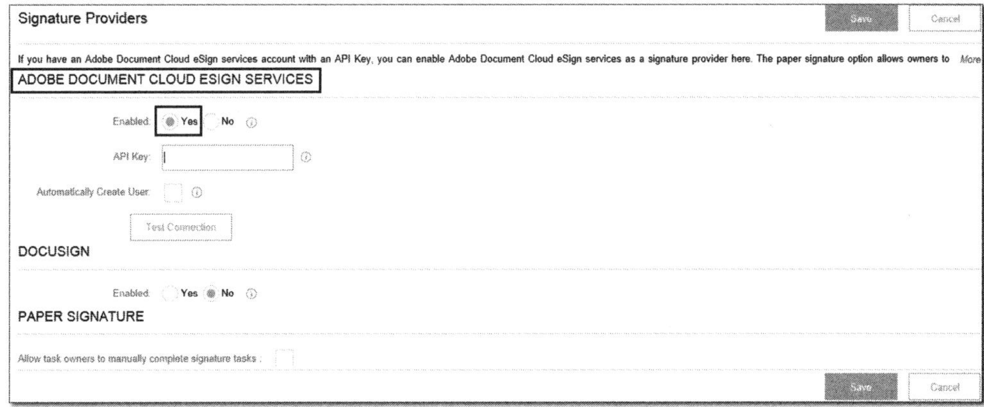

Figure 3.35 Enabling eSign Services

3. Enter the customer-provided eSign Services account API Key.
4. Check the AUTOMATICALLY CREATE USER box if and only if the customer has provided written confirmation (see Figure 3.36).

> **Note**
>
> Checking the AUTOMATICALLY CREATE USER box will create a user automatically under the customer's corporate eSign account. The creation of users can incur licensing fees.

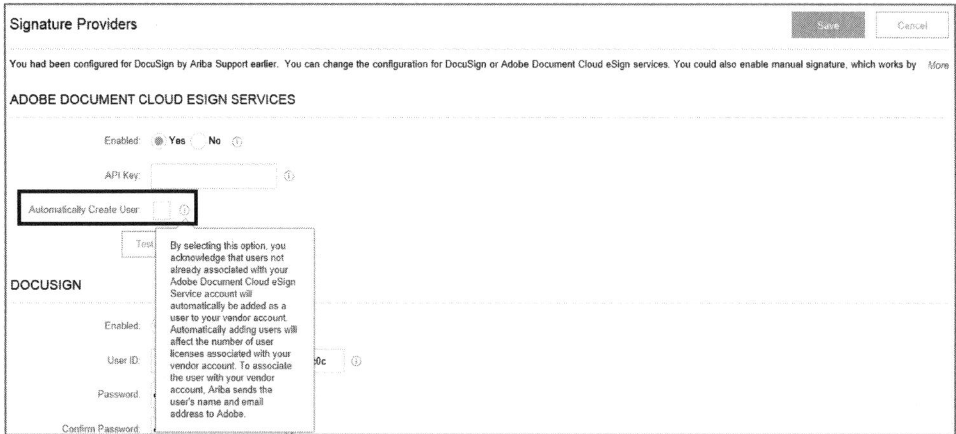

Figure 3.36 Enabling Automatic eSign User Account Creation

5. Click SAVE to save configurations

3.2.5 Best Practices

This section will provide you with some best practices for your SAP Ariba Contract Management implementation. These best practices are based on several SAP Ariba Contract Management implementations across various verticals such as utilities, energy services, healthcare, oil and gas, and telecommunications. The best practices are categorized into configuration components, including the contract legacy load process.

- **Master data**
  - Push customers to define and finalize the commodity codes at the earliest possible point during the project. Too many projects are delayed because commodity codes are not defined on time.

  - Define the benefits of using UNSPSC codes for commodity codes and the integration implications of commodity codes with SAP Ariba Network and SAP Ariba P2P.
  - Try to maintain the level of commodity codes to up to four levels, as only up to four levels are reportable, even though seven levels of commodity codes can be loaded.
  - If SAP Ariba Spend Visibility is in the landscape, make sure to understand the common master data between SAP Ariba Spend Visibility and SAP Ariba Contract Management. The following master data is shared between SAP Ariba Spend Visibility and SAP Ariba Contract Management:
    - Enterprise users
    - Units of measure
    - Currency conversion rates
  - Identify the suppliers that need to be loaded either as a batch process or through registration using SAP Ariba Supplier Information Management.
  - Customer-specific groups for approvals and access must be defined. These groups will inherit roles from one or more parent system groups. Care should be taken while defining these custom groups.
- **Contract authoring**
  - Contract authoring is a very advanced feature that will require a good knowledge of SAP Ariba Contract Management. It is advisable to use a phased approach for rolling out contract authoring.
  - When working with assembled contract documents:
    - Do not use manual (literal) paragraph numbering.
    - Remove any empty paragraphs before loading—do not use empty paragraph for vertical spacing. Change paragraph style in Microsoft word and increase the spacing before or after the paragraph.
    - Prepare clean versions of the Microsoft Word documents—Microsoft Word documents contain embedded data used for formatting and other operations. The embedded data can vary depending on the Microsoft Word version used, and opening a document created using one version of Microsoft Word with a newer version of Microsoft Word does not update all the embedded data to the newer version.

  - Remove soft returns before loading the document. You should also remove soft returns within paragraphs that will be clauses. Assembled documents do not support soft returns or page breaks inside clauses. Soft returns are created when users type Shift+Enter into a Microsoft Word document. Soft returns might also appear in contract documents with text copied from an HTML web page, or another format with markup syntax.
- Keep in mind that a lot can be achieved within SAP Ariba Contract Management without the contract authoring process.

- **Header fields**
  - Don't create fields that will not be used. In SAP Ariba Contract Management deployment, up to 10 custom fields are included with the deployment. In order to create more, the customer will have to purchase additional set of fields. Also, from a usability standpoint, 10 fields is ideal.
  - Name fields consistently across solutions such as SAP Ariba Sourcing and SAP Ariba Contract Management. Doing so will allow data to flow from one solution to another. For instance, a value maintained in a custom field with the same name in SAP Ariba Sourcing and SAP Ariba Contract Management will automatically fill when an SAP Ariba contract is created from an SAP Ariba sourcing award. Also, fields with the same name in different modules in the SAP Ariba upstream can share the same pick lists. Finally, a consistent naming scheme will lead to across-the-board standardization, making the solution will more intuitive for business users.
  - Make fields required when they are to be used in reporting.
  - Position fields logically.
- **Contract types**
  - Customers often want to include multiple contract types in a drop down list at the header of SAP Ariba contract workspace. In SAP Ariba, it is important to note that some contract types may not refer to classification, but may instead refer to the functionality within SAP Ariba. For instance, an amendment maybe defined as a contract type by customers, but in SAP Ariba, there is a built-in functionality to define the status of the contract as an amendment.

- **Workspace questions**
  - Workspace questions are not reportable. Care must be taken while choosing between using a custom field or a workspace question.
  - Workspace questions can be very useful in guiding the user through the contracting process, and can be used as a condition throughout the workspace to hide or show certain tasks, documents, etc. Questions that do not need to be reported should be created as questions to save on the count of custom fields.
  - Template questions cannot be translated. A workaround is to show multiple languages in the question. If customer team is not centralized, it may be a good idea to create separate templates based on various languages.
- **Project tasks**
  - Do not define too many contract tasks. This could result in lesser or slower user adoption. Best practice is to keep the number of tasks below 10. If this is hard to achieve, keep the number of required tasks as low as possible.
  - Approval and review tasks can be linked to the complete folder, or even workspace. Therefore, you do not have to create separate approval and review tasks for each document.
  - Task attributes are extremely useful. Make sure to define them appropriately. For instance, make sure to set Repeat for each Document Draft to Yes for approval workflow tasks.
- **Contract legacy loads**
  - Contract legacy loads is a time demanding activity to collect all the necessary data. Advice customers to start this process early in the project.
  - Provide small set of data in advance to customers.
  - Pay attention to special characters: project names can contain them, but documents cannot.
  - Disable emails during legacy loads to ensure users are not spammed with emails.
  - A separate and simpler contract template is usually defined for legacy loads.
- **Task notifications**

It is very important to review the notifications for each task with the customer. This will reduce the frustration business users may encounter upon receiving several emails from SAP Ariba. Email notification preferences can be used by individual users to disable or enable notifications.

3.3 Summary

Our goal in this chapter was to describe the benefits of implementing the SAP Ariba Contract Management solution. The features defined in this chapter such as contract authoring and integration to electronic signature providers can be easily enabled to create a complete end-to-end paperless contracting solution that considerably improves the contracting process, resulting in greater efficiency, lower costs, and improved relationships. Lastly, this chapter recommends tried-and-tested best practices for quickly and efficiently implementing SAP's cloud solution for contract management.

This chapter focuses on operational procurement, a set of processes in what SAP Ariba broadly calls "downstream." Operational procurement includes SAP Ariba Procure-to-Pay and its variations and SAP Fieldglass, a leading vendor management system for contingent labor procurement.

4 Operational Procurement

Once the earlier activities of sourcing and setting up a contract have occurred, procurement in the traditional sense can begin. Several SAP Ariba and SAP Fieldglass solutions support operational procurement activities: SAP Ariba Procure-to-Pay (P2P), SAP Ariba Procure-to-Order (P2O), SAP Ariba Procurement Content (SAP APC), and the SAP Fieldglass Vendor Management System (VMS). The SAP Fieldglass Vendor Management System manages all categories of external labor, including contingent workers, independent contractors, and specialized talent pools. In other words, for contract workers, it addresses the intersection between HR and procurement and helps organizations keep an eye on and analyze their contingent workforces.

This chapter outlines SAP Ariba Procure-to-Pay, SAP Ariba Services Procurement, SAP Ariba Procurement Content, and SAP Fieldglass VMS. It connects the dots between the solutions' functionalities, and shows how to implement them.

4.1 SAP Ariba P2P, SAP Ariba P2O, SAP APC, and SAP Ariba Services Procurement

SAP Ariba Procure-to-Pay (P2P) supports the end-to-end procurement process through payment in SAP Ariba, whereas SAP Ariba Procure-to-Order (P2O) stops short at ordering, and then integrates with an SAP ERP backend system for goods/services receipts and invoicing/payment.

Viewed another way, SAP Ariba Procure-to-Pay (P2P) covers the processes of requesting, approving, and procuring an item/service (as seen in Figure 4.1), as well as invoice processing and cash management. Compare this to SAP Ariba P2O, which only covers the first part of this process. Figure 4.2 shows the SAP Ariba home page, which leverages a portal approach to provide the user with a gateway to all the SAP Ariba solutions they can access.

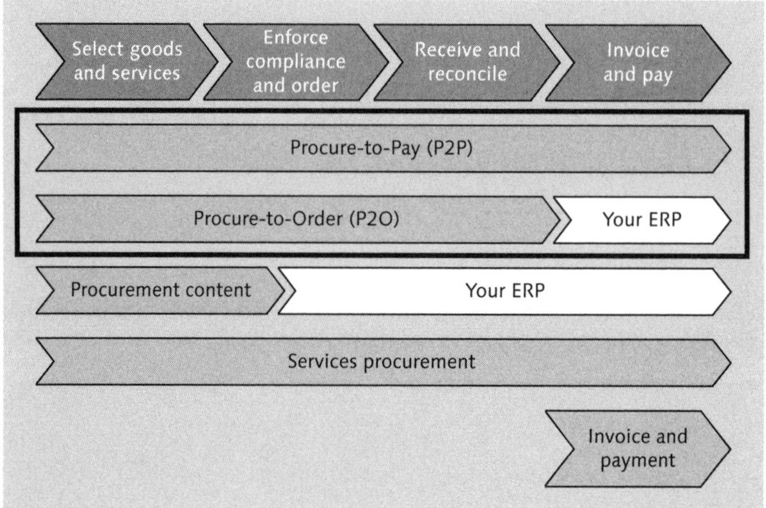

Figure 4.1 What is SAP Ariba P2X/SAP Ariba P2P?

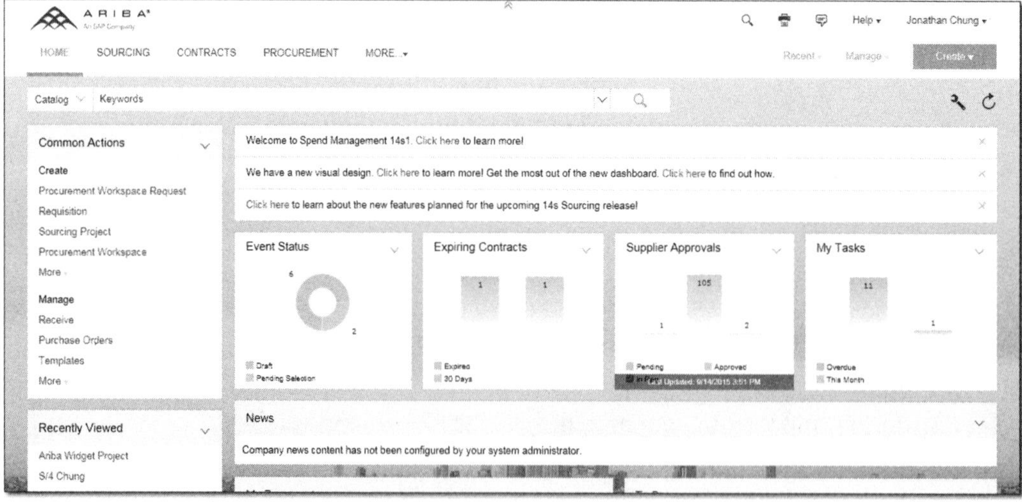

Figure 4.2 Home Page—SAP Ariba

Supporting both SAP Ariba P2P and SAP Ariba P2O is SAP Ariba Procurement Content (SAP APC). SAP Ariba Procurement Content provides users with a catalog platform in the SAP Ariba Network for accessing content from suppliers via their SAP Ariba Network loaded catalogs, directly to a catalog hosted by a supplier (punch out), or customer-loaded catalog in SAP APC. Choosing an item from a catalog ensures pricing and item consistency, as well as contract consumption/ adherence in the procurement process, and is usually a best practice approach.

In the following sections, we will cover when and where to deploy SAP Ariba P2X and the two variations of SAP Ariba P2X: SAP Ariba P2P and SAP Ariba P2O. For contingent workforce management, we will review SAP Fieldglass solutions and implementations. We will also cover integration approaches with SAP ERP environments.

4.1.1 SAP Ariba Procure-to-Pay and Procure-to-Order

This section outlines when and where to leverage SAP Ariba P2P and SAP Ariba P2O, the overall processes covered by these solutions, and how they work with other solutions including SAP Ariba Discovery, SAP Ariba Spot Quote, and SAP Ariba Procurement Content (SAP APC).

Procure to Order (SAP Ariba P2O)

Chapter 2 and Chapter 3 of this book, as well as the steps in Figure 4.3, cover sourcing activities. In these steps, a demand is registered or forecast and a source of supply identified using the RFX or by assigning one of the category suppliers directly as the source of supply for the purchasing. If the supplier is new, they are typically vetted and then added as a supplier to the supplier master for the company. Once the supplier relationship is established during this sourcing process, a user can log into SAP Ariba P2O or SAP Ariba P2P and request an item/service, navigate the approvals process established internally by their company, order the item, and receive the item in SAP Ariba P2O or SAP Ariba P2P. A user can order both catalog items and non-catalog items, as per Figure 4.4.

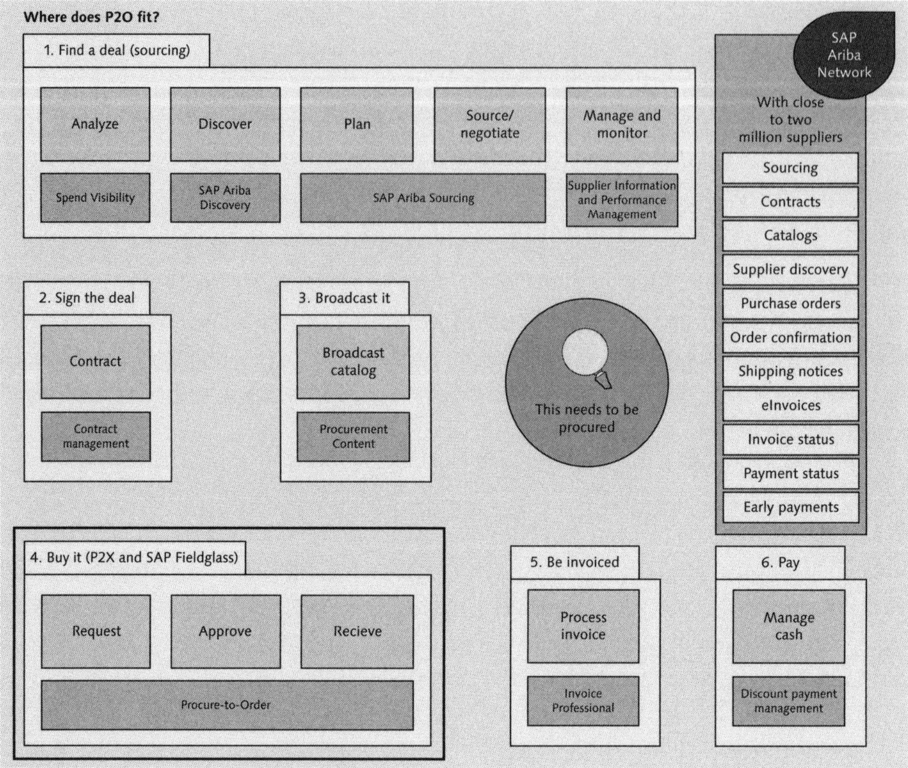

Figure 4.3 Where Does SAP Ariba P2O Fit?

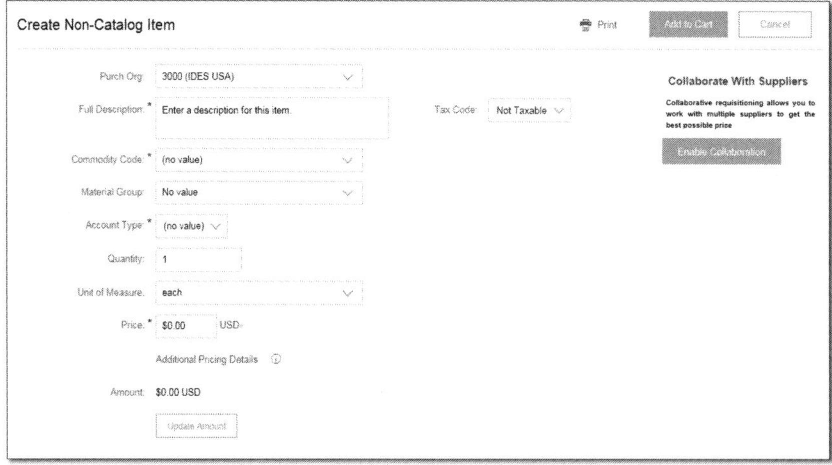

Figure 4.4 SAP Ariba P2P: Create a Non-Catalog Item

In SAP Ariba P2O, the invoice then arrives in the SAP ERP environment for processing from the supplier. SAP Ariba P2O and SAP Ariba P2P both have the ability to update connected SAP ERP environments so that the accounts payable department can make a three-way match based on the documents generated in SAP Ariba. For lightweight integrations where only payment to the supplier is required (such as SAP Ariba P2P), an "OK2Pay" message is sent to the SAP ERP/payment system once all of the transaction steps from request item/service to invoice processing have been completed in SAP Ariba.

SAP Ariba P2O's process also covers the requisition to order in SAP Ariba, with follow on invoicing occurring in another system, typically an SAP ERP-based process. As such, SAP Ariba P2O covers the requisition process, receiving, catalogs, contract compliance, interactions/collaborations on purchase orders (POs) with supplier in the SAP Ariba Network (including supplier determination, PO confirmation, and ship notice), as well as PO delivery to suppliers via the SAP Ariba Network and/or one of the supported transmission methods.

SAP Ariba P2O users and catalog managers can access SAP Ariba Procurement Content catalogs, and these catalogs can be loaded from the business network using cXML and CIF file formats. Level 1 (hosted on the business network) and level 2 (hosted by the supplier) punchout catalogs can also be accessed via SAP APC. In both instances, the business network handles the authentication step. Keyword search, dynamic filters for categories, suppliers, price ranges, manufacturers, and favorites, are all supported in SAP Ariba P2O connections with SAP APC. In addition, both SAP Ariba P2O and SAP Ariba P2P approaches in SAP APC support kits and filtered views.

Per Figure 4.5, Budget checks in SAP Ariba P2O can leverage imported budget data from your finance systems in SAP ERP, and can export updates on budget consumption as the procurement is approved. Once approved, you can send the resulting purchase order via a number of delivery formats, including fax, email, cXML, electronic data interchange (EDI), and/or manual delivery. Purchasing cards (p-cards) are also supported, along with p-card reconciliation.

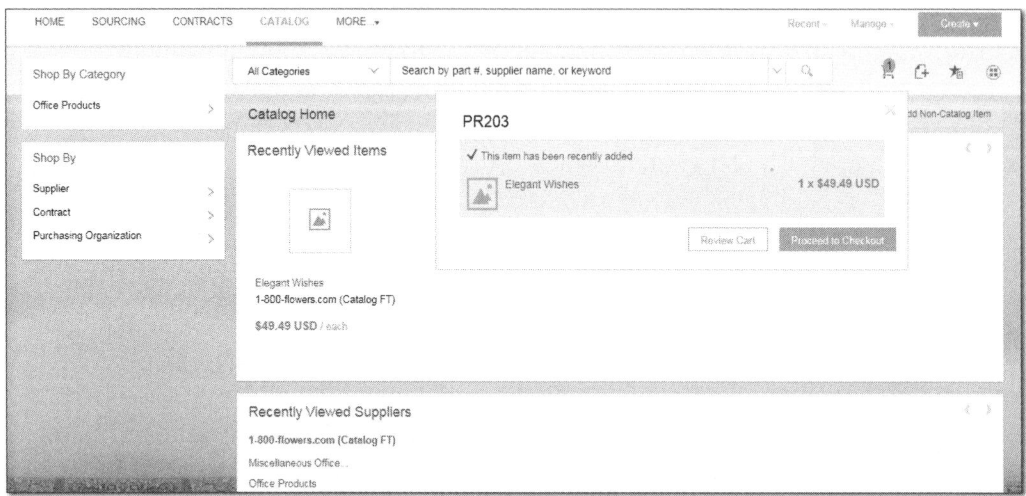

Figure 4.5 SAP Ariba P2P Shopping Cart with Catalog

While suppliers can receive the purchase orders in various formats from SAP Ariba P2O, suppliers transmit advanced shipping notifications and order confirmations only via the SAP Ariba Network. Suppliers must have an active account to upload these types of documents on the network. Upon receipt, SAP Ariba P2O users can leverage the following features:

- Desktop and central receiving
- Receiving against contracts for non-PO spend
- Automated, date-specified receiving for imported requisitions
- Asset information capture and reporting
- Returns management
- Receipt import

You can also configure procurement workspaces in SAP ARIBA SAP Ariba P2O, using the CREATE menu on the dashboard, workspace requests, purchase requisitions, and templates, in order to manage procurement as a project.

These workspaces/templates in Figure 4.6 can include tasks, approvals, and designated fields. Requisitions, purchase orders, receipts, and invoices, as well as subprojects such as sourcing and supplier performance management projects, can be linked to the workspace.

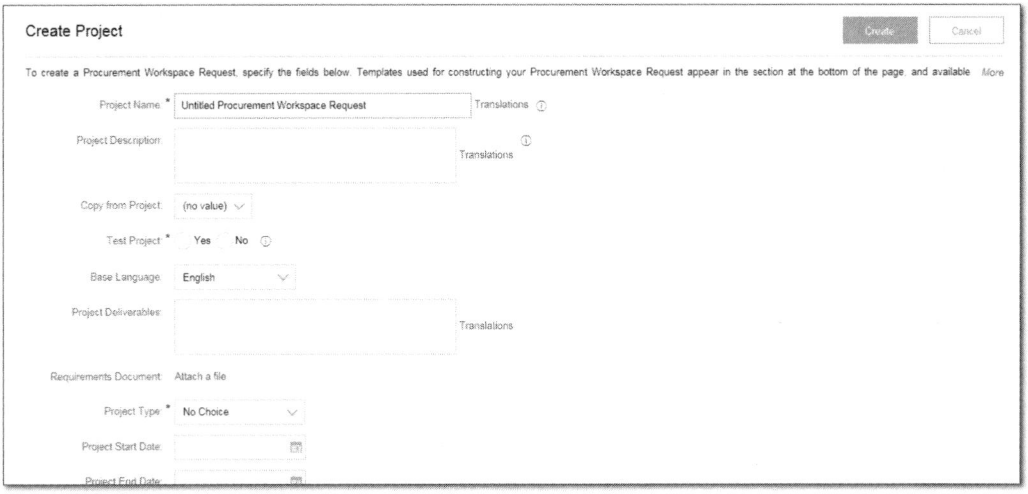

Figure 4.6 SAP Ariba P2P Project Workspace

Procure-to-Pay (SAP Ariba P2P)

Per Figure 4.7, SAP Ariba P2P provides the same process coverage as SAP Ariba P2O, while extending into the invoice-to-payment area. This means invoices are reconciled in SAP Ariba P2P and the invoice submission coordinated in the SAP Ariba Network, and/or via one of the supported formats. Internal invoices (created by the buyer), punch-in invoice, remittance, and status advice are also supported as part of the process, in conjunction with the SAP Ariba Network. As with SAP Ariba P2O, updates and process support can be integrated with the associated SAP ERP environment.

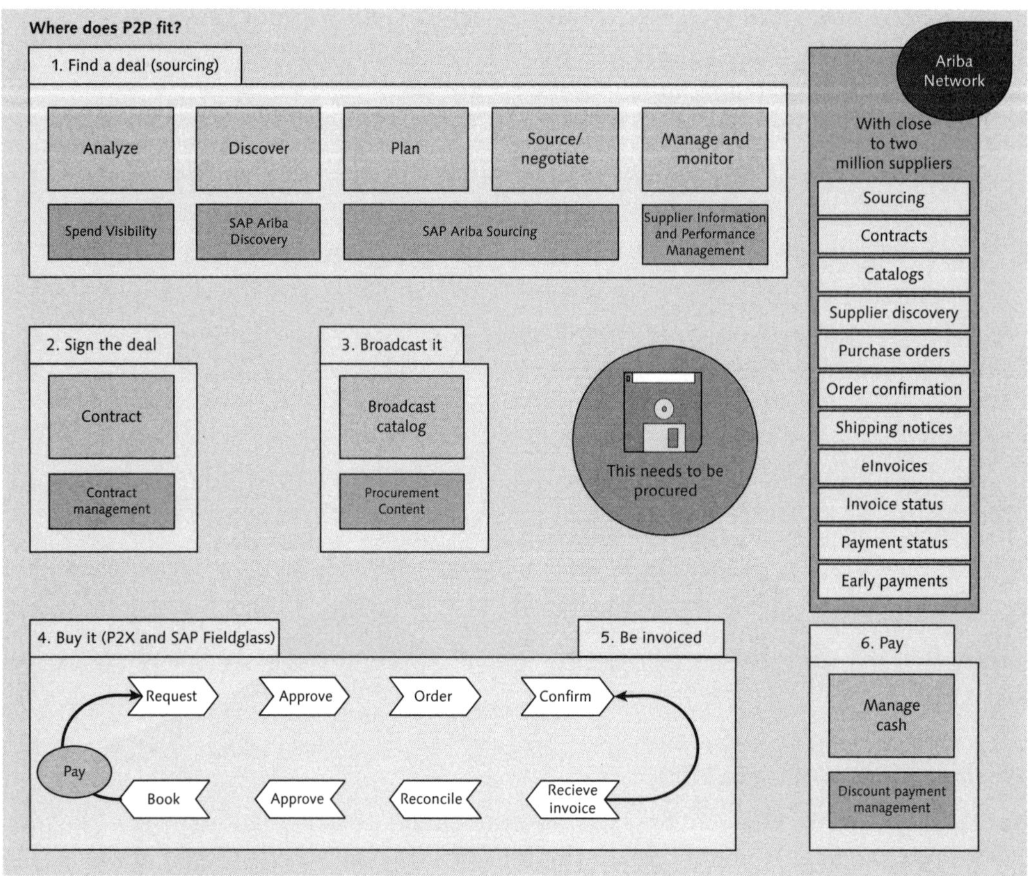

Figure 4.7 Where Does SAP Ariba P2P Fit?

SAP Ariba Discovery and SAP Ariba Spot Quote

You may configure items in SAP Ariba P2O and SAP Ariba P2P to require pre-order collaboration with a supplier in order to define the specifications, scope, and service levels associated with the item before a requisition is submitted for approval. Such an item will send a collaboration request to one or more suppliers via SAP Ariba Network, and suppliers can respond with bids or proposals. Buyers can enforce obtaining bids from multiple suppliers in SAP Ariba P2O/SAP Ariba P2P for high-value purchases. Note that this threshold can be changed by adjusting the `Application.Discovery.Requisition.Amount` parameter. If the supplier is not already on the SAP Ariba Network, buyers have the option to invite suppliers to register.

You can also publish requisitions to SAP Ariba Discovery, which was discussed at length in Chapter 2. SAP Ariba Discovery also plays a role in SAP Ariba Spot Quote, which is a shared scenario with SAP Ariba Sourcing. SAP Ariba Spot Quote addresses an area of spending that is often neglected: low-cost items with tight timelines that are not available in a company catalog. Often one-time or rush order buys, Spot Quote items are under-managed and under-served categories that nonetheless require quick turnaround. A Spot Quote item typically starts in an SAP ERP system when a non-procurement buyer creates demand after discovering that the item/service is not available. Buyers generally lack efficient or effective methods to source these categories. SAP Ariba Spot Quote seeks to improve this situation with a tool and process that allows the buyer to go out and source the item on a one-time basis, leveraging the power of SAP Ariba Discovery to find new and optimal sources of supply.

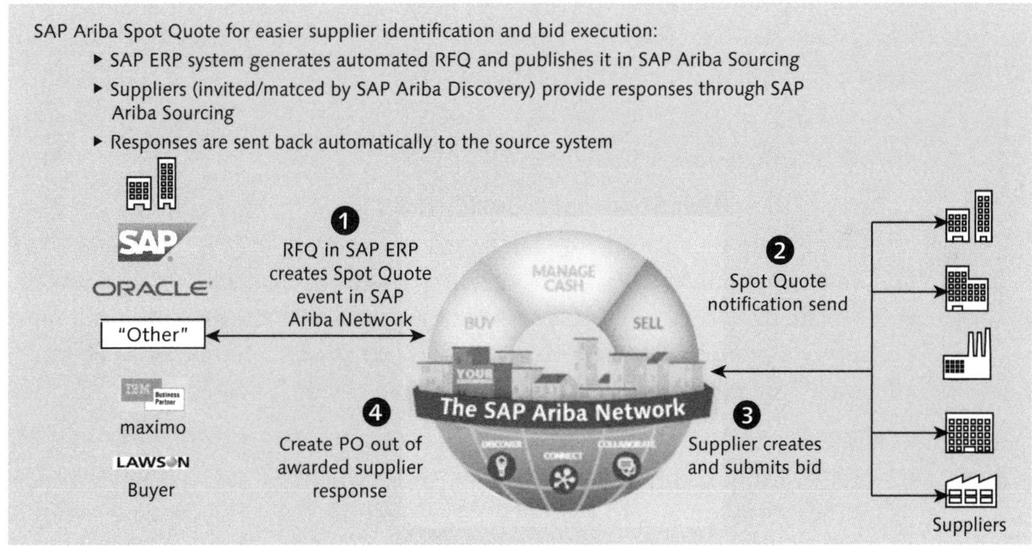

Figure 4.8 SAP Ariba Spot Quote Process Flow (SAP ERP)

Per Figure 4.8, a demand is generated in SAP ERP, but this demand could also come from a SAP Ariba P2P-based process where a user does not find the item they need in one of the SAP APC catalogs. Once the buyer determines they cannot find the item in any of their existing catalogs and/or contracts, and that the item is in low enough quantities/frequency that a long term contract or procurement cycle is not necessary, he uses SAP Ariba Sourcing to send a Spot Quote notification to SAP Ariba Discovery. SAP Ariba Discovery matches supplier and product, and the resulting bids are sent back through SAP Ariba Sourcing (see Figure 4.9).

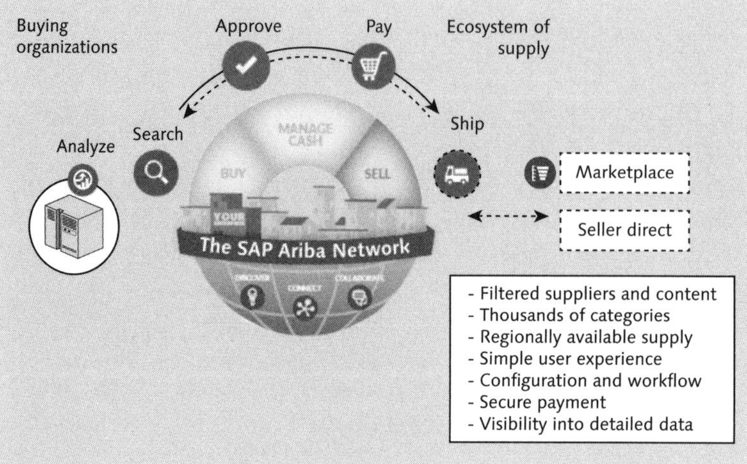

Figure 4.9 SAP Ariba Spot Buy—Find and Buy Non-Sourced Goods

SAP Ariba Procurement Content (SAP APC)

The most efficient type of order is usually one that is sourced with a preexisting agreement from a defined item maintained in a catalog. This "procurement content," housed in a catalog, helps prevent typos from manually entered orders, while enabling users to quickly find what they need with the help of search functionality, descriptions, pricing, part numbers, terms and conditions, availability, and other core items for supporting a successful ordering process.

SAP Ariba P2X leverages SAP Ariba Procurement Content (SAP APC) to provide this functionality and content to the end users, as well as a streamlined maintenance process to the suppliers. SAP APC supports fuzzy search, parametric refinement, and side-by-side comparisons of selected items.

SAP APC can also support non-SAP Ariba P2X processes, such as SAP ERP procurement processes, as featured in Figure 4.10. Here, the user "punches out" to SAP APC to pull item/service content, and then brings this info back into the SAP ERP Materials Management (MM) or SAP Supplier Relationship Management (SRM) procurement environment.

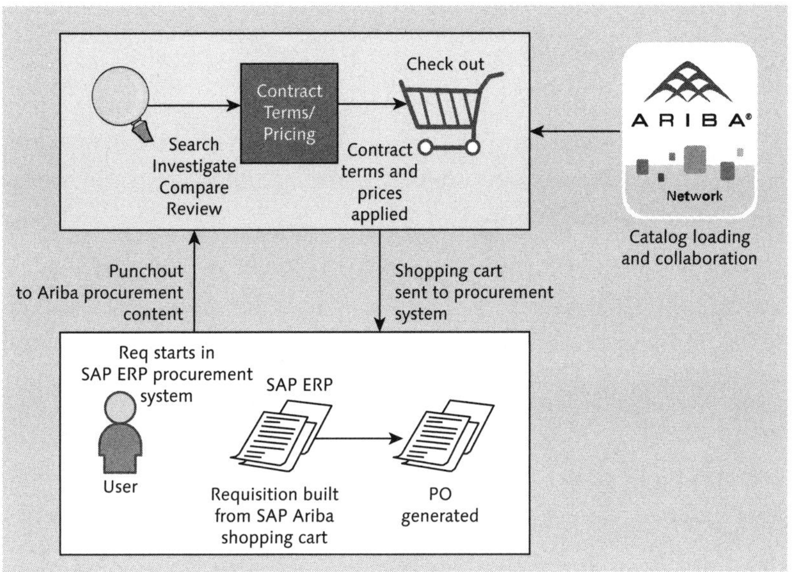

Figure 4.10 SAP Ariba Procurement Content Process Flow

To enable an SAP APC catalog with SAP Ariba, SAP Ariba provides the following setup services:

- Upload and activate test and production catalogs
- Configure catalog filters (views)
- Edit the catalog hierarchy
- Create and configure catalog kits
- Index catalog data
- Perform catalog refreshes
- Conduct supplier catalog education sessions

Additional functionality can be enabled by SAP Ariba upon request, such as kits and filtered views. Kits are packages of items that can be pulled from the catalog into a shopping cart/requisition in one click, bringing multiple items as part of the selection. Kits are useful for onboarding new employees (onboarding kit with laptop, badge, manuals, etc.), repetitive purchasing activities requiring the same bundle of goods (such as new store set up kits), and for larger items that are assembled out of multiple defined smaller items such as the bill of materials (BoM) concepts in direct procurement scenarios. Filtered views allow for different items or subsets of selections to be displayed to different users and/or organization.

Another key area for catalogs is having a robust search functionality. Here, SAP APC offers keyword search, dynamic filters by category, suppliers, price ranges, and manufacturers, as well as relevance ranking, side-by-side comparison, favorites, and catalog hierarchy (UNSPSC).

You can set up contracts in SAP Ariba P2O via the SAP APC user interface or by importing contracts directly via SAP APC, while controlling access to those contracts. SAP APC contracts can be based on suppliers, material categories, or items, and include the following conditions:

- Release required
- Contract hierarchies
- Effective expiration dates
- Limits
- Simple and advanced pricing terms
- Blanket purchase orders (BPOs)

Contracts in SAP APC enforce term compliance on the shopping carts to which they are assigned. Contracts can be manually assigned to purchase orders and track usage of contracts in purchasing activities with the designated supplier.

Most catalog scenarios involve tightly defined items that your company orders frequently, so as to standardize as much of the order as possible. However, not all purchasing activities conform to this scenario. Some orders require further discussion and definition with the supplier prior to ordering. Yet parts of the process, such as initial selection and definition of general item or service remain largely the same, order by order. For this type of order, SAP APC offers collaboration options.

You can configure items in SAP APC to require pre-order collaboration with a supplier to facilitate definition of the specifications, scope, and service levels associated with the item before a requisition is routed for approval. Upon selection of the item in SAP APC, a collaboration request is sent to one or more suppliers via the SAP Ariba Network, and suppliers can respond with bids or proposals. Buyers can then continue the ordering process by reviewing, negotiating further, and accepting proposals. Buyers can enforce obtaining bids from multiple suppliers for high-value purchases to extract better discounts. Buyers can also invite suppliers who are currently not enabled on SAP Ariba Network to register, in order to build relationships with new suppliers and explore cost-saving opportunities.

You administer SAP APC through a separate login page, used solely for administration. The search functionalities in SAP APC support general, wildcard, refined, and parametric searches, as well as favorites. SAP APC supports kits, or a collection of items bundled for a specific purpose/product, as well. Kit examples include a new store setup, employee onboarding kits, and configurable items requiring multiple decision points. The kit appears as a single line item in SAP APC, but once it is added to a requisition or shopping cart, the kit unpacks into the underlying line items and can belong to multiple suppliers.

Another variation on the catalog is the punchout catalog, which SAP APC also moderates. The punchout process involves the buyer, the supplier, and the SAP Ariba Network. Punchout messages are routed through the SAP Ariba Network for validation and authentication. This process follows these steps:

1. First, the user selects a punchout item in the SAP Ariba Procurement Solution catalog. This selection sends a request to the SAP Ariba Network to establish a connection with the remote catalog.
2. The SAP Ariba Network authenticates the buying organization and forwards the request to the supplier's punchout site.
3. The supplier sends back a URL of a webpage on the supplier's punchout site designed specifically for the buyer. The procurement system redirects the user to this URL. The remote shopping site appears in the user's window, and the user begins shopping.
4. After shopping, the user clicks the site's checkout button, which moves the contents of the shopping cart from the supplier site back to SAP Ariba Procurement Content.

For their part, the customer needs to define the in-scope catalogs and suppliers, as well as the types of catalogs required from each supplier. The suppliers need to onboard on the SAP Ariba Network and create, upload, and maintain catalogs on in this environment, or use the punchout approach detailed earlier. SAP Ariba catalog specialists are available to assist suppliers in this process.

For importing catalogs into SAP APC, suppliers and catalog managers can leverage multiple approaches:

1. Suppliers can load catalogs on the SAP Ariba Network. This type of catalog is a *network catalog* or *network subscription*.
2. You or your catalog manager can load the catalog into SAP Ariba Procurement Content directly. This is called a *local catalog* or *local subscription*.
3. You can also load content from a contract through a *generated subscription*.

Each method has a different process with different advantages and use cases. Most organizations leverage network subscriptions outlined in the first example, to automate their catalog process as much as possible and reduce the workload for catalog managers.

4.1.2 SAP Ariba Services Procurement for Operational Sourcing and SAP Ariba P2P/SAP Ariba P2O

Please note that from a product roadmap standpoint, SAP has replaced much of SAP Ariba Services Procurement with SAP Fieldglass functionality and no longer actively sells SAP Ariba Services Procurement. Customers currently evaluating services procurement solutions from SAP are actively encouraged to prioritize SAP Fieldglass for services procurement scenarios.

Services procurement differs from traditional material procurement in a couple of ways. As per Table 4.1, pricing, quantity, and requirements are much more dynamic in services than with the procurement of an item.

	Material Procurement	Services Procurement
Prices	Prices are fixed	Prices are negotiable and agreeable to using various approaches (fixed fee, time and materials, etc.)
Quantity	Item is fixed, apart from configurable items. If contract or catalog item, the item is further defined.	Item can be project or bucket of hours—more dynamic than a material item as to what is required.
Requirements	Material is shipped, usually in a consumable unit, and oftentimes the entire order is shipped together.	Service is delivered, usually over a defined time period, with the customer paying by unit of time or upon project completion.

Table 4.1 Services vs. Material Procurement

Procuring services oftentimes requires further steps that are not required for materials. For example, you may need to select from a pool of potential providers and interview the candidate tasked with delivering the services, or with joining your department for a set duration as a third-party provider.

The boxes in Figure 4.11 depict the standard procure-to-pay process for a material. As you can tell, a procurement of service often requires more steps and iterations during the order process to arrive at the PO, and may have a more fragmented billing process as the time sheets are submitted over a period for individual invoicing.

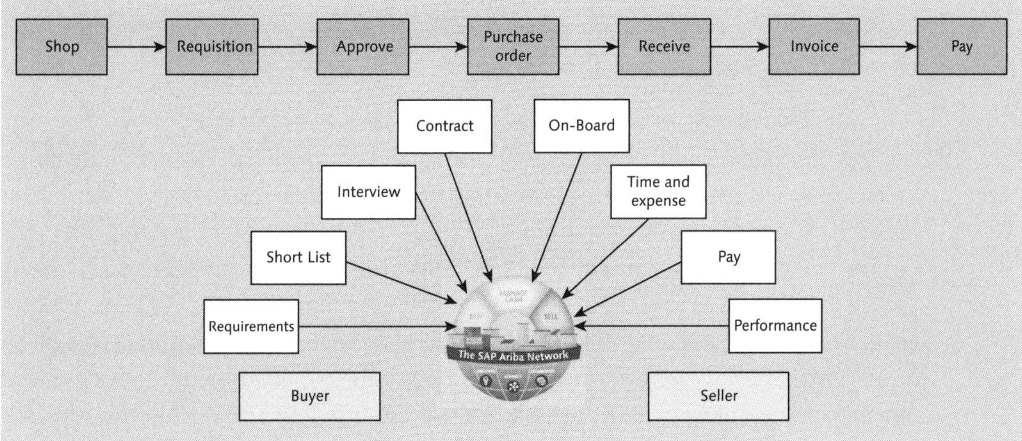

Figure 4.11 SAP Ariba Services Procurement Process

To address these differences and challenges, SAP Ariba Services Procurement allows you to:

- Use procurement categories to control the policies for specific types of line items
- Collaborate with suppliers on the SAP Ariba Network to negotiate favorable pricing and to define the details of a particular line item, such as temporary labor
- Set the transparency (openness) of the collaboration process by selectively exposing information on a supplier's proposal to the supplier's competitors

- Set up temporary workers as contractors in the system so that they have special permission to work in the SAP Ariba Procurement Solution
- Enable time sheets, which contractors fill out to track hours worked, and which can be converted to invoices automatically

For catalog-based procurement, SAP Ariba Services Procurement allows you to manage groups of catalog items in SAP Ariba Procurement Content as service items, specifying permissions, default values, policies, and other constraints. When a user selects one of these services items in the catalog, he can fill out the remaining information according to the rules specified for the item. For services procurement, there is much more emphasis placed on iterations and collaboration during the procurement process, as well as interview and evaluation steps not required during material procurement.

On the other hand, in most organizations, indirect procurement is viewed as a cost center, and thus an area to be managed and controlled for cost minimization and increased efficiency. However, indirect procurement, though a significant portion of overall company spending activities, oftentimes does not receive much prioritization for management, and is left therefore to grow organically, using whatever processes and methods are available or cobbled together. As these processes and company customs around indirect procurement become increasingly convoluted and expensive, a need for comprehensive, system-based solutions increases in tandem in many areas of the procurement process, from the sourcing and contracts areas, through procurement processes, and on down to the invoice-to-pay scenarios.

In a procure-to-pay scenario, most companies initially concern themselves with approval aspects of indirect procurement, making sure the requisitioning employee's manager signs off on the spending. In system-less/lite environments, this can occur in the form of an email, or a literal signature on a purchase order.

This process of signing off on whatever the employee manages to source in an indirect procurement activity does not usually scale well, and overlooks discounts and spend categorization areas, not to mention the system-based procurement structures that inform a supplier regarding the exact product requested, terms expected, and the delivery points. Finance eventually grows weary of finding out about spending after the fact, as this type of spending impacts their cash-flow management efforts and overall working capital management.

Enter SAP Ariba P2P and SAP Ariba P2O. With both of these solutions, you can bring order to the unruliness of an organically evolved procurement process. As a strategy and principal, it helps to focus initially on the areas causing the most difficulty and cost in an organization. For indirect procurement, approval adherence will often drive initial discussions. Companies are subject to various reporting and compliance regulations, and these are oftentimes not followed if the approval relies on the signature of a manager for any category type or spending threshold. Approval workflow is thus a key area of focus, and SAP Ariba's workflow in SAP Ariba P2X scenarios provides clarity, sequencing, and record-keeping for various approval scenarios. So-called "maverick" spending can be minimized with a defined approval structure in-system, combined with recordkeeping of each individual order's approval string and approvers.

Costs resulting from one-off orders placed without contract or terms, and with poorly described items, are another fertile area of focus for identifying and addressing the key performance indicators (KPIs) of an SAP Ariba P2X implementation. The ideal order will have a purchase order created using a contract and/or catalog item from suppliers, with defined terms and relationships with your company. This way, the order is fulfilled with minimal costly manual interventions to correct orders with the supplier. The resulting order leverages pricing that has been negotiated with the supplier.

Once the order is placed, a supplier will submit a request for payment, typically in the form of an invoice. This is also another source of costs and inefficiencies if not managed, as the invoice needs to be received, scanned, and processed/reconciled with the original order and the receiving documents. If these documents are strewn throughout the company in various file cabinets or receipts, the process can become quite laborious. In addition, suppliers assess penalties if the terms of their order are not followed on the payment-side. Late payments can create additional costs for the company, and, equally important, can miss out on early payment discount opportunities provided by suppliers if negotiated during the payment cycle. SAP Ariba P2X covers the basic invoicing and payment areas in SAP Ariba, SAP Ariba Invoice Automation, and SAP Ariba Payment Automation. These areas and additional SAP Ariba solutions around invoice, discount management, and payment, are discussed in Chapter 5 of this book.

A negotiation for obtaining better pricing drives off volumes and overall terms. In order to understand the volumes, a company first has to understand the categories of items it buys, and how their suppliers perform according to their relationships with the company. Doing so requires analytics and reporting. In a SAP Ariba P2X project, this means utilizing SAP Ariba Spend Visibility and SAP Ariba Supplier Information and Performance Management (SIPM) which are outlined in Chapters 8 and 6 respectively of this book. However, putting the data into an organized format and process for analysis is very much the focus area and value-add for an SAP Ariba P2X project. In SAP Ariba P2X, the tactical aspects of procurement are defined and structured, so that analysis can be performed and valuable insights on volumes and performance can be brought to bear with suppliers in further negotiations and contract cycles.

4.2 Implementing SAP Ariba P2P, SAP Ariba P2O, and SAP Ariba Services Procurement

These next sections focus on implementing the two main versions of SAP Ariba P2X, as well as a brief overview of SAP Ariba Services Procurement. SAP Ariba Services Procurement is technically no longer offered by SAP, having been replaced by SAP Fieldglass, though it is still supported. However, some customers still run this solution for services procurement.

4.2.1 SAP Ariba P2X Projects

SAP Ariba P2P and SAP Ariba P2O, and variations of the two, are traditionally called SAP Ariba P2X. SAP Ariba P2X can include the following implementation steps:

1. **Supplier enablement**
   When a customer implements SAP Ariba P2X, they typically look to onboard suppliers not yet transacting in the SAP Ariba Network. Suppliers can join at a number of levels, but at minimum they need to be set up to receive a PO.

2. **Flight planning**
   Flight planning is more of a project management topic, as it relates to supplier enablement. SAP Ariba projects are typically rolled out in phases, and coordination with suppliers during the different phases, as well as coordination of resources and timelines, are usually required. Flight plans help automate and standardize this process of onboarding suppliers into the new system in their designated roles and in an optimal manner.

3. **Catalog enablement**
   As discussed in a previous section of this chapter, catalogs required by the customer can be managed in the SAP Ariba Network via SAP Ariba Procurement Content. Suppliers can log into the business network and upload catalogs. Suppliers can also host punchout catalogs and allow for SAP Ariba P2X users to "punch out" to their hosted catalogs. Lastly, the suppliers can send data to the customer for review, and can upload the data into a customer-maintained catalog in SAP APC.
4. **Change management**
   Often overlooked, change management is a very important element of SAP Ariba P2X projects. Unlike specialized applications or processes, affecting a limited number of employees, the procurement processes established in SAP Ariba P2X typically impact a large number of employees and company suppliers in their day-to-day activities. Inadequate training and communication with the different community members, the main ones being administrators, buyers, requisitioners, approvers, and suppliers, can lead to the failure of an otherwise flawless implementation and system. The customer change management is typically lead by the customer's resources, with guidance from SAP Ariba or third party consultants.
5. **Technical workstream**
   This area includes integrating/interfacing procurement documents and processes with the customer's ERP environment and the SAP Ariba Network. This is sometimes included in the SAP Ariba P2X workstream, with SAP Ariba P2X supporting various initial requisitioning and PO steps of the process, before transferring down the requirements to SAP ERP. Topics such as integration, master data conversions, and data optimizations all fall under the technical workstream of a SAP Ariba P2X implementation.

This section provides a high-level overview of the integration options, while Chapter 9 provides detailed approaches and configuration steps to some of the main options for integration of SAP Ariba P2X with SAP ERP.

Supplier Enablement

Supplier enablement requires planning and execution steps for a SAP Ariba P2X project. In traditional on-premise software environments, suppliers still require notification and support during the transition to a new system on the customer-side.

New master data requirements, order formats, and transmission methods all can affect a supplier and how they conduct business with a customer. Due to SAP Ariba P2X's interaction with the SAP Ariba Network, supporting your supplier's transition to transacting via SAP Ariba P2X with you is paramount, as the supplier not only needs to understand the new process, but may also need to join the SAP Ariba Network if they are not already enrolled. Both supplier enablement and flight plan in SAP Ariba P2X pertain to enabling and migrating suppliers to the new SAP Ariba P2X environment. The supplier enablement process is covered at length in Chapter 7.

Flight Planning

Procurement is a business area which necessarily interacts with the outside world in order to obtain the goods and services a company requires as inputs for production (direct procurement), and as supporting goods and services underpinning operations (indirect procurement). Without cooperation from suppliers, no procurement solution will be entirely successful. A flight plan addresses this by providing a guide for enablement of suppliers and categories of spend to ensure successful adoption of SAP Ariba solutions.

On an SAP Ariba project, flight plans are created using a combination of automated tools, which include best practices, as well as fine-tuning the plan to meet customer-specific needs and goals. Flight plans are created and refined throughout SAP Ariba implementation, including during the sales phases of the project and continuing on once the project enters production, as outlined in Figure 4.12.

You will manage the flight plan creation throughout the various phases. Depending on the phase, the creation and build out could be managed by different stakeholders and process owners. The main phases can be broken out into three distinct steps: data preparation, flight plan generation, and customer-specific updates, per Figure 4.13. Oftentimes, the data preparation phase occurs at a high level during the sales phase. A customer provides SAP Ariba with supplier data in order to verify which suppliers are already active on the SAP Ariba Network. As the prospect begins transitioning into a customer, the flight plan is generated and honed during the project. The customer then reviews the plan and provides additional feedback to fine-tune this flight plan to their needs and constraints.

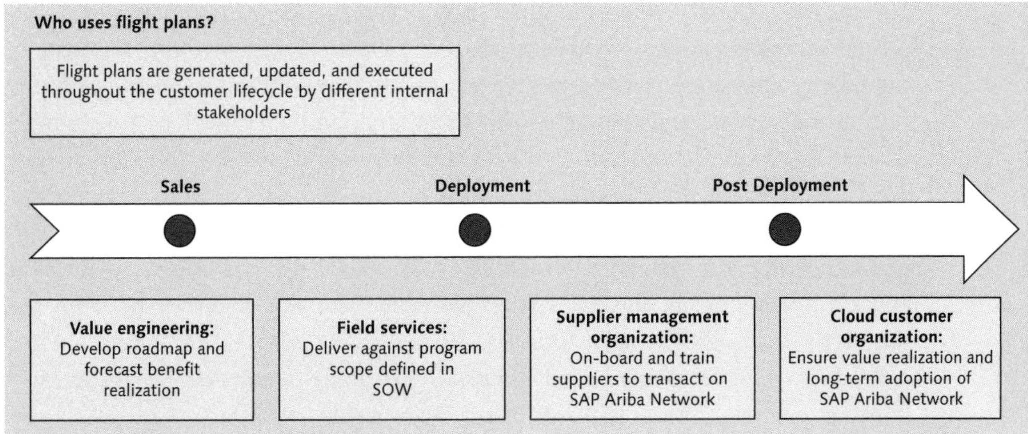

Figure 4.12 Who Uses Flight Plans?

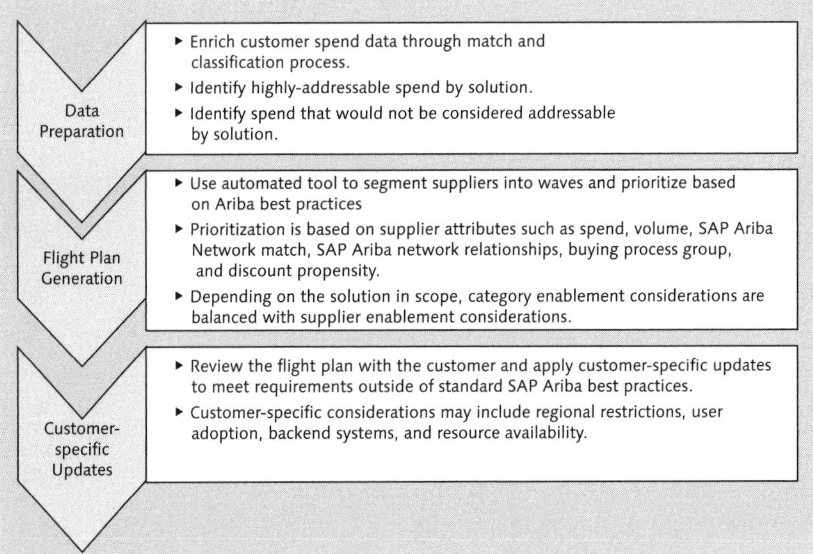

Figure 4.13 Flight Plan Creation

Suppliers are selected for the various onboarding waves according to a variety of criteria. The automated analysis looks at percentage of spend, buying process, transaction volumes, geography, discount propensity, and existing SAP Ariba Network scores, and provides an overall score based on this assessment.

The customer then overlays this analysis with internal considerations, such as the business units most focused on the project (if a business unit is driving this project, then their suppliers will likely receive special attention during the flight plan process). The customer and project are also dependent on the availability of resources, as well as required integration to backend systems. (Does the supplier need to receive documents directly into their system or will they be logging into the SAP Ariba Network to process documents?). While integrated suppliers are typically higher volume and spend, the integration may take longer than suppliers who can process documents in the SAP Ariba Network, influencing the timeframe and phase in which certain suppliers can onboard. Lastly, if there are additional SAP Ariba P2X design items required to support particular transactions with the supplier, or general considerations on the customer-side, these factors can also influence the sequencing of supplier onboarding.

Ultimately, the shared goal of all parties involved is to realize the most savings, revenues, and efficiency as quickly as possible. A typical flight plan output will look to capture as much of the addressable spend of the project as quickly as possible, phase-wise.

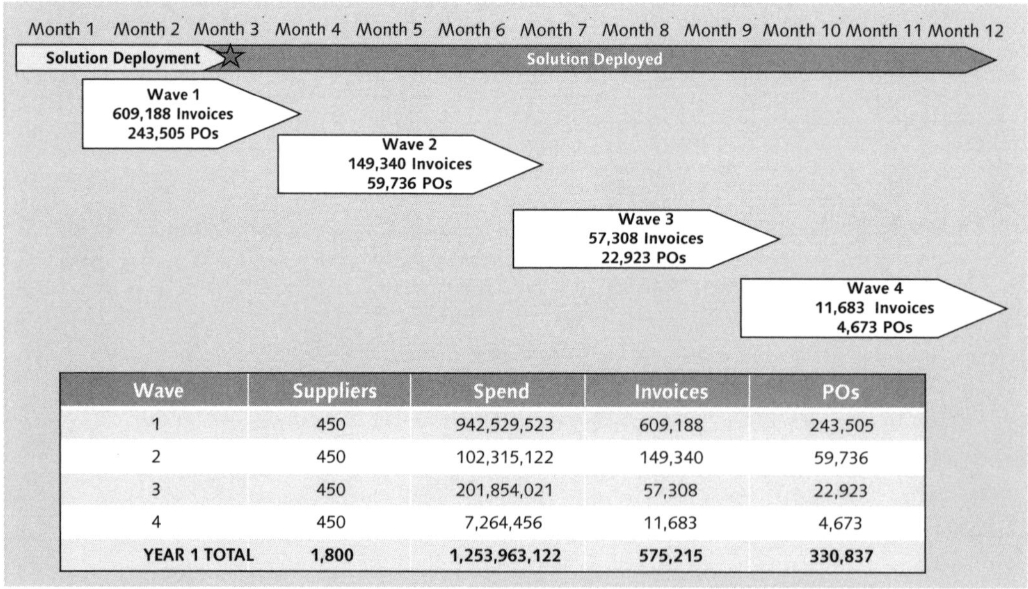

Wave	Suppliers	Spend	Invoices	POs
1	450	942,529,523	609,188	243,505
2	450	102,315,122	149,340	59,736
3	450	201,854,021	57,308	22,923
4	450	7,264,456	11,683	4,673
YEAR 1 TOTAL	**1,800**	**1,253,963,122**	**575,215**	**330,837**

Figure 4.14 Flight Plan Output

In the flight plan shown in Figure 4.14, the majority of the addressable spend, POs and invoices are covered in the initial wave. This is a best practice and goal for the creation of flight plans—address the "low-hanging fruit" first, and then focusing on the remaining, oftentimes more difficult or infrequent, suppliers and their transactions. The flight plan provides both summary level and supplier level analyses for customer review.

There are three main stages to a flight plan: planning and recommending, architecting, and deployment:

1. **Planning Phase**
   Here, you meet with stakeholders, define the spend and supplier selection, and analyze the current process.
2. **Architecting Phase**
   During the architecting phase, you define the business and functional requirements, develop the design specifications, and validate the concepts with both the project stakeholders and the suppliers directly.
3. **Deployment Phase**
   During the deployment phase, you configure the solution and enable suppliers, contracts, catalogs, and invoicing. Finally, you initiate training for the categories deployed in the system and communicate the launch.

Finally, the plan is tracked according to its actual execution over the different waves.

Catalog Enablement

In addition to the catalog functionality, the core features of SAP Ariba Procurement Content are:

- Contract compliance: SAP APC allows for items to have a contract number maintained, which references an existing contract in SAP Ariba Contract Management and allows for enforcement and cascading of terms from the contract, as well as consumption and reporting during and after the transaction.
- Collaborative shopping cart: This is an in-catalog shopping cart option to tune catalog item orders further before going through approvals.

- Approval rules: Approval rules allow for catalog managers to manage content, as well as additional optional workflows in catalog to augment approval flows for user profile changes, shopping carts, and contract requests.
- Reporting: Catalog managers have standard reports to view content usage and other key performance metrics.

The three types of catalogs that can be loaded or accessed in SAP APC are supplier provided/loaded catalogs, customer loaded catalogs, and punch out catalogs hosted directly by the supplier.

The punchout process involves the buyer, the supplier, and the SAP Ariba Network. Punchout messages are routed through the SAP Ariba Network for validation and authentication. This process involves the following steps:

1. The user selects a punchout item in the SAP Ariba Procurement Solution catalog. This selection sends a request to the SAP Ariba Network to establish a connection with the remote catalog.
2. The SAP Ariba Network authenticates the buying organization and forwards the request to the supplier's punchout site.
3. The supplier sends back a URL of a webpage on the supplier's punchout site designed specifically for the buyer. The procurement system redirects the user to this URL. The remote shopping site appears in the user's window and the user begins shopping.
4. After shopping, the user clicks the site's CHECK OUT button, which moves the contents of the shopping cart from the supplier site back to SAP Ariba Procurement Content.

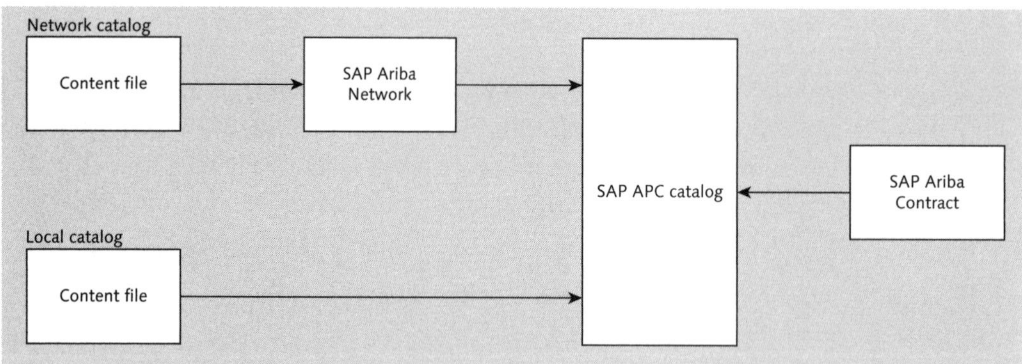

Figure 4.15 SAP Ariba Procurement Content Catalog Load Options

Per Figure 4.15, there are two main loading options for catalogs. The first and more efficient option is to allow suppliers to provide catalogs via the SAP Ariba Network, which can be done via network, local, or generated subscription, as discussed earlier.

Parameters can be found in the Catalog Manager section of the Core Administration tool to control automatic downloading of catalogs.

The subscription section in SAP APC displays current catalog subscriptions, their versions and statuses. From here one can:

- Activate or deactivate a subscription.
- Delete versions or entire subscriptions.
- Compare versions within the same subscriptions to understand differences.
- The resulting report can be emailed or printed.
- View supplier details.
- View version validation information or content.
- Fix validation errors online by editing the erroneous catalog item. Click on a specific version marked VALIDATION ERROR.

The second option is to load customer catalogs via catalog interchange format (CIF) catalogs. Not all catalogs may be supplier provided via the SAP Ariba Network. Some catalogs are internal to your company, containing items such as material masters from SAP ERP or from suppliers who do not offer catalogs via the SAP Ariba Network. These catalogs can be uploaded to SAP APC using the Administration Console in SAP APC. The typical format for these catalogs is "CIF".

CIF files are different from Excel spreadsheets and should not be edited in Excel. CIF files are more similar to CSV files and should be edited only in a text editor. CIF Full Load leverages the `LOADMODE` parameter setting for SAP APC. The `LOADMODE` parameter in the CIF header determines whether SAP Ariba Procurement Content will perform a full, destructive load of the items or an incremental update. Use "F" for full and "I" for incremental. CIF catalogs contain a header, body, and body trailer sections. The CIF also contains the commodity classification code for each item so that they can be properly mapped into your commodity code structure.

The SAP APC timestamp on a CIF file determines whether the file is an update or existing. This prevents the same file from being uploaded more than once. This means that your catalog managers should update existing catalogs using the same CIF file name as previous versions, leveraging the timestamp as the trigger for updates, along with setting the updates to incremental. Each customer typically creates their own CIF template for catalog managers to maintain and update for customer-loaded catalogs. Catalog managers populate their catalogs using the template and then upload the templates directly into SAP APC or into a loading area, where periodically SAP APC pulls the new materials up into the system.

A typical content management project or project-phase includes lining out the different types and number of catalogs in scope, update frequency required, loading processes, and optional configuration items, such as additional workflows to be configured internally in SAP APC. Catalog managers and SAP Ariba P2X subject matter experts (SMEs) drive this project and delivery and ongoing maintenance of SAP APC, typically. More than other solution areas, catalogs are continually updated and added or removed in procurement. As such, defining ongoing maintenance and subscription protocols are of utmost importance. Catalog managers also need to be included at the onset, so as to learn how to manage their new SAP APC environment on an ongoing basis.

Change Management

Within any system implementation project affecting end users, some change management is required. With SAP Ariba P2X implementations, the need for organized, well-executed change management is particularly acute, given the large and casual user population typically requisitioning at a company. These users require communication and training, as do the buyers, suppliers, and approvers of the new system. Change management entails:

- Executing activities related to human performance impacts
- Managing the "people aspects" of new technology and processes
- Providing stakeholders with the knowledge to be successful
- Ensuring users have what they need to embrace a new way of doing the job
- Mitigating risk associated with the project

A big risk for any project involving technology and people is the possibility that end users of the new system do not end up adopting the new systems and processes, thereby undermining the project's objectives. In the worst case scenario, an organization can experience negative productivity impacts and losses as users devise workarounds and paper-based or manual processes to avoid working in and with the new system. Change management is thus of the utmost importance, and is a central theme for any SAP Ariba project.

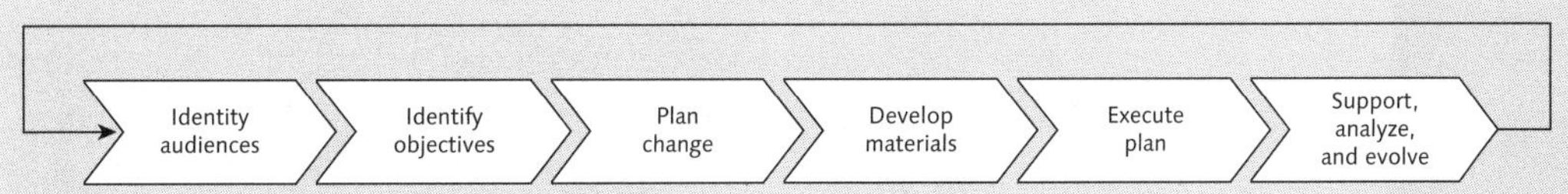

Figure 4.16 SAP Ariba Change Management

The steps in an SAP Ariba change management project comprise six distinct, phases as per Figure 4.16. In each step, the following actions are taken:

1. **Identify audiences:** For a SAP Ariba P2X project, the stakeholders for change management are primarily the suppliers and end users doing the requisitioning, as well as the buyers and approvers. In addition, there are accounts payable processes and people to take into consideration, as well as manufacturing, forecasting, materials management, and sales and distribution groups which may have specific touch points with the system and processes.
2. **Identify objectives:** Here a review is conducted of the strategic objectives of the program, audience, and timeline.
3. **Plan change:** In order to facilitate the change process within the company and supplier base, a plan around timing, required resources, and core phases is finalized.
4. **Develop materials:** Any education, communication, or training materials is then created to support the program rollout.
5. **Execute plan:** Here all of the strategy, objectives definition, and supporting materials converge in the execution phase.
6. **Support, analyze, and evolve:** During the "run" phase of the project, further tuning and analysis is required to expand the footprint and success of the project with suppliers and users alike.

Technical Workstream

The technical-related workstreams are supported primarily by the SAP Ariba shared services group and corresponding onsite customer, consultant, and partner resources. These workstreams focus on:

- Master data: Conversion of master data, such as supplier information, units of measure, categories, etc., for eventual upload into SAP Ariba P2X.
- Integration toolkit (CSV): Integration topics for SAP Ariba P2X linking an SAP ERP environment with SAP Ariba P2X activities (more on this area in Chapter 9).
- Web services: Calls from SAP Ariba P2X to source system to check validity/ availability of items and cost assignments for example.
- Ok2Pay (SAP Ariba P2P): Message sent from SAP Ariba P2X to an ERP backend, endorsing payment of an invoice.
- Other technical related services:
  - Application management: General support and management of application.
  - Adapter integration: Integration of SAP ERP for document exchange via adapter or direct connection.

For a many SAP Ariba P2O deployments, clients will choose to have invoices sent directly to their SAP ERP system. As a result, purchase orders and/or invoices are sometimes exchanged between the SAP Ariba Network and another procurement application, such as SAP ERP.

Such process flows may necessitate integrations between SAP Ariba P2O and SAP ERP, typically for PO and receipt exports.

There may also be additional integrations from SAP ERP and the SAP Ariba Network required. These integrations often leverage adapters, such as SAP Business Suite Add-On or SAP Process Orchestration with the SAP Ariba Network Adapter, as part of the architecture. Adapters enable document conversion from the original format to cXML, in order to communicate with the AN.

Systems integrations leads (SILs), are SAP Ariba resources familiar with adapter-specific implementations. These resources explain the project plan and can work with the client team to define document mappings. For SAP integrations, further functional and technical specialists assist on the SAP ERP-side, to cover the integration nuances in the SAP ERP environment.

4.2.2 SAP Ariba P2X Deployment

A SAP Ariba P2X deployment project does not follow the traditional SAP ASAP methodology per se, and goes beyond the high-level framework of the new SAP Activate. A SAP Ariba P2X project is more of an amalgam between a packaged service implementation using a start-deploy-run approach and the phases that a traditional an SAP Activate project typically covers: preparation, explore, realize and deploy. In addition, like many Shakespearean masterpieces, there is a play within a play, or a project within a project, in the form of the supplier enablement and change management projects described in the previous sections of this chapter.

An SAP Ariba P2X deployment divides into two main sections: architect and enable phase, and solution setup. Unlike traditional on-premise projects, where kickoffs and project prep oftentimes comprise a single week, more focus and investment is made in this area up front, in order to determine the readiness of the organization and resources for delivering of this project.

Figure 4.17 shows the various streams that flow in tandem from the point of deployment kickoff. Not only are the change management and adoption programs running in tandem to the configuration and custom requirements realization, the design and planning phase of the project is considerably condensed and the solution set up steps overlapping. (Design can be conducted while build and prep are going on for other project elements).

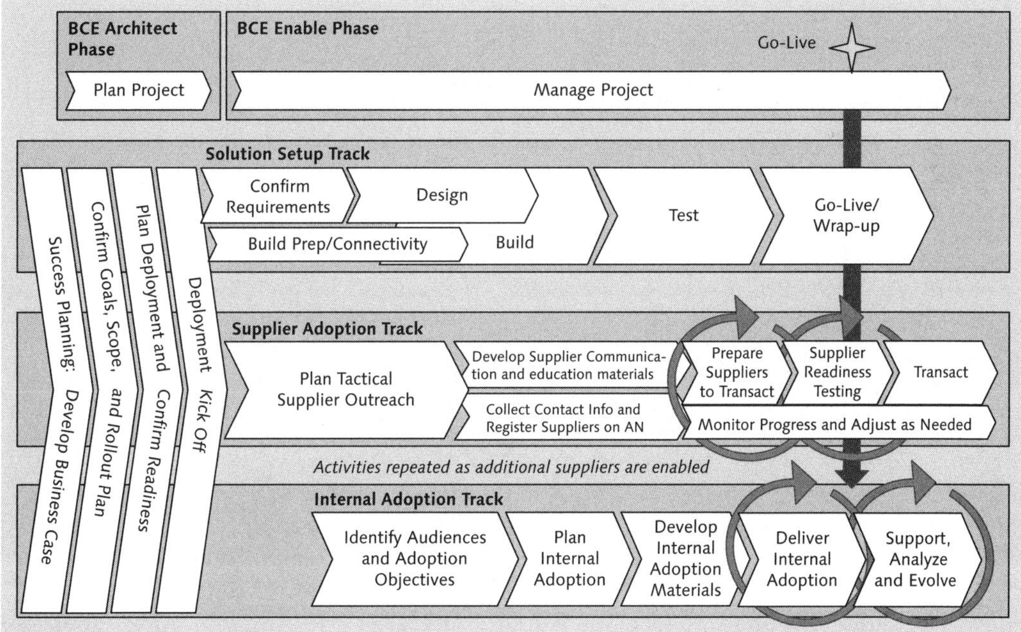

Figure 4.17 SAP Ariba Downstream Project—SAP Ariba P2X

In addition, given the nature of supplier enablement and change management, the overall rollout of SAP Ariba P2X can comprise multiple go-lives, as each wave of suppliers and internal org units join the system in subsequent stages. Oftentimes this is main path for onboarding large supplier-bases, as a "big bang" approach can quickly overwhelm a company's internal supplier resources and procurement departments. As shown in Figure 4.18, the focus of the initial project is typically to plan for the overall rollout/go-live approach and then target the first go-live.

Often known as a pilot approach model, a SAP Ariba P2X project designs the solution in the solution setup track as in Figure 4.17, with subsequent roll outs involving slight adjustments to the initial templates from the solution setup track. The main work is done in the solution adoption tracks and internal adoption track, which includes rolling the solution out to a new part of the organization and to the supply base. Figure 4.18 shows these as SAP Ariba milestones—each subsequent roll out phase is a milestone, with the initial roll out as the initial milestone. Once the first go-live/milestone has been completed, SAP Ariba project resource involvement can transition further to customer-lead resources for the further roll outs.

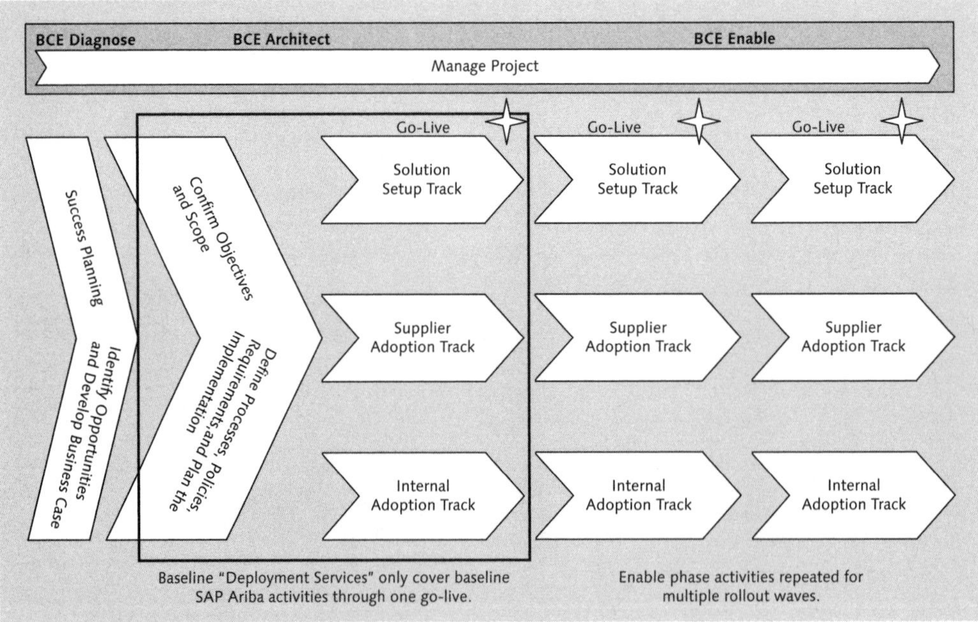

Figure 4.18 SAP Ariba's Milestones for Downstream Delivery

In addition to a multiple waves approach towards implementation, the SAP Ariba milestones methodology provides:

- Better project planning and preparation: Using milestones acknowledges the organizational limitations of rolling out everything in a big bang approach, while also acknowledging the full scope of the roll out, via the milestones. This approach ensures that regions and supplier groups are accounted for in the overall roadmap, and can help focus design discussions and the project in general.
- Alignment of all delivery services work in a common methodology: One methodology covering the entire scope of work including the go-live and the preparation to adopt, all managed from a single project plan, and built around clearly defined milestones.
- Separates requirements from design: Milestones for further supplier groups and rollouts do not necessarily get folded into the initial design phase, allowing the focus to initially center on the reaching the first milestone and pilot organization.

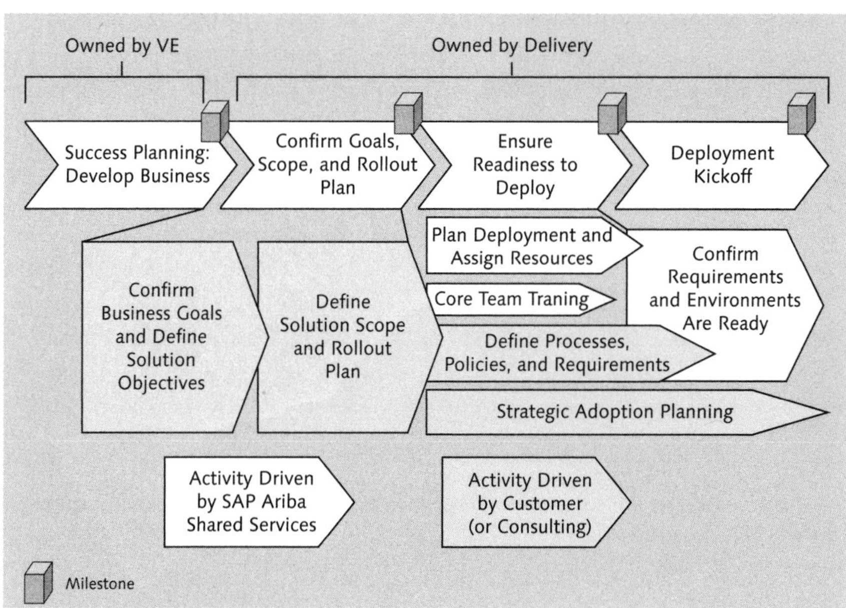

Figure 4.19 Methodology for Project Planning

In Figure 4.19, the first phase, SUCCESS PLANNING: DEVELOP BUSINESS CASE, is driven largely by the SAP Ariba account team, value engineering, and the customer's requisitioning team responsible for the purchase of the system/ subscription. Although this phase comes before those we've laid out in this book, objectives and business cases defined during this phase underpin much of the delivery, as do the project sponsors deriving from this process. As such, most successful projects start with a solid handover from this phase, with the business goals and high-level solution objectives reiterated to the delivery team and to-be project team members. The first item of business for the arriving delivery team on the customer side is to confirm the business goals and define the solution objectives in alignment and the handover from the value engineering team and their colleagues on the purchasing side of the decision to implement SAP Ariba.

Onsite SAP Ariba and/or SAP Partner consultants play a supporting role in the CONFIRM GOALS, SCOPE AND ROLLOUT PLAN phase, but a key role on large projects, by helping guide the customer resources in setting up a successful implementation. Once these areas have been defined, SAP Ariba shared services is engaged to begin aligning on the plan, assigning resources, and delivering core team training. The company implementing SAP Ariba begins to parse out the supporting streams of change management and supplier enablement. Once shared services confirms the requirements for setting up the instances, or "realms," as termed by SAP Ariba, you have essentially finished project planning stage and are ready for kickoff.

Architect and Enable Phase

Next, we will go into a little more detail on Figure 4.19. For each phase, we will give an overview of what happens, discuss the major milestone, and describe the importance of that phase within the bigger picture.

Beginning with the first phase after handoff, CONFIRM GOALS, SCOPE AND ROLLOUT PLAN, the main goals/objectives from this phase are to confirm business goals, define solution objectives that will achieve goals, and define solution scope to realize the goals. Table 4.2 outlines the steps and responsibilities for each project participant type.

Step	Shared Services	Customer	SAP Ariba/Partner Consulting
Define business goals and solution objectives	Walk the customer through an exercise to confirm and document their business goals and solution objectives.	▸ Define/confirm 3-5 top priority business goals and associated solution objectives. ▸ Perform any due diligence needed to make these decisions.	Do the heavy lifting analysis to identify top priority goals and objectives—either via success planning or extra consulting.
Confirm scope through go live	Walk the customer through an exercise to confirm solution scope through one go-live. Cover these topics: ▸ Processes ▸ Categories ▸ Suppliers ▸ Departments ▸ Systems ▸ Content	▸ Make decisions to clearly define and confirm solution scope. ▸ Develop and document any rollout planning beyond first go-live.	▸ Support the customer through defining solution scope. ▸ Develop expected ROI based on spend volume included in scope and savings/value identified in business case across all rollout waves.

Table 4.2 Confirm Goals, Scope, and Roll Out Plan

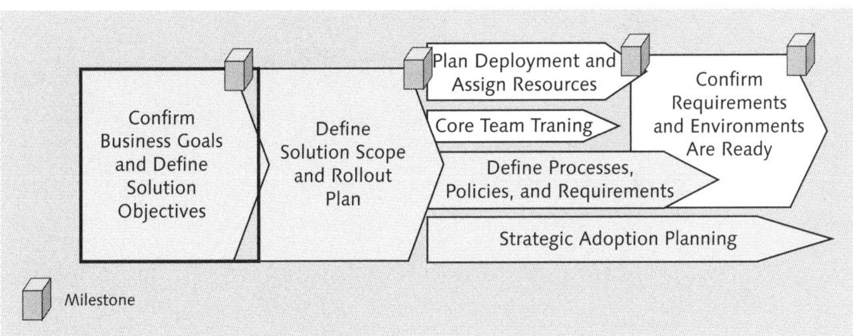

Figure 4.20 Confirm Business Goals and Define Solution Objectives Phase

In this phase circled in Figure 4.20, the customer will identify the business case, business/savings goals, and what objectives must be met to attain them. These need only cover the upcoming/pending deployment wave. The major milestone in this phase is to have the goals and objectives defined. You must understand the business goals and objectives before you can evaluate whether your solution (scope) will deliver them, as per table Table 4.3.

Step	Shared Services	Customer	SAP Ariba/Partner Consulting
Analyze	▸ Ask customer to provide 12 months of spend data. ▸ Analyze the data and identify savings opportunities based on industry benchmarks (if not already done).	Provide last 12 months' spend data in SAP Ariba's supplier spend/transaction data file format.	N/A
Review analysis	▸ Review, understand and confirm customer's business goals/business case and expected savings and benefits. ▸ Document customer's business goals in the solution goals and objectives guide.	▸ Provide customer's business goals/ business case, showing the savings/outcomes customer expects to obtain from the SAP Ariba solution. ▸ Perform any analysis necessary to confirm the business case.	Develop a high-level program vision and strategy, resulting in a detailed business case and high level roadmap to drive benefit realization.

Table 4.3 Confirm Business Goals and Objectives

Step	Shared Services	Customer	SAP Ariba/Partner Consulting
Perform due diligence	▶ Lead meeting to help customer identify how the solution will deliver the desired business results, and what major capabilities will be needed to drive the expected savings or operational outcomes. ▶ Document these critical capabilities as solution objectives in the solution goals and objectives guide.	▶ Participate in the review to identify how the solution can deliver the expected savings/outcomes. ▶ Perform any due diligence necessary to confirm how major solution capabilities will drive savings through better price compliance, operational efficiencies, negotiating leverage, etc.	Perform any due diligence necessary to confirm how major solution capabilities will drive savings through better price compliance, operational efficiencies, negotiating leverage, etc.

Table 4.3 Confirm Business Goals and Objectives (Cont.)

In the second phase, DEFINE SOLUTION SCOPE AND ROLLOUT PLAN, as in Figure 4.21, the scope of the current/pending rollout wave is confirmed, documented and finalized. Scope definition must include all six dimensions of scope: business processes, categories, suppliers, systems, regions/departments/users, and content. The major milestone is having the solution scope defined. You must understand the scope of the solution before you can plan and confirm whether it will be possible to deliver it with the resources available.

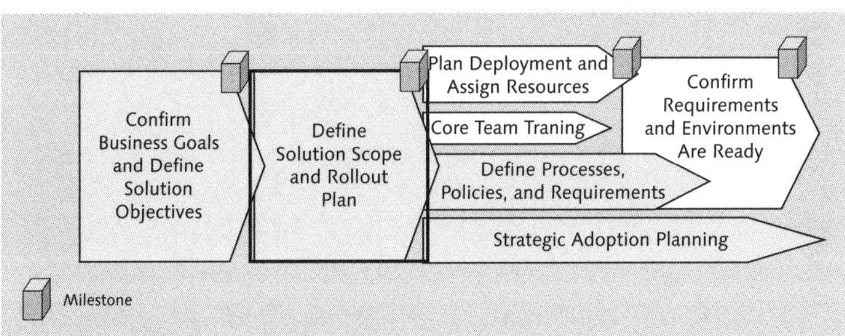

Figure 4.21 Define Solution Scope and Rollout Plans

<table>
<tr><th>Step</th><th>Shared Services</th><th>Customer</th><th>SAP Ariba/Partner Consulting</th></tr>
<tr><td>Analyze/decide</td><td>Lead customer through SAP Ariba's scope confirmation exercise to align the in-scope business processes, spend categories and suppliers with the systems, departments and content needed to support their transactions.</td><td>Decide which spend categories, business processes, suppliers, systems, departments and content to include in the scope of the SAP Ariba solution and with what rollout timing.</td><td>Lead customer through analyzing business goals, value levers and organizational limitations to identify the Solution scope and rollout plan that will maximize ROI and ease of rollout.</td></tr>
<tr><td>Document scope</td><td>Document scope through a single go-live, covering the following scope dimensions in the solution scope alignment document:
1. Spend categories
2. Purchasing processes
3. Customer's suppliers who provide those categories:
▸ Systems/technology
▸ Users/departments/regions
▸ Content (catalogs, contracts, etc.)</td><td>▸ Review and sign off the solution scope alignment document.
▸ Develop and document any rollout planning needed beyond the initial go-live and any wave by wave cost-benefit or ROI plan needed to drive program support.</td><td>Develop a category rollout plan that documents the scope of each wave (processes, categories, suppliers, systems, departments and content) along with the cost, effort and expected savings based on transaction volume and operational improvements identified in the business case, across all planned rollout waves.</td></tr>
</table>

Table 4.4 Define Solution Scope and Roll Out

In order to arrive at a meaningful definition of scope as per the steps in Table 4.4, the following areas should be covered in the scope document:

- Categories: This is how the customer will tie it to volume, savings and business impact.

- Business processes: This will drive what systems, features and functionality are needed
- Suppliers
- Systems
- Departments/Regions/Users
- Content (catalogs, contracts, reports, etc.)

The next phase (as seen in Table 4.5 and Figure 4.22), PLAN DEPLOYMENT AND ASSIGN RESOURCES is when a project plan covering all activities from kickoff through go-live and SAP Ariba roll-off is completed and signed off on. All project resources understand their responsibilities and have committed to completing their assignments on time. The major milestone is when the deployment project plan is complete and resources have been assigned. A project plan is only valid if it is realistic, and if the team buys into it and commits to delivering on time.

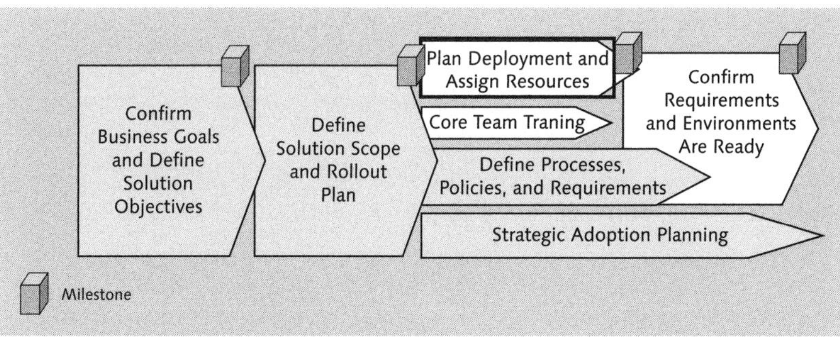

Figure 4.22 Plan Deployment and Define Resources

Step	Shared Services	Customer	SAP Ariba/Partner Consulting
Review deployment	Walk customer through deployment methodology to help them understand the nature, effort and skills needed for the major project tasks.	Review methodology and tasks and estimate time and effort needed to perform customer owned tasks.	Assist customer in estimating time and effort to complete project tasks for their specific scope and organization.

Table 4.5 Plan Deployment and Define Resources

Step	Shared Services	Customer	SAP Ariba/Partner Consulting
Assign resources	Assign SAP Ariba resources to SAP Ariba project roles.	Assign customer resources to customer project roles.	Assist customer in defining project and post-project responsibilities and evaluating candidates.
Timeline definition	Lead customer through developing a detailed project plan that delineates tasks, ownership and timing of all deployment activities needed to reach go-live.	Contribute customer tasks and timing to the project plan and sign off the completed project plan.	▸ Work with customer to identify internal events and initiatives that might impact or be impacted by the SAP Ariba program and build them into the project plan. ▸ Suggest timing and risk mitigation steps to address these dependencies.
Project management framework definition	Propose the project management framework including recurring meetings, status reporting, risk and issue management and partner with customer to define the management framework for this project.	Participate in defining the project management framework.	Work with customer to develop project management framework appropriate for the scope and customer culture.

Table 4.5 Plan Deployment and Define Resources (Cont.)

Step	Shared Services	Customer	SAP Ariba/Partner Consulting
Kickoff presentation	Draft the deployment kickoff presentation and plan the deployment kickoff to align the core project team on project goals, scope, methodology, activities, roles, responsibilities, timing, communication and administration.	Contribute to, review, and approve the deployment kickoff presentation.	Work with customer to engage project stakeholders and tailor kickoff material to specific customer audiences.
Assessment	N/A	Identify and assess project impact on other departments and proactively communicate with stakeholders and leaders of impacted departments to obtain their support and cooperation.	After solution scope is defined, lead Customer through assessment of project impact on other departments and through proactively communicating with stakeholders and leaders of impacted departments to obtain their support and cooperation.

Table 4.5 Plan Deployment and Define Resources (Cont.)

The next two phases, Core Team Training and Define Processes, Policies, and Requirements, as seen in Figure 4.23 and Table 4.6, are important to ensure success of the overall project. Firstly, core team training is necessary to provide the team members with a baseline understanding of the solution they are designing and implementing. Defining processes, policies, and requirements is essential to guiding the project's focus and ultimately understanding whether the project was successful or not by these definitions after delivery.

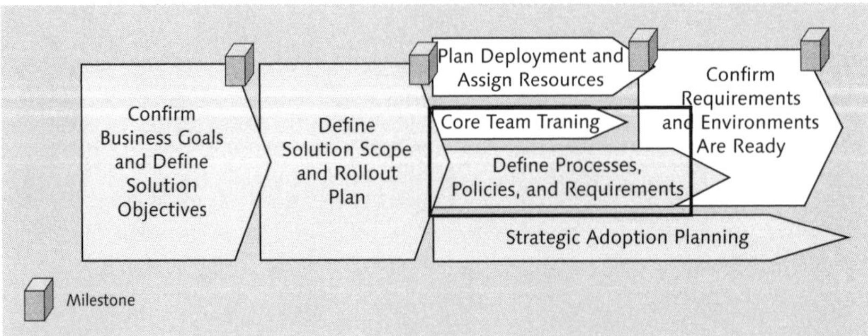

Figure 4.23 Training and Define Processes, Policies, and Requirements

Step	Shared Services	Customer	SAP Ariba/Partner Consulting
Training	Provide SAP Ariba features and functions training.	Send customer team members to SAP Ariba features and functions training as necessary.	Provide SAP Ariba features and functions training to additional customer team members as scoped.
Operations analysis and future state definition	N/A	Determined by customer.	Lead customer through analyzing their operations and define the future state business processes, policies and requirements that the solution will need to handle in-scope categories down to the level of detail needed to support solution design.

Table 4.6 Training and Define Processes, Policies, and Requirements

The second-to-last phase, as seen in Figure 4.24 and Table 4.7, CONFIRM REQUIREMENTS AND ENVIRONMENTS ARE READY is where, in addition to confirming that resources have been assigned and the project has been planned, you must confirm that customer understands their requirements and that all test environments are ready and accessible. The project will hit delays if either the customer requirements are not well understood or the teams do not have access to both SAP Ariba and customer systems. The major milestone for this phase is being ready for kickoff!

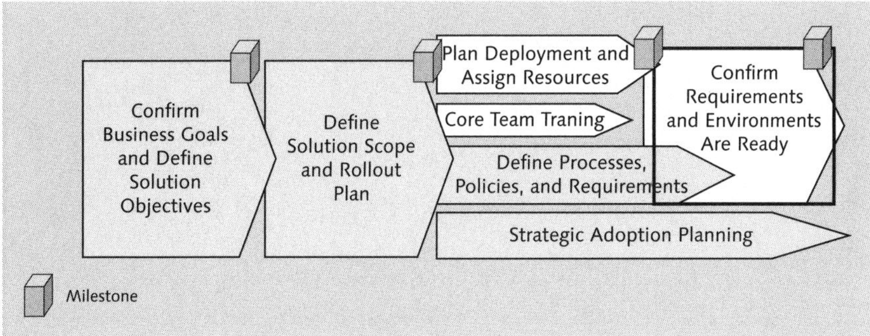

Figure 4.24 Confirm Requirements and Environments are Ready

Step	Shared Services	Customer	SAP Ariba/Partner Consulting
Complete requirements assessment questionnaire	Using the requirements assessment questionnaire, ask customer basic questions about their business requirements to assess whether the requirements cover all in scope functional topics and are well enough understood to proceed with detailed requirements confirmation and design.	▸ Answer all questions in the SAP Ariba requirements assessment questionnaire. ▸ Research and identify decision makers as necessary.	If SAP Ariba has done detailed process, policy and requirements definition for customer, we should not have to assess state of requirements unless much time has passed since they were defined and signed off.

Table 4.7 Confirm Requirements and Environments are Ready

Step	Shared Services	Customer	SAP Ariba/Partner Consulting
Review requirements assessment questionnaire	Review requirements assessment questionnaire and all other business process and requirements documentation provided by customer to ascertain readiness.	Provide most up-to-date business process flows and requirements documentation.	Conduct detailed review of defined future state process, policy and requirements with customer and assist customer to validate that they accurately represent the desired future state.
Confirm system availability	Confirm that customer's instances of SAP Ariba on-demand applications have been created and are available to use.	Confirm that the project team will have access to all customer system environments and tools that will be needed to conduct the project.	Help customer identify and document who will need access to which environments and tools and verify that that access has been granted.

Table 4.7 Confirm Requirements and Environments are Ready (Cont.)

The final phase, as seen in Figure 4.25 and Table 4.8, is STRATEGIC ADOPTION PLANNING in which the system is assessed for its potential to integrate at an organizational level into every day processes, essentially becoming your company's platform for procurement. There are no milestones associated with strategic adoption planning, other than that it needs to be completed along with the requirements/environments workstream.

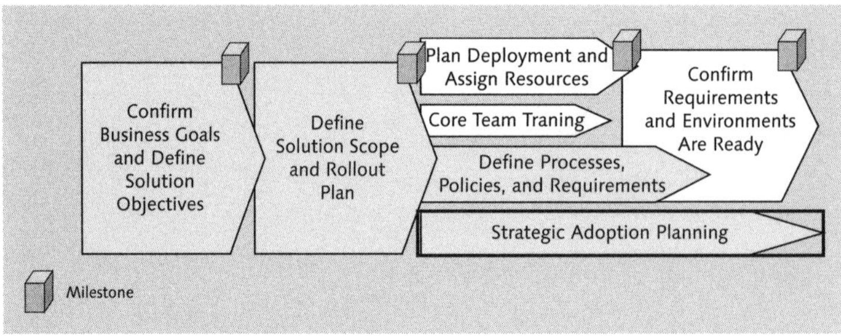

Figure 4.25 Strategic Adoption Planning

Step	Shared Services	Customer	SAP Ariba/Partner Consulting
Solution assessment	Answer customer questions on the typical impact of the SAP Ariba solution and SAP Ariba best practices for managing impact on suppliers and stakeholders.	▸ Assess the solution's impact on suppliers. Assess customer relationships with impacted suppliers and ascertain whether there are other active or pending initiatives that affect the suppliers. ▸ Identify appropriate level of communication to each critical supplier. ▸ Develop a supplier campaign plan to recommend activities and approaches to get customer's suppliers to transact through the SAP Ariba solution in the way that maximizes value for both customer and the suppliers. ▸ Identify other departments likely to be impacted by the solution and the critical stakeholders whose support will be needed to drive adoption. ▸ Assess relationships between department sponsoring the project and other departments and ascertain whether there are other pending changes that could complicate those departments adoption of the solution. ▸ Identify appropriate level of communication to affected departments and the stakeholders to engage.	▸ Assess solution's impact on suppliers. ▸ Assess customer relationships with impacted suppliers and ascertain whether there are other active or pending initiatives that affect the suppliers. ▸ Identify appropriate level of communication to each critical supplier. ▸ Develop a supplier campaign plan to recommend activities and approaches to get customer's suppliers to transact through the SAP Ariba solution in the way that maximizes value for both customer and the suppliers.

Table 4.8 Strategic Adoption Planning

Solution Set Up

Once the architect phase has been completed for the core planning and workstreams, the actual workstreams begin. Per the overview in Figure 4.17, these are:

1. Solution Setup Track
2. Supplier Adoption Track
3. Internal Adoption Track

In this section, we will discuss the solution setup track, which begins with a final confirmation of the requirements.

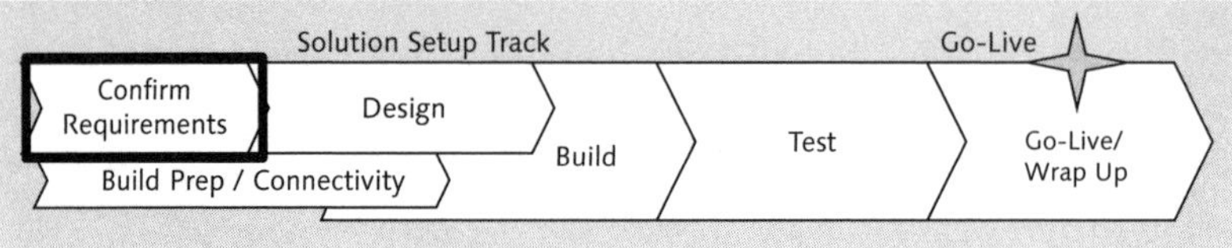

Figure 4.26 Confirm Requirements

For SAP Ariba P2X projects, the phase in Figure 4.26 covers a wide array of areas. Workflow, process, material/service category definition, connection to and integration with other SAP Ariba solutions in the landscape, such as SAP Ariba Sourcing, SAP Ariba Invoice Professional, or SAP Ariba Supplier Information and Performance Management (SIPM) on the analytics-side, all need to be defined in the context of SAP Ariba P2X, as in Table 4.9.

Step	Shared Services	Customer	SAP Ariba/Partner Consulting
Demo	Hold solution demos	Attend solution demos. Learn what the SAP Ariba solution can do.	Attend solution demos.
Requirements review	Walk customer through the business requirements workbook (BRW). Help them understand requirements questions.	Participate in BRW review. Answer questions to provide requirements.	Participate in BRW review. Add context and advice relevant to customer's situation.

Table 4.9 Sourcing Setup Track: Confirm Requirements

Step	Shared Services	Customer	SAP Ariba/Partner Consulting
Best practice discussion	Advise on general best practices by responding to customer questions	Perform research and analysis necessary to define requirements.	Help customer define their requirements by analyzing customer's organization and operations in order to make customer-specific recommendations
Review and sign off	Review requirements decisions with customer to verify that requirements are complete, consistent, and clear.	Sign off on completed requirements.	Proactively drive and facilitate requirements decisions.

Table 4.9 Sourcing Setup Track: Confirm Requirements (Cont.)

Much of the requirements gathering is done using SAP Ariba workbooks, or business requirements workbooks (BRWs). The data and requirements defined in these workbooks form the underpinning for the SAP Ariba P2X system and configuration.

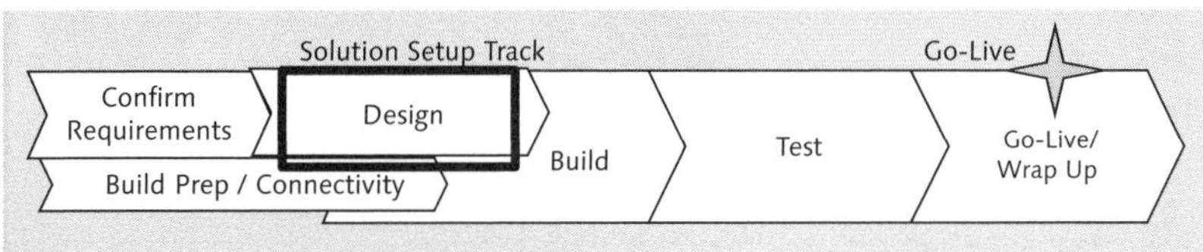

Figure 4.27 Solution Setup Track Design

Once a requirement area has been confirmed, a design phase follows as in Figure 4.27 and Table 4.10, either for that area or for the entire set of requirements. Requirements without overlapping, dependent areas that need definition to proceed, can begin their design phase while remaining requirements are still being defined. This is somewhat a departure from a traditional on-premise project, where requirements are typically all laid out prior to commencing design. While it is oftentimes easier and less risky to begin design only after all of the requirements have been defined, beginning the design for areas prior to their definition allows for time efficiencies on the project, and may actually help make the overall set of requirements more realistic, if the design steps uncover dependencies that influence other requirements. For example, if certain material classification is defined in a requirement in the beginning, and the design phase uncovers additional field dependencies for the material code extensions, further requirement definition around these fields in invoice and other related documents may need to follow suit.

Step	Shared Services	Customer	SAP Ariba/Partner Consulting
Configuration design	Identify and document configurations to SAP Ariba applications that would best handle the defined requirements.	Design and document holistic solution. Review suggested system configurations and assess whether they are right for the customer.	Lead design and documentation of holistic solution: business processes, user actions, workarounds, admin and support functions in addition to system functionality.
Design review and sign off	Explain system configurations and functionality to customer	Understand, provide feedback and sign off the holistic design and system configurations.	Facilitate review of system configurations and holistic solution design. Drive signoff on both.

Table 4.10 Solution Setup Track Design

During the Design and Confirm Requirements phases, an additional phase is running in parallel as per Figure 4.28 and Table 4.11.

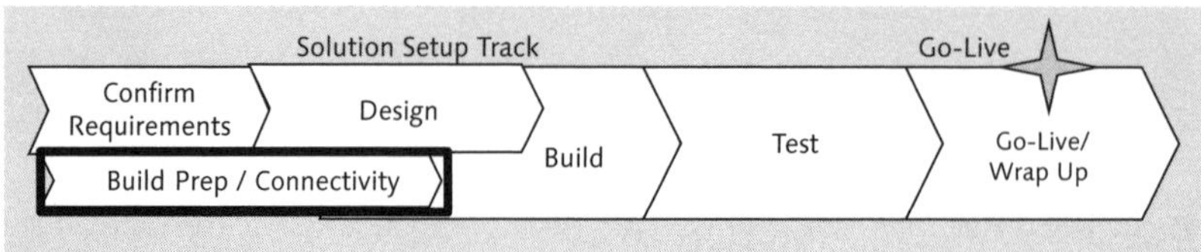

Figure 4.28 Solution Setup Track Build-Prep-Connectivity

During this phase, the connectivity and infrastructure necessary to support the solution, the requirements, and resulting design is established. Although on-demand SAP Ariba solutions are hosted in the cloud, some setup and connection may be required within the customer's realm in order to enable various solutions to communicate with one another, as well as external integration with third-party systems and data sources.

Step	Shared Services	Customer	SAP Ariba/Partner Consulting
Technical knowledge transfer—integration	Teach customer the technical capabilities of SAP Ariba tools	Build out all necessary infrastructure and connectivity between customer and SAP Ariba systems.	Work with customer to configure SAP Ariba tools and customer systems to talk to one another.

Table 4.11 Solution Set Up Track—Build Prep/Connectivity

Once the basic connectivity, configuration requirements, and design have been completed, the next step is to begin the build phase, as per Figure 4.29 and Table 4.12.

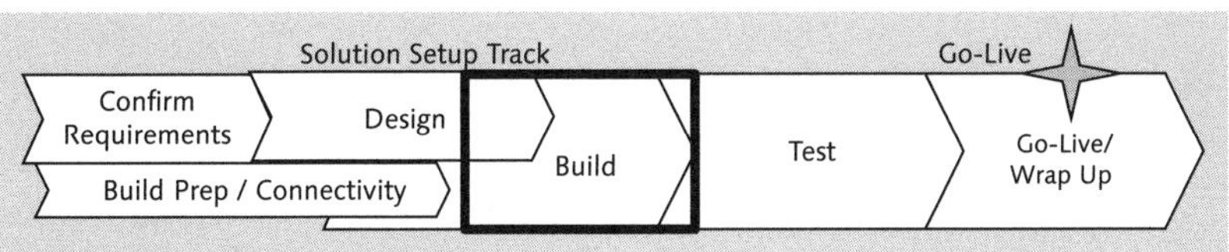

Figure 4.29 Solution Setup Track Build

Here, the workbooks completed during the CONFIRM REQUIREMENTS and DESIGN phases are handed over to the SAP Ariba shared services team to begin building out the solution in the customer's realm. Shared services performs the majority of this build activity, as this group has access to the configuration points in the multi-tenant cloud environment to action these types of changes. Having shared services as the central point of configuration for build helps control access to the system and validate the configuration changes in line with the other configuration and interdependencies.

Step	Shared Services	Customer	SAP Ariba/Partner Consulting
Build	Build/configure elements of the SAP Ariba applications to which customer does not have access.	Configure all customer-facing elements of the SAP Ariba applications (AN rules, approval rules, configuration data, etc.) and build all interfaces between customer applications and SAP Ariba interfaces.	Work with customer to configure customer facing aspects of the SAP Ariba applications including master data and transactional interfaces.
Test plan definition	Provide sample test plan.	Plan entire testing program.	Plan entire testing program.
Test script definition	Provide sample test use cases and scripts.	Develop customer-specific test use cases and scripts.	Develop customer-specific test use cases and scripts.

Table 4.12 Solution Set Up Track Build

The last two items in Table 4.12 relate to the following phase, TEST. Testing is typically a customer-led effort, given that customer is ultimately validating the solution to ensure it meets their requirements.

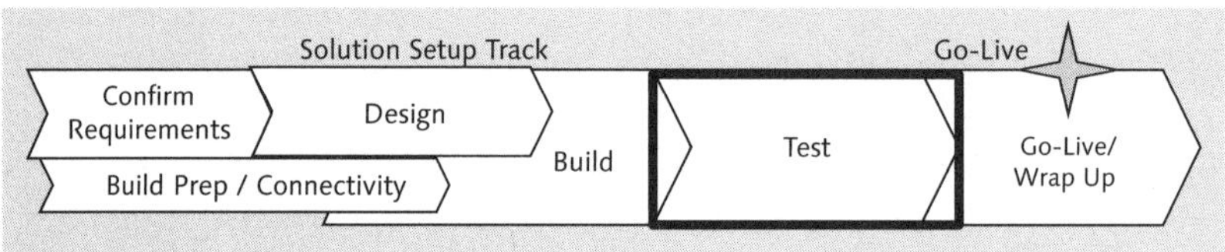

Figure 4.30 Solution Set Up Track Test

As with an on-premise solution implementation, the test phase in Figure 4.30 exists to validate that the key functions and business processes are supported in the new solution, and that this solution will effectively support the business and the scenarios in scope at go-live. During this phase, you ensure that all of these areas work as they have been designed and built, and address any issues that arise during testing. Per Table 4.13, break/fix work is typically handled by SAP Ariba or the consulting partner, whereas testing is led by the customer.

Step	Shared Services	Customer	SAP Ariba/Partner Consulting
Execute test	Provide advice on general best practices for testing.	Manage and execute testing.	Manage testing and assist in executing system test.
Defect resolution	Debug and resolve test defects with SAP Ariba applications	Identify test defects. Debug and resolve test defects with customer systems.	Work side by side with customer to research and debug test issues.

Table 4.13 Solution Setup Track Test

Once testing is complete, it is time to go live and wrap up the project. Before this can happen, the project needs to effectively gate out of testing, as with a quality gate in SAP Activate methodology, and the project leadership and sponsors need to validate whether testing has been successfully completed. If there are items that were raised during testing that have not been completely addressed by go-live, an additional decision as to whether the project can accept this outstanding issue at go-live needs to be made. Some minor issues can be addressed post go-live if necessary, whereas showstopper issues require analysis on shifting the go-live date to address and the impacts associated with this route.

Per Figure 4.31, once the project management and steering committee have agreed on the go-live, the project is ready to cut over into production. SAP Ariba on-demand projects typically have two instead of three environments, and limited transport paths. This is unlike traditional on-premise SAP software projects, where you move most configuration items up from development to quality assurance onwards to production. Here, there is mainly a quality assurance realm and a production realm, and the configuration is essentially replicated from quality into production at the time of go live. Conversions and interfaces need to be established in tandem as part of the go-live, as per Table 4.14.

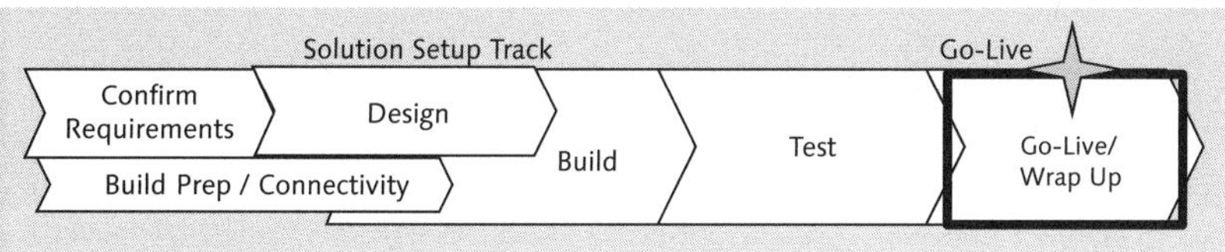

Figure 4.31 Solution Set Up Track—Go Live and Wrap-Up

Step	Shared Services	Customer	SAP Ariba/Partner Consulting
Cutover planning	Work with customer to plan SAP Ariba system production cut-over.	Plan holistic cutover of all impacted systems and data.	Work with customer to plan holistic cutover of all impacted systems and data.
Cutover execution	Execute non-customer-facing production cutover tasks for SAP Ariba applications	Execute customer-facing production cutover tasks of SAP Ariba applications as well as cutover tasks for customer systems.	Work with customer to execute customer-facing production cutover tasks of SAP Ariba applications as well as cutover tasks for customer systems.

Table 4.14 Solution Setup Track—Go Live and Wrap Up

Note that multiple systems may require adjustments during go-live of an SAP Ariba P2X solution, as certain legacy systems are replaced by SAP Ariba P2X, and SAP Ariba P2X is connected to other systems for periodic batch updating or transactions within the customer's landscape.

In the Confirm Readiness phase, which is the change management part of go live/wrap up phase in Table 4.15, you complete the following steps:

1. Draft change management project plan
2. Assign resources
3. Confirm commitment and finalize plan
4. Define/confirm requirements
5. Train resources
6. Assess readiness
7. Strategic adoption planning

Step	Shared Services	Customer	SAP Ariba/Partner Consulting
Change management project plan	Draft project plan covering SAP Ariba deployment through one go-live and walk customer through assigning names and dates to plan tasks.	Assign names and dates to SAP Ariba deployment project plan. Raise and include any customer-specific events or activities and sign off project plan.	Work with customer to align SAP Ariba deployment project plan to any related customer projects or events.
Assessment	Assess customer's readiness to deploy: resources, systems, business requirements, and sponsorship.	Get ready to deploy.	Lead customer through analyzing and defining business requirements and gaining sponsor and stakeholder commitment.
Communication and impact assessment	Answer questions on typical organizational impact and adoption planning for SAP Ariba solutions	Assess impact on suppliers and end users. Develop a strategic adoption plan for obtaining support and participation from customer organization and suppliers.	Lead customer through assessing solution impact and developing a strategic adoption plan.

Table 4.15 Go Live and Wrap Up—Change Management Planning

4.2.3 Standalone Implementations

Standalone implementations are not quite independent of any system, but focus on supporting as much of the process in SAP Ariba as possible. This means SAP Ariba P2O implementations, where invoicing and reconciliation of invoices occur outside of the system, are less likely candidates for standalone, while SAP Ariba P2P implementations can fit this category up to the point of when payment is required, where a payment request is sent to your bank or OK2Pay is transmitted to SAP ERP accounts payable.

Figure 4.32 outlines the landscape and process. A requisition originates in SAP Ariba P2P, with the PO moving out to the SAP Ariba Network. From the SAP Ariba Network, the supplier pulls the PO and can create ship notifications. The item is received in SAP Ariba P2P and the invoice submitted by the supplier via SAP Ariba Network to SAP Ariba P2P. Finally, invoice remittance advice is issued to the supplier from SAP Ariba P2P via SAP Ariba Network, advising the supplier of invoice payment.

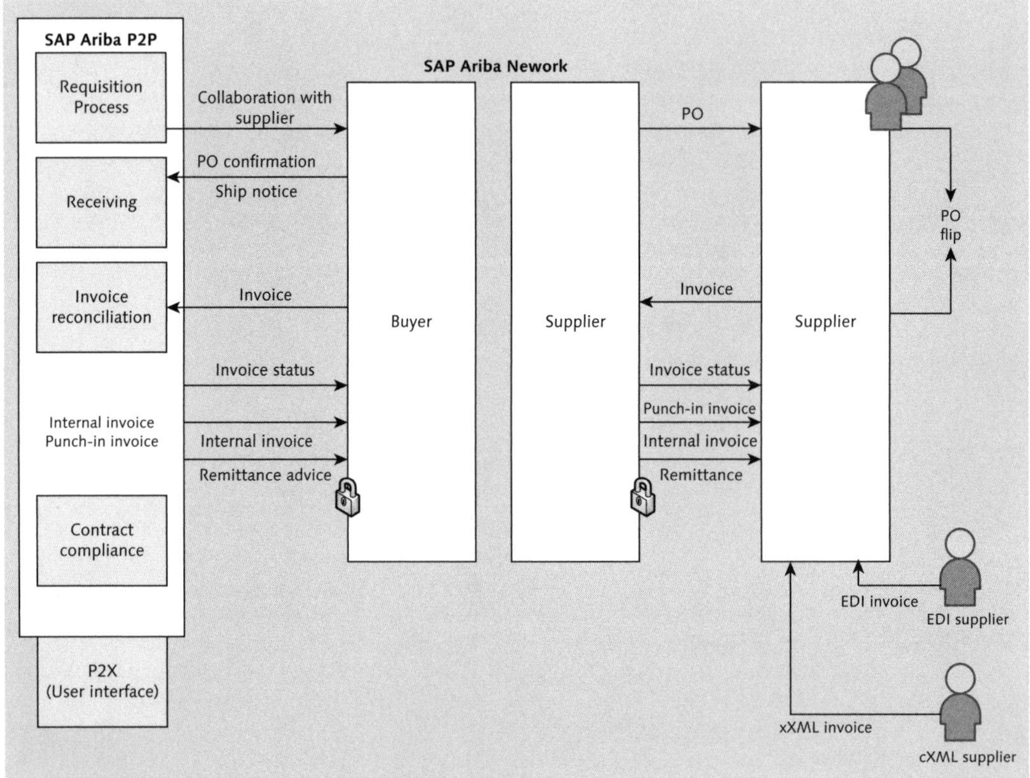

Figure 4.32 Standalone SAP Ariba P2P with Receiving

4.2.4 Integrated Implementations

There are a number of integration options for SAP Ariba P2P, SAP Ariba P2O, and SAP APC with other systems in your procure-to-pay process. The main one is integration with your SAP ERP environment for some or all of the documents, as well as enabling transfer back and forth of documents originating in SAP ERP, including direct procurement requisitions from materials requirements planning (MRP) runs in SAP ERP, as well as invoice and remittance advice in the SAP Ariba P2P scenario.

Figure 4.33 shows a lighter integration with SAP ERP, with exports of requisitions from SAP ERP and imports of POs created in SAP Ariba P2P. In addition, an OK2Pay is delivered from SAP Ariba P2P to trigger the actual payment of an invoice. These integration points can be built out to a level where the process documents are both reflected in SAP ERP and SAP Ariba P2P, with leading documents being created directly in SAP ERP, as well.

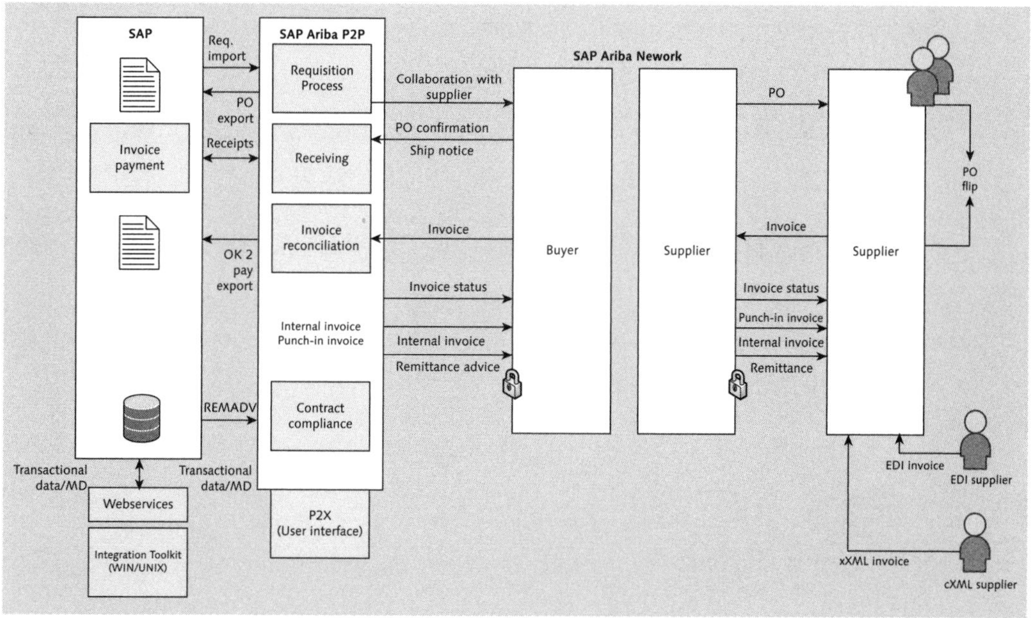

Figure 4.33 SAP Ariba P2P Integrated with ERP Backend

As a catalog solution that can be accessed using an SAP defined catalog protocol called "Open Catalog Interface" (OCI), SAP Ariba Procurement Content offers numerous ways you can integrate with SAP on-premise procurement systems, such as Material Management for purchasing in SAP ERP and/or SAP Supplier Relationship Management (SRM). Here, a web service call is made from SAP ERP/ SAP SRM out to SAP APC, as if the system were accessing a third-party catalog hosted by a supplier. Once an item has been selected, the item is returned using the same call and protocol-type. As long as SAP APC communicates back to the originating system in the fields and format that can be used on the purchasing document, which can either be set up in SAP APC directly with SAP Ariba, or via a user exit in SAP ERP or SAP SRM, your order then populates in the procurement system and the order is approved/sent to the supplier.

An alternative approach is to do the entire shopping cart process along with the approvals in SAP APC, sending back the order information to SAP ERP to be issued. Figure 4.34 outlines a process whereby the user creates a PR in SAP ERP, then punches out to SAP APC and conducts the requisitioning and ordering process leveraging processes and content of SAP APC, returning to SAP ERP for PO creation and follow on processes. Suppliers upload CIF catalogs via the SAP Ariba Network, which are threaded into applicable SAP APC customers—these catalogs and supplier-hosted punch out catalogs, are called via SAP APC during the requisitioning process. Once the catalog content is leverage to create a complete order, the purchase order is generated in SAP ERP. Leveraging the SAP Business Suite Add-On or an adapter, such as the SAP Ariba Network Adapter, the PO is then sent to the supplier via the SAP Ariba Network and Invoice submitted in the same manner.

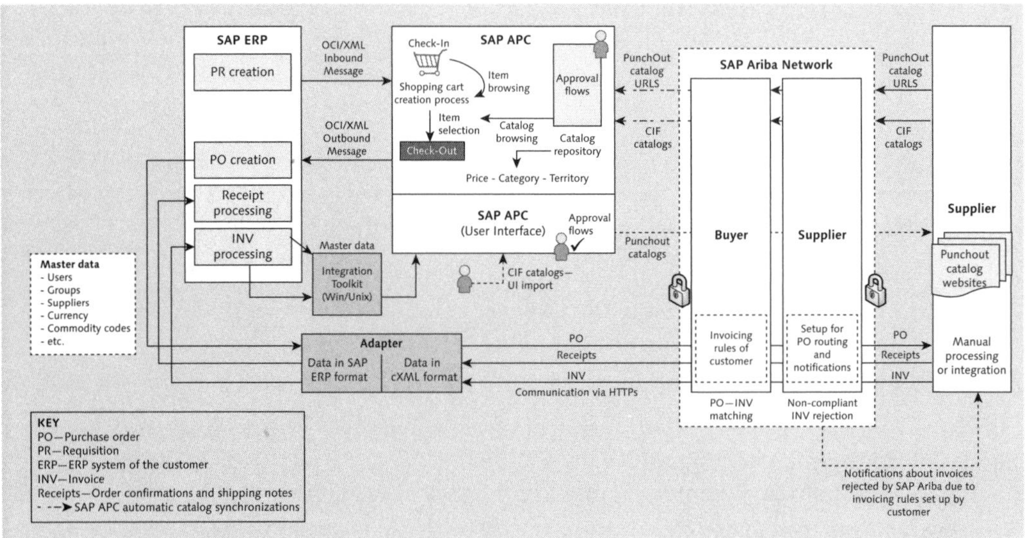

Figure 4.34 SAP APC with Procurement Automation

Figure 4.35 details the main approaches for further integrations with SAP ERP. From SAP ERP, SAP APC is called via a webservice, and the user then creates a shopping cart in SAP APC. Once sourced, this shopping cart is sent back to SAP ERP and creates a PO in SAP ERP. In SAP ERP, the PO is finalized and then transmitted back to the SAP Ariba Network via an adapter. The supplier then acknowledges the PO and fulfills it in the SAP Ariba Network. Upon receipt, the customer logs a goods receipt in their SAP ERP environment, and again this goods receipt is transmitted out to the SAP Ariba Network, where the supplier can now invoice. The invoice document is replicated back to the customer's SAP ERP environment. Intermediate communications/documents, such as advanced shipping notifications (ASNs) and PO confirmations can also be transmitted via the adapter approach.

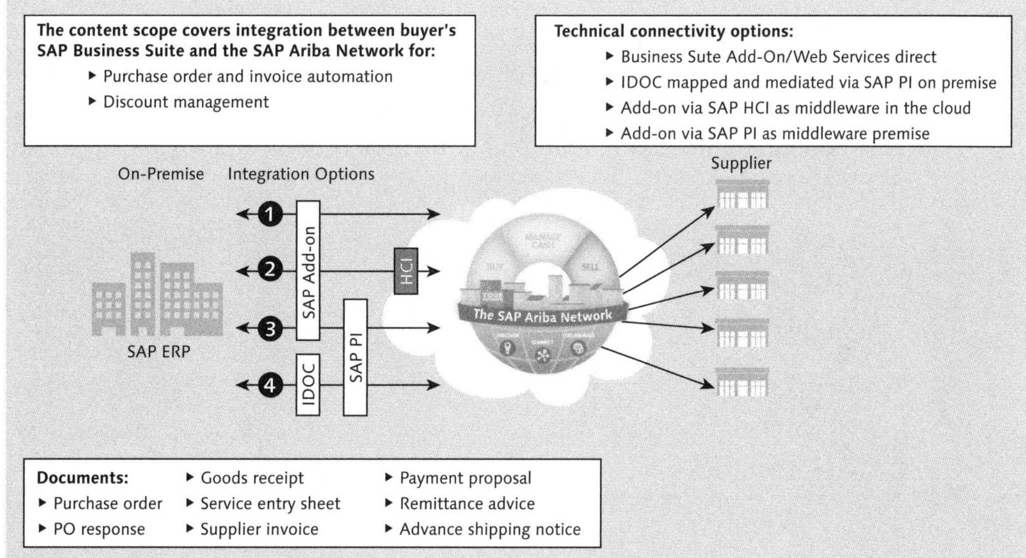

Figure 4.35 SAP Ariba Network Integration for SAP—Full Buyer Enablement

Figure 4.35 outlines the main integration options for SAP Business Suite with the SAP Ariba Network. There are several integration options, which can be confusing when analyzing which route to take for integration. The options are essentially driven by three factors. First, the Business Suite Add-On is a new approach and aims to replace the SAP Ariba Adapter built on SAP PI, prior to the acquisition of Ariba by SAP. The second factor is the need for some customers to "mediate" the connection via SAP PI, for centralization purposes (customer seeks to use a middleware platform such as SAP PI for all interactions with third-party systems, or security, as some security protocols do not allow for direct access to SAP ERP from the internet. Lastly, while SAP Ariba Network and most SAP Ariba solutions "speak" cXML when communicating with 3rd party systems, SAP ERP needs translation of these messages. Messages can be translated to iDocs, which is the old method for exchanging data intersystem with SAP ERP or webservices-based communication, in order to communicate back and forth.

Essentially, the main integration options for connecting SAP ERP to the SAP Ariba Network are to leverage the SAP Business Suite Add-On to directly connect SAP ERP with the SAP Ariba Network, to connect via SAP's middleware platform (SAP Process Integration) either in a mediated fashion between the Business Suite Add-On and the SAP Ariba Network, or via iDocs and a SAP PI-based adapter. As fourth option, you can integrate leveraging the SAP HANA Cloud Integration (SAP HCI). Chapter 9 of this book covers these integration approaches. The document types covered by these integration approaches are:

1. Purchase order
2. PO response
3. Advance shipping notice
4. Goods receipt/service entry sheet
5. Supplier invoice
6. Payment proposal
7. Remittance advice

In addition, SAP Ariba Discount Management can be implemented for SAP ERP leveraging these integration approaches. SAP Ariba Discount Management allows for discount negotiation at the time of invoice in exchange for earlier payments than terms require.

Viewed another way (see Figure 4.36), there are two options for connecting directly:

1. SAP Business Suite Add-On installed directly on SAP ERP
2. SAP HANA Cloud Integration

There are also two SAP PI-mediated options:

1. SAP Business Suite Add-On mediated via SAP PI. This approach is often taken for security requirements and/or if SAP PI is the main integration platform for the ERP environment.
2. SAP Ariba Network Adapter. Based on SAP PI, the SAP Ariba Network Adapter was the original approach for integrating SAP ERP to SAP Ariba, prior to the acquisition of Ariba by SAP.

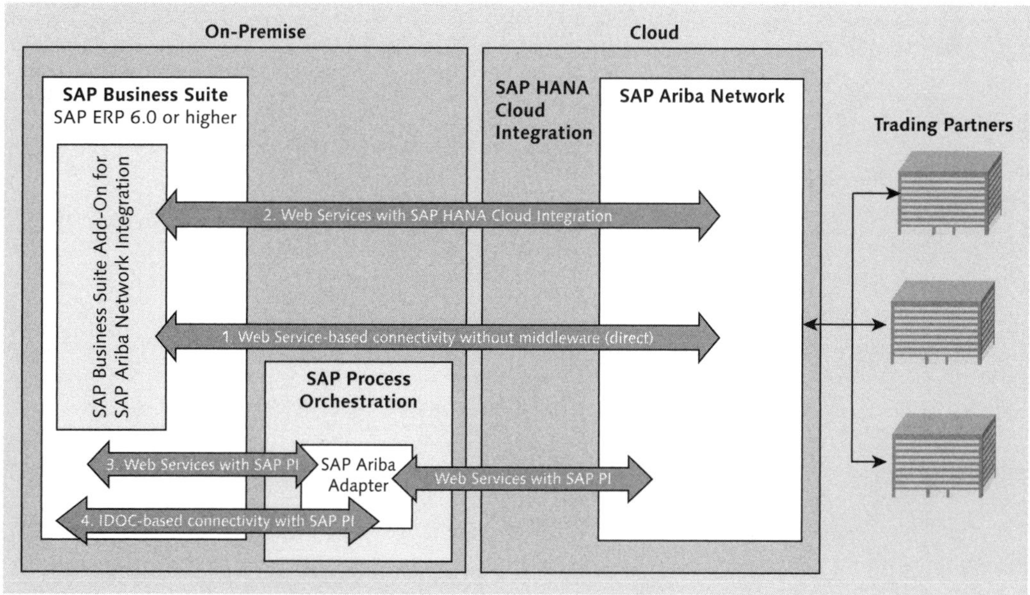

Figure 4.36 System Landscape and Technical Connectivity Options for the SAP Ariba Network

4.2.5 Defining Project Resources and Timelines

Having the right resources and colleagues on a SAP Ariba P2X project can be the difference between a successful or mediocre execution. Table 4.16 describes the key SAP Ariba and/or consulting partner roles on a SAP Ariba P2X project.

SAP Ariba P2X Role	Description
SAP Ariba Customer Engagement Lead	▸ Provide customer ownership. ▸ Establish clear lines of accountability within SAP Ariba. ▸ Reduce confusion for customer when dealing with SAP Ariba. ▸ Establish high quality relationships with our customers with a goal of becoming a trusted advisor. ▸ Establish a point of contact to manage contract extension. ▸ Contact to discuss events or changes within customer organization that would impact the use of SAP Ariba products/services. ▸ Focus on customer success and collaborative commerce adoption. ▸ Faster return on customer investment. ▸ More spend under control and managed cost effectively. ▸ Rapid deployment to improve ability to capture achievable potential.
SAP Ariba Program Manager	▸ Point of contact for overall deployment. ▸ Ensure resources are available and properly assigned. ▸ Manage overall project timeline (all workstreams) to help ensure timely completion of project tasks. ▸ Identify and address resource needs. ▸ Provide project roles, responsibilities, and issue escalation path. ▸ Participate in the steering committee. ▸ Confirm customer goals and project scope. ▸ Establish project management framework. ▸ Point of contact for issue escalation. ▸ Identify and escalate, as appropriate, project issues. ▸ Provide timely project communication and facilitates regular status meetings. ▸ Distribute project wrap-up collateral at the conclusion of the project.

Table 4.16 SAP Ariba and Consulting Partner SAP Ariba P2X Project Roles and Responsibilities

SAP Ariba P2X Role	Description
SAP Ariba P2P Workstream Lead	▸ Responsible for management of the SAP Ariba P2P deployment workstream. ▸ Responsible for the SAP Ariba P2P workstream timeline. ▸ Responsible to report SAP Ariba P2P workstream status on regular basis. ▸ Coordinates and facilitates SAP Ariba P2P design and configuration phase. ▸ Point of contact for day to day configuration questions.
Functional Consulting: Subscription Services	▸ Facilitate business process review and configuration session(s). ▸ Configure the solution according to customer requirements. ▸ Responsible for keeping track of all issues and coordinating issue resolution. ▸ Assist with resolution of issues during system test and user acceptance test.
Functional Consulting: Incremental Services	▸ Assist customer with gathering all spend category information. ▸ Collects high level business requirements. ▸ Assist customer with mapping business processes and procurement categories into SAP Ariba P2P processes. ▸ Assists customer with making SAP Ariba P2P configuration decisions. ▸ Assists customer with test script preparation.
Technical Consulting: Subscription Services	▸ Educate customer technical team on master data extract, mapping and load into SAP Ariba system. ▸ Review data for completeness and assist in data issue resolution. ▸ Assist with technical aspects of site configuration. ▸ Perform customizations. ▸ Educate customer on functionality and setup of SAP Ariba integration tools.

Table 4.16 SAP Ariba and Consulting Partner SAP Ariba P2X Project Roles and Responsibilities (Cont.)

SAP Ariba P2X Role	Description
Technical Consulting: Subscription Services (Cont.)	▸ Educate customer site administrators on administrative tasks throughout deployment. ▸ Assist with resolution of issues during system test and user acceptance test.
Technical Consulting: Incremental Services	▸ Support customer technical team to design and build integration interfaces with their SAP ERP and backend systems. ▸ Provide customer with best practices to develop the integration architecture.
Supplier Enablement Lead	▸ Responsible for management of the enablement services workstream. ▸ Responsible for reporting enablement workstream status. ▸ Responsible for the enablement workstream timeline. ▸ Provide input and obtain approval for suppliers' communications and education. ▸ Manage buyer and supplier interactions. ▸ Prepare customer and suppliers to transact using the SAP Ariba Network.
Catalog Services Team (SAP APC Only)	▸ Contacts supplier to assist with catalog enablement process including publishing a catalog on the SAP Ariba Network. ▸ Reports to SAP APC project manager on supplier enablement status. ▸ Customizes supplier education material creation.
Supplier Enablement Lead (Applicable for Invoice Automation/ Professional)	▸ Contacts suppliers to assist with enablement process including registering on the SAP Ariba Network and configuring their account. ▸ Reports to SE lead on supplier enablement status. ▸ Customizes supplier education material creation.
Supplier and Catalog Enablement Services Team (Applicable for SAP Ariba P2X, Suite Integration, SAP APC, and Invoice Automation)	▸ Contacts suppliers to assist with enablement process including registering on the SAP Ariba Network and configuring their account. ▸ Contacts supplier to assist with catalog enablement process including publishing a catalog on the SAP Ariba Network. ▸ Reports to SE lead on supplier enablement status. ▸ Customizes supplier education material creation.

Table 4.16 SAP Ariba and Consulting Partner SAP Ariba P2X Project Roles and Responsibilities (Cont.)

SAP Ariba P2X Role	Description
Electronic Supplier Integration Manager (N/A for SAP APC)	▸ Creates integration guidelines for cXML/EDI suppliers. ▸ Answers technical questions during the integration process of cXML/EDI suppliers.
Systems Integration Lead (Applicable for Invoice Professional, SAP Ariba P2P/SAP APC with Invoice Automation, and SAP Ariba Invoice Conversion Services)	▸ Educate customer on SAP Ariba Network adapter architecture, capabilities, and potential configurations. ▸ Provide SAP Ariba cXML documentation and list of data fields for each in-scope transaction. ▸ Support SAP Ariba Network adapter installation. ▸ Support adapter related design decisions. ▸ Support customer with adapter-related data mappings and configurations. ▸ Support customer in testing transactions between SAP ERP and the SAP Ariba Network. ▸ Support customer with adapter test issue resolution. ▸ Develop customizations to customer's SAP Ariba Network account. ▸ Develop custom CSV invoice upload template. ▸ Assist with testing and resolve SAP Ariba Network-related issues.
Education Services	▸ In case of SAP APC: Deliver catalog administration training ▸ In case of SAP Ariba P2X or Invoice Pro: Deliver core team training ▸ In case of SAP Ariba P2X or Invoice Pro: Deliver train-the-trainer end user training. This training requires the project team to knowledge share with the super users and key change management instructors, to enable the individuals in change management to act as multipliers for the rest of the organization at go-live.

Table 4.16 SAP Ariba and Consulting Partner SAP Ariba P2X Project Roles and Responsibilities (Cont.)

SAP Ariba P2X Role	Description
Invoice Conversion Services	OPEN ICS: ▸ Advise customer on best practices. ▸ Answer customer questions regarding Open ICS solution. STANDARD ICS: ▸ Manage the invoice conversion services workstream. ▸ Host requirements/design workshops to educate customer on invoice conversion functionality and configurability (including ICS master data transfer, invoice data capture, and exception handling). ▸ Help customer understand their business requirements in the context of the ICS solution. ▸ Gather customer requirements for capturing paper invoice data into electronic fields and transmitting that data to SAP Ariba. ▸ Review ICS configuration documents provided by the ICS provider with the customer. ▸ Answer customer questions about ICS functionality. ▸ Review customer's test cases and scripts, if requested by the customer. ▸ Assist with testing and resolving ICS related issues.

Table 4.16 SAP Ariba and Consulting Partner SAP Ariba P2X Project Roles and Responsibilities (Cont.)

Customer roles are equally as important for a successful SAP Ariba P2X project. Table 4.17 lists the customer roles along with a description of their tasks. Please note that project commitment time indicates what percentage of an individual's working hours would be occupied by the project. For roles where the project commitment time varies widely project-to-project, we have not indicated a percentage.

Customer SAP Ariba P2X Role	Description
Project Sponsor	▸ Project commitment time: 10-20%. ▸ Establish and communicate overall project vision. ▸ Provide senior leadership communication in support of the project. ▸ Mandate appropriate change management across leadership of all affected departments. ▸ Monitor status reports and timelines. ▸ Resolve escalated issues including those which involve customer resources, lack of participation, or supplier compliance messaging.
Program Manager	▸ Project commitment time: 100% ▸ Confirm customer goals and project scope. ▸ Help plan the project activities and timeline. ▸ Ensure adequate resources are assigned. ▸ Manage participation of all required resources. ▸ Coordinate stakeholders as needed (accounts payable, purchasing, receiving, finance, etc.) ▸ Coordinate signoff on all SAP Ariba deliverables. ▸ Manage project timeline and adherence to schedule. ▸ Participate in project status meetings. ▸ Identify, manage and escalate project issues and risks as appropriate. ▸ Develop go-live cutover plan and manage cutover execution. ▸ Single point of contact for overall deployment.

Table 4.17 Customer Roles and Responsibilities

Customer SAP Ariba P2X Role	Description
Functional Lead (ideally not the same person as the Program Manager	▸ Project commitment time: 100% ▸ Participate in configuration workshops. ▸ Define and document business requirements pertaining to all in-scope processes, transactions and SAP Ariba solutions. ▸ Gather business input from all involved functional resources and departments: procurement, A/P, accounting, finance, etc. ▸ Define business process and requirements and make decisions on solution configurations to handle those requirements. ▸ Write `<customer>` functional design document. ▸ Develop test cases and test scripts for testing. ▸ Plan, manage, and conduct system testing and user acceptance testing of the entire solution. ▸ Validate that master data and application configuration data functions as desired. ▸ Identify, escalate, and resolve project issues. ▸ Help develop go-live cutover plan and manage cutover execution. ▸ Experiment with system behavior and configuration to support customer decisions on system configurations. ▸ Learn the detailed SAP Ariba functionality all the way through the procure-to-pay process and learn how the system configurations, customizations and data drive the system functionality. ▸ Assist in writing design document. ▸ Post-deployment role: supporting use of the system. ▸ Answer customer questions on how the system will support the business and technical requirements raised by all involved customer departments.

Table 4.17 Customer Roles and Responsibilities (Cont.)

Customer SAP Ariba P2X Role	Description
Technical Team	▸ Project commitment time: 80-100% ▸ SAP ERP technical resource. ▸ Participate in configuration workshops. ▸ Contribute to SAP ERP related aspects of solution design ▸ Develop and test SAP ERP interface/integration functionality (for both master data and transactional data). ▸ Extract and format master data from SAP ERP systems and load it into SAP Ariba. ▸ Assist with testing and resolve SAP ERP-related issues. ▸ Conduct cutover activities. ▸ Middleware technical resource. ▸ Install, configure and test SAP Ariba integration toolkit or web services interfaces. ▸ Develop and test middleware transmission and mapping functionality. ▸ Configure integration error handling and notification functionality. ▸ Define scheduling scripts for automatic data integrations and email notifications. ▸ Configure corporate network to support end-user authentication (if needed). ▸ Configure corporate network to enable inbound and outbound transmissions with appropriate security controls. ▸ Assist with testing and resolve integration related issues.

Table 4.17 Customer Roles and Responsibilities (Cont.)

Customer SAP Ariba P2X Role	Description
Change Management/Training Lead	▸ Project commitment time: 10-20% ▸ Assess the impact of the project's business process, policy, organizational and cultural changes on end users and other affected employees. ▸ Develop and execute change management plan to address impacts from all changes related to the SAP Ariba program. ▸ Manage communication plan development and project-wide communications to key stakeholders. ▸ (If end-user training is needed) Develop training approach. ▸ (If end-user training is needed) Develop training documentation. ▸ (If end-user training is needed) Plan and manage training delivery. ▸ (If end-user training is needed) Ensure training needs are addressed/issues escalated appropriately.
Administrator	▸ Project commitment time: 50% ▸ Customer technical expert on SAP Ariba on-demand site ▸ Administer configurable aspects of the SAP Ariba on-demand site such as group permissions, user-group assignments, approval rules, invoice exception types and configuration data. ▸ Raise any technical issues with the On-Demand site.

Table 4.17 Customer Roles and Responsibilities (Cont.)

Customer SAP Ariba P2X Role	Description
Process Experts/Pilot Users/ Power Users	▸ Participate in configuration workshops and contribute to business requirements and solution design. ▸ Participate in test case/script development. ▸ Participate in system test and UAT. ▸ Identify power users within each department to act as experts by providing assistance to peers and input to overall process. ▸ Help roll out supplier compliance mandate within their respective departments. ▸ Help define and execute internal change management program within their respective department. ▸ Act as knowledge expert on SAP Ariba Network and SAP Ariba Solutions ongoing.
Designated Support Contact (DSC)	▸ Establish production support model. ▸ Main contact to SAP Ariba support after deployment. ▸ Granted "Designated Support Contact" (DSC) access to *http://connect.ariba.com* ▸ On-demand (OND) liaison to SAP Ariba for end user issues and requested system changes. ▸ Authorize administrative requests, including site customizations and enhancement requests. ▸ Track status of issues and requests on *http://connect.ariba.com* ▸ Work with SAP Ariba to manage volume of issues. ▸ Manage and communicate impact of SAP Ariba upgrades and downtime on the organization. ▸ DSCs automatically receive the following types of notifications: ▸ Notifications of scheduled/unscheduled downtime and security information/bulletins; and ▸ Notifications of new product releases, features, and service pack availability.

Table 4.17 Customer Roles and Responsibilities (Cont.)

Customer SAP Ariba P2X Role	Description
Supplier Enablement Lead	▸ Primary liaison between customer, suppliers and SAP Ariba enablement team. ▸ Manage supplier compliance and escalation process for non-compliance. ▸ Works with SAP Ariba enablement supplier enablement lead to manage the project and drive project milestones ▸ For multi-country programs, need a country/regional lead. ▸ Enforce program goals within organization. ▸ Approve lists of suppliers targeted for SAP Ariba Network enablement. ▸ Manage the gathering of supplier contact data and validate results from SAP Ariba data collection effort. ▸ Plan and support supplier communications. ▸ Approve supplier communications and education materials to be shared with suppliers. ▸ Participate in system test and UAT. ▸ Reinforce supplier enablement program compliance with identified suppliers and internal stakeholders. ▸ Manage supplier relationships, monitor and enforce supplier compliance. ▸ Facilitate supplier training sessions (if any). ▸ Participate in regular status meetings. ▸ Promote the initiative internally with category managers and business relationship owners, AP group and externally with suppliers.
Catalog Lead	▸ Catalogs: Communicate and educate suppliers on catalog requirements and catalogs they must provide. ▸ Catalogs: Test catalogs with suppliers to ensure successful publication. ▸ Catalogs: Ensure suppliers provide correct catalog content in correct format.

Table 4.17 Customer Roles and Responsibilities (Cont.)

Customer SAP Ariba P2X Role	Description
Supplier Enablement Lead	▸ Each functional lead serves as the champion for the Program within their respective business unit. ▸ Participate in requirements gathering and configuration workshops. ▸ Provide process documentation for "as is" state and support to create the "to be" process. ▸ Plan, manage, and conduct user acceptance testing. ▸ Identify power users within each business unit to act as "expert" providing assistance to peers and input to overall process. ▸ Execute internal change management program coordinating training across their respective department. ▸ Act as point of escalation for issues related to processes or identified supplier, both during the program and ongoing
AP, IT, Finance, and Procurement	▸ Supplier selection. ▸ Data collection. ▸ Vendor master maintenance. ▸ Develop new suppliers process. ▸ Training (internal). ▸ Go-live preparation. ▸ Supplier compliance.
SAP Ariba Network Account Admin	▸ Responsible for administration tasks related to SAP Ariba Network account (company profile). ▸ User administration (create, delete, users, roles and permissions). ▸ Account configuration (transaction business rules). ▸ Application management. ▸ Data management.

Table 4.17 Customer Roles and Responsibilities (Cont.)

As with other modules, timelines for SAP Ariba P2P and SAP Ariba P2O projects, as well as federated process control versions of these projects (see Section 4.2.6 for more information on federated process control), depend on the complexity and scope of the implementation. Many A/P implementations are done in tandem or embedded in an overall SAP Ariba Procure-to-Pay (SAP Ariba P2P) project, representing the "invoice-to-pay" process in the procedure. For baseline implementations of the various solutions, the timelines in Figure 4.37 and Figure 4.38 are provided as examples.

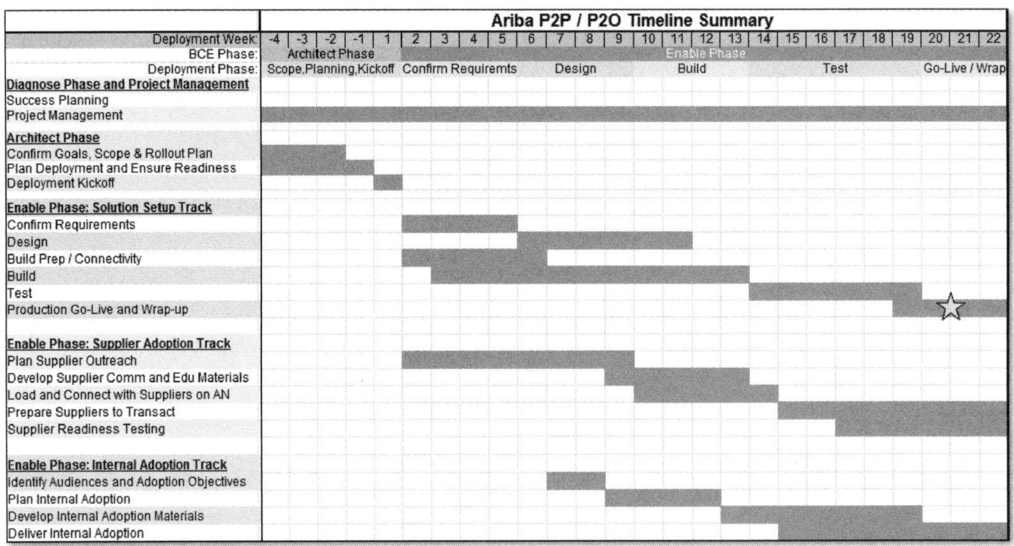

Figure 4.37 SAP Ariba P2P/SAP Ariba P2O Timeline Summary

Figure 4.37 covers 22 weeks in six core phases. This includes both the supplier adoption and internal adoption tracks running during the second half of the project timeline.

For projects leveraging federated process control (FPC), additional time is required as per Figure 4.38, primarily in the DESIGN and TEST phases of the implementation.

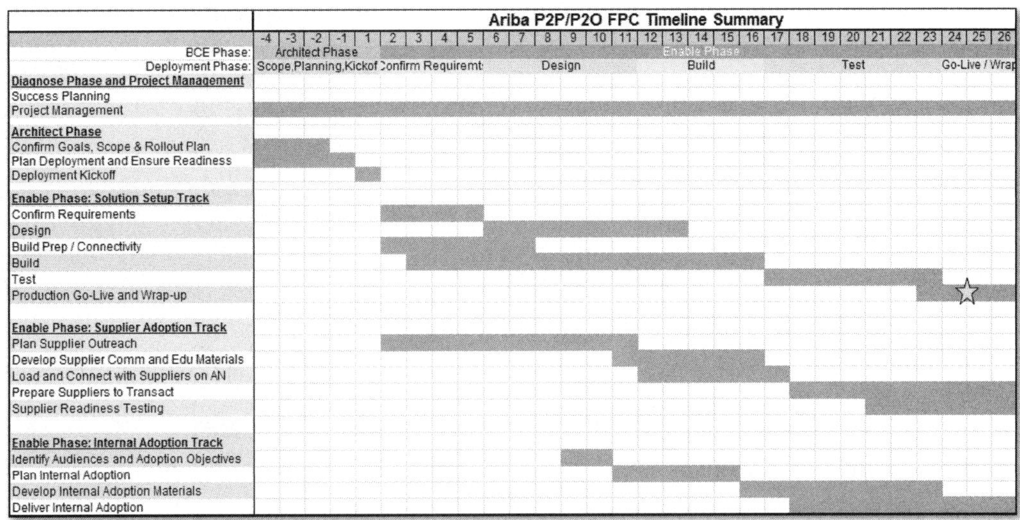

Figure 4.38 SAP Ariba P2P/SAP Ariba P2O FPC Timeline Summary

4.2.6 Federated Process Control

If you have multiple SAP ERP backends or business units in various parts of your systems landscape, and need to isolate these systems on a one-to-one basis with the SAP Ariba front-end solutions, SAP Ariba offers federated process control for SAP Ariba P2P and SAP Ariba P2O. The parent site is a control center that defines enterprise-wide procurement policies (approval rules, system parameters, and customizations), manages catalog content, and consolidates the master data that is shared across the enterprise.

The parent site publishes these policy, content, and data components to the child sites, either through subscription or inheritance. The child site (or sites) are where all of the actual procurement transactions (requisitions, orders, invoicing, and receiving) occur. Each child site is configured to support one Enterprise Resource Planning (ERP) system connected to the child site. Each child site can be integrated with only one SAP ERP system. In most cases, SAP ERP-specific master data is loaded directly into the child site. Note that modifications in child sites can override customizations inherited from the parent.

The FPC child sites can be configured in three different variants:

1. Single variant: Data is highly shared between parent and child sites. All data objects are typically maintained in the parent site. This option is only available if the parent and child ERP variants are the same.
2. Multi-variant: Common data is shared between parent and child sites, but ERP-specific data is loaded directly into the child site.
3. Disconnected/basic: Data is not shared between parent and child sites.

Depending on the child site configuration, a variety of features are available, as per Table 4.18.

Feature	Basic	Single Variant	Multi-Variant
Cross Site Reporting	X	X	X
Cross Site Global Contracts		X	X
Shared Content	X	X	X
Invoice Reassignment	X	X	X
Site Switcher	X	X	X
Services procurement (categories imported in children only)	X	X	X
Common Data Server Integration		Parent	Parent
Suite Integration		X	X

Table 4.18 FPC Feature Availability by Child Site Configuration Type

Configuration capabilities vary by child configuration type, as described in Table 4.19.

Configuration Capability	Basic	Single Variant	Multi-Variant
Default language	Configured in child	Child can override parent configuration	Child can override parent configuration
Default currency	Configured in child	Child can override parent configuration	Child can override parent configuration

Table 4.19 Configuration Capabilities by Child Site Configuration Type

Configuration Capability	Basic	Single Variant	Multi-Variant
Catalogs	Configured in child	Configured in parent; child cannot override	Configured in parent; child cannot override
Catalog hierarchy	Configured in child	Configured in parent; child cannot override	Configured in parent; child cannot override
Catalog views	Configured in child	Configured in child	Configured in child
Customizations	Configured in child	Child can add to parent configuration	Child can add to parent configuration
Approval rules	Configured in child	Child can override parent configuration	Child can override parent configuration
Rule CSV files	Configured in child	Child can override parent configuration	Child can override parent configuration
Enumerations	Configured in child	Child can override parent configuration	Child can override parent configuration
Flex master data templates	Configured in child	Child can add to parent configuration	Child can add to parent configuration
Parameters	Configured in child	Child can override parent configuration	Child can override parent configuration
String resources	Configured in child	Child can override parent configuration	Child can override parent configuration

Table 4.19 Configuration Capabilities by Child Site Configuration Type (Cont.)

For suite integration, both single- and multi-variants support master data synchronization, SAP Ariba contract management and compliance workflow, single sign-on, suite integrated dashboard, and suite integrated flexible fields.

A data rationalization process must be completed before beginning an SAP Ariba P2O federated process control deployment. Data rationalization is the process of analyzing an enterprise's master data, business policies, and configuration requirements and determining what can be shared across the enterprise versus what must remain unique to specific business units.

Examples of data rationalization include:

- User data, with power users common across realms.
- Supplier data, with common suppliers versus site-specific suppliers.
- Accounting data, with chart of accounts typically being ERP-specific and loaded into child sites.
- Site configuration data, including exception types, expense policies, and so forth.

Before beginning an SAP Ariba Procure-to-Order FPC deployment, customers must conduct a data rationalization exercise to determine the following:

- The number of child sites needed
- Parent and child site variant types
- Child site configuration types
- Common or shared data, policies, and customizations
- SAP ERP-specific data

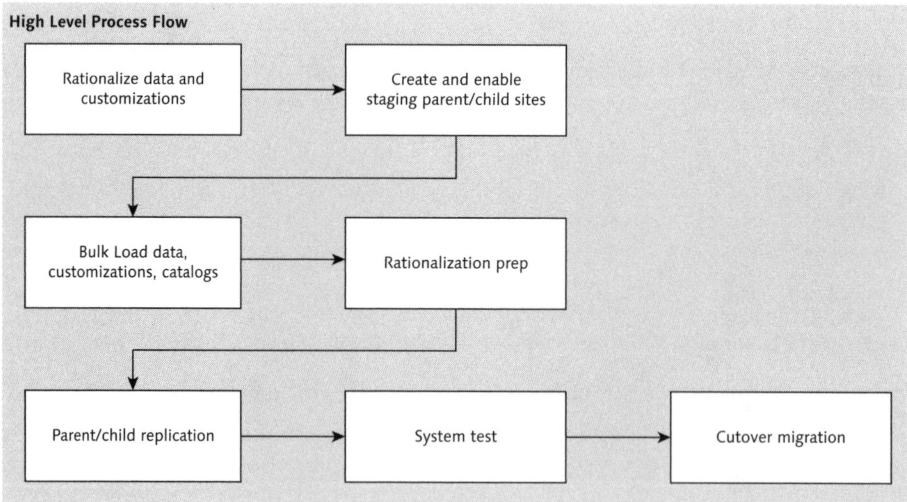

Figure 4.39 Multi-SAP ERP (Federated Process Control) Migration Tools

Figure 4.39 outlines the general steps required to roll out FPC in an SAP Ariba parent-child configuration. Note that all of the "children" need to be either SAP Ariba P2P or SAP Ariba P2O, as FPC does not support mixing different versions of SAP Ariba P2X. Migration is not available for Invoice Professional sites, nor for sites with differing SAP Ariba Network IDs. You cannot maintain two different reporting sites in an FPC configuration.

4.3 SAP Fieldglass Vendor Management System

SAP Fieldglass' cloud-based vendor management system (VMS) manages all categories of external labor, including contingent workers, statement of work (SOW) projects and services, independent contractors, and specialized talent pools. SAP Fieldglass' VMS addresses the intersection between HR and procurement, and helps organizations gain visibility into their contingent workforces.

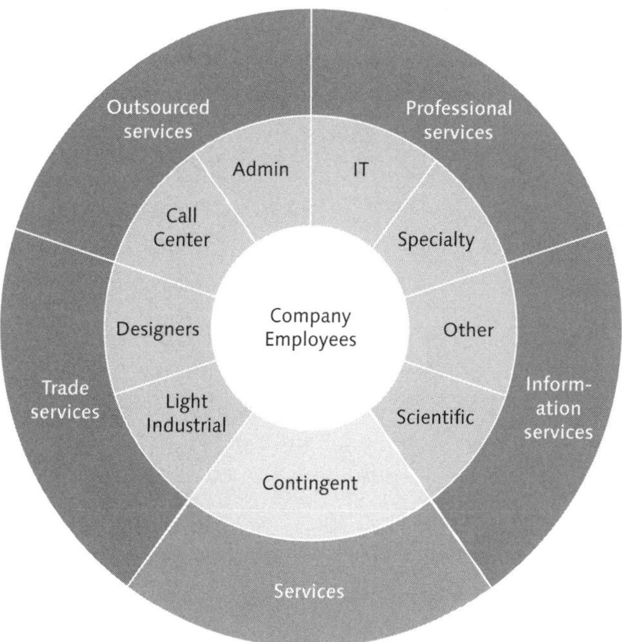

Figure 4.40 SAP Fieldglass—Unified Platform for All External Services

As shown in Figure 4.40, SAP Fieldglass manages all categories of non-payroll labor spend, including:

- Contingent labor in numerous categories
- SOW projects and services
- Independent contractors
- Specialized talent pools, such as retirees and alumni

SAP Fieldglass Vendor Management System manages the entire lifecycle of procuring goods and services from the initial requisition to extensive reporting. The solution also goes beyond these with core functionalities in five key areas, which address issues with contingent labor procurement, a knotty issues for procurement systems. These key areas are:

- **Visibility**
  This has always been a difficult issue for services, especially with regards to contingent labor. Many countries and states have laws regulating the use of contingent labor, so it is paramount to understand what types of services are being purchased. In SAP ERP and other systems, workarounds involving misclassification of services to materials are sometimes used in order to make the procurement process conform to a single master data set or process. This leads to difficulty in reporting on services, if misclassifications have been put in place in order to streamline the SAP ERP environment. SAP Fieldglass provides a platform to bring this information back into the forefront with accurate classifications and measurements to enable precise management of this spend category.
- **Efficiency**
  Groups operating in SAP ERP often devise their own methods for procuring services, leading to process fragmentation. Some groups may go through a strict review and resume approvals, while others may cut blanket POs and bring in contract workers the next day. Having a common platform and process via SAP Fieldglass brings this into a more uniform environment, which increases efficiency.
- **Program and worker quality**
  Many procurement systems do not have detailed rating options and performance tracking for contract workers, as these types of functions are more commonly associated with HR-centric applications. A procurement or logistics system may be able to rate damaged goods and supplier on-time performance, but it is typically difficult to register issues with a particular individual

contractor in system. As such, companies are often doomed to repeat the same mistakes down the line, as they lack institutional awareness of past issues. SAP Fieldglass allows for this information to be memorialized in system and provide a register for future interaction with the service suppliers and individual contractors, increasing quality.

- **Cost savings**
  Once you have begun to accurately measure your spend in operational procurement using SAP Fieldglass, your additional knowledge becomes leverage to drive savings during negotiations and consolidate spend for further reductions in costs.
- **Risk mitigation and compliance**
  As discussed in the initial bullet point, there are numerous laws that vary by state and even local entity. Compliance is often impossible to achieve in a fragmented procurement system, where fields and processes are not available in the system. In many cases, an offline, cumbersome process is devised to try and stay in compliance and mitigate risk. With SAP Fieldglass, all of this is collected in one environment and platform, which in turn is integrated with contracts and other compliance drivers on the commercial side of the equation.

Having one focused area for VMS activities, SAP Fieldglass provides an open integration platform that supports all major enterprise systems. With extensive integration with both SAP Ariba and SAP applications, SAP Fieldglass can seamlessly fit into an existing SAP ecosystem and yield many process efficiencies through integrations with accounting or AP systems for invoicing or with SAP Ariba for PO attachment and compliance to total-spend management policies. Chapter 9 of this book provides more detail on integration approaches for SAP Fieldglass, SAP Ariba, and SAP ERP.

Per Figure 4.41, services are a challenging area for most SAP Ariba P2P systems, as the entire document stream is more dynamic and changing than materials procurement. Many engagements have to be negotiated via an RFx process, as the work is often one-off and non-repeatable in nature. This type of negotiation produces a tailored SOW and purchase order. Once the work is performed, the actual duration of a service item often does not amount to the original amount quoted, and time entry supplants goods receipts as main matching process for accounts payable to pay an invoice.

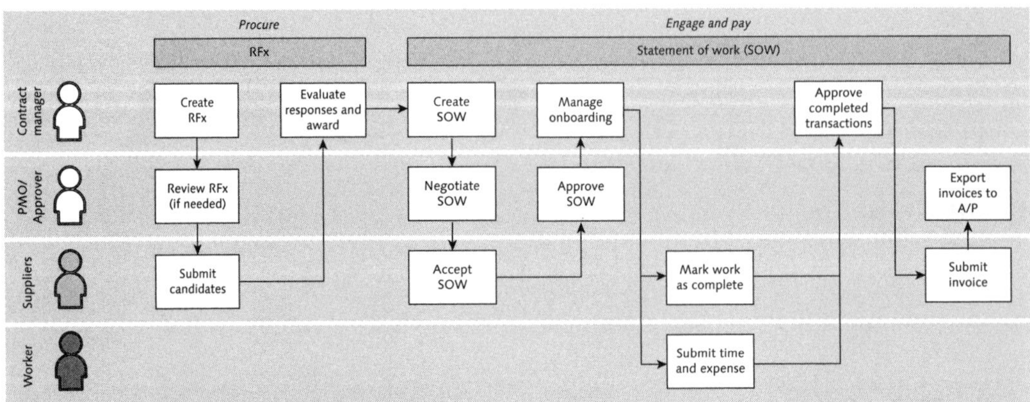

Figure 4.41 Services Process Flow

Add contingent labor management challenges, where vetting the service provider's employee, onboarding/offboarding, and tracking time and performance becomes even more pronounced, and you have the business case for an overarching VMS.

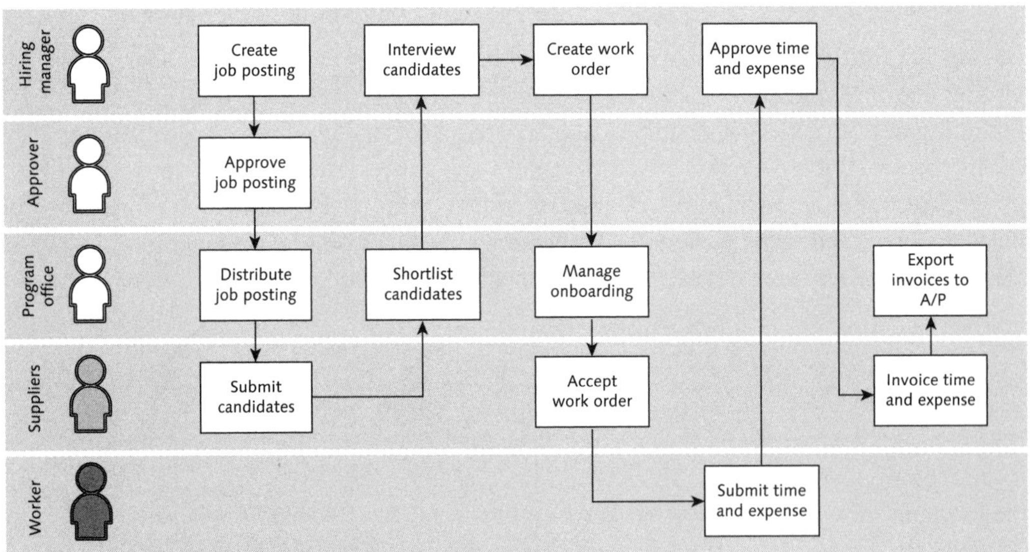

Figure 4.42 Typical Process Flow: Contingent Labor

For contingent labor in Figure 4.42, vetting the individual who is being engaged to perform the work is oftentimes as important as the work definition with the supplier. Here, interviewing and HR management are factors, which make this area of services procurement more complex. Not only is the procurement systems area put upon to act dynamically with the changes of services procurement, but a tie-in with HR systems and processes has to be established to manage workers who do not technically belong to your company.

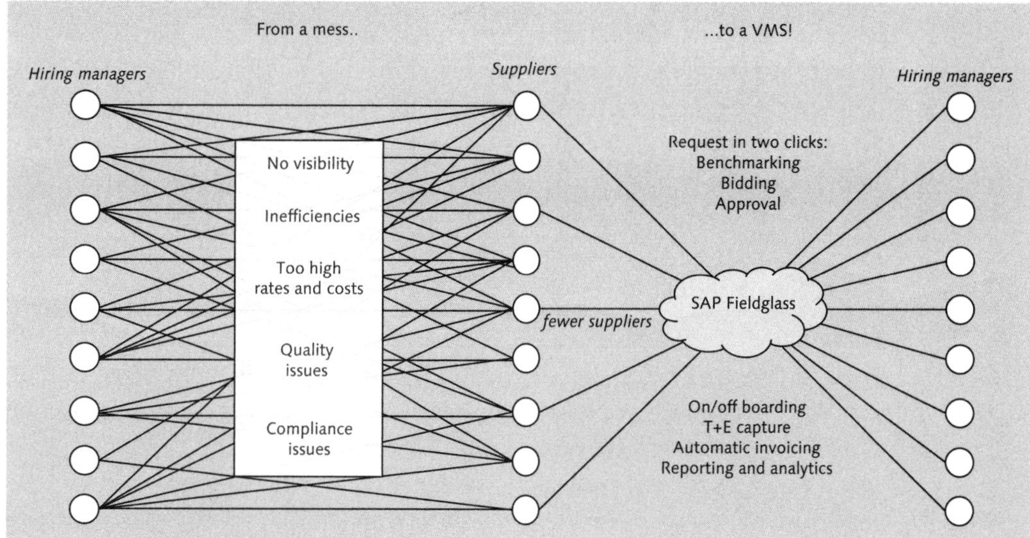

Figure 4.43 The Contingent Labor Challenge

Per Figure 4.43, common issues organizations have in managing their external workforce include:

1. **No qualifications standards**
   Large quantity of suppliers that have different qualifications to perform various services; inefficient processes make it difficult for managers and suppliers to comply with policies and existing agreements; and a limited view into how much others pay for a service results in the managers paying too much.
2. **Cost savings**
   Whether managers are sole sourcing engagements to friends and family, suppliers are not adhering to the terms and conditions of the agreement that exist with them, or the scope of projects is creeping out of control, SAP Fieldglass helps firms drive cost savings of 8–12% in these areas.

3. **Lack of efficiency**
   The process of engaging workers and services is complex. It can take 20+ phone calls and emails per request. A lot of time is spent onboarding and offboarding workers and on reconciling invoices. SAP Fieldglass has simplified the process with a two-click requisition and prepopulated SOW templates.
4. **Quality and analysis**
   Without a VMS, organizations commonly approach measuring quality through providing a survey to managers on a quarterly or semi-annual basis. If managers respond at all to the survey, they typically zero in on the last or the worst activity from the suppliers they have worked with. With SAP Fieldglass, feedback can be provided at a line-item level throughout the life cycle of the assignment. Measurement of quality is made easier and provides very specific feedback about what can be done to continuously improve on the overall service being provided.
5. **Compliance**
   With an emphasis being placed on security and safety today, insuring compliance to your policies on these topics is paramount. How is safety training completed? After workers are terminated, who ensures that they no longer have access to your systems? SAP Fieldglass helps drive compliance to internal policies such as a "do not hire" rule, as well as compliance with broader legislative rules and regulations. SAP Fieldglass provides auditable proof to ensure that policies are adhered to and tracked in a centralized manner.

SAP Fieldglass is a technology platform that sits in the middle of buyers and suppliers. A common concern is that it will disintermediate the relationship with your suppliers, but the reality is that SAP Fieldglass facilitates that relationship. For buyers, the requisition is simplified; suppliers are able to provide services in an expedited fashion, no longer held up by complex or unfamiliar on-and-off-boarding or approval policies. These highly manual processes are streamlined with SAP Fieldglass. Buyers can create requisitions in two clicks, competitively bid for services, benchmark their needs against the broader market, on-and-off-board workers, capture time and expenses, automate invoicing and receive detailed reporting and analytics.

As in Figure 4.44, a requisition for contingent labor is created in SAP Fieldglass, approved and passed to SAP Ariba P2X, where it is processed further and turned into a PO. The work order is moved back up through SAP Fieldglass to the supplier. Once the supplier resource submits a timesheet, is the requisition again passed through SAP Fieldglass, approved, and the resulting invoice is passed to the business network for reconciliation in SAP Ariba. Once SAP Ariba P2X matches the invoice with the PO and the approvals, the invoice is paid via SAP Ariba's OK2Pay message to a FI/CO accounts payable system, such as SAP ERP.

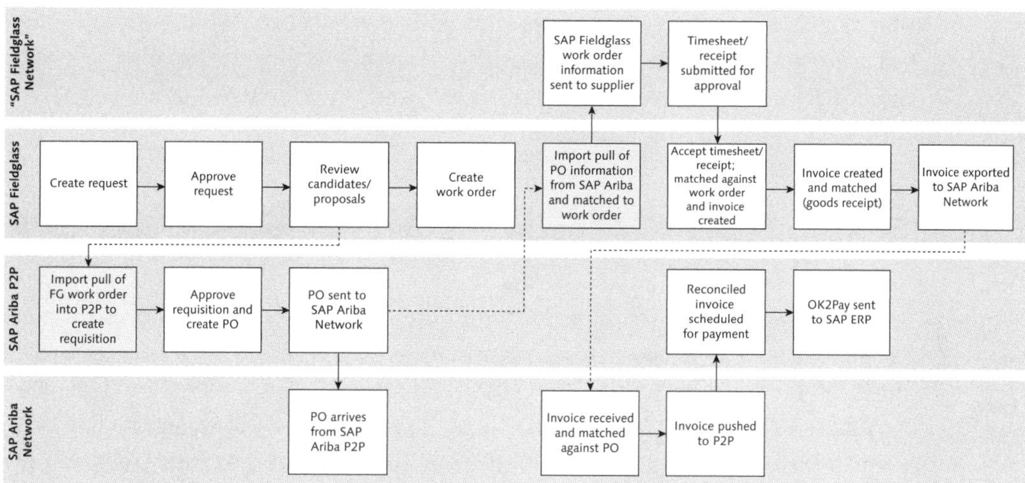

Figure 4.44 Integrated Workflow Between SAP Ariba and SAP Fieldglass

The SAP Ariba Network can now intelligently integrate with SAP Fieldglass via the Cloud Integration (CI) adapter detailed in Chapter 9. This integration provides business benefits for both buyers and suppliers.

As a buyer, you can:

- Use your existing integration with the SAP Ariba Network to route SAP Fieldglass invoices to your SAP ERP system.
- Give your suppliers visibility into the status of SAP Fieldglass invoices on the SAP Ariba Network.
- Realize lower IT maintenance costs by avoiding two integrations.
- Pay your suppliers faster.

As a supplier, you can:

- (If you were a SAP Fieldglass-only supplier) get exposure to more business through the SAP Ariba Network.

- Check the status of your SAP Fieldglass invoices on the SAP Ariba Network.
- Receive payment faster.

Combined with the collaborative, network-based procurement capabilities of SAP Ariba and the human resources expertise of SAP SuccessFactors, SAP delivers a platform for businesses to manage their entire workforce—both temporary and permanent staff—from initial recruiting and onboarding to ongoing development, performance management, retention, and retirement.

4.4 Implementing SAP Fieldglass Vendor Management System

SAP Fieldglass has subscription model typical of the VMS space. Here, customers receiving invoices do not pay subscription fees or for basic set up services to join the SAP Fieldglass network. The SAP Fieldglass network is similar to the SAP Ariba Network, but there is a difference in scale and focus—over $20 billion in invoices are submitted over the SAP Fieldglass network annually, whereas the SAP Ariba Network has a $750 billion run rate and supports a much wider variety of transaction types and scenarios.

A supplier submitting an invoice on the SAP Fieldglass network pays a modest fee for doing so; this revenue model drives tight focus on enabling customers as quickly as possible on the network. SAP Fieldglass does this with a highly focused delivery organization, which engages as soon as the commercial side has been completed for a customer.

In the following sections we will cover the preparatory steps you should take prior to beginning an SAP Fieldglass project and discuss the project resources, phases, and timelines associated with such a project.

4.4.1 Planning your Implementation

Prior to beginning an SAP Fieldglass project, there are five key areas to cover:

1. **Define objectives, metrics and key performance indicators (KPIs)**
   Similar to SAP Ariba projects, one of the first things you should do when kicking off VMS implementation is develop the scope of the project and determine the goals it should accomplish. Is the priority to control costs through rate cards

or retiree reuse, or would you prefer to focus on optimizing cost savings by analyzing the use of fixed bid, project-based statements of work (SOWs), or time and materials? Perhaps your priority is to mitigate risk by better managing compliance with tenure regulations and on- and offboarding processes. Once the goals are defined, you then manage the entire project to those goals.

Similar to SAP Ariba Supplier Performance Management projects, some companies are more concerned with improving the quality of the workforce by using a scoring system and supplier/candidate evaluations. Other common objectives include ensuring adoption of the VMS automation, so that more spend is managed; decreasing the time to hire; and shortening onboarding times. Comparing these goals with the capabilities of your suppliers helps further refine the scope. If your suppliers do not specialize in or support certain goals that were initially defined, these goals and/or the in-scope supplier group need to be adjusted.

Once the program goals are established, you will want to determine how to measure and track results in a systematic and meaningful way. Tying specific metrics and KPIs to each objective is crucial for understanding the performance of the program. With SAP Fieldglass VMS in place, reports should be available for tracking these important metrics. If you have a third party managed service provider (MSP) or vendor on-premise (VOP) partner, you can also link the KPIs directly to the service level agreements (SLAs) of these suppliers in areas such as response times, resume delivery, rates and invoice accuracy.

2. **Build the team and develop a clear communication strategy**
   As with most projects, it is important that the correct people are involved from the beginning of a SAP Fieldglass implementation project, in order to ensure that the process, potential scope and timeline are understood by all parties. Your internal team should include a program sponsor, a project manager, and someone with technical aptitude. Ensure that your resources are dedicated to the project with enough bandwidth and have the appropriate skill level and knowledge. This team should provide updates to your senior management periodically concerning the status of the project. A project sponsor helps maneuver through political or organizational roadblocks. Buy-in at senior levels of management will greatly aid in adoption of the VMS system. Once executives understand the enormous cost savings and efficiencies offered by the SAP Fieldglass VMS platform, they will drive the project's success and the adoption of the system.

The project manager and team should also offer regular updates on the project status, and communicate the value to specific segments of the organization, such as time savings and higher quality workers. Doing so is critical to drive further internal adoption and usage of the SAP Fieldglass platform. A VMS deployment requires change management similar to SAP Ariba P2P implementations. User adoption and the changing of buying habits and processes are keys to a successful rollout. Therefore, it is necessary to address this important aspect of change management and organizational impacts throughout the implementation. Determine how to deal effectively with change in your end user community. Communication, both crisp and continuous, is a lynchpin in a VMS project rollout. The project leaders and the executive sponsor need to continually communicate the importance of the project throughout the organization.

One challenge not immediately apparent for SAP Fieldglass projects is obtaining commitment from your internal IT organization for integration and user management topics. Because SAP Fieldglass has a very light IT footprint, both from a cloud standpoint and in terms of costs to your organization, it is possible for project leadership to overlook or downplay the important role IT still needs to play on some SAP Fieldglass projects. For example, SAP Fieldglass may need to integrate with existing on premise systems or other cloud systems. Your internal IT department may be the only group with specialized knowledge to assist in the design and eventual access points to these systems. Having the business sign off on the case for SAP Fieldglass is a great first step, but obtaining an IT sign off on identified integration, process, and user management areas prior to starting the implementation is oftentimes just as important.

3. **Establish business processes, assign approval workflows and understand data requirements**
   Documenting your business rules and system design is the best way to set expectations and avoid misunderstandings throughout the course of the project. In addition, the written materials can act as a reference during the system configuration process, and can help curb changes to the scope and design that cause delays. Using process flows will help you make important decisions about approvals. Collecting data such as users, workers and jobs can be one of the more tedious aspects of the implementation. It is best to determine upfront what will be required, including file formats, to avoid complications when it

comes time to load and test the data elements in the tool. Make sure to also take the time to identify custom field requirements and functionality. As with all cloud implementations, customization options are more limited than with on-premise, but a design phase still may be able to line out achievable enhancements and customizations.

4. **Determine integration requirements early**
   Many SAP Fieldglass VMS implementations include system integrations to existing applications that touch various phases of the worker lifecycle, such as SAP HCM, SAP SuccessFactors, SAP ERP, AP and SSO (single sign-on). Often the sharing of data needs to be bi-directional. Integrations can be scheduled to occur on in batch mode on a periodic basis or configured to occur only on demand. On-demand calls to an SAP ERP system from an external system are sometimes not possible, due to internal IT department rules, operating procedures, and firewall constraints. In these instances, batch receipt of data from SAP ERP can be scheduled at regular intervals.

   A few integration factors to consider:

   - Identify required/desired interfaces and required resources.
   - Prioritize interfaces realistically and clearly: phased approaches work, provided the interfaces being phased in either have no overlapping data or have been tested thoroughly prior to the phased roll out.
   - Account for the corporate integration policy and process requirements in the project plan.
   - Integration designs and realization are sometimes an iterative process, where the initial design and functionality requires tuning once in place.
   - Ensure proper testing by applicable resources and stakeholders is conducted prior to any roll outs.

5. **Enable your supplier community**
   As with SAP Ariba projects, supplier adoption is as critical to the VMS's success as your internal user adoption. It is important to maintain an open dialogue between your program owners and suppliers to help ease resistance to new processes, potential fees, and the system itself. Some potential areas to address include the lack of clarity on how to handle workers staffed by noncompliant suppliers and suppliers that try to modify the MSP or VMS agreements.

If executed properly, your suppliers will recognize their own benefits from the VMS implementation such as faster payments, reduced sales costs and potential sales increases by receiving more requisitions through the system.

4.4.2 Defining Project Resources, Phases and Timelines

An SAP Fieldglass implementation schedule typically lasts 8 to 12 weeks, depending on complexity and integration requirements of the implementation. During that time, the customer works closely with its VMS project team (and that of its managed service provider (MSP), if the program is not self-managed).

Fieldglass implementations are more cross organizational than most, leveraging at times subject matter experts (SMEs) from HR, IT, and procurement organizations. The first thing to obtain is strong project sponsorship that can span these different organizations. This may require a C-level executive on the finance or operations-side, to embrace the cost savings and compliance benefits offered by SAP Fieldglass.

From HR, the group or individual managing contingent labor employees is a logical choice as a SME. From IT, for SAP Fieldglass integrations, it is recommended to have a lead familiar with both systems and the network requirements. For example, if SAP HCM needs to be integrated with SAP Fieldglass, in order to provide contingent worker information from SAP HCM, having an SAP HCM SME who owns this information in SAP HCM on the project would be recommended. If no integrations are planned, then employees need to have internet access and the training to leverage the system. In such cases, the project is more of an HR/ procurement-driven initiative and change management exercise. Contingent workforce managers in HR and services procurement people in procurement need to be involved from the onset and through roll-out, to ensure the design is properly tailored to the company's requirements, and that the roll-out is accepted by both internal users and the suppliers.

From a project phase perspective, SAP Fieldglass implementations can leverage the SAP Ariba methodology and roles similar to those in SAP Ariba projects (see Table 4.20 and Table 4.21). Additional regions, suppliers, and company divisions can be expanded in SAP Fieldglass once the initial pilot implementation is complete, using the same milestone methodology.

SAP Fieldglass Role	Description
SAP Fieldglass Project Manager	▶ Point of contact for overall deployment. ▶ Ensure resources are available and properly assigned. ▶ Manage overall project timeline to help ensure timely completion of project tasks. ▶ Identify and address resource needs. ▶ Provide project roles, responsibilities, and issue escalation path. ▶ Participate in the steering committee. ▶ Confirm customer goals and project scope. ▶ Establish project management framework. ▶ Point of contact for issue escalation. ▶ Identify and escalate, as appropriate, project issues. ▶ Provide timely project communication and facilitates regular status meetings. ▶ Distribute project wrap-up collateral at the conclusion of the project.
SAP Fieldglass Workstream Lead	▶ Responsible for management of the SAP Fieldglass deployment workstream. ▶ Responsible for the SAP Fieldglass workstream timeline. ▶ Responsible to report SAP Fieldglass workstream status on regular basis. ▶ Coordinates and facilitates SAP Fieldglass design and configuration phase. ▶ Point of contact for day to day configuration questions.
Functional Consulting: Subscription Services	▶ Facilitate business process review and configuration session(s). ▶ Configure the solution according to customer requirements. ▶ Responsible for keeping track of all issues and coordinating issue resolution. ▶ Assist with resolution of issues during system test and user acceptance test.

Table 4.20 SAP Fieldglass Roles

SAP Fieldglass Role	Description
Functional Consulting: Incremental Services	▸ Assist customer with gathering all spend category information. ▸ Collects high level business requirements. ▸ Assist customer with mapping business processes and procurement categories into SAP Ariba P2P processes. ▸ Assists customer with making SAP Ariba P2P configuration decisions. ▸ Assists customer with test script preparation.
Technical Consulting: Subscription Services	▸ Educate customer technical team on master data extract, mapping and load into SAP Fieldglass system. ▸ Review data for completeness and assist in data issue resolution. ▸ Assist with technical aspects of site configuration. ▸ Perform customizations. ▸ Educate customer on functionality and setup of SAP Fieldglass integration tools. ▸ Educate customer site administrators on administrative tasks throughout deployment. ▸ Assist with resolution of issues during system test and user acceptance test.
Technical Consulting: Incremental Services	▸ Support customer technical team to design and build integration interfaces with their SAP ERP and backend systems. ▸ Provide customer with best practices to develop the integration architecture.
Supplier Enablement Lead	▸ Responsible for management of the enablement services workstream. ▸ Responsible for reporting enablement workstream status. ▸ Responsible for the enablement workstream timeline. ▸ Provide input and obtain approval for suppliers' communications and education. ▸ Manage buyer and supplier interactions. ▸ Prepare customer and suppliers to transact using the SAP Fieldglass Network.

Table 4.20 SAP Fieldglass Roles (Cont.)

Customer Fieldglass Role	Description
Project Sponsor	▸ Project commitment time: 10% ▸ Establish and communicate overall project vision. ▸ Provide senior leadership communication in support of the project. ▸ Mandate appropriate change management across leadership of all affected departments. ▸ Monitor status reports and timelines. ▸ Resolve escalated issues including those which involve customer resources, lack of participation, or supplier compliance messaging.
Project Manager	▸ Project commitment time: 100% ▸ Confirm customer goals and project scope. ▸ Help plan the project activities and timeline. ▸ Ensure adequate resources are assigned. ▸ Manage participation of all required resources. ▸ Coordinate stakeholders as needed (accounts payable, purchasing, receiving, finance, etc.) ▸ Coordinate signoff on all SAP Fieldglass deliverables. ▸ Manage project timeline and adherence to schedule. ▸ Participate in project status meetings. ▸ Identify, manage and escalate project issues and risks as appropriate. ▸ Develop go-live cutover plan and manage cutover execution. ▸ Single point of contact for overall deployment.
Functional Lead (ideally not the same person as the Project Manager)	▸ Project commitment time: 100% ▸ Participate in configuration workshops. ▸ Define and document business requirements pertaining to all in-scope processes, transactions and SAP Fieldglass solutions. ▸ Gather business input from all involved functional resources and departments: procurement, A/P, accounting, finance, etc.

Table 4.21 Customer SAP Fieldglass Roles

Customer Fieldglass Role	Description
Functional Lead (ideally not the same person as the Project Manager) (Cont.)	▸ Define business process and requirements and make decisions on solution configurations to handle those requirements. ▸ Write <customer> functional design document. ▸ Develop test cases and test scripts for testing. ▸ Plan, manage, and conduct system testing and user acceptance testing of the entire solution. ▸ Validate that master data and application configuration data functions as desired. ▸ Identify, escalate, and resolve project issues. ▸ Help develop go-live cutover plan and manage cutover execution. ▸ Experiment with system behavior and configuration to support customer decisions on system configurations. ▸ Learn the detailed SAP Fieldglass functionality all the way through the procure-to-pay process and learn how the system configurations, customizations and data drive the system functionality. ▸ Assist in writing design document. ▸ Post-deployment role: supporting use of the system. ▸ Answer customer questions on how the system will support the business and technical requirements raised by all involved customer departments.
Technical Team	▸ Project commitment time: 80-100% if integration required ▸ SAP ERP/HR technical resource. ▸ Participate in configuration workshops. ▸ Contribute to SAP ERP related aspects of solution design ▸ Develop and test SAP ERP interface/integration functionality (for both master data and transactional data). ▸ Extract and format master data from SAP ERP systems and load it into SAP Fieldglass. ▸ Assist with testing and resolve SAP ERP-related issues.

Table 4.21 Customer SAP Fieldglass Roles (Cont.)

Customer Fieldglass Role	Description
Technical Team (Cont.)	▶ Conduct cutover activities. ▶ Middleware technical resource. ▶ Install, configure and test SAP Fieldglass integration toolkit or web services interfaces. ▶ Develop and test middleware transmission and mapping functionality. ▶ Configure integration error handling and notification functionality. ▶ Define scheduling scripts for automatic data integrations and email notifications. ▶ Configure corporate network to support end-user authentication (if needed). ▶ Configure corporate network to enable inbound and outbound transmissions with appropriate security controls. ▶ Assist with testing and resolve integration related issues.
Change Management/ Training Lead	▶ Project commitment time: 10-20% ▶ Assess the impact of the project's business process, policy, organizational and cultural changes on end users and other affected employees. ▶ Develop and execute change management plan to address impacts from all changes related to the SAP Fieldglass program. ▶ Manage communication plan development and project-wide communications to key stakeholders. ▶ (If end-user training is needed) Develop training approach. ▶ (If end-user training is needed) Develop training documentation. ▶ (If end-user training is needed) Plan and manage training delivery. ▶ (If end-user training is needed) Ensure training needs are addressed/issues escalated appropriately.

Table 4.21 Customer SAP Fieldglass Roles (Cont.)

Customer Fieldglass Role	Description
Administrator	▸ Project commitment time: 50% ▸ Customer technical expert on SAP Fieldglass on-demand site ▸ Administer configurable aspects of the SAP Fieldglass on-demand site such as group permissions, user-group assignments, approval rules, invoice exception types and configuration data. ▸ Raise any technical issues with the On-Demand site.
Process Experts/Pilot Users/ Power Users	▸ Participate in configuration workshops and contribute to business requirements and solution design. ▸ Participate in test case/script development. ▸ Participate in system test and UAT. ▸ Identify power users within each department to act as experts by providing assistance to peers and input to overall process. ▸ Help roll out supplier compliance mandate within their respective departments. ▸ Help define and execute internal change management program within their respective department. ▸ Act as knowledge expert on SAP Fieldglass Network and SAP Fieldglass Solutions ongoing.
Supplier Enablement Lead	▸ Primary liaison between customer, suppliers and SAP Fieldglass enablement team. ▸ Manage supplier compliance and escalation process for non-compliance. ▸ Works with SAP Fieldglass enablement supplier enablement lead to manage the project and drive project milestones ▸ For multi-country programs, need a country/regional lead. ▸ Enforce program goals within organization. ▸ Approve lists of suppliers targeted for SAP Ariba Network enablement. ▸ Manage the gathering of supplier contact data and validate results from SAP Ariba data collection effort.

Table 4.21 Customer SAP Fieldglass Roles (Cont.)

Customer Fieldglass Role	Description
Supplier Enablement Lead (Cont.)	▸ Plan and support supplier communications. ▸ Approve supplier communications and education materials to be shared with suppliers. ▸ Participate in system test and UAT. ▸ Reinforce supplier enablement program compliance with identified suppliers and internal stakeholders. ▸ Manage supplier relationships, monitor and enforce supplier compliance. ▸ Facilitate supplier training sessions (if any). ▸ Participate in regular status meetings. ▸ Promote the initiative internally with HR, category managers and business relationship owners, AP group and externally with suppliers.

Table 4.21 Customer SAP Fieldglass Roles (Cont.)

4.5 Summary

In this chapter, we have reviewed "downstream solutions", as SAP Ariba classifies them, for both SAP Ariba and SAP Fieldglass. These areas cover both procure-to-pay processes, as well as augmenting solutions in the areas of content and contingent labor procurement. Broadly, this area is called operational procurement, as these systems support different kinds of tactical procurement at an operational level.

This chapter examines the SAP Ariba solutions for managing invoices in accounts payable processes as well as obtaining further discounts using SAP Ariba Discount Professional.

5 Invoice Management

The final part of the procure-to-pay process resides with accounts payable. Traditionally, suppliers have submitted paper invoices in various formats, which creates a document-management challenge and multiple inefficiencies. At its worst, a paper-based invoice-to-payment process entails the supplier writing up an invoice by hand and sending it via traditional mail. The customer then receives the invoice and rekeys the document into their system (potentially with errors from illegible handwriting or typing mistakes), while faxing or going around the office to confirm that the invoice aligns with the goods delivered/services performed. If the invoice does not match with the terms or delivered items, a dialogue is initiated with the supplier to correct the mistake, multiple cumbersome official communications take place, and a supplier eventually issues a new invoice or a credit using the same method. The customer receives the new invoice, and then sorts and re-queues it for processing. By this time, the customer may be out of compliance with the terms of the original purchase order for payment and spending considerable amounts of time and money to finally initiate payment via a check run, which itself is another laborious task that involves issuing, printing, and mailing checks to suppliers. With all of this overhead, some invoice processing operations can cost as much as $60 per invoice processed; processing costs sometimes eclipse the amount of the actual invoice to be paid, not to mention they forego opportunities for discounts and working capital management.

You can overcome these profit-sapping, manual invoice-to-payment processes with the use of SAP Ariba's invoice management and payment solutions. Using the rules and tools of SAP Ariba Invoice Professional, SAP AribaPay, and SAP Ariba Discount Professional solutions, an accounts payable team can quickly return invoices with missing or erroneous information to the supplier for correction. With SAP AribaPay, you can further avoid late-payment fees and inefficiencies caused by paper checks. The eponymous SAP Ariba Discount Management module manages discounts: prorated, dynamic discounting, automatic and ad hoc dynamic discounts, discount groups, and so on.

This chapter covers Ariba's solutions in the area of accounts payable. This includes SAP Ariba Invoice Automation, SAP Ariba Invoice Professional, SAP AribaPay, SAP Ariba Payment Automation, and SAP Ariba Discount Professional. This chapter will outline the solutions' functionalities, business benefits, and implementation approaches.

5.1 Accounts Payable Solutions

In this section, we begin by giving you an overview of how SAP Ariba's available solutions support the invoicing process. Next, we will delve into the specifics of SAP Ariba Invoice Automation and SAP Ariba Invoice Professional, SAP Ariba Discount Management, SAP AribaPay, SAP Ariba Payment Automation, and SAP Ariba Payment Professional.

5.1.1 Overview of SAP Ariba's Invoice Management Solutions

SAP Ariba's invoice management solutions leverage the SAP Ariba Network, in which over two million suppliers, including many of your existing suppliers, already interact. Leveraging the SAP Ariba Network and SAP Ariba Exchange for community collaboration, SAP Ariba Invoice Automation and SAP Ariba Invoice Professional enable uniform invoice submission by multiple suppliers. This includes invoice validation against more than 80 business rules; invoicing against contracts and service-entry sheets; VAT/tax/legal compliance; account coding; two-, three-, and four-way matching; invoice routing, approval, and reporting; and analytics. To bridge the final systems involved in invoice processing, SAP Ariba Invoice Automation and SAP Ariba Invoice Professional offer invoice processing via supplier portal, EDI, cXML, CSV, and paper-conversion services.

Invoice-processing errors can impact the majority of invoices in paper-based environments. Transposing invoices into another system and misreading handwritten or poorly scanned invoices ends up creating errors and delays in payment. SAP Ariba Invoice Automation and SAP Ariba Invoice Professional automate many of these process, which increases accuracy and reduces processing time. This is often used as the core justification in business cases supporting invoice automation projects.

SAP Ariba Invoice Automation comprises the invoice and conversion, or "flipping," of purchase orders into invoices on the SAP Ariba Network, while SAP Ariba Invoice Professional encompasses the advanced workflow features that expand the solution cross-system to align invoice processing in SAP Ariba with distinct customer business processes.

Once you process the invoice, as seen in Figure 5.1, the next step is payment. Traditionally, paying suppliers has been challenging to automate, as suppliers cannot check on pending payments or where things are in the payment process, and thus begin calling for updates. SAP AribaPay leverages the power of the SAP Ariba Network to extend back-office systems to transmit ACH payments to suppliers. For suppliers, having SAP AribaPay integrated with the SAP Ariba Network provides updated information on the status of payments and allows them to update their account details directly.

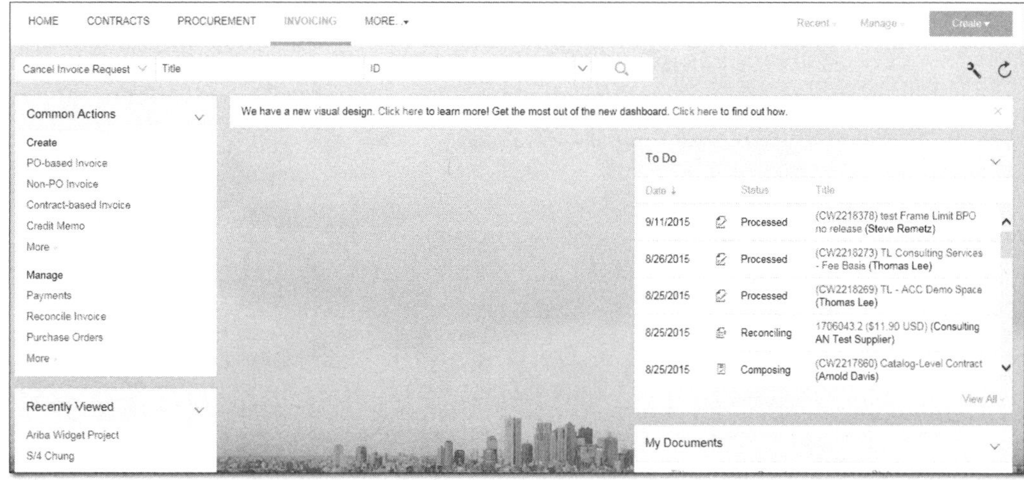

Figure 5.1 SAP Ariba Invoicing Options

SAP Ariba invoicing, payment, and discount solutions support a general, overarching process for accounts payable. First, an invoice is created, referencing either a PO, contract, or with no reference. You can create the invoice in the following ways:

- In your external SAP ERP system and loaded into your SAP Ariba solution through SAP Ariba Network. This option is only available if your solution includes SAP Ariba Invoice Professional, and typically requires integration to be set up with SAP ERP to realize.
- By the supplier on SAP Ariba Network and transmitted to your SAP Ariba solution.
- Manually by a buyer on your site, using a paper invoice sent by a supplier.
- Manually by a supplier punching into your site from their SAP Ariba Network account to create an invoice. This type of invoice typically references a contract.
- By an invoice conversion service (ICS) provider that converts paper invoices into an electronic format and sends them to your site through SAP Ariba Network.

Once an invoice is submitted using one of these methods, SAP Ariba creates an approvable invoice document. When the invoice is approved, SAP Ariba automatically creates the following two associated, approvable documents:

1. An invoice reconciliation (IR) document, which invoice exception handlers use to resolve any discrepancies between the invoice, associated orders or contracts, and receipts, in order to validate accounting and other information.
2. A payment request (PR) document, which can generate a payment once the invoice is reconciled.

The automatic reconciliation processor tries to match the IR to existing purchase orders, contracts, and receipts, and then validates them according to your site's configuration. At this point, one of the following two processes occurs:

1. If there are no discrepancies in the IR, or if the discrepancies are within you're company's pre-configured tolerances, the IR is sent directly to the responsible group or person for approval to pay the supplier. During this part of the process, discount negotiations leveraging SAP Ariba Discount Professional can also begin.
2. If there are unacceptable discrepancies in the IR, they show up as exceptions on the IR document and require manual reconciliation. One or more exception handlers resolve exceptions, and the IR is sent to the responsible group or person for approval to pay the supplier, or to commence discount negotiations with SAP Ariba Discount Professional.

If your site is configured to handle final approval of the IR, then at this point the invoice moves to reconciled. If your site is configured to send the IR for final reconciliation and approval in your SAP ERP system, the invoice moves to reconciling status until receiving that final approval.

Once the invoice is reconciled, the payment is scheduled through the payment request.

SAP AribaPay's capabilities cover the complete automation of your payment processes, including electronic payments, detailed remittance statements, a supplier self-service portal, and supplier bank-routing information verification. Using these tools, you can accelerate supplier-participation rates (in-house ACH programs often struggle with onboarding suppliers), increase accounts payable productivity and capability, and reduce fraud cases and late-payment fees. Combining SAP Ariba Invoice Management solutions with SAP AribaPay delivers a one–two punch to inefficiency and waste in accounts payable. Using the rules and tools of electronic invoicing, your accounts payable team can quickly return invoices with missing or erroneous information to the supplier for correction. With SAP AribaPay, you further avoid late-payment fees and inefficiencies caused by paper checks. A summary is provided in Table 5.1.

Task	Common Challenges	How SAP Ariba Helps	SAP Ariba Solutions	Value Drivers
Invoicing	▸ Manual processes ▸ Lack of visibility	▸ Automated invoicing ▸ Buyer and supplier visibility	▸ SAP Ariba Invoice Automation ▸ SAP Ariba Invoice Professional	▸ Reduce invoice processing cost by >50% and cycle time to 1–5 days ▸ Better forecasting for buyers and suppliers
Working capital	▸ Inconsistent payment terms ▸ Rigid, buyer-initiated payment terms	▸ Strategically manage and extend payment terms ▸ Buyer/supplier initiated discounts	SAP Ariba Discount Professional	▸ $1M–$2M in early payment discounts per $1B targeted spend ▸ 1–4 day DPO extension

Table 5.1 Accounts Payables Challenges and SAP Ariba Solutions

Task	Common Challenges	How SAP Ariba Helps	SAP Ariba Solutions	Value Drivers
Payment	▸ Secure storage of supplier bank account info ▸ Converting checks to electronic format	▸ Supplier bank account data removed from buyer servers ▸ Check to electronic conversion service	▸ SAP AribaPay, SAP Ariba Payment Automation	▸ Enhanced controls related to supplier bank account data ▸ $2–$3 savings per check converted to electronic

Table 5.1 Accounts Payables Challenges and SAP Ariba Solutions (Cont.)

5.1.2 SAP Ariba Invoice Management: SAP Ariba Invoice Automation and SAP Ariba Invoice Professional

SAP Ariba Invoice Automation and SAP Ariba Invoice Professional helps you optimize invoice processing and lower operating costs by significantly reducing paper, exception handling, and supplier inquiry calls. These solutions support more than 70 currencies, digital signature authentication, VAT/tax compliance, and data archival.

Given the scope of the business network, many suppliers in your supply base are likely already transacting on the business network. During the supplier enablement stream of an SAP Ariba Invoice Automation, as well as SAP Ariba Invoice Professional, the project on boards targeted suppliers onto the business network as part of the project and follow-on phases. As with SAP Ariba P2X projects, customers typically onboard their suppliers in waves, so as to adequately support the onboarding and set up processes for the new invoicing approach.

SAP Ariba Invoice Automation focuses on the general invoice processing functionality enabled in the business network between buyer and supplier. Buyers can configure rules which ensure that suppliers submit conforming invoices at the line item, country, and supplier group levels. SAP Ariba provides more than 30 templates for these invoices, which conform to various country and invoice-type requirements.

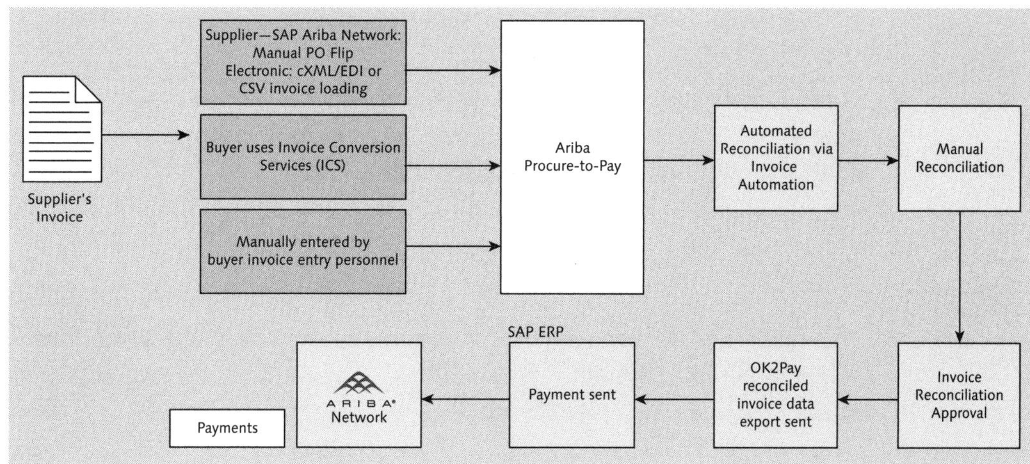

Figure 5.2 SAP Ariba P2P Invoice Automation Process

Figure 5.2 provides more granular details for the SAP Ariba Procure-to-Pay workflow, based on the high level invoice process. The steps in this process are as follows:

1. The supplier creates an invoice. Invoices are created in one of the following ways:
   - Supplier submission via SAP Ariba Network
   - Buyer uses ICS
   - Buyer can receive and submit invoices to ICS, or supplier can submit directly to ICS
   - Buyer submits invoice by keying supplier's paper invoice data into the SAP Ariba invoicing solution
   - Invoice is submitted
2. SAP Ariba receives the invoice data and generates an invoice reconciliation document.
3. The SAP Ariba automatic reconciliation process tries to match the invoice reconciliation document to existing purchase orders, contracts, and receipts data, such as price, terms, quantity, etc., then validate them according to your configuration.

4. SAP Ariba lists details from the invoice, purchase orders, contracts, and receipts on the invoice reconciliation document:
   - If no discrepancies are found, or if the discrepancies are within your company's pre-configured tolerances, the invoice reconciliation document is sent directly to the invoice manager for approval.
   - If unacceptable discrepancies are found, they are listed as exceptions on the invoice reconciliation document and must be manually reconciled.
5. After an invoice has been reconciled and approved by the invoice manager, a payment approvable is generated. This takes the form of an OK2Pay file that is sent to your SAP ERP system. Validate it is OK2Pay based on the supplier's payment method and terms (net 30, etc.).
6. You may configure SAP ERP systems to communicate payment status updates back to your SAP Ariba invoicing solutions and the SAP Ariba Network systems. In both SAP Ariba Invoice Automation and SAP Ariba Invoice Professional scenarios, you view payment status details by navigating to the PAYMENTS tab of a given invoice. Suppliers can view payment information for their SAP Ariba Network invoice, as well.

Supplier connectivity and invoicing options include the SAP Ariba supplier portal, which accessible via a browser and an Internet connection. For those suppliers that insist on sending paper invoices, or other scenarios/jurisdictions where paper invoices are required, SAP Ariba Invoice Conversion Services is available to scan and convert those paper invoices electronically.

On the other hand, SAP Ariba Invoice Professional is, at its core, a workflow rules engine and an integration conduit for SAP ERP. SAP Ariba Invoice Professional allows you to configure more than 70 business workflow rules for invoice validation. SAP Ariba Invoice Professional also reconciles non-purchase order invoices, or other applicable business rules.

The steps and processes for SAP Ariba Invoice Professional are similar to the SAP Ariba Procure-to-Pay invoice process, as can be seen in Figure 5.3. However, with SAP Ariba Invoice Professional, once the IR is approved, the approved invoice export is sent to the SAP Ariba Network Adapter. The Business Suite Add-On, or the SAP Ariba Network Adapter, then sends the updated invoice status (approved) to the SAP Ariba Network and the buyer's SAP ERP system. SAP ERP systems can be configured to communicate payment status updates back to your SAP Ariba invoicing solutions and the SAP Ariba Network systems. You can then view payment status details by navigating to the PAYMENTS tab of a given invoice. Suppliers can view payment information for their SAP Ariba Network invoice, as well.

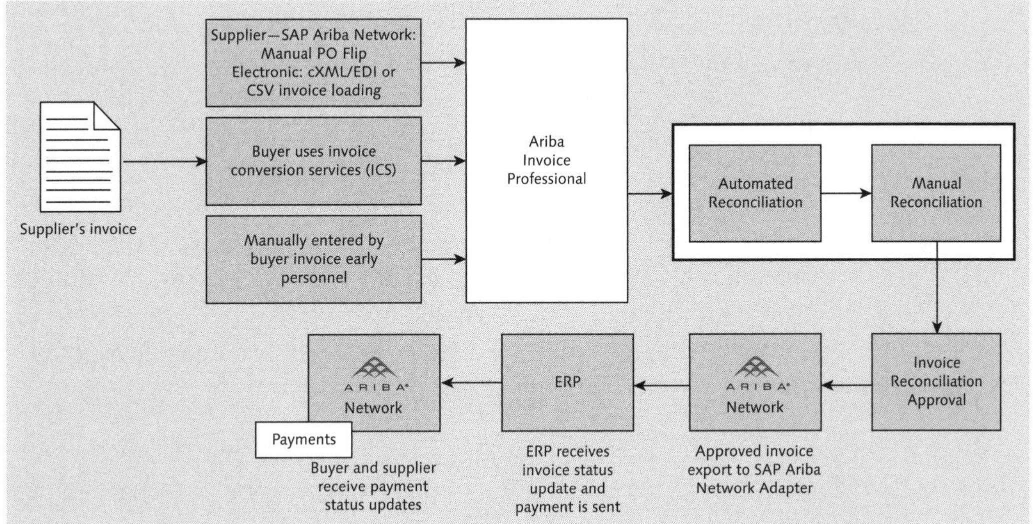

Figure 5.3 SAP Ariba Invoice Professional Invoice Process

Via workflow rules, with SAP Ariba it is possible for an organization to achieve close to 100 percent touchless processing of their invoices. You can also extract tax table data from your SAP ERP system or third-party tax application and load it into SAP Ariba Invoice Professional on a reoccurring basis, and validate taxes submitted on an invoice at the line level.

Self-service tools for suppliers include online dashboards, which centralize all documents and communications. In these dashboards, suppliers can view approvals, payments, rejected orders, etc. By streamlining invoice processing with SAP Ariba Invoice Automation and SAP Ariba Invoice Professional, organizations can maintain or extend days payable outstanding (DPO). With this efficiency in place, the payment process provides you with greater flexibility in payment scheduling, including obtaining discounts for earlier payment than negotiated terms (using SAP Ariba Discount Professional, discussed later in the chapter). Working capital/terms and on-time payment analytics aligned with SAP Ariba Invoice Professional enable you to analyze in-depth the performance of these associated account payables topics.

Invoices with errors or omissions are rejected and returned to suppliers for correction and re-submission. With compressed invoice approval cycle times, driven by SAP Ariba Invoice Professional and SAP Ariba Invoice Automation, organizations can leverage the speed and efficiency of their invoice processing to maximize early payment discounts.

Your suppliers can submit PO and non-PO invoices online through the business network user interface, or via EDI/XML. They can also convert, or "flip," a purchase order received on the network in order to create a PO invoice.

Suppliers can use the SAP Ariba Network to view status updates for invoices that are supplier-entered, buyer-entered, entered through SAP Ariba Invoice Conversion Services, or copied from the buyer's SAP ERP system. This reduces the number follow-up calls and confusion in your payment processes. For archiving purposes, both buyers and suppliers can request an archival invoice ZIP file.

You also have optional features for SAP Ariba Invoice Automation, such as SAP Ariba contract and services invoicing. The features in SAP Ariba contract and services invoicing include:

- Create invoices from contracts through the user interface.
- Create service sheets for service purchase orders through the user interface.
- Creation of service sheets by uploading them as CSV files or transmitting them electronically as cXML documents.
- Creation of contact invoices by uploading them as CSV files or transmitting them electronically as cXML or EDI documents.
- Flip buyer-approved service sheets into service invoices.
- Search functionality for checking and reporting on service sheets and contract invoices.
- Buyers can set up contracts in the user interface and validate service sheet submissions against these contracts with access control and master data approval.

Lastly, SAP Ariba provides optional services for SAP Ariba Invoice Professional, which include:

- Expanded site configuration
- Invoice CSV upload

- Acceleration or update to Ariba's country guide
- Tax invoicing for Mexico
- Tax invoicing for Brazil
- SAP Ariba eArchive powered by Logica
- SAP Ariba invoice conversion services
- SAP Ariba open invoice conversion services

5.1.3 SAP AribaDiscount Professional

With the efficiency and agility improvements provided by SAP Ariba Invoice and SAP AribaPay, you can turn your accounts payable department into a profit center. Initially, you'll achieve this via improved management of days payable outstanding (DPO). In a high-interest-rate environment, DPO management by itself provides you with better cash flow and additional profitability. In a low-interest-rate environment, in which returns on deposits are much less than one percent, obtaining and managing supplier discounts for early payments can provide the lion's share of profitability gains.

Many suppliers would prefer to provide a discount for early payment, rather than resorting to factoring or other methods to buttress cash flow. With SAP Ariba Discount Professional, you can fully automate early payment discount management from initial offer up to agreement, including transactions involving prorated or dynamic discounting. SAP Ariba Discount Professional provides you with control over the amount of cash to apply and the suppliers to target for discount programs. For support in maximizing the savings with SAP Ariba Discount Professional, SAP Ariba's working capital management services team can provide expertise and payment term data as part of a consulting engagement, to help you formulate an effective DPO improvement and dynamic discounting program.

SAP Ariba Discount Professional automates early-payment discount management with a robust toolset from initial offer to agreement, as well as a services arm (SAP Ariba working capital management services) to support you in the formulation of an effective DPO-management program.

SAP Ariba Discount Professional supports prorated, dynamic discounting; automatic and ad-hoc dynamic discounts; discount groups; full treasury control;

alerts/notifications; and reporting. For suppliers, in addition to better cash flow management and control, SAP Ariba Discount Professional also provides a cash-flow-optimizer tool and invoice/payment visibility. Standing early payment terms apply discount terms automatically to every applicable approved invoice. Standing term offer parameters define discount term offers and include face discount percent, APR percent, net day, discount day, pro-rated discount scale (Y/N), and the supplier or group of suppliers to whom the offer applies.

In SAP Ariba Discount Professional, you can set up multiple offers from which a supplier or group of suppliers can choose, and then notify you automatically with the terms of offer, date of change, and request to review the offer, when an early payment term is created or changed.

You can also create buyer-defined dynamic discounts, applying discount terms agreed to by a supplier on an ad hoc, invoice-by-invoice basis, using a wide array of parameters. Your suppliers have access to the notifications and to a supplier cash optimization tool, which allows suppliers to identify the invoices required for early payment approval and the corresponding discounts to meet a supplier-defined cash flow need. Suppliers have the ability to initiate their own dynamic discount proposals based on this analysis, and in general.

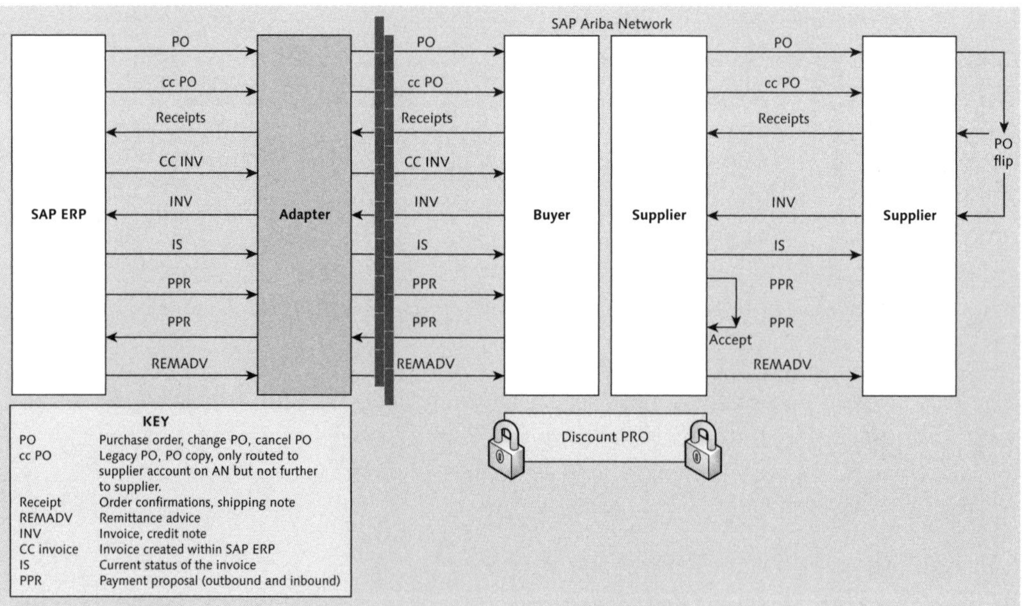

Figure 5.4 SAP Ariba Discount Professional Landscape/Process

As per Figure 5.4, SAP Ariba Discount Professional resides at the nexus of buyer and supplier on the business network. However, in many implementations, the integration points extend beyond the business network, back to the buyer's ERP environment of the, and even out to the supplier's SAP ERP environment. Integrated with SAP ERP, SAP Ariba Discount Professional allows finance/AP to expand and develop discount opportunities and agreements directly in the accounts payable environment in SAP ERP, using SAP Ariba Discount Management as the mediation point in the business network. This allows SAP ERP to send payment proposals up to the network, and allows the supplier to respond within the business network, while receiving notification of remittance advice (REMADV in Figure 5.4) or status either in the business network, or sent to the supplier's SAP ERP.

5.1.4 SAP Ariba Payment Management: SAP AribaPay and SAP Ariba Payment Automation

This section focuses on the payment aspect of the invoicing process and the applicable SAP Ariba solutions, after the invoice has been submitted. SAP AribaPay manages payment aspects at the end of a procure-to-pay process in SAP Ariba. Many SAP ERP customers revert to SAP ERP for accounts payable from their SAP Ariba solutions. SAP AribaPay offers the option for managing payment in SAP Ariba, further consolidating the processes in SAP Ariba and circumventing the oftentimes cumbersome Automated Clearing House process (ACH) leveraged for payments in most payment scenarios, including SAP ERP.

SAP AribaPay

Once the initial invoice has been validated and reconciled, it is time to address the payment portion of the process. For this, SAP AribaPay serves as the business network-based payment solution, facilitating payments from buyers to their suppliers. Buyers can create individual or batch payment requests in their individual SAP ERP systems, which are then transferred via the business network to a payment service provider, and then on to the originating and receiving financial institutions. During this process, SAP AribaPay provides visibility of payments via track and trace functionality, facilitates faster reconciliation, and confirms expected invoice and payment amounts.

As in Figure 5.5, SAP AribaPay enables you to pay your suppliers over the business network, providing improved visibility, cash flow controls (when payment is to be made), dual user verification, simple UIs facilitating self-service, and, ultimately, reduced costs, as well as greater efficiencies than traditional ACH processes.

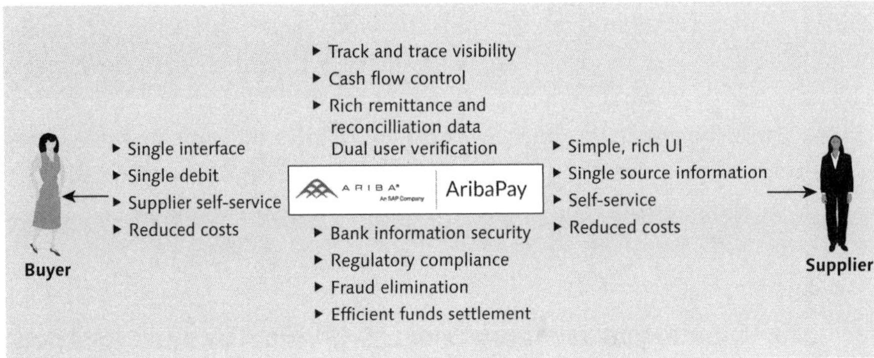

Figure 5.5 SAP AribaPay

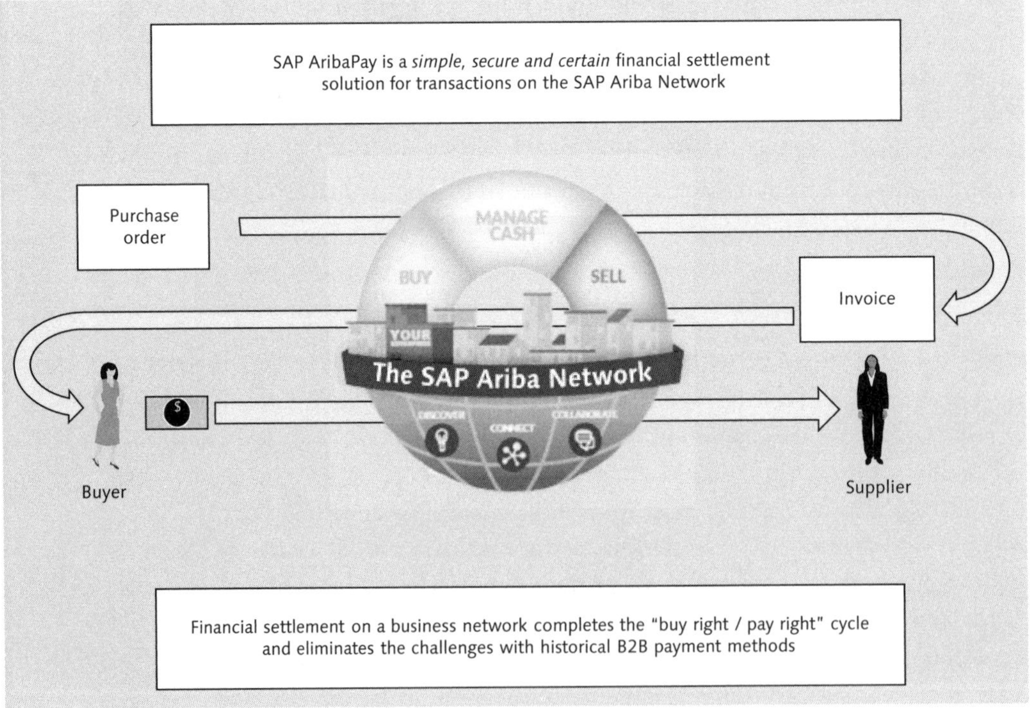

Figure 5.6 SAP AribaPay and Traditional B2B Payment Process

Traditional ACH processes, as detailed in Figure 5.6, re-establish for each transaction the information that already is static in the business network in secure areas. With ACH, it can be challenging to determine where a payment is, and the surcharges on payment typically run three percent of the total payment amount.

With SAP AribaPay, leveraging the business network from SAP Ariba allows for more efficient payment process than ACH. The differences are lined out in Table 5.2.

Functional Area	ACH	SAP AribaPay
Traditional ACH disbursement services	Yes	Yes
Multiple, supplier friendly remittance formats	No	Yes
Secure storage of supplier bank account details	No	Yes
Supplier responsible for updating bank account details	No	Yes
Supplier self-service: on-line payment visibility	No	Yes
Supplier enablement, education and support	No	Yes
SAP Ariba receives 1st line invoice/payment inquiry phone calls	No	Yes
Collection and sharing of "hard to get" supplier information: W-9's, proof of banking, etc.	No	Yes

Table 5.2 ACH vs. SAP AribaPay

Combining the power of the business network for supplier information and transaction support with focused accounts payable solutions on the payment-side provides SAP AribaPay with an offering that extends well beyond traditional ACH approaches to payment.

SAP Ariba Payment Automation

SAP Ariba Payment Automation requires SAP Ariba Invoice Automation or SAP Ariba Procure-to-Pay. Customers can maintain existing payment (ACH) connections with their banks and use SAP Ariba Payment Automation to deliver remittance information only to suppliers; provide status updates to buyers and suppliers; deliver remittances to suppliers (email, EDI, cXML, or directly via the business network); and support supplier self-service of remittance name, address, and bank account information.

SAP Ariba Payment Professional

You can choose to use SAP Ariba Payment Professional both for the delivery of remittance information to suppliers and the transmission of ACH payment instructions to your bank. Payment instructions are transmitted to your bank in accordance with the bank's transmission standards. Payment instruction transmission is the key difference between SAP Ariba Payment Professional and Automation. As with SAP Ariba Payment Automation, suppliers can view payment status updates through the SAP Ariba Network. When exceptions occur, SAP Ariba Payment Professional processes ACH return information from the bank and updates payment status. You can configure SAP Ariba Payment Professional to send ACH instructions in the following ways:

- Using supplier-maintained information in SAP Ariba Payment Professional that identifies suppliers' bank accounts.
- Using bank account information from SAP ERP and passed along in the payment file.
- Issuing ACH only if bank account information in the payment proposal and SAP Ariba Payment Professional match exceptions that have been flagged using business controls.
- $0 PreNote validation of supplier bank accounts.

For any bank that is new to SAP Ariba, a bank integration project is required.

SAP Ariba Payment Professional delivers reports on supplier bank account changes for suppliers with trading relationships with a buyer.

5.2 Implementing SAP Ariba Invoice Professional, SAP AribaPay, and SAP Ariba Discount Professional

Once you have decided on the solutions in invoicing and accounts payable, it is time to implement. This section will cover the various solutions and implementation approaches. SAP Ariba Invoice Professional and SAP AribaPay address the invoicing process, whereas SAP Ariba Discount Professional focusses on squeezing additional discounts out of existing processes during the invoicing and payment process. As such, the implementation approaches are similar, but the participants and change management efforts required vary by solution.

5.2.1 SAP Ariba P2P Downstream Implementation

The SAP Ariba Invoice Professional, SAP Ariba Discount Professional, and SAP AribaPay implementation approaches leverage the SAP Ariba P2P downstream implementation methodology, detailed in Chapter 4, where an overarching project management team runs three main tracks—solution setup, supplier adoption, and internal adoption. As with SAP Ariba P2P, these solutions require the project to include change management and the supplier onboarding components, in addition to the standard solution set up track. In this section we will cover the initial steps you need to take for all three tracks, and guide you through each individual track.

Project Planning

Per Figure 5.7, the first four phases in your implementation project are:

- Planning for success by developing a business case
- Confirming your goals, scope, and rollout plan
- Planning your deployment and confirming readiness
- Deployment/kickoff

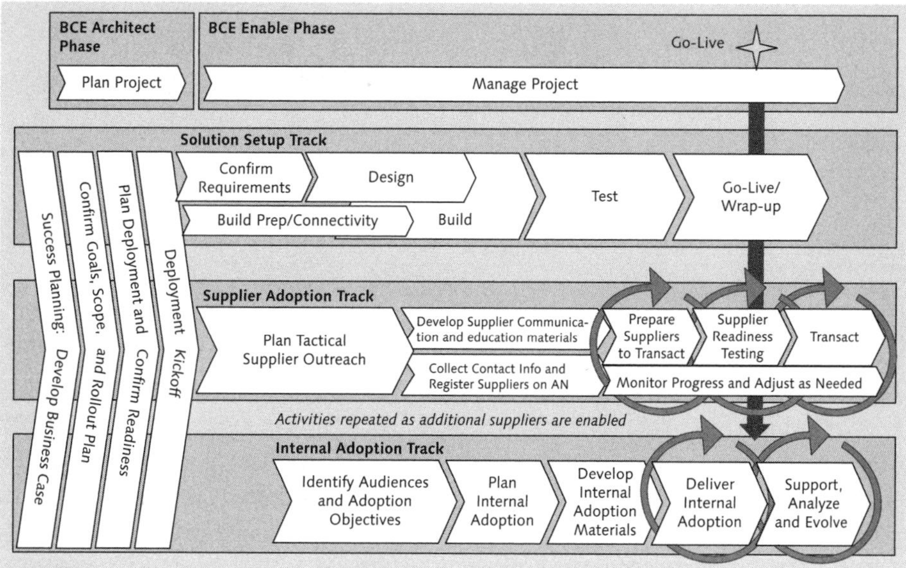

Figure 5.7 SAP Ariba Deployment Methodology for SAP Ariba Invoice Management, SAP Ariba Discount Management, and SAP AribaPay

It should be noted these four phases apply to all three delivery tracks: solution setup, supplier adoption, and internal adoption.

As seen in Figure 5.8, the key activities when you are confirming your goals, scope, and rollout plan are analysis of spend/payment data, and consequent goal and scope definition. For invoice analysis, identifying the largest sources and savings, whether supplier- or process-driven (or both), is the key insight required for defining scope in all three solution areas. For example, during an analysis for SAP Ariba Invoice Professional you might determine that process efficiency and faster invoice processing with your largest suppliers will provide the most ROI, and so those suppliers should be grouped and the savings quantified as a target. Likewise for SAP AribaPay and SAP Ariba Discount Management: if your largest returns are to be had with particular suppliers or processes, this fact needs to drive the scope and understanding during this phase of the project, and provide a navigation lodestone for later phases. At the end of the project, these goals and metrics are what you will use to define success and justify the investment.

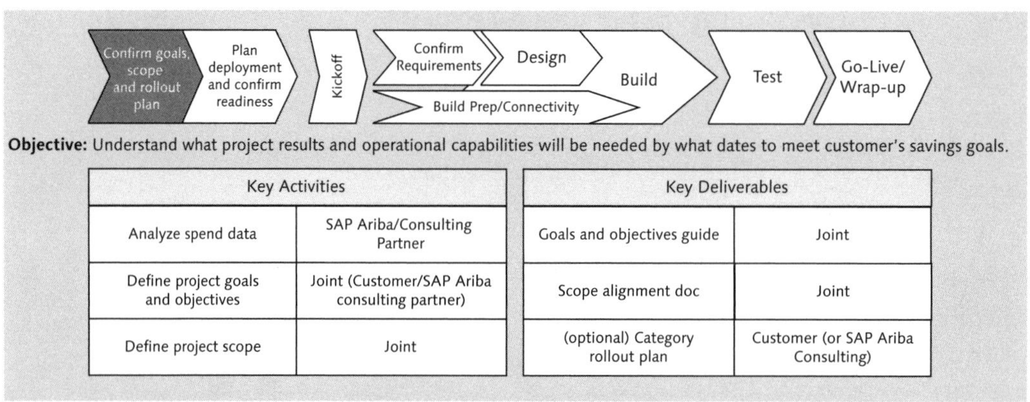

Key Activities	
Analyze spend data	SAP Ariba/Consulting Partner
Define project goals and objectives	Joint (Customer/SAP Ariba consulting partner)
Define project scope	Joint

Key Deliverables	
Goals and objectives guide	Joint
Scope alignment doc	Joint
(optional) Category rollout plan	Customer (or SAP Ariba Consulting)

Figure 5.8 Confirm Goals and Roll Out Planning

The next phase in Figure 5.9, is where you plan the deployment and ensure everything is ready, is known as "pre-kickoff," as it is the final step prior to kick off. During this phase, SAP Ariba consulting or a consulting partner provide the customer with best practices related to readiness, building a program to support invoice submission via SAP Ariba Invoice Professional, payment submission via SAP AribaPay, and/or discount facilitation via SAP Ariba Discount Professional, as well as measurement.

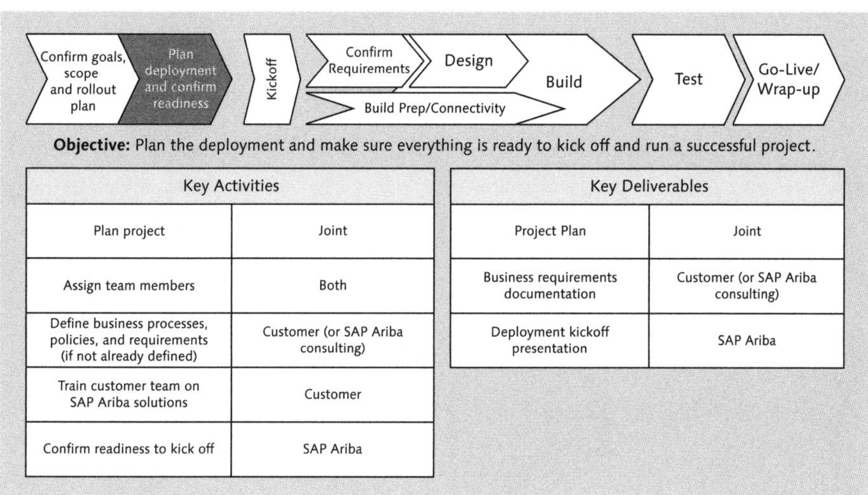

Key Activities	
Plan project	Joint
Assign team members	Both
Define business processes, policies, and requirements (if not already defined)	Customer (or SAP Ariba consulting)
Train customer team on SAP Ariba solutions	Customer
Confirm readiness to kick off	SAP Ariba

Key Deliverables	
Project Plan	Joint
Business requirements documentation	Customer (or SAP Ariba consulting)
Deployment kickoff presentation	SAP Ariba

Figure 5.9 Plan Deployment Readiness

Regarding customer key deliverables and activities, the first step is to assign applicable internal team members who have a complete understanding of the current scope and timeline of the program. Prior to kickoff, the customer should also begin to gather identified suppliers' data to deliver SAP Ariba in the vendor collection template for the applicable aspects of supplier strategy development, specifically flight planning and supplier strategy/onboarding development.

At a supplier data level, the customer needs to collect all required supplier data elements for outreach for identified suppliers. This includes the supplier ID, supplier name, supplier contact, full address, phone, email, remittance address, category manager at customer, days payable outstanding (DPO), PO vs. non-PO, contract expiration data, contract term, invoice number, and invoice copy for top suppliers in outreach program. There may be additional data elements which you need to include, based on the industry, spend category, and solution.

For individual solutions, you should initiate discussions with accounts payable for all three solution areas, while focusing on the invoice submission process/areas for SAP Ariba Invoice Professional, and payments and bank interaction for SAP AribaPay and SAP Ariba Payment Automation/Professional. These internal customer groups typically reside in accounts payable, but could be distinctly different at a subgroup level. Payment methods, banking relationships, legacy systems, and company culture all need to be accounted for in the evaluation.

For SAP Ariba Discount Professional projects, this is the time to begin discussions with treasury/finance to obtain the SAP Ariba Discount Professional program hurdle rate. SAP Ariba delivery and consulting partner deliverables include sharing best practices related to readiness, building an early payment program, and measurement strategy definition.

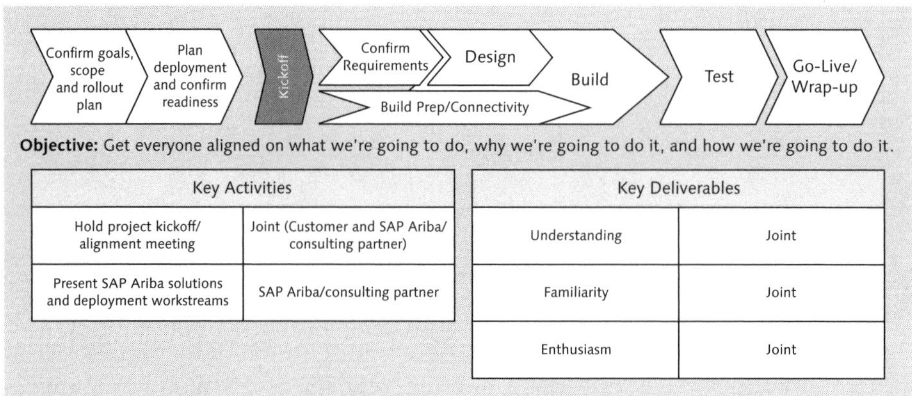

Confirm goals, scope and rollout plan
Plan deployment and confirm readiness
Kickoff
Confirm Requirements
Design
Build
Build Prep/Connectivity
Test
Go-Live/ Wrap-up
Objective: Get everyone aligned on what we're going to do, why we're going to do it, and how we're going to do it.
Key Activities
Hold project kickoff/ alignment meeting
Joint (Customer and SAP Ariba/ consulting partner)
Present SAP Ariba solutions and deployment workstreams
SAP Ariba/consulting partner
Key Deliverables
Understanding
Joint
Familiarity
Joint
Enthusiasm
Joint

Figure 5.10 Kickoff

Next, we begin the kickoff phase. The most important deliverable of the kickoff phase is the actual kickoff meeting. While this meeting, outlined in Figure 5.10, is oftentimes viewed as a formality in projects, it serves a real purpose to align the different teams and stakeholders, create understanding and familiarity amongst the teams, and, perhaps most importantly, generate enthusiasm! This goes for all three tracks on these types of project, as users and suppliers of the system benefit from communication around the project kickoff.

On the SAP Ariba/partner consulting side, this is when SAP Ariba shared services begin to play a significant role in the project. For smaller implementations, shared services will oftentimes run the kickoff meeting with the customer, as this group handles most of the project deliverables going forward. On larger projects with more complex requirements and onsite teams, the SAP Ariba delivery teams and/or consulting partners lead the preparation and delivery of the kickoff presentation.

Customer key deliverables and activities are equally important during kickoff, and include:

- Participate in the kickoff meeting to confirm scope of the aspects of the program, goals/objectives, and high-level timeline.
- Customer program sponsor delivers program's message to internal stakeholders supporting particular aspects of that program.

Joint key deliverables and activities for customer and SAP Ariba delivery/consulting partner include:

- Agreeing on aspects of the plan, timeline, and milestones.
- Reviewing key success factors for the aspects of the program.
- Initiating governance structure and approach for the aspects of the program.

Unlike the following phases, the kickoff phase has the same goals and objectives for SAP Ariba Invoice Management, SAP Ariba Discount Management, and SAP AribaPay.

Solution Setup

Once the kickoff meeting is complete, the project/program is officially underway. In this section, we will walk you through the remaining phases for the solution setup track.

Confirm Requirements Phase

The next step is to confirm the requirements, which are a direct reflection of the planning and scope defined in the phases leading up to this phase. For an SAP Ariba project, these requirements are typically gathered in workbooks. The SAP Ariba delivery, shared services, and partner consultants will define the to-be processes with the customer, showing the solution via demos where applicable. The customer then sends responses/data in the workbook format back to Ariba. Ultimately, these workbook responses are leveraged to build out the solution in the customer's "realms" which are the individual customer areas in the SAP Ariba cloud environment.

To confirm the requirements for SAP Ariba Invoice Professional, the data required revolves mainly around workflow. First, the invoice needs to make it through a potentially large number of customer-defined rules. These rules can prevent invoices from even entering the workflow, saving valuable cycles and human interventions. These rules, however, need to be defined and refined in order to ensure that the optimal amount of automation occurs up-front, without filtering out legitimate invoices or frustrating suppliers to the point that they resume submitting via paper-based processes.

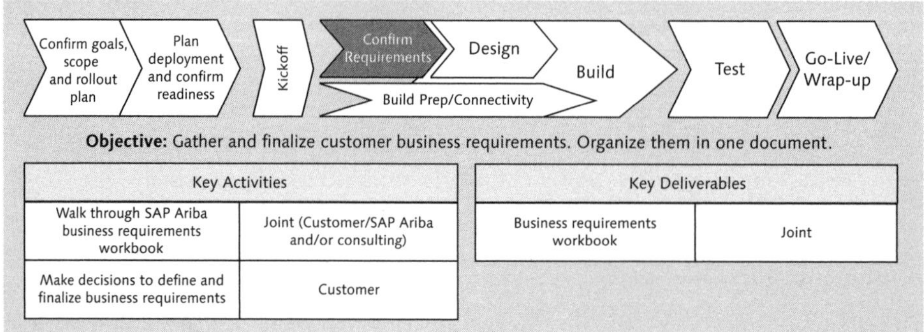

Figure 5.11 Confirm Requirements

Once the invoice has passed muster with the submission rules in SAP Ariba Invoice Professional, it is ready to move through workflow. This workflow can be set up throughout the landscape of processes and solutions around invoice submission, including who approves the initial invoice, to whom the invoice is then forwarded to for reconciliation, when discount requests activate (if applicable, SAP Ariba Discount Management processes are also included).

To confirm the requirements for SAP Ariba Discount Management, defining thresholds, supplier/scenario targets, and savings strategies for the different types of discounts in SAP Ariba Discount Professional (automatic, ad hoc user-driven, ad hoc supplier-driven) is a key part of the workbook deliverable.

To confirm the requirements for both SAP Ariba Payment Automation and SAP Ariba Payment Professional, the key requirements hinge on understanding your bank's transmission standards, as well as reporting requirements around transactions.

Design Phase

As per Figure 5.12, the next phase, design, revolves around key deliverables for all three solution areas (SAP Ariba Invoice Management, SAP Ariba Discount Management, and SAP AribaPay). To start, SAP Ariba and/or consulting partners propose the configuration of any or all of the three aforementioned SAP Ariba solutions, based on the requirements gathered and follow-on design sessions, and also provide configuration documents. The customer then defines any custom interfaces to third-party systems for either master data, transactions, or both. Finally, SAP Ariba delivery and/or consulting partners work in tandem with the customer to define the configurations and document the holistic design.

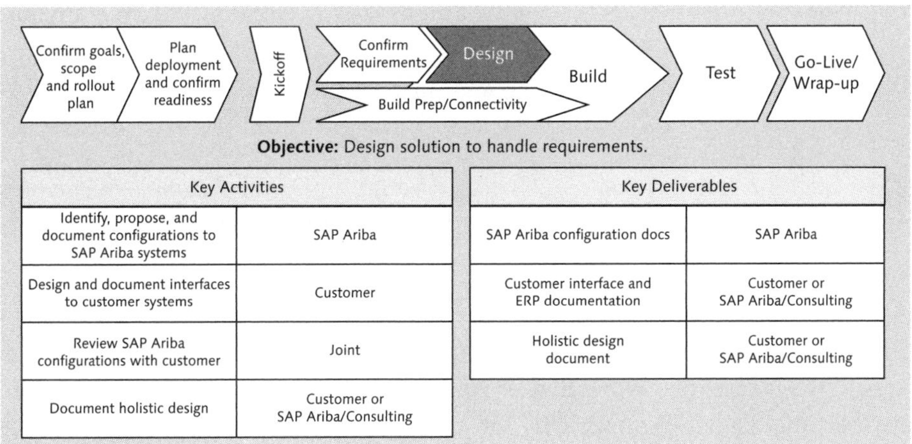

Confirm goals, scope and rollout plan
Plan deployment and confirm readiness
Kickoff
Confirm Requirements
Design
Build Prep/Connectivity
Build
Test
Go-Live/ Wrap-up
Objective: Design solution to handle requirements.
Key Activities
Identify, propose, and document configurations to SAP Ariba systems
SAP Ariba
Design and document interfaces to customer systems
Customer
Review SAP Ariba configurations with customer
Joint
Document holistic design
Customer or SAP Ariba/Consulting
Key Deliverables
SAP Ariba configuration docs
SAP Ariba
Customer interface and ERP documentation
Customer or SAP Ariba/Consulting
Holistic design document
Customer or SAP Ariba/Consulting

Figure 5.12 Design

In the design phase for SAP Ariba Invoice Automation and SAP Ariba Invoice Professional, you are required to both create rule definitions based on the requirements gathered in the previous phase and to perform workflow build out. To realize certain checks or approvals, the most elegant option may not be to import the requirements verbatim into the system as defined in the requirements. Achieving the rules and workflow requirement goals in an efficient, elegant manner should be the overarching goal of this phase.

For SAP Ariba Discount Management, the design phase focuses on the one-time activities of design, setup, and configuration. The success of any customer–supplier project is just as dependent on supplier participation as it is customer initiative. As part of design, the supplier track requires SAP Ariba delivery and/or consulting partner assistance for the customer to develop the final flight plan and develop the early payment terms in support of the SAP Ariba Discount Professional aspects of the program.

SAP Ariba Discount Management deliverables and activities in the design phase include:

- Finalizing the flight plan.
- Reviewing the best practices document with the customer on building and managing a successful early payment program, including templates around messaging.
- Payment terms, DPO goals, supplier groups, wave planning, and program hurdle rate definition.
- Complete scoping questionnaire and analysis.
- Providing supplier data and payment terms.
- Finalize and agreement on SAP Ariba Discount Professional campaign between customer and SAP Ariba delivery or consulting partner.

In the design phase for SAP AribaPay, SAP Ariba Payment Automation, and SAP Ariba Payment Professional, the requirements defined should serve as a straightforward underpinning for the design of these processes. As the payment processes involve less workflow and/or rules, there is less room for improvisation. Establishing the bank connectivity for transactions and status (in the case of SAP Ariba Payment Professional), and advice of remittance messaging for suppliers for both solutions, remain the key drivers for the design, build, and ultimately, the SAP AribaPay portions of the project.

Build Preparation/Connectivity Phase

During the build preparation/connectivity phase (Figure 5.13), core connectivity is established for SAP Ariba realms and the customer's users (both internal and supplier users). SAP Ariba delivery and/or consulting partners establish or build linkages between customer systems and SAP Ariba realms in scope, as defined in the requirements. SAP Ariba provides access to the technology and processes required to allow an identified supplier to participate in the program, however, this access is validated, for now, without onboarding the suppliers until later in the project (for more information on the supplier adoption track deliverables, please see the section on supplier adoption). The majority of the steps and deliverables in the build preparation phase apply to SAP Ariba Invoice Management, SAP Ariba Discount Management, and SAP AribaPay. For SAP Ariba Invoice and Discount Management projects, the focus is on the connectivity points between the business network, suppliers, and the customer backend SAP ERP systems involved. For SAP AribaPay, customer bank connectivity is the focus, along with the business network and any customer SAP ERP environments in scope.

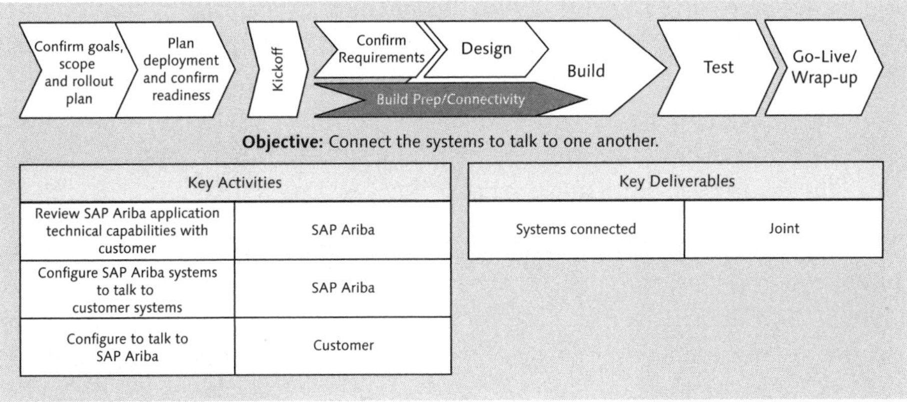

Key Activities	
Review SAP Ariba application technical capabilities with customer	SAP Ariba
Configure SAP Ariba systems to talk to customer systems	SAP Ariba
Configure to talk to SAP Ariba	Customer

Key Deliverables	
Systems connected	Joint

Figure 5.13 Build Preparation

Build Phase

During the build phase, shown in Figure 5.14, the SAP Ariba delivery or consulting partner configure the solution(s) in conjunction with SAP Ariba shared services (for configuration items that can only be accessed by shared services). Data collection, testing, and interfaces to customer systems are typically owned by the customer. The customer and the SAP Ariba delivery or consulting partners agree when the system is ready for testing.

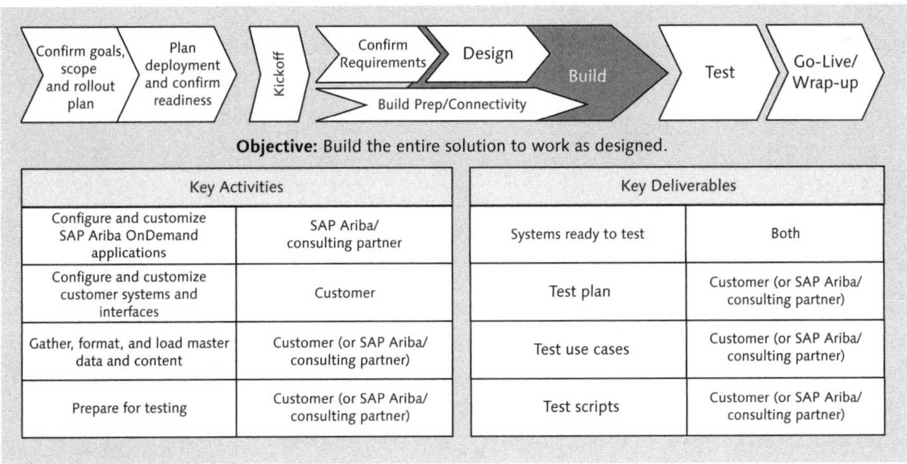

Key Activities	
Configure and customize SAP Ariba OnDemand applications	SAP Ariba/ consulting partner
Configure and customize customer systems and interfaces	Customer
Gather, format, and load master data and content	Customer (or SAP Ariba/ consulting partner)
Prepare for testing	Customer (or SAP Ariba/ consulting partner)

Key Deliverables	
Systems ready to test	Both
Test plan	Customer (or SAP Ariba/ consulting partner)
Test use cases	Customer (or SAP Ariba/ consulting partner)
Test scripts	Customer (or SAP Ariba/ consulting partner)

Figure 5.14 Build

The build phase for SAP Ariba Invoice Automation turns primarily on the rules set up. Project participants ensure the rules defined in the requirements and design phases to enable the automatic payment of conforming invoices are configured in the system. For SAP Ariba Invoice Professional projects, the focus main is on setting up workflow requirements in the system to pass approvals up and down the defined chains of approvers.

During the build phase for SAP Ariba Discount Professional, SAP Ariba delivery and/or consulting partners assist the customer in configuring early payment term offers in SAP Ariba Discount Professional, and additionally provide SAP Ariba Discount Professional buyer and seller training and user guides to the customer.

The customer is typically responsible for configuring approved early payment term offers in SAP Ariba Discount Professional, and for incorporating SAP Ariba Discount Professional aspects of the program into the overall change management plans.

Jointly, both the customer and SAP Ariba delivery and consulting partners establish year one and year two financial goals, based on agreeable metrics and key performance indicators (KPIs).

For SAP Ariba Payment Professional, both linkages (status and payment issuance) with banks have to be established during the build phase, as well as the corresponding linkages with the SAP Ariba Network. For SAP Ariba Payment Automation, there is more internal focus on remittance advice enablement in the SAP Ariba Network, as the customer maintains their existing ACH payment configuration with the bank.

Test Phase

The customer typically drives the test phase in Figure 5.15, as this phase is used to ratify much of the design and configuration, as well as the end product/solution be delivered to the customer and their stakeholders. However, the SAP Ariba delivery and consulting partners play a key role in addressing any bugs/defects noted during testing, and assume expanded roles in testing where required. Key focus areas in each of the three testing areas include end-to-end integration testing between any SAP ERP, SAP Ariba, and other systems; payment throughput; invoice submission capabilities of the system; and general connectivity for users.

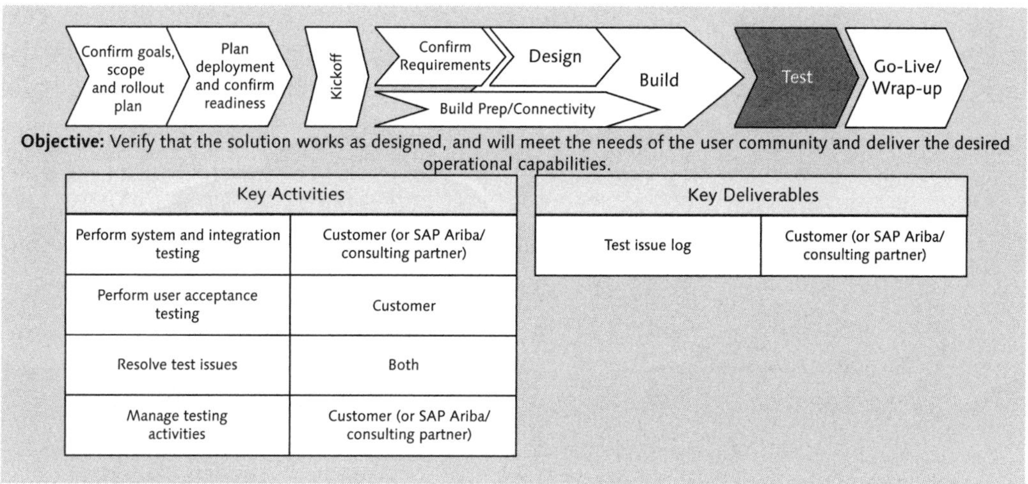

Figure 5.15 Test

Go-Live/Wrap-Up

Going live in Figure 5.16 represents the most significant milestone for any SAP Ariba project. The customer and SAP Ariba delivery or consulting partners plan the cutover and confirm the resulting plan.

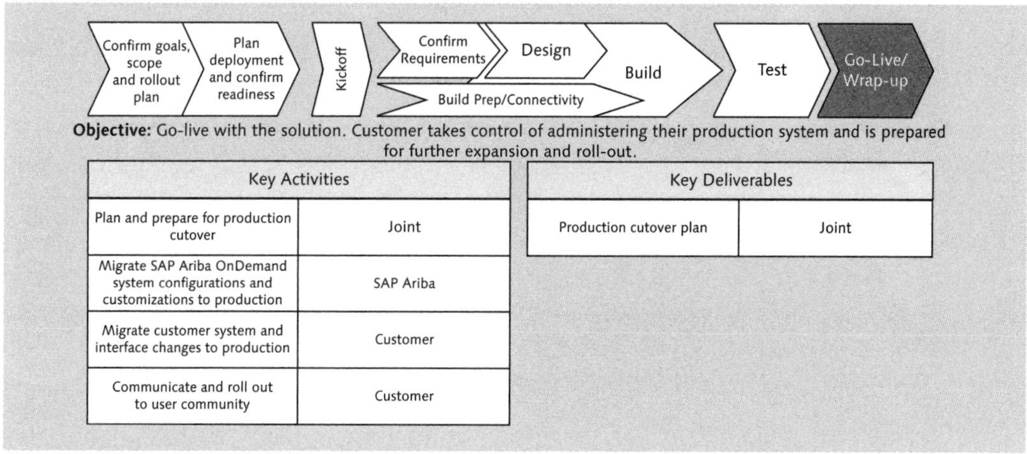

Figure 5.16 Go Live

SAP Ariba shared services migrates the system configuration and customizations to production in tandem with the customer migrating any interface changes and customer system configuration to production, while the customer spearheads the change management activities. Ongoing program and enablement activities include making weekly SAP ERP updates to reflect current pay discounts based on the SAP Ariba report provided from supplier terms selection fields, as well as ensuring executive-level participation in program kickoff and quarterly updates. Lastly, further supplier waves are planned and initiated post go-live as part of the wave approach to expanding the supplier user communities on the new solutions.

Supplier Adoption

The importance of supplier adoption and participation in Figure 5.17 regarding the new solutions being rolled out cannot be overstated. Without supplier participation, the new solution quickly becomes a one-sided tool and few of the targeted efficiencies can be realized. For this reason, a supplier adoption track is managed in tandem to the actual SAP Ariba implementation project. To this end, a customer typically enables SAP Ariba personnel or SAP Ariba third-party providers to call identified suppliers and onboard them to the new system. Particularly with SAP Ariba Discount Professional, a certain amount of education for the supplier is necessary, in order for them to understand the value that early payment discounting brings to them, in the form of working capital and cash flow flexibility.

Strategy definition for the supplier adoption track occurs throughout the last two shared phases of the overall methodology (PLAN DEPLOYMENT AND CONFIRM READINESS, as well as DEPLOYMENT/KICKOFF), such that when the project kicks off, you are already in a position to begin lining out the tactical supplier outreach. Similar to communication planning for the project's other stakeholders, the customer spend is first analyzed, and from this analysis the supplier groups are defined. As the overall project kicks off, the supplier adoption track formulates outreach plans to bring the most applicable suppliers on board with the program once the project is ready to go live, with interim education and selling steps to prepare these suppliers for the new system.

Supplier adoption efforts are driven by the amount of change and adoption required on the part of the supplier. For SAP AribaPay and SAP Ariba Invoice Management solutions, this is typically lower than for SAP Ariba Discount Management areas. However, all three require analysis, strategy definition, and tactical execution of the plan.

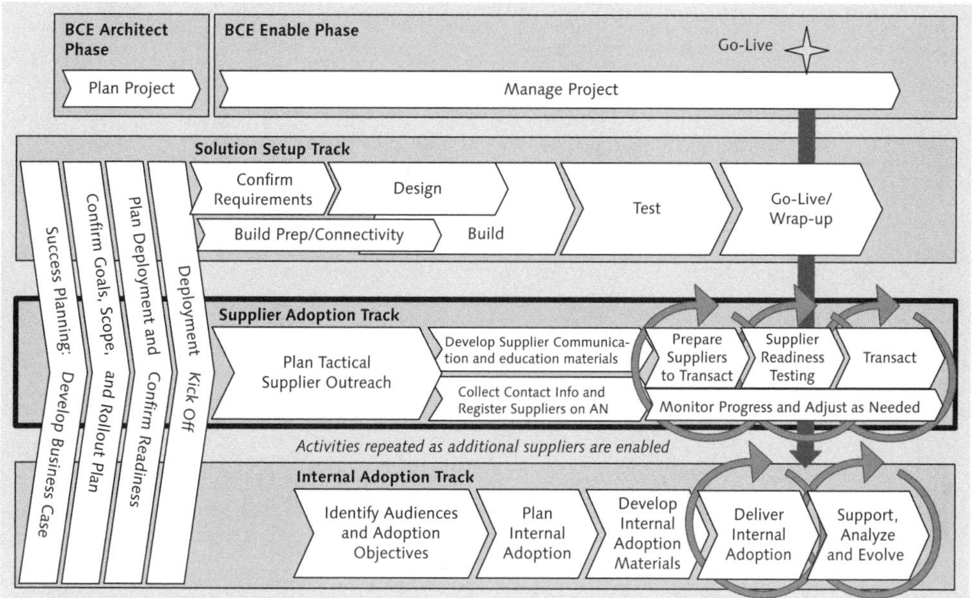

Figure 5.17 SAP Ariba Supplier Adoption Track

For SAP Ariba Discount Professional in the supplier adoption track, the SAP Ariba supplier enablement group and/or consulting partner manages identified suppliers' progress and provide summary reports to track their status as related to the Discount Professional aspects of the program. As these supplier contacts will be making discounting decisions based on cash-flow needs and other management strategies, the enablement of SAP Ariba Discount Management suppliers is typically more involved than bringing on board a supplier into the SAP Ariba Network to process POs and submit invoices. The SAP Ariba Discount Management enablement activities include:

- Delivery of SAP Ariba Discount Professional education materials as part of the supplier education sessions.
- Identification of appropriate decision-maker at the identified supplier.
- Emails and calls to identified suppliers to position the SAP Ariba Discount Professional Services and upsell the benefits of participating.
- Delivery of cash management web seminars for identified suppliers.
- Delivery of targeted email marketing campaigns to identified suppliers to position cash acceleration and understand changes in their liquidity.

- For larger identified suppliers, develop relationships with key decision makers and model cash strategies across the SAP Ariba Network.
- Verify availability of proper contacts on the SAP Ariba Network.
- Include identified suppliers in cash management surveys.
- Review of identified suppliers' liquidity needs (through Dun and Bradstreet and public financials).
- Reach out to new identified suppliers that have not opted in.
- Host monthly/quarterly discount reviews with customer and propose growth strategies.
- Ongoing management of the SAP Ariba Discount Professional aspects of the program.

Customer key deliverables and activities include:

- Maintain and update the customer-specific SAP Ariba Discount Professional education content on the supplier information portal.
- Ensure change management specific to SAP Ariba Discount Professional has been rolled out to affected stakeholders, per the rollout plan.
- Participate in joint meetings with the identified suppliers, where appropriate; stay engaged and maintain active and available resources.
- Continue to develop and monitor KPIs, and maintain regular management meetings.
- Require suppliers to complete terms selection, but do not require selection of an early payment term.
- Offer a range of early payment options and establish monthly KPIs to evaluate program success.
- Provide appropriate internal resourcing to support the SAP Ariba Discount Professional solution supplier onboarding and roll out.

Internal Adoption

For SAP Ariba Invoice Management, SAP Ariba Discount Management, and SAP AribaPay solutions, the internal adoption track addresses various stakeholder groups by solution. Change management with these types of solutions typically begins, as it does with supplier adoption, with analysis and strategy definition, based not on spend volumes as much as by stakeholder and eventual user groups. Communication plans, executive sponsorship/buy in for the corresponding groups, education/training, and, finally, super user training to assist individuals and groups at a tactical level once the solution is live, are all core to effective internal adoption programs.

For SAP Ariba Invoice Management solutions, the accounts payable groups involved with processing invoices and leveraging the efficiencies of touchless invoice automation and payment are key internal stakeholders. You need to include these groups need in the initial assessments, requirements gathering, design and roll out of the solutions. Initiating departments, such as procurement, also require change management, so as to dovetail into the new invoicing processes.

SAP Ariba Discount Management requires, a similar approach. Treasury and finance have a bigger stake in this solution than in other, more accounts payable solutions. As such, special inclusion and discussion needs to be driven within finance and treasury for a successful rollout of SAP Ariba Discount Professional.

For SAP AribaPay, finance also has a larger stake in managing the resulting cash flow implications from payments and terms. Procurement needs to ensure the proper terms are being set in negotiations further up in the process, and thus it needs to be included. At the heart of the process are the accounts payable groups and individuals focusing on payments and banking transactions.

Change management plans are tailored to the organization or geography in which they are being applied. Successful change management programs all bear the hallmarks of proper stakeholder analysis, strategic objective definition, measurable usage/KPI targets, communication plans with frequent communication (repetition is your friend oftentimes in a challenging change management exercise), engaged change management leaders, and unequivocal sponsorship from the executive layer of the company.

5.2.2 Standalone Implementations

There are SAP Ariba Invoice Management, SAP Ariba Discount Management, and SAP AribaPay options that can run almost entirely between SAP Ariba solutions. The benefits of running everything in SAP Ariba is the light integration requirements with SAP ERP and IT—all systems, excepting a financial update once the invoice payment has been requested, are managed by SAP Ariba. Not only does the user get one look and feel for the entire process in SAP Ariba, the user also has tight linkages to the SAP Ariba Network throughout the process for collaboration on invoicing, possible avoidance of ACH and the resulting complexities and fees, and document optimization.

As depicted in Figure 5.18, SAP Ariba can run the entire transaction in SAP Ariba P2P and the SAP Ariba Network. For smaller organizations with less intensive accounting requirements and IT infrastructure, this may provide the most efficient solution for procurement activities. However, if larger concerns and systems, which need to be updated in real time throughout the transaction in SAP Ariba, exist within the organization then integration to SAP ERP may be the best option for satisfying this requirement.

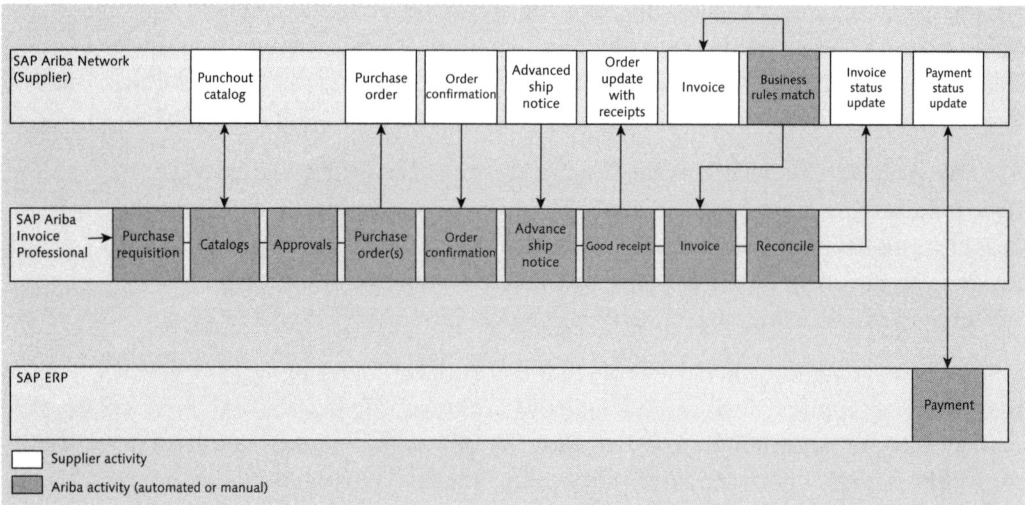

Figure 5.18 Standalone Implementation of P2P with Payment Update to SAP ERP

5.2.3 Integrated Implementations

Many customers are not in a position to decouple the procurement process from their existing SAP ERP environments, especially FI/CO. A typical process for invoicing in an integrated landscape may look like Figure 5.19.

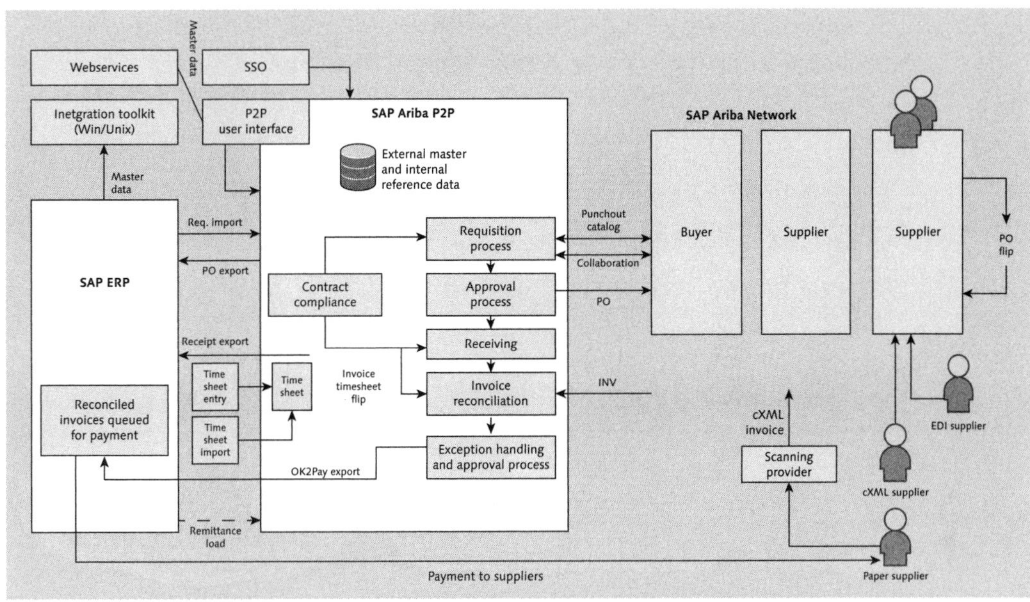

Figure 5.19 P2P Landscape Integrated with SAP ERP for SAP Ariba Invoice Management

Figure 5.19 depicts integration with SAP ERP via SAP Ariba Invoice Professional at a process level. Here, documents are sent down to SAP ERP, beginning with the purchase order. The purchase order copy updates SAP ERP's budget in finance, allowing the finance department to understand their outstanding liabilities in real time as they are created in SAP Ariba. Next, the order is confirmed and the supplier sends an optional inbound delivery notification in SAP Ariba. These documents also update in SAP ERP, in order to notify the inventory management and production planning departments of a pending order.

Inventory management/receiving then creates a goods receipt in the SAP ERP environment. This receipt takes the item into inventory (in some cases), and can queue financial processes in the event that the goods receipt was valuated for the item. In some instances, finance can begin including the valuated items in capital depreciation runs, in the case of an asset, and inventory value calculations in SAP ERP, while the invoice is being reconciled and payment is being actioned in SAP Ariba and SAP Ariba Invoice Professional (Figure 5.20). More details on the integration scenarios of SAP Ariba with SAP ERP are provided in Chapter 9.

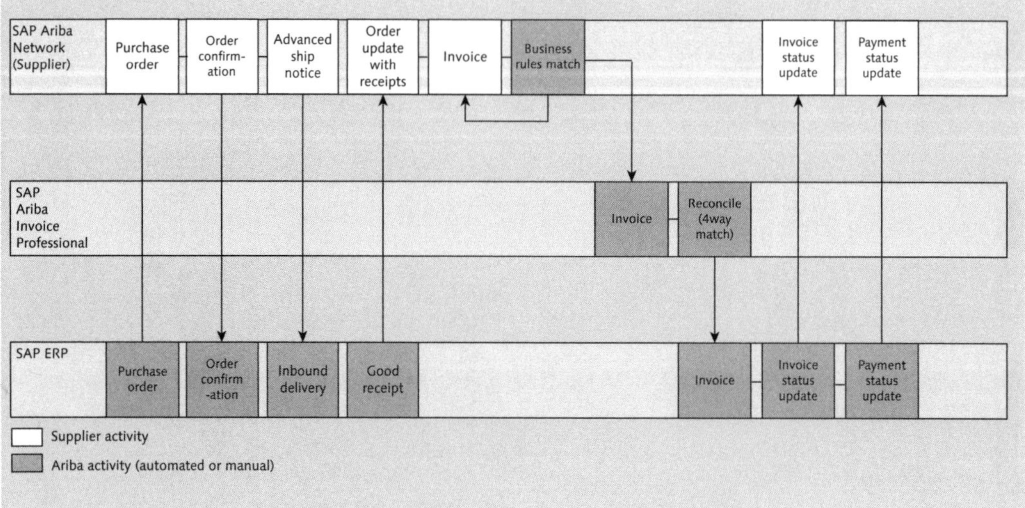

Figure 5.20 SAP Ariba Invoice Professional Integrated with SAP ERP

5.2.4 Defining Project Resources and Timelines

Timelines for SAP Ariba Invoice Management, SAP Ariba Discount Management, and SAP AribaPay projects depend on the complexity and scope of the implementation. Many of these A/P implementations are done in tandem, or embedded in an overall SAP Ariba Procure-to-Pay (P2P) project, representing the "invoice to pay" process in the procedure. For baseline implementations of various solutions, the following timelines serve as examples:

- SAP Ariba Payment Professional: 20 week implementation, with customer providing project manager, functional lead, technical lead, training lead, and pilot users.
- SAP Ariba Payment Automation: SAP Ariba Payment Automation, like Invoice Automation, is typically implemented during an SAP Ariba P2P overall project implementation. The SAP Ariba P2P project timeline in Figure 5.21 runs 26 weeks, with customer providing sponsor, project manager, technical, functional, supplier enablement, change management, support, testers, training lead, and business SMEs.

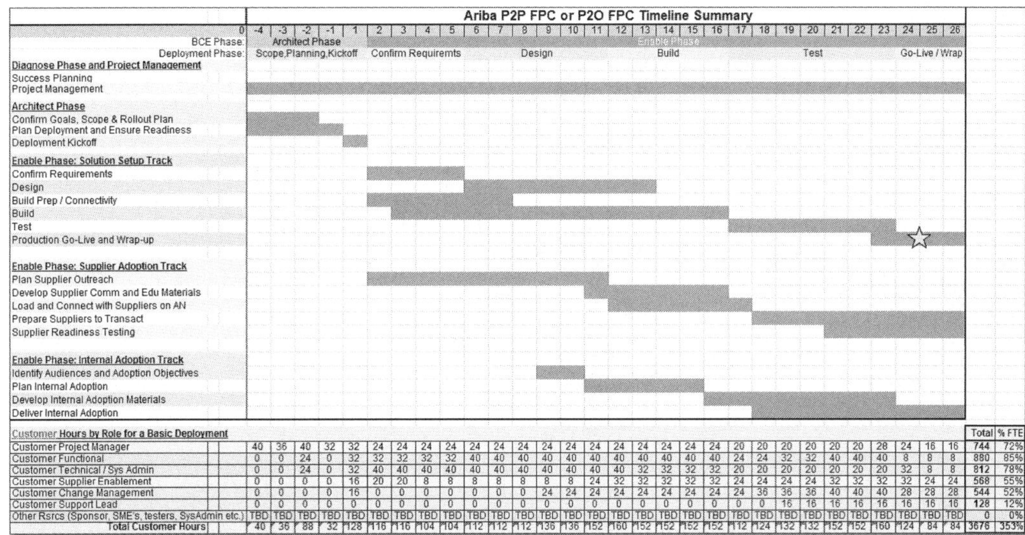

Customer Hours by Role for a Basic Deployment	-4	-3	-2	-1	1	2	3	4	5	6	7	8	9	10	11	12	13	14	15	16	17	18	19	20	21	22	23	24	25	26	Total	% FTE
Customer Project Manager	40	36	40	32	32	24	24	24	24	24	24	24	24	24	24	24	24	24	24	24	20	20	20	20	20	20	28	24	16	16	744	72%
Customer Functional	0	0	24	0	32	32	32	32	32	40	40	40	40	40	40	40	40	40	40	40	24	24	32	32	40	40	40	8	8	8	880	85%
Customer Technical / Sys Admin	0	0	24	0	32	40	40	40	40	40	40	40	40	40	40	40	32	32	32	32	20	20	20	20	20	20	20	32	8	8	812	78%
Customer Supplier Enablement	0	0	0	0	16	20	20	8	8	8	8	8	8	8	24	32	32	32	32	32	24	24	24	24	32	32	32	32	24	24	568	55%
Customer Change Management	0	0	0	0	16	0	0	0	0	0	0	0	24	24	24	24	24	24	24	24	24	36	36	36	40	40	40	28	28	28	544	52%
Customer Support Lead	0	0	0	0	0	0	0	0	0	0	0	0	0	0	0	0	0	0	0	0	0	0	16	16	16	16	16	16	16	16	128	12%
Other Rsrcs (Sponsor, SME's, testers, SysAdmin etc.)	TBD	TBD	TBD	TBD	TBD	TBD	TBD	TBD	TBD	TBD	TBD	TBD	TBD	TBD	TBD	TBD	TBD	TBD	TBD	TBD	TBD	TBD	TBD	TBD	TBD	TBD	TBD	TBD	TBD	TBD	0	0%
Total Customer Hours	40	36	88	32	128	116	116	104	104	112	112	112	136	136	152	160	152	152	152	152	112	124	132	132	152	152	160	124	84	84	3676	353%

Figure 5.21 SAP Ariba P2P Project Timeline Example

- SAP AribaPay: 22-week implementation with customer providing sponsor, project manager, integration lead, training lead, and business SMEs (see Figure 5.22).

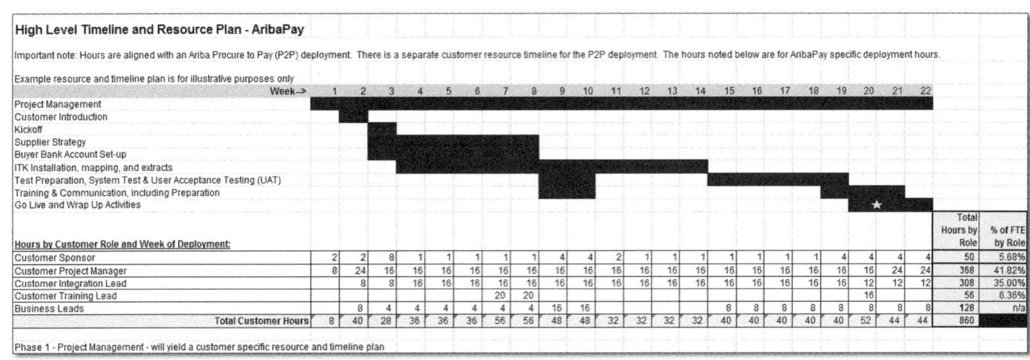

Hours by Customer Role and Week of Deployment:	1	2	3	4	5	6	7	8	9	10	11	12	13	14	15	16	17	18	19	20	21	22	Total Hours by Role	% of FTE by Role
Customer Sponsor	2	2	8	1	1	1	1	1	4	4	2	1	1	1	1	1	1	1	4	4	4	4	50	5.68%
Customer Project Manager	8	24	16	16	16	16	16	16	16	16	16	16	16	16	16	16	16	16	16	16	24	24	368	41.82%
Customer Integration Lead		8	8	16	16	16	16	16	16	16	16	16	16	16	16	16	16	16	16	12	12	12	308	35.00%
Customer Training Lead							20	20												16			56	6.36%
Business Leads		8	4	4	4	4	4	4	16	16					8	8	8	8	8	8	8	8	128	n/a
Total Customer Hours	8	40	28	36	36	36	56	56	48	48	32	32	32	32	40	40	40	40	40	52	44	44	860	

Phase 1 - Project Management - will yield a customer specific resource and timeline plan

Figure 5.22 SAP AribaPay Project in Conjunction with SAP Ariba P2P Project—Example Timeline

- SAP Ariba Invoice Professional: 25-week project, with customer providing sponsor, project manager, functional, technical, and business SMEs (see Figure 5.23).

Invoice Pro Deployment - High Level Customer Timeline																										
Example Resource and Timeline Plan for illustrative Purposes only																										
Week	1	2	3	4	5	6	7	8	9	10	11	12	13	14	15	16	17	18	19	20	21	22	23	24	25	
General Project Management and weekly Meetings																										
Solution Planning																										
Functional Configuration Workshop																										
Supplier Catalog Enablement Activities																										
Additional Build/Configuration Activities																										
Test Prep, System Test, User Acceptance Testing (UAT)																										
Training and Communication, incl. Preparation																										
Go Live and Wrap Up Activities																										
Hours by Customer Role and Week of Deployment																										Total Hours
Customer Project Manager	24	24	20	20	12	12	12	12	12	12	12	12	12	12	12	12	12	12	12	12	12	14	14	14	14	348
Customer Functional		32	32	32	32	32	32	32	32	32	32	32	32	32	32	32	32	32	32	32	32	32	32	32	12	748
Customer Enablement		32	32	32	32	32	32	32	32	32	32	32	32	32	32	32	32	32	32	32	32	32	32	32	12	748
Customer Technical		32	32	32	32	32	32	32	32	32	32	32	32	32	32	32	32	32	32	32	32	20	20	20	12	712
Customer Adapter/Technical Lead		32	20	20	20	20	20	20	20	20	20	20	20	12	12	12	12	12	12	12	12	8	12	4	4	376
Customer Training Lead											24	24										20	20	20	20	128
Process Expert Users		TBD	TBD	TBD	TBD	TBD	TBD	TBD	TBD	TBD	TBD	TBD	TBD	TBD						TBD	TBD	TBD	TBD	TBD		TBD
Total Hours by Customer Role	24	152	136	136	128	128	128	128	128	128	152	152	128	120	120	120	120	120	120	120	120	126	130	122	74	
Note: Phase 1 Resource Planning will yield Customer-specific Timeline and Resource Plan																										

Figure 5.23 SAP Ariba Invoice Professional Project Timeline Example

- SAP Ariba Invoice Automation: SAP Ariba Invoice Automation is typically implemented during an SAP Ariba P2P overall project implementation. The SAP Ariba P2P project timeline in Figure 5.24 runs 26 for weeks, with customer providing sponsor, project manager, technical, functional, supplier enablement, change management, support, testers, training lead, and business SMEs.

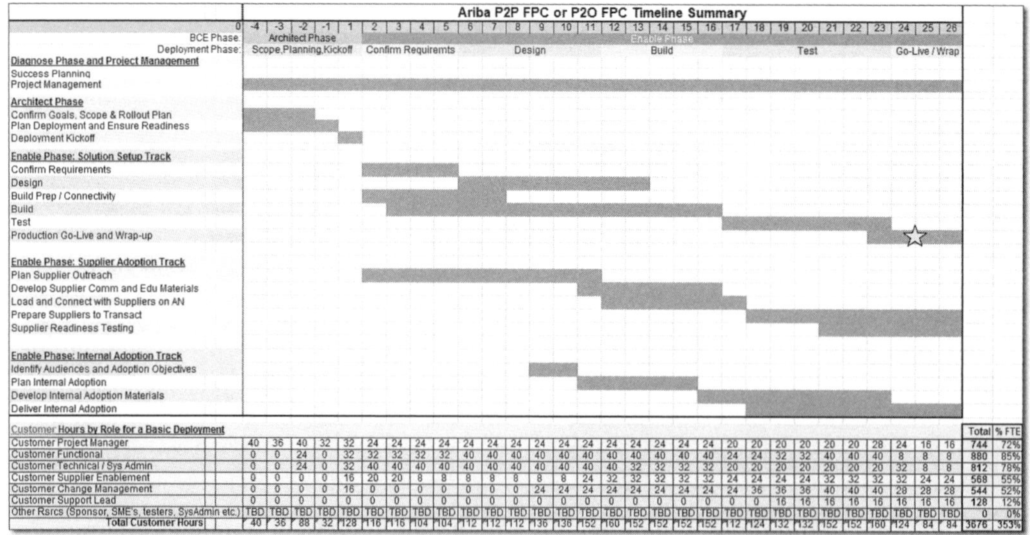

Customer Hours by Role for a Basic Deployment	-4	-3	-2	-1	1	2	3	4	5	6	7	8	9	10	11	12	13	14	15	16	17	18	19	20	21	22	23	24	25	26	Total	% FTE
Customer Project Manager	40	36	40	32	32	24	24	24	24	24	24	24	24	24	24	24	24	24	24	24	20	20	20	20	20	20	28	24	16	16	744	72%
Customer Functional	0	0	24	0	32	32	32	32	32	40	40	40	40	40	40	40	40	40	40	40	24	24	32	32	40	40	40	8	8	8	880	85%
Customer Technical / Sys Admin	0	0	24	0	32	40	40	40	40	40	40	40	40	40	40	40	32	32	32	32	20	20	20	20	20	20	20	32	8	8	812	78%
Customer Supplier Enablement	0	0	0	0	16	20	20	8	8	8	8	8	8	8	24	32	32	32	32	32	24	24	24	24	32	32	32	32	24	24	568	55%
Customer Change Management	0	0	0	0	16	0	0	0	0	0	0	0	24	24	24	24	24	24	24	24	24	36	36	36	40	40	40	28	28	28	544	52%
Customer Support Lead	0	0	0	0	0	0	0	0	0	0	0	0	0	0	0	0	0	0	0	0	0	0	16	16	16	16	16	16	16	16	128	12%
Other Rsrcs (Sponsor, SME's, testers, SysAdmin etc.)	TBD	TBD	TBD	TBD	TBD	TBD	TBD	TBD	TBD	TBD	TBD	TBD	TBD	TBD	TBD	TBD	TBD	TBD	TBD	TBD	TBD	TBD	TBD	TBD	TBD	TBD	TBD	TBD	TBD	TBD	0	0%
Total Customer Hours	40	36	88	32	128	116	116	104	104	112	112	112	136	136	152	160	152	152	152	152	112	124	132	132	152	152	160	124	84	84	3676	353%

Figure 5.24 SAP Ariba P2P Project Timeline Example

Project roles and responsibilities on SAP Ariba Invoice Management, SAP Ariba Discount Management, and SAP AribaPay projects have been laid out in Table 5.3, which discusses roles and responsibilities for SAP Ariba/consulting partners, and Table 5.4, which discusses roles and responsibilities for customers.

SAP Ariba or Consulting Partner Role	Responsibilities
Project Sponsor	▸ Serve as the program sponsor and champion within SAP Ariba ▸ Help define overall project vision ▸ Provide senior leadership communication in support of the project ▸ Drive program workstreams to achieve business case goals ▸ Develop supplier and network strategy in support of business goals ▸ Monitor status reports and timelines ▸ Provide guidance for high-level issue resolution ▸ Liaison to the commercial team for scope issues
Project Manager	▸ Confirm customer goals and project scope ▸ Plan the project activities and timeline ▸ Ensure adequate resources are assigned ▸ Establish project management framework (meetings, status, issue management, etc.) ▸ Coordinate activities and input from SAP Ariba project resources ▸ Manage project timeline and adherence to schedule ▸ Ensure timely project communication and status updates ▸ Identify, manage and escalate project issues and risks, as appropriate ▸ Point of contact for overall deployment

Table 5.3 Consulting Partner Roles and Responsibilities

SAP Ariba or Consulting Partner Role	Responsibilities
SAP Ariba OnDemand Functional Lead	▸ Host requirement/design workshops to educate customer on SAP Ariba solution functionality and configurability, and help customer understand their business requirements in the context of the SAP Ariba solution. ▸ Answer customer questions about functionality of SAP Ariba On-Demand application and SAP Ariba Network ▸ Propose solution configurations and customizations to handle customer requirements ▸ Document configurations to SAP Ariba On-Demand application and SAP Ariba Network ▸ Review customer's test cases and scripts, if requested by the customer ▸ Monitor testing progress and resolve SAP Ariba related issues
SAP Ariba OnDemand Technical Lead	▸ Educate customer on SAP Ariba master data and transactional data integration capabilities, formats and mapping ▸ Educate customer on customer-facing aspects of site configuration ▸ Build customer's configurations and customizations into the OND system ▸ Answer customer questions about OND site functionality ▸ Assist with testing and resolve SAP Ariba-related issues
SAP Ariba Network Adapter Tech Resource(s)	▸ Educate customer on SAP Ariba Network adapter architecture, capabilities, and potential configurations ▸ Provide SAP Ariba cXML documentation and list of data fields for each in-scope transaction. ▸ Support SAP Ariba Network adapter installation ▸ Support adapter-related design decisions ▸ Support customer with adapter-related data mappings and configurations ▸ Support customer in testing transactions between their SAP ERP and the SAP Ariba Network ▸ Support customer with adapter test issue resolution

Table 5.3 Consulting Partner Roles and Responsibilities (Cont.)

SAP Ariba or Consulting Partner Role	Responsibilities
SAP Ariba Network Adapter Tech Resource(s) (Cont.)	▸ Develop customizations to customer's SAP Ariba Network account UI ▸ Assist with testing and resolve SAP Ariba Network related issues
SAP Ariba Supplier Enablement Lead	▸ Manage the enablement services work stream ▸ Advise customer on how to perform supplier enablement activities ▸ Lead supplier data collection efforts ▸ Develop supplier communication and education materials ▸ Monitor supplier registration progress and address supplier enablement related issues ▸ Manage resources to facilitate education and testing of integrated suppliers ▸ Automation-only: document configurations to customer SAP Ariba Network account
SAP Ariba Supplier Management Team	▸ Contact suppliers to instruct and encourage them to register on the SAP Ariba Network.

Table 5.3 Consulting Partner Roles and Responsibilities (Cont.)

Customer Roles	Responsibilities
Project Sponsor	▸ Establish and communicate overall project vision ▸ Provide senior leadership communication in support of the project ▸ Mandate appropriate change management across leadership of all affected departments ▸ Monitor status reports and timelines ▸ Resolve escalated issues, including those which involve customer resources, lack of participation, or supplier compliance messaging.

Table 5.4 Customer Roles and Responsibilities

Customer Roles	Responsibilities
Project Manager	▸ Confirm customer goals and project scope ▸ Help plan the project activities and timeline ▸ Ensure adequate resources are assigned ▸ Manage participation of all required resources ▸ Coordinate stakeholders as needed (accounts payable, purchasing, receiving, finance, etc.) ▸ Coordinate signoff on all SAP Ariba deliverables ▸ Manage project timeline and adherence to schedule ▸ Participate in project status meetings ▸ Identify, manage, and escalate project issues and risks, as appropriate ▸ Develop go-live cutover plan and manage cutover execution ▸ Single point of contact for overall deployment
Functional Lead	▸ Participate in configuration workshops ▸ Define and document business requirements pertaining to all in-scope processes, transactions, and SAP Ariba solutions ▸ Gather business input from all involved functional resources and departments: procurement, A/P, accounting, finance, etc. ▸ Define business process and requirements and make decisions on solution configurations to handle those requirements. ▸ Write customer functional design document ▸ Develop test cases and test scripts for testing ▸ Plan, manage, and conduct system testing and user acceptance testing of the entire solution

Table 5.4 Customer Roles and Responsibilities (Cont.)

Customer Roles	Responsibilities
Functional Lead (Cont.)	▸ Validate that master data and application configuration data functions as desired ▸ Identify, escalate, resolve project issues ▸ Help develop go-live cutover plan and manage cutover execution ▸ Become the expert on system functionality and documentation, and customer-specific system use
Customer Functional Systems Analyst	▸ Participate in configuration workshops ▸ Experiment with system behavior and configuration to support customer decisions on system configurations ▸ Learn detailed SAP Ariba functionality all the way through the procure-to-pay process, and learn how the system configurations, customizations and data drive the system functionality. ▸ Answer customer questions on how the system will support the business and technical requirements raised by all involved customer departments
Customer Functional Resources/Testers/Pilot Users	▸ Participate in configuration workshops and contribute to business requirements and solution design ▸ Participate in test case/script development ▸ Participate in system test and UAT ▸ Identify power users within each department to act as experts by providing assistance to peers and input to overall process. ▸ Help roll out supplier compliance mandate within their respective departments ▸ Help define and execute internal change management program within their respective department

Table 5.4 Customer Roles and Responsibilities (Cont.)

5.2.5 Data Sources and Solution Landscape Inventory

This chapter has covered several different data sources for the invoice-to-pay process to consider both during the project and at run time. During the project's requirements gathering phase, master data elements for the new system need to be defined. Are these sources of data to remain the system of record once SAP

Ariba's solutions are in place; i.e., will SAP Ariba need to have their tax tables updated from a tax system/file cabinet and purchasing groups from SAP ERP, or will SAP Ariba become the system of record and these systems effectively become the children in a parent-child relationship, where SAP Ariba updates the various systems? Will the systems be maintained independently? Please note that maintaining systems independently is always a dangerous proposition if you expect any interaction between the systems going forward. Many of these decisions made during the project phases and at run time have implications for the overall system performance, and for ROI.

Understanding where the rules and tolerances are defined and kept in the current system and process is crucial. The rule, terms, and tolerances could be maintained in an existing system being replaced, or in a file cabinet in a paper-based operation. These are part of the conversion activities to inventory what needs to be converted from where, and also interface activities for any ongoing required updates once the SAP Ariba solution is live. You must also consider and account for banking relationships in the design of your solution, so as to ensure communication is seamless and payments are made as required by the process and systems.

Regarding the landscape of an overall invoice-to-pay solution in Ariba, much of the interplay between systems will take place between systems of record with information and transaction capabilities relevant to the process. This includes SAP ERP systems, as well as invoice processing solutions for scanning documents, such as OpenText VIM, tax solutions that are either connected to SAP ERP already and updating SAP Ariba tables, or integrated at some level with SAP Ariba directly. Banking and payment solutions may also require integration at some level.

In Figure 5.25, paper invoices are received and scanned via SAP ERP, OpenText VIM or SAP Ariba ICS. These invoices are sent up to the SAP Ariba Network for processing, which in turn routes to SAP Ariba Invoice Professional once the rules have been applied in SAP Ariba Invoice Automation to filter any discrepancies with the format and field entries. Once the invoice is reconciled in SAP Ariba Invoice Professional, it is sent to SAP ERP for payment.

There are many different ways to configure the process and the system landscape to integrate SAP Ariba Ariba's invoice-to-payment solutions into your accounts payable operations. Invariably, these solutions relieve the administrative burden of manual, paper-based processes, and drive greater flexibility in a diverse set of strategic areas of the business. Whether working capital, supplier satisfaction/alignment, or greater overall efficiencies for finance and accounts payable, SAP Ariba invoice-to-payment solutions offer a wide variety of potential uses and payoffs for the financial operations aspects of procurement.

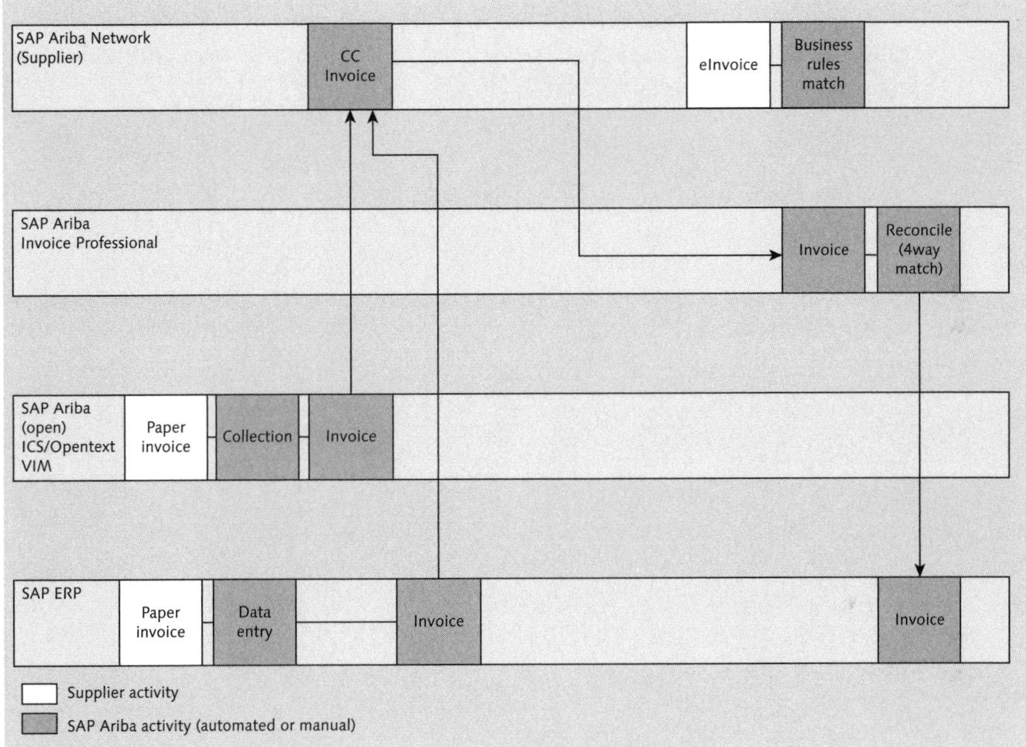

Figure 5.25 SAP Ariba Invoice-to-Payment Process Landscape with ERP/OpenText VIM/ICS

5.3 Summary

Accounts payable has long focused on the reconciliation of supplier-submitted invoices with the sourcing and purchasing documents, along with supporting workflow approvals and intermediate steps in order to initiate payment to the supplier. This reconciliation effort can be very difficult, tedious, and, ultimately, expensive in a paper-based transaction—even more so with a verbally initiated transaction. SAP Ariba's solutions in this area, with SAP AribaPay, SAP Ariba

Invoice Professional, and SAP Ariba Discount Management, leverage the processes you have built out on the transaction side in SAP Ariba to provide a much more cost efficient accounts payable experience. With payment speed and capabilities to reconcile in an efficient manner, SAP Ariba customers can further leverage this agility to obtain early-payment discounts negotiated as part of a strategy with the supplier or on the fly. This agility achieves cost savings at the end of the procure-to-pay process, at a critical juncture where money is changing hands. And this juncture is oftentimes a key area for realizing savings and additional, operational efficiencies.

Supplier relationship management begins and ends with analysis—the supplier needs to be assessed for viability, onboarded in the system, and ultimately measured on performance. This chapter reviews SAP Ariba Supplier Information and Performance Management and its implementation approaches.

6 Supplier Information and Performance Management

SAP Ariba Supplier Information and Performance Management (SIPM) reduces the cost of managing and updating supplier information by housing a supplier data repository, offering backend vendor master integration with third-party systems, using a single supplier record across all systems, and handling online buyer and supplier training. SAP Ariba SIPM provides additional reporting and analysis functionality to analyze supplier performance in your various procurement activities. Essentially, SAP Ariba SIPM is comprised of two individual products: SAP Ariba Supplier Information Management (SIM) and SAP Ariba Supplier Performance Management (SPM). SAP Ariba SIM handles supplier record management, while SAP Ariba SPM aggregates performance metrics and feedback from your various systems. Together, SAP Ariba SPM and SAP Ariba SIM create an actionable performance profile for the supplier and supplier groups, which you can further enrich by layering third-party data from providers onto it in order to increase your risk management.

This chapter outlines the SAP Ariba solutions for understanding and managing supplier relationships, with a focus on SAP Ariba SIPM functionality and implementation of the various components.

6.1 SAP Ariba Supplier Information and Performance Management

SAP Ariba Supplier Information and Performance Management (SIPM) combines SAP Ariba Supplier Information Management and SAP Ariba Supplier Performance Management solutions into comprehensive supplier information and performance analytics solutions. These solutions can be implemented in sequence or individually. SAP Ariba Supplier Information Management and SAP Ariba Supplier Performance Management are two modules of the overall SAP Ariba Supplier Management solution, which represent a centralized approach for managing the entire lifecycle of your company's relationship with its suppliers, from discovery and onboarding to risk and performance management.

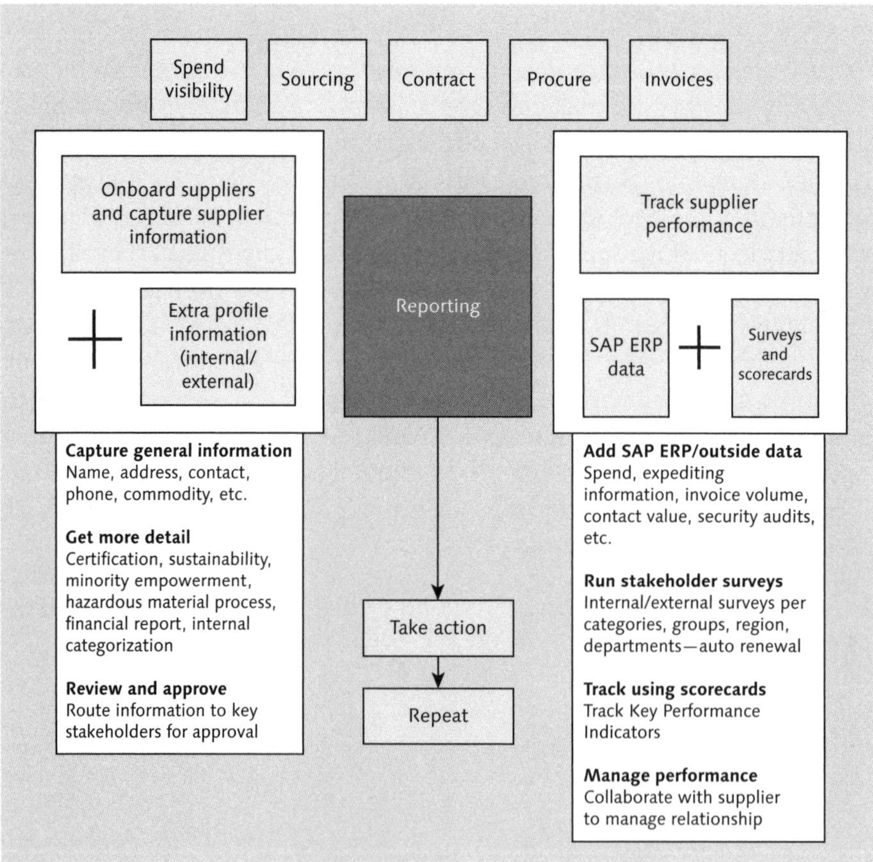

Figure 6.1 How SAP Ariba Supplier Management Works

Per Figure 6.1, there are two parts to analyzing and improving supplier performance. The first part is organizing the supplier data within the system. As supplier data constantly changes, suppliers need to have the proper access points to maintain their data validity in your system in the most efficient and economic manner possible. In a word, this allows supplier maintenance within your internal system, something that is oftentimes a time-consuming exercise for internal employees, to shift to the supplier. Adequate access and prompting for the supplier to do this updating themselves supports this effort. SAP Ariba SIM enables this functionality, and provides the baseline reporting capabilities for a supplier's product category offerings, certifications, locations, and terms. For performance-related assessments, further system data and external data sources need to be tapped, as well as supplier management-driven surveys and score carding.

Whether you're looking at on-time delivery data, objective and subjective surveys results, or pricing variance and score card data, different processes and systems need to provide the data to overlay the supplier record with a SAP Ariba Supplier Performance Management view. The SAP Ariba Supplier Performance Management view ultimately allows for action to be taken that will further improve the interactions between your company and its supply base. Figure 6.2 shows the entry point to various SAP Ariba SPM reports.

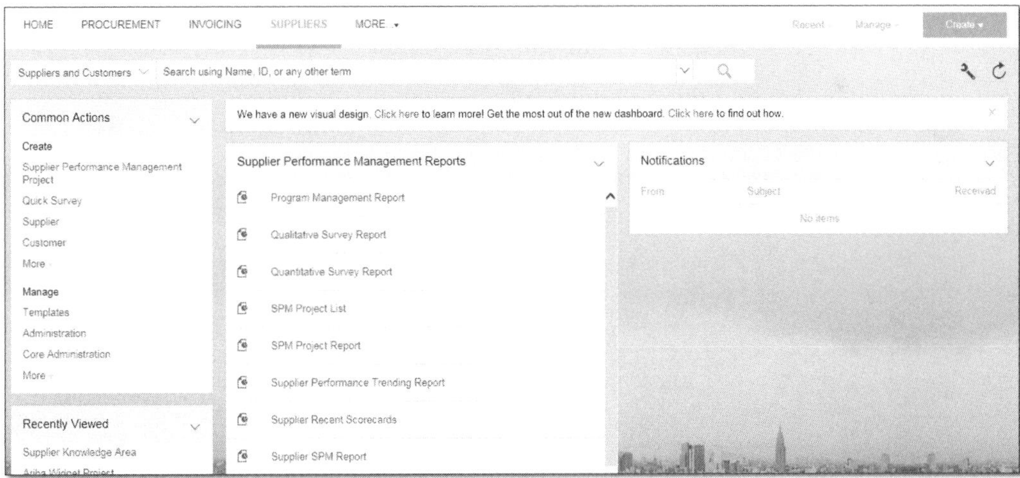

Figure 6.2 SAP Ariba SPM Report Overview

In the following sections, we will cover the functionalities of both SAP Ariba SIM and SAP Ariba SPM, followed by a discussion of some strategies for continuous supply chain optimization, as well as for supplier consolidation.

6.1.1 SAP Ariba Supplier Information Management

The SAP Ariba Supplier Information Management (SAP Ariba SIM) solution features process management functionality that allows you to create standardized, repeatable processes for managing suppliers, and also to store and update supplier profiles in one centralized location. SAP Ariba SIM also provides standard onboarding and approval processes for new suppliers. The following are some of the key SAP Ariba Supplier Information Management features:

- A centralized supplier workspace, providing a holistic view of the supplier, which both suppliers and supplier managers can create and update.
- Easy access to SAP Ariba Discovery, a solution for uncovering new suppliers on the SAP Ariba Network by product category and other variables/requirements.
- Specialized user groups for managing and approving suppliers.
- Defined onboarding and management processes, including approval and information collection, with notifications and workflow tasks that allow you to collaborate with internal and external users in order to create, review, and revise supplier profiles, and to provide requested materials.
- Automatic routing of supplier self-registrations and profile updates to individual supplier managers based on commodity, region, and other criteria.
- Collaborative project areas that enforce repeatable and measurable best practices through templates and relevant phases, tasks, and milestones.
- Supplier certificate management, allowing supplier managers to prompt suppliers to upload certificates and to upload new certificates when the original ones expire.
- A repository for associated documents such as supplier presentations, and the ability to search those documents. SAP Ariba Supplier Performance Management can also include scorecards, surveys (see Figure 6.3), corrective action plans, and yearly goals and objectives.
- Reporting and analysis for supplier management data, including prepackaged reports and the ability for authorized users to create, modify, and share custom reports.

Event Doc573764971 - Quick Supplier Survey Next Exit

These rules control every aspect of how the event works. You may change them to suit your event or accept the defaults.

1 Rules
2 Participants
3 Content
4 Summary

Timing Rules

Response start date: * When I Click the **Publish** button on the Summary page
Schedule For the Future:

Due date: * Duration: 30 minutes Reminder (Edit)
Fixed time:

Bidding Rules

Enable scoring on participant responses: Yes No

Market Feedback

Figure 6.3 SAP Ariba SIPM Supplier Survey

The SAP Ariba SIM supplier profile captures key common supplier data that is usable across all business, commodities, etc. within the company. Additionally, this profile is useful for reporting in SAP Ariba against sourcing, contracts and spend management projects. This information is also capable of syncing with an RFx so that a supplier's responses are the default values in the RFx, and so that any updates made via the RFx also sync with the profile. A profile example is provided in Figure 6.4.

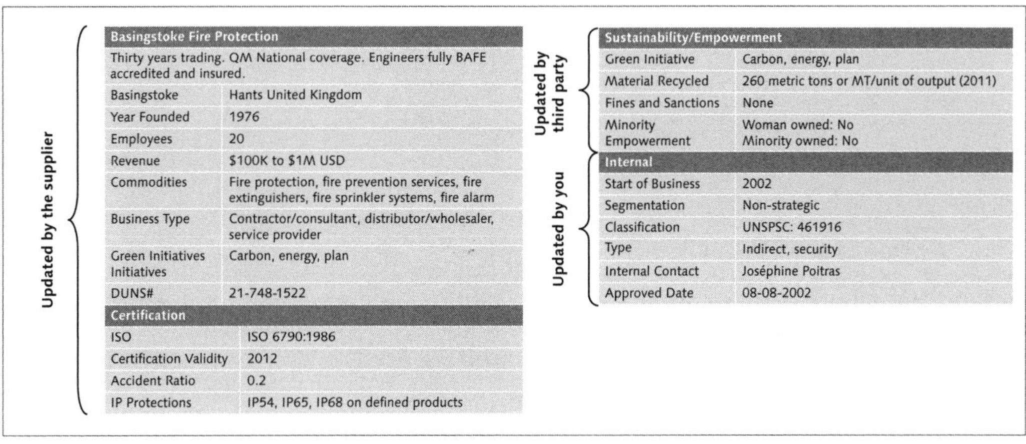

Basingstoke Fire Protection	
Thirty years trading. QM National coverage. Engineers fully BAFE accredited and insured.	
Basingstoke	Hants United Kingdom
Year Founded	1976
Employees	20
Revenue	$100K to $1M USD
Commodities	Fire protection, fire prevention services, fire extinguishers, fire sprinkler systems, fire alarm
Business Type	Contractor/consultant, distributor/wholesaler, service provider
Green Initiatives Initiatives	Carbon, energy, plan
DUNS#	21-748-1522
Certification	
ISO	ISO 6790:1986
Certification Validity	2012
Accident Ratio	0.2
IP Protections	IP54, IP65, IP68 on defined products

Sustainability/Empowerment	
Green Initiative	Carbon, energy, plan
Material Recycled	260 metric tons or MT/unit of output (2011)
Fines and Sanctions	None
Minority Empowerment	Woman owned: No Minority owned: No
Internal	
Start of Business	2002
Segmentation	Non-strategic
Classification	UNSPSC: 461916
Type	Indirect, security
Internal Contact	Joséphine Poitras
Approved Date	08-08-2002

Figure 6.4 SAP Ariba Supplier Information Record

6.1.2 SAP Ariba Supplier Performance Management

Once you have suppliers and their data in place in SAP Ariba Supplier Information Management, SAP Ariba Supplier Performance Management (SAP Ariba SPM) allows you to use consistent measurements for supplier performance to identify any performance problems. Using SAP Ariba SPM helps organizations determine whether suppliers deliver on contracted expectations outlined in service-level agreements. The data derived from SAP Ariba SPM allows users to have fact-based conversations with suppliers regarding their performance, and can improve negotiation outcomes with those suppliers. The following are some of the key SAP Ariba Supplier Performance Management features:

- Templates that allow users to create SAP Ariba SPM projects, scorecards, and surveys using approved business processes as in Figure 6.5. The template that can be used to create SAP Ariba SPM projects represents the standard process that your group must follow for these projects.

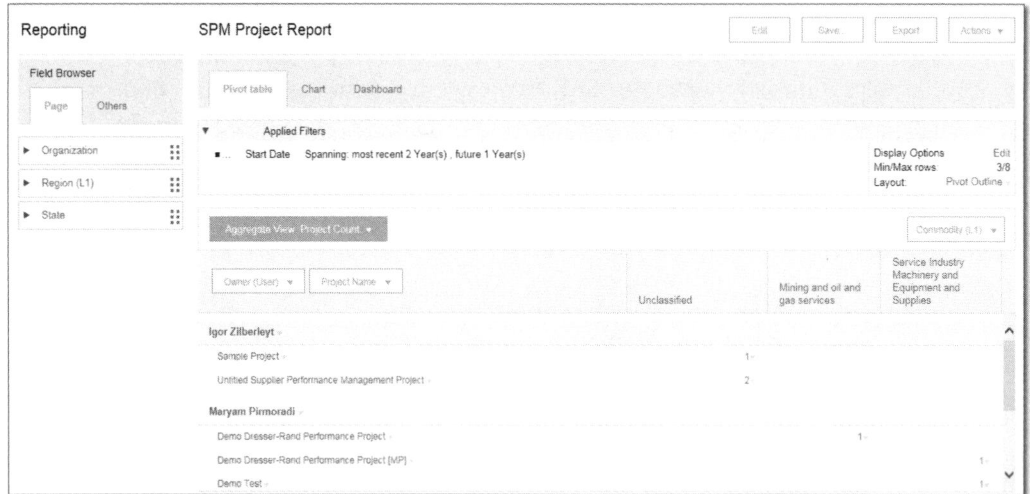

Figure 6.5 SAP Ariba SPM Project Overview

- Performance criteria translated into key performance indicators (KPIs) that map between SAP Ariba SPM scorecards and surveys. Several groups (such as human resources, manufacturing, or marketing) with similar performance goals for suppliers can leverage the same or similar criteria and their corresponding KPIs. SAP Ariba SPM provides:

- Prepackaged SAP Ariba SPM reports
- Collaboration with suppliers to improve processes
- Visibility into performance issues to suppliers and buyers alike

The way SAP Ariba Supplier Performance Management surveys are initiated is via the project framework. A user creates a project and defines KPIs. Then, the user defines the surveys and scorecards to map to these KPIs. Once the surveys are complete, the data is consolidated and scores defined by KPI for each supplier.

6.1.3 Strategies for Continuous Supply Chain Optimization

There is no "one size fits all" strategy for supply chain optimization as it relates to procurement and suppliers, continuous or otherwise. One theory behind supply chain optimization includes Albert Hirschmann's *Exit, Voice, and Loyalty,* (see ISBN 978-0674276604) which postulates a binary set of options for responding to decreasing quality, rising prices, or other difficulties with a supplier. Either the customer exits and finds another supplier, or he voices his displeasure and attempts to salvage the relationship and make it stronger. Popular manufacturing approaches today favor "just-in-time" and "lean" manufacturing. These approaches are driven by the need to keep as little inventory as possible up and down the manufacturing process. Inventory creates costs, ages and becomes outdated, and has even been known to "shrink" in porous environments or loosely controlled warehouse situations. Inventory is also a marker of trust levels with suppliers. If you are not confident that your supplier can provide you with a material or service when you want it or at the required quality level, you build inventory to buffer this area, so as to avoid shut downs to the manufacturing process. Similarly, if you do not have a strong relationship with a supplier and will replace them at the first sign of trouble with another, you may carry more inventory to help you bridge the supplier switch.

Just-in-Time production and "lean" manufacturing are examples of "voice" approaches, because the customer integrates their operations with a supplier, and thus forms a relationship that is not easily severed. In successful instances, voice supplier relationships can lead to supplier-driven product innovation for the customer, such as key potato suppliers breeding new kinds of potatoes for a fast-food restaurant, or an automobile supplier assisting with automotive designs to better leverage their components. In unsuccessful instances, where a voice supplier relationship has gone bad, voice supplier relationships can severely impact profits, or even threaten a company's survival, due to an overreliance on a once symbiotic relationship with a supplier. For direct procurement items, such as components used to assemble the final product, depending on the criticality of the component, most supplier relationships lie somewhere between voice and exit. Whereas for indirect or commodity items, such as office paper and pens, there is a larger preference for exit. There is no need to work with a supplier of deteriorating quality if another supplier can be found easily at comparable (or even lower) costs and the item is not a critical item in your value delivery process as a company.

Factors for supply chain optimization consideration, at least from a procurement standpoint, include:

- **The industry in which you operate**
  If your industry requires complex interplay between supplier and customer, in order to obtain to a winning finished product, choosing a supplier empowering/dialogue approach may be more suitable.
- **The industry in which the supplier operates**
  As will be discussed in Chapter 8 with SAP Ariba Spend Visibility, if there is a fragmented supply base, there is an opportunity for savings by staying flexible and leveraging the exit strategy. In industries where there are only a couple of players (oligopolies/monopolies), exiting and switching suppliers may not be a desirable option, due to costs and/or a supply disruption. Simply put, in a consolidated market, there may be no less costly alternative on offer from the limited number of other suppliers.
- **The type of item being purchased**
  If this is a core component to one of your end products, then having a relationship with the supplier may be more important than if you are buying paper clips.
- **Manufacturing/production strategy**
  If your production strategy requires tight synchronization with suppliers, in order to minimize inventory and increase speed, then having suppliers you can trust from a quality and delivery perspective in this value chain is important, even if those suppliers charge slightly more.

From an SAP Ariba SIPM standpoint, once you understand your strategy and industry position, you can gather and standardize the supplier information with SAP Ariba SIM, and analyze supplier performance with SAP Ariba SPM. In the event that performance deterioration is identified, or performance improvements are required to support your own processes from the supplier, SAP Ariba SIPM bolsters your understanding and case to frame an exit or voice decision.

6.1.4 Supplier Consolidation Strategy

Another overarching strategy, if neither voice nor exit is compelling in-and-of-itself as a supply chain optimization strategy, is to continuously whittle down your supply base to create further efficiencies and volume discounts. While some of the reasons for reducing your number of suppliers are more obvious (increased volumes, discounts, and time savings), other benefits to supplier consolidation include a reduction in supplier records and relationships to manage, analyze, and assess in the system landscape. Each one of these supplier relationships and records requires updating in the system. So when suppliers are consolidated, your system management also becomes simpler.

Consolidating suppliers is not a cure-all, and doing so can cause issues if you tip the balance into putting all of your risk and reliance into too few suppliers. Not only does this impact your negotiating ability when the supplier knows you have few alternatives, but you may also overlook geographical relationships and products that require a regional supplier for supply chain or regulation purposes. This ambiguity is yet another reason to understand your supplier relationships using SAP Ariba SIPM and SAP Ariba Spend Visibility as much as possible before acting rashly, as hasty decisions that appear sound based on a single data point could, in fact, be quite shaky in other areas where analysis is still required.

6.2 Implementing SAP Ariba Supplier Information and Performance Management

This section will outline the different approaches and resources required for implementing SAP Ariba SIPM. This solution straddles both ends of the project spectrum. SAP Ariba Supplier Information Management (SAP Ariba SIM) needs to be up and running from day one to help suppliers begin maintaining their information, whereas SAP Ariba SIPM may not be used for several months after go-live, when it will collect system performance metrics prior to doing a review. As with all analysis, you need a relevant data set before you can really start. Other aspects of a system need to be generating data in order for relevant analysis to work.

6.2.1 Defining Project Resources, Phases, and Timelines

The following sections details project resources, project phases, and timelines suited for SAP Ariba SIPM implementations. A summary of the process for implementing SAP Ariba SIPM is presented in Figure 6.6. Another core phase of a SAP Ariba SIPM project not included in Figure 6.6 is pre-kick off and data collection planning. Conducting analysis as to the data involved, prior to project kickoff assists with project focus from kickoff onwards.

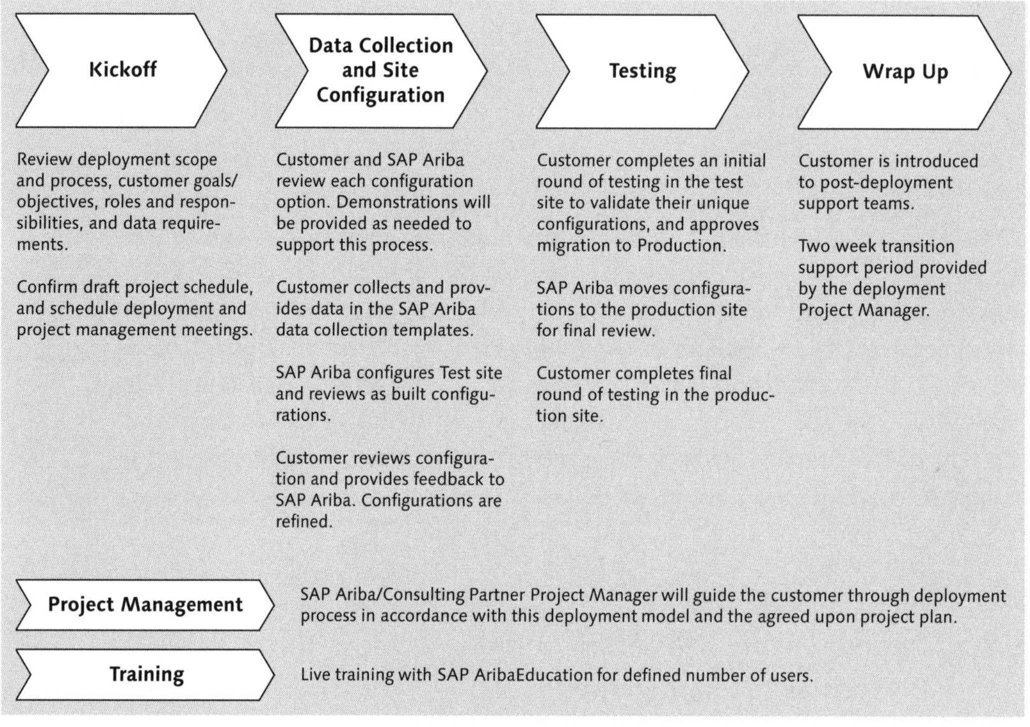

Figure 6.6 SAP Ariba On-Demand Deployment Process—SAP Ariba SIPM

SAP Ariba SIPM projects follow a slightly different approach from SAP Ariba P2P projects, where supplier onboarding and project management run in parallel for different areas. In a SAP Ariba SIPM project, the emphasis is on data collection, though there are still project management and training tracks, which would equate to the internal adoption track of a SAP Ariba P2P project. Although there is no official track for supplier adoption, during each phase of the project, the focus is on the supplier. For SAP Ariba Supplier Information Management, suppliers need to be onboarded in order to furnish correct information in the format required by SAP Ariba SIM, if their information is not already available on the SAP Ariba Network to some degree. As a result of these characteristics, supplier data is malleable, dynamic, and error-prone. Supplier data updates benefit from the SAP Ariba Network, as a supplier can update their record directly once in the network, and can have that record used by multiple customers. Supplier data can be cleansed, to a degree, and needs to be kept up-to-date as much as possible for proper payment and certifications/eligibility. This is especially true in on-premise procurement systems: companies typically have thousands of supplier records that are redundant and/or out of date.

For the performance management part of SAP Ariba Supplier Information and Performance Management, supplier communication is important during the review phases, so that the supplier is aware how they are being measured and has proper expectations set. In general, the quality of reporting and analytics will drive primarily on the quality of the data fed into the system.

Separating the data collection and site configuration phases, as seen in Figure 6.7, allows for further definition by phase of main activities. Table 6.1 discusses the different stages of deployment for SAP Ariba SIPM in more detail.

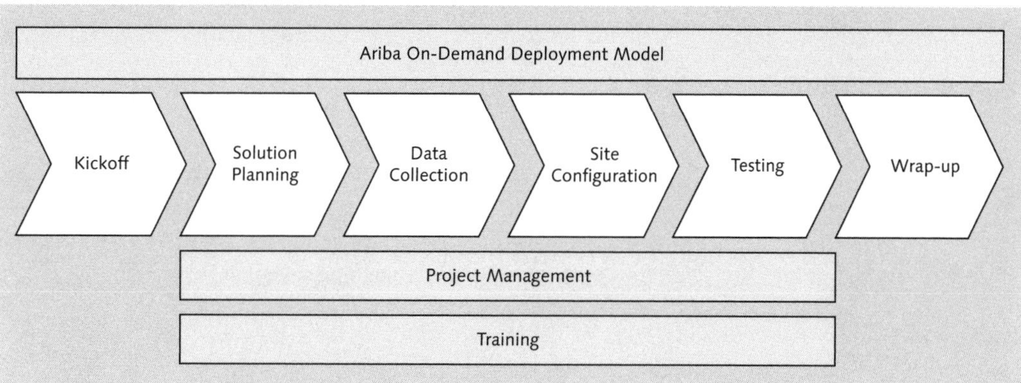

Figure 6.7 Stages of Deployment—SAP Ariba SIPM

Phase	Description
Kickoff meeting	Review deployment scope and process, customer goals/objectives, roles and responsibilities, and data requirements. Confirm correct users have been added to the test site. A project plan is provided post kickoff and regular project management and deployment meetings are scheduled.
Solution planning	Customer and SAP Ariba/consulting partner define the current and to-be processes for onboarding suppliers, and update the SAP Ariba SIM and SAP Ariba SPM process matrices.
Data collection	Customer and SAP Ariba/consulting partner discuss configuration options. SAP Ariba/consulting partner conducts demos as needed to assist in data collection requirements. Customer collects and provides data in the appropriate data collection templates. Data includes master data, custom header fields, performance management process, survey/scorecard data, supplier onboarding process, supplier profile questionnaire, form development, custom fact table development, and document attachments.
Site configuration	SAP Ariba configures site with provided data and conducts demos of the configurations. SAP Ariba refines the configuration based upon customer feedback. Configurations are initially completed in the test site.
Testing	Test to confirm the configurations are completed. Customer completes testing in the test site first. SAP Ariba updates configurations based on test results and then the configuration is transferred to the production site for final review. During this review, customer verifies any customer-specific information.
Wrap-up	Move configurations from test site to production site. Transition to customer support and customer success.
Project management	Project plan guiding SAP Ariba/consulting partner and customer from beginning to end. Deliverable is a project plan and structure to manage successful deployment.
Training	SAP Ariba/consulting partner demonstrates software functionality as part of the configuration sessions. Recorded trainings are available in the HELP menu. Live training with SAP Ariba Education is included limited number of users. Additional training typically is an optional add-on.

Table 6.1 SAP Ariba SIPM Stages of Deployment

In the following breakdown, we will discuss the key deliverables of each of the phases and streams mentioned in Table 6.1:

- **Kickoff**
  The kickoff phase key deliverables include: master data, custom header fields, D-form, custom report, SAP Ariba SPM process (tasks, process configuration, and related documents), SAP Ariba SPM surveys/scorecards, supplier onboarding workflow, and supplier profile questionnaire. It is also important during this initial phase to identify concerns and goals, define the project plan, and create and deliver the project's kickoff presentation. The project workshop schedule needs to be laid out during the kickoff phase. Key workshops include the enablement workbook-driven sessions, supplier workspace template definition, SAP Ariba SPM project templates, scorecards, and surveys, knowledge transfer planning, and optional workshops on D-forms, custom facts, and custom reporting.
- **Solution planning**
  For SAP Ariba SIPM implementations, the focus areas during the solution planning phase divide along the lines of SAP Ariba SIM and SAP Ariba SPM. For SAP Ariba SIM implementations, during the solution design phase, it is important to define the following:
  - The to-be process for onboarding new suppliers, and ongoing maintenance of supplier information for previously on-boarded suppliers.
  - Identify any additional documents to be created or consumed during the SAP Ariba SIM project.
  - Supplier onboarding process is built within a unique template named default supplier workspace.
  - Only one supplier onboarding process template per site, as this template is specially designed to integrate with the supplier profile questionnaire

  For SAP Ariba SPM implementation and deployment, you need to address the following items during the solution planning phase:
  - Document the SAP Ariba SPM process to support planning, monitoring, and corrective action activities associated with their supplier's performance
  - One SAP Ariba SPM process template is typically configured as part of a standard deployment.

  - Additional templates can be purchased from SAP Ariba as required.
  - KPI library, survey, and scorecard configuration

- **Data collection and site configuration**
  Although data collection and site configuration phases are essentially two different phases, they can, on occasion, be combined in an SAP Ariba SIPM project, provided the solution design phase has yielded clear configuration requirements for this data collection and site configuration phase. As an initial step, you confirm the SAP Ariba SPM and SAP Ariba SIM process design matrices and use these to drive the configuration of your SAP Ariba test site, also referred to as a *realm*. The master data collection is framed by the enablement workbook provided by SAP Ariba or your consulting partner. Here, you define and format your data required for the in-scope reports. Custom header, form, supplier profile questionnaires (SPQs), and analytical reports can also be finalized and implemented in this phase, as the report definition is oftentimes an iterative process with SAP Ariba or your consulting partner. Use supplier profile questionnaires to gather relevant information from your suppliers, and to underpin approval flows and award decisions during sourcing events.

- **Testing**
  After data collection and configuration are complete, either for the whole SAP Ariba SIPM implementation or for independent parts, testing can begin. Ideally, a system freeze is put in place for the test realm, with no further configuration allowed unless to address an issue uncovered during testing. SAP Ariba or a consulting partner can provide sample test scripts, but the customer typically conducts and leads testing. As configuration is confirmed during testing, it moves into the production realm. Users in the system, especially if live, are not able to access the reports and functionality just yet.

- **Wrap-up and go-live**
  Once testing is complete, the remaining configuration moves from the test realm into production. Access is enabled for the production users, and support for the system is transferred internally at SAP Ariba to the customer support and the customer success teams.

- **SAP Ariba SIPM project roles**
  Per Table 6.2, a SAP Ariba SIPM project requires a number of resources from both the customer and the SAP Ariba/consulting partner.

Role	Description
SAP Ariba Project Manager	▸ Responsible for day-to-day project management, including managing scope, project plan, and SAP Ariba resources ▸ Provides functional knowledge of SAP Ariba software capabilities ▸ Facilitates configuration sessions and conducts functionality demonstrations ▸ Distributes project documentation at the conclusion of the project
SAP Ariba Configuration Lead	▸ Responsible for technical aspects of the deployment, including data loading and functionality configuration ▸ Facilitates testing by providing a test script and responding testing related issues ▸ Provides administrative demonstrations
Manager, Upstream Deployment	▸ Escalation point of contact
Customer Engagement Executive	▸ Acts as the day-to-day operational advocate ▸ Assists/manages issues escalation ▸ Assists in coordinating with SAP Ariba teams throughout the length of your contract ▸ Contact to discuss events or changes within your organization that would impact your use of SAP Ariba products/services ▸ Offers ongoing adoption support during the length of your contract ▸ Point of contact to manage contract extension
Customer Project Sponsor	▸ Act as champion for the project and provide overall project vision ▸ Escalation contact for deployment issue resolution ▸ Drive change management and high level communication in support of the project

Table 6.2 SAP Ariba SIM, SAP Ariba SPM, and SAP Ariba SIPM Roles

Role	Description
Customer Project Manager	▸ Primary point of contact for overall deployment ▸ Partners with SAP Ariba project manager to manage project timeline and on time deliverables ▸ Manages all customer resource activities including internal meetings and decision making ▸ Resolve issues and escalate as necessary to ensure the deployment remains on track
Functional Lead	▸ Define business process and participate in data collection and configuration efforts ▸ Complete unit testing throughout deployment ▸ Responsible for customer testing ▸ Lead roll out and training efforts post deployment
Process Experts/Pilot Users	▸ Provide input to configuration decision ▸ Participate in testing as needed

Table 6.2 SAP Ariba SIM, SAP Ariba SPM, and SAP Ariba SIPM Roles (Cont.)

- **Project Timeline**
  A typical project timeline for SAP Ariba SIPM is around three months. However, depending on the project's scope and complexity, this timeline can extend further. The longest project phase for this type of project is the data collection and configuration phase. The project timeline can also extend further for supplier onboarding waves into the SAP Ariba Network, and can vary depending on internal resource availability. For supplier onboarding, a phased approach is typically selected do to the finite nature of internal resources able to support the new suppliers and processes in SAP Ariba SIPM. Oftentimes, groups of suppliers and product categories are rolled out, or specific divisions and types of procurement are phased in after go-live.

In terms of the timeline, as you can see in Figure 6.8, there is a 12 week overall timeline for a basic SAP Ariba SIPM project. Unlike other solution implementations, an emphasis is placed pre-kick off in understanding data and planning the overall project to bring this data into SAP Ariba SIPM processes.

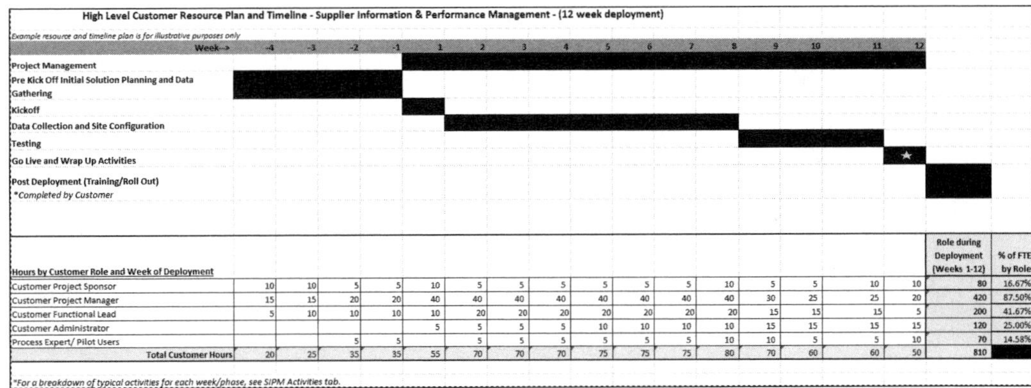

High Level Customer Resource Plan and Timeline - Supplier Information & Performance Management - (12 week deployment)

Example resource and timeline plan is for illustrative purposes only

Week-->	-4	-3	-2	-1	1	2	3	4	5	6	7	8	9	10	11	12
Project Management																
Pre Kick Off Initial Solution Planning and Data Gathering																
Kickoff																
Data Collection and Site Configuration																
Testing																
Go Live and Wrap Up Activities															★	
Post Deployment (Training/Roll Out) *Completed by Customer																

Hours by Customer Role and Week of Deployment																	Role during Deployment (Weeks 1-12)	% of FTE by Role
Customer Project Sponsor	10	10	5	5	10	5	5	5	5	5	5	10	5	5	10	10	80	16.67%
Customer Project Manager	15	15	20	20	40	40	40	40	40	40	40	40	30	25	25	20	420	87.50%
Customer Functional Lead	5	10	10	10	10	20	20	20	20	20	20	20	15	15	15	5	200	41.67%
Customer Administrator					5	5	5	5	10	10	10	10	15	15	15	15	120	25.00%
Process Expert/ Pilot Users			5	5		5	5	5	5	5	5	10	10	5	5	10	70	14.58%
Total Customer Hours	20	25	35	35	55	70	70	70	75	75	75	80	70	60	60	50	810	

*For a breakdown of typical activities for each week/phase, see SIPM Activities tab.

Figure 6.8 SAP Ariba SIPM 12 Week Project Schedule

6.2.2 Implementation Considerations

The first thing to consider before beginning your implementation for any of the variations of SAP Ariba Supplier Information Management is how the supplier information will enter the system. There are three main routes for setting up and maintaining a supplier record:

1. Supplier self-registration.
2. Company user, or user group working with supplier, can enter supplier record creation request, which then goes through an approval workflow and possible follow-on workflow for record updates/enrichment, to gain final entry into the supplier database.
3. Direct entry of supplier master data into the system without approvals by designated users with proper authorizations, as per Figure 6.9.

For SAP Ariba Supplier Information Management implementations and, to some degree, SAP Ariba Supplier Performance Management, the focus turns on gathering uniform supplier data necessary for conducting transactions and evaluations. What are the data requirements for your company? For example, what data is required in the supplier record and what information should be optional? Is a supplier allowed to see the information entered by the customer in their supplier record, or is this information, or parts thereof, to be confidential? Do suppliers need to win a contract, or purchase from your company in order to be entered into your supplier data? Does this require a qualification step in addition to the purchasing scenario, or can a supplier become prequalified and entered into the supplier records without actually having done business with your company? Lastly, will all necessary supplier data derive from the supplier record entries obtained from the supplier directly or one of the customer users, or is additional survey or external data enrichment required?

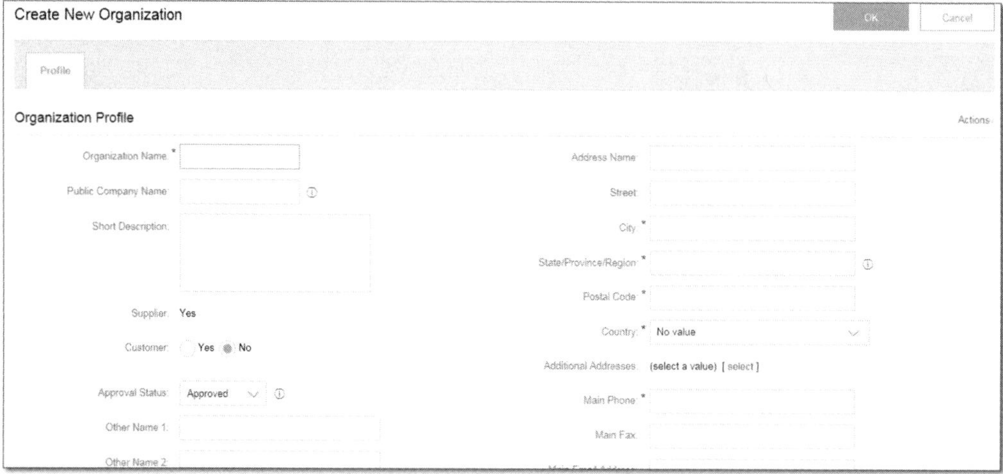

Figure 6.9 Create Supplier in SAP Ariba

Once the process is defined/refined, workflows around supplier record approval need to be lined out. Who approves and based on what supplier data? Do any special approvers need to be engaged for certain types of suppliers, such as IT or safety, health, and environmental? Which users require access to supplier records? Figure 6.10 outlines a basic SAP Ariba SIPM overview process.

The first step for the SAP Ariba SIPM process is supplier creation. During the design of your process, you defined how the supplier is created or creates and updates this information in SAP Ariba SIM directly, as well as the specific fields and data required. After the record has been submitted, most companies have an approval flow in place to ensure the supplier has submitted all of the required data and is eligible for inclusion in the SAP Ariba SIM area for suppliers. Once the supplier has been approved and entered into your supplier area, performance management and update notifications for expiring certifications processes can be applied. If there are time-sensitive areas of a supplier record, such as certifications and insurance fields, an expiration and notification process needs to be defined.

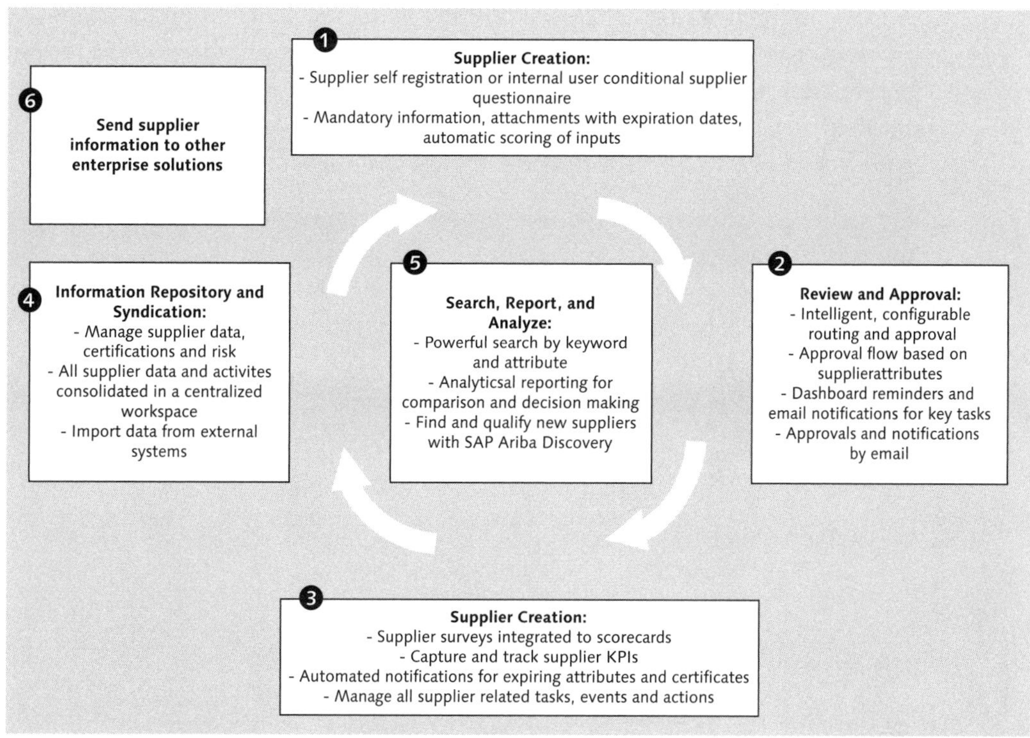

Figure 6.10 Supplier Information and Performance Management Process

The fourth step of the SAP Ariba SIPM process involves syndication and integration with other data sources to enrich existing supplier records and/or add suppliers from other transacting systems in your company's landscape, as well as to share supplier records with other systems in your landscape at the end of the SAP Ariba SIPM process. Once the supplier records are in place for SAP Ariba SIM, and performance is being tracked according to your focus areas, analysis is a further, and critical, step. If your analysis reveals that further suppliers are required for certain product areas, SAP Ariba Discovery provides a quick and easy way to find new suppliers. Your analysis may also reveal the opposite—that fewer suppliers are required and consolidation is possible.

Once the analysis step is complete, a final step may be required in SAP Ariba SIPM to update supplier records in your landscape in other systems sharing this data. Typically, SAP Ariba SIM plays a central role in supplier management, due to the ease of updating possible in the SAP Ariba Network, as well as the depth of existing, up-to-date supplier records already in the SAP Ariba Network. There are sometimes other systems which require these supplier records, and which can benefit from the updating capabilities of SAP Ariba SIM and performance management insight from SAP Ariba SPM for suppliers. Integration options and approaches with SAP Ariba SIPM are discussed at the end of this chapter.

Per Figure 6.11, the SAP Ariba SPM process begins with project creation, where the survey manager/buyer identifies key stakeholders and defines milestones/timelines. The next step is to identify the supplier base and the criteria for inclusion in the event, based on the supplier's characteristics and capabilities.

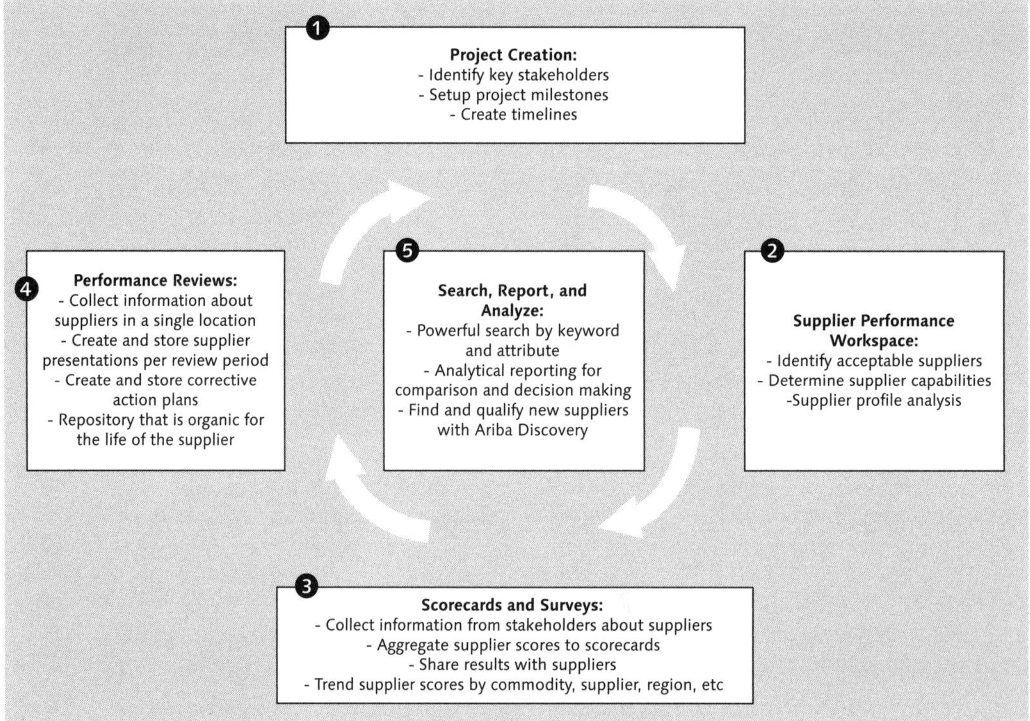

Figure 6.11 SAP Ariba Supplier Performance Management Process

SAP Ariba SPM is a project, essentially, where supplier segments are identified, metrics are defined, surveys/scorecards are completed, supplier reviews are conducted, and finally further analysis and queries are performed. Most SAP Ariba SPM activities are iterative and cyclical.

When implementing SAP Ariba SIPM, the underpinning for a successful implementation rests on several areas of your company and its IT and process infrastructure. Having a standardized system across the organization for supplier performance management is a larger goal, and may require additional process definition and socialization, not to mention clean data, to be create up-front. If a standardized process is not possible for the organization due to its size or complexity, a standardized process for performance management for the divisions using the system is an alternative. Suppliers in the SAP Ariba Network should have a higher data quality level than a typical supplier record in a corporate on-premise system, as suppliers are transacting in the SAP Ariba Network and need to keep their information up-to-date for multiple customers. Nonetheless, ensuring data cleanliness for a reporting project is always a high priority, and record quality should be validated, particularly custom fields that may not be standard in the general information of suppliers on the network. Custom header field examples include supplier type, scorecard type, supplier categorization, spend area, plant location, or strategic supplier (yes/no).

Forms provide a data entry point for suppliers and your reviewers, and typically also require customization and design work. Forms in SAP Ariba SIPM are searchable and reportable, and can contain header and line item level data/fields. Forms can include certificates of liability, asset tracking, project resource sheets, incident forms, deal sheets, as well as product information.

Defining key performance indicators (KPIs) and measures help suppliers understand where they will be measured, and focus your company's analytics upon indicators driving the business. Setting succinct, meaningful KPIs that allow for application in more than an individual supplier/division allows for larger relevance and report consumption.

As far as the consumers of SAP Ariba SIPM reports, it is important to identify the stakeholders and the resources to align with the roles required by the project. Ideally, some of the project participants, especially the subject matter experts, should come from the stakeholders groups, and represent their interests and needs on the project. Supplier organizations and their users will need to be loaded during deployment into SAP Ariba SIPM.

User authentication is a topic for all solutions, cloud-based or otherwise. SAP Ariba offers two primary ways to access on-demand solutions: either via corporate authentication or corporate authentication with single sign on (SSO). In the former, users log on to systems using their corporate ID and password. In the latter, users log on to their corporate network and the authentication allows access to SAP Ariba solutions when needed. In order to enable either option, a user database and web connection needs to be present for your in-scope users. You also must provide SAP Ariba your public RSA key, the URL of your remote authentication relay page, and the URL of the logout page.

Other general questions to answer for a SAP Ariba SIPM project:

1. Once the configured site has been deployed, what is the plan for post-deployment? Has an internal, post-deployment implementation plan been determined? What are the cycles for evaluation and data updates, as well as processes? Some of these questions can be answered by the SAP Ariba SPM and SAP Ariba SIM process matrices.
2. Have you selected the strategic suppliers which will be used for the initial SAP Ariba SIPM rollout? Typically, SAP Ariba SPM and SAP Ariba SIM are rolled out in phases, as your company's purchasing department would otherwise become overwhelmed with the sheer volume of suppliers, reporting cycles, and reports. During a SAP Ariba SIM roll out, you also determine which existing suppliers require re-validation, similar to the process new suppliers follow.
3. Will the application release to a smaller group of power users before rolling out to the full team? This is a valuable approach, because power users are multipliers in an organization and can serve as a first line of defense. However, some projects do not have the additional time required for a power user first pilot, and so they integrate power users into their project teams, so that when the system goes live on day one, power users have had the additional training and exposure to the system in order to assist in training and adoption efforts for their colleagues.

6.2.3 Data Source and Solution Landscape Inventory

For a SAP Ariba SIPM project, multiple data sources can be in-scope for the initial deployment, and even ongoing run time. The focus of SAP Ariba SIM is the supplier record, so if you have a supplier database in an SAP ERP environment or other system that needs inclusion in the reporting and general SAP Ariba system, a comparison of your supplier records, and which suppliers are already transacting on the SAP Ariba Network, is a good first step. Though not as pronounced as in the SAP Ariba P2P and other project streams, and not included in this chapter's project plans, onboarding and even conversion of suppliers in other systems could be required if those suppliers are not in the SAP Ariba Network prior to the project, and required for reporting and assessment purposes in SAP Ariba SIM and SAP Ariba SIPM. A supplier will need to log on to the SAP Ariba Network in order to maintain their data, although suppliers not on the network can still be analyzed as part of SAP Ariba SIPM.

Spend data, expediting information, invoices, security audits, and contract value may also require extraction from SAP ERP. If the system of record is to be SAP ERP going forward for these data points, then further integration/interface and ongoing push/pulls into SAP Ariba SIPM is required. Integration between SAP Ariba SIPM and SAP Master Data Governance for Supplier (SAP MDG-S) is one of the features of the SAP Ariba 14s release. This feature provides open APIs for web services between the two systems, but you still need to map the SAP ERP supplier fields. In tandem with SAP MDG-S, these APIs also provide web services integration between SAP Ariba SIPM and SAP ERP. Standard (direct) integration via an adapter is not available today with SAP Ariba SIPM and SAP ERP, due to cXML limitations. This scenario is being addressed in the 15s sourcing roadmap, which will be the next mainline release for SAP Ariba SIPM.

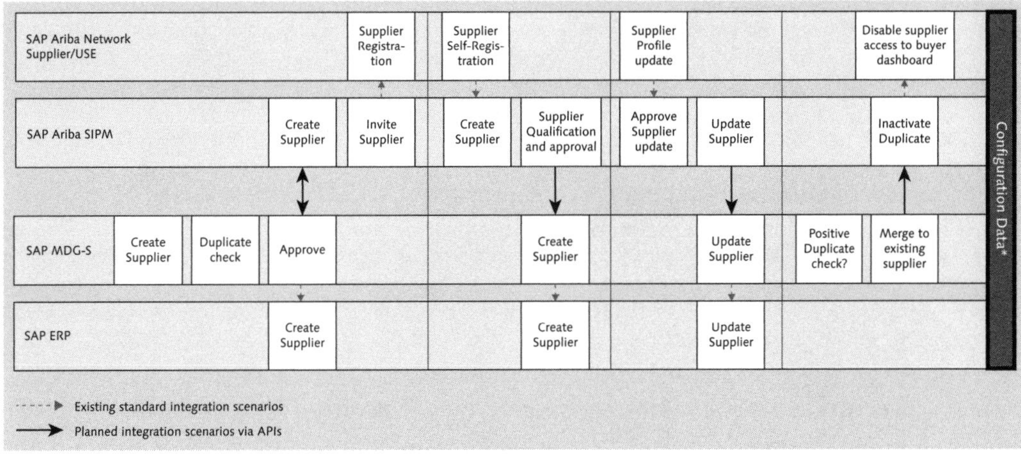

Figure 6.12 Sourcing with SAP Ariba SIPM Integration Flow Diagram to SAP ERP and SAP MDG-S

Per Figure 6.12, the supplier creation can be centrally managed in SAP MDG-S as a system of record, and then pushed out to SAP Ariba and back to SAP ERP for further usage. A supplier can also self-register and, once approved, have the supplier record pulled back from the SAP Ariba Network/SAP Ariba SIM into SAP MDG-S and SAP ERP. Further supplier-driven updates to SAP MDG-S can be front-ended by SAP Ariba SIM and the SAP Ariba Network, or from SAP MDG-S up to the SAP Ariba SIM. Figure 6.13 shows the screenshots and fields for this new functionality in 14s.

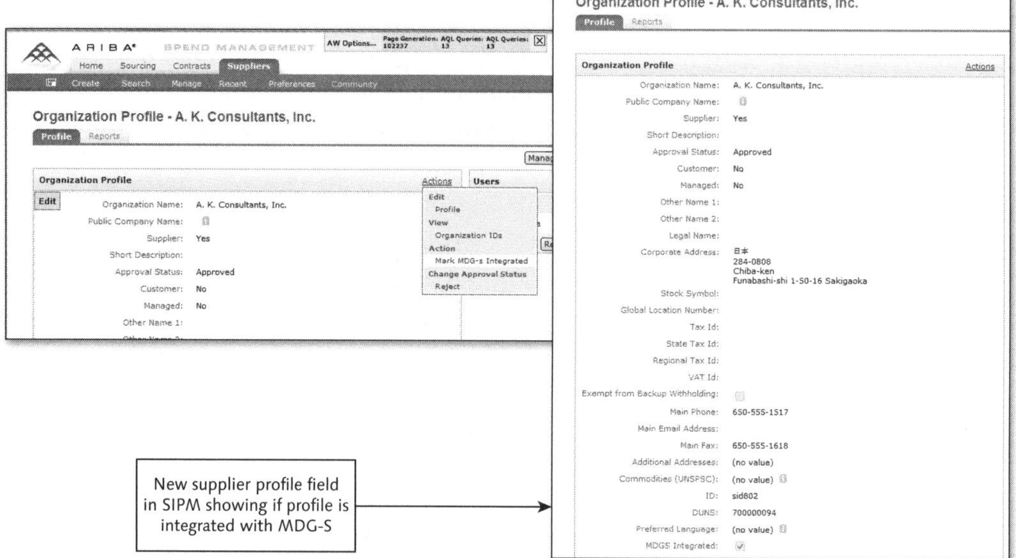

Figure 6.13 SAP MDG-S Action 14s Profile Field

You can find more on integration approaches for SAP Ariba and SAP ERP, including some detailed setup steps, in Chapter 9 of this book.

6.3 Summary

SAP Ariba Supplier Information and SAP Ariba Supplier Performance Management combined form the SAP Ariba SIPM solution outlined in this chapter. You may choose to implement one or the other, depending on requirements and priorities. Typically, however, you need to be able to manage your supplier information before you can conduct surveys or report on performance management beyond the basic reports available in system based on objective performance data such as on-time delivery. Running a coherent supplier performance management program usually indicates that a company has a high level of focus on its supply base. SAP Ariba SIPM allows you address both your data management needs, with the supplier helping manage their information for you in SAP Ariba SIM, and the subjective and objective performance measurements via SAP Ariba SPM.

Supplier collaboration is used to establish a real time electronic service between your entire supply base and buyer processes in the SAP Ariba Network, enabling suppliers with outsource-service capabilities and self-service tools to reach their full potential.

7 Supplier Collaboration

As consumer and users, we tap into personal networks like Facebook, Twitter, Amazon, and eBay to learn, share, and shop better. Leading companies are managing business networks to more efficiently engage with their trading partners. The SAP Ariba Network is SAP Ariba's business network solution addressing this need.

In this chapter, you will see the manner in which the supplier enablement process works and the tools and insight required for a smooth transition into the SAP Ariba Network. While you are probably familiar with the general supplier enablement steps, this chapter will provide you with an understanding of supplier onboarding, required permissions in the application, enablement process, portal and task configuration, supplier monitoring, and reporting.

7.1 The SAP Ariba Network

With the SAP Ariba Network, SAP Ariba delivers a connection-centric approach where buyers and suppliers can establish trading relationships in the cloud. Today suppliers and buyers can manage all customer relationships through a single unified interface which enables accurate and timely seller and buyer information providing one single company profile in the SAP Ariba Network. This is an ease-of-access profile screen through a unified cloud solution, providing greater efficiency through a many-to-many supplier-to-buyer relationship approach.

SAP Ariba is your place for business commerce, from sourcing to contract management, purchasing or invoicing. SAP Ariba is the single place where you can obtain relevant leads of buyers who are ready to buy; a place for suppliers to get their product catalogs in front of requisitioners and submit proposals to buyers; a place to negotiate contracts and perform collaborative redlining, receive orders, and submit invoices. The SAP Ariba Network is not a private network for just one customer and one supplier, but for multiple customers and suppliers, all collaborating on one platform. And this platform for suppliers, called the SAP Ariba Network for sellers, helps sales, marketing, and eCommerce professionals find buyers by putting products and services in front of end users—the hundreds or thousands of employees at each customer who make buying decisions every day. This, in turn, helps suppliers accelerate the sales cycle, and helps close deals faster, leading to improved performance, which results in improved customer retention and suppliers receiving payment faster.

The SAP Ariba Network provides a seller collaboration console as a new way to enhance the seller experience with greater exposure, convenience, and control, in order to "consumerize" business commerce. SAP Ariba brings all aspects of the buyer/seller collaboration under one umbrella. Prior to the introduction of the seller collaboration console, supplier users had multiple IDs to the SAP Ariba Network and separate SAP Ariba profiles. Now, through the seller collaboration console, you can use your SAP Ariba Commerce Cloud user ID and access all your SAP Ariba information and customer relationships in one place, utilizing a shared profile and document repository.

The seller collaboration console includes:

- Centralized administration, a single user ID for all SAP Ariba commerce cloud seller solutions, common terms of use, and a common SAP Ariba cloud profile.
- Leads through SAP Ariba Discovery
- Proposals through SAP Ariba Sourcing
- Contracts through SAP Ariba Contract Manager
- Orders and invoices through SAP Ariba Network.

As a supplier, there are multiple benefits for you to join the network and collaborate with customers. As a large company transacting with other large companies, it will improve your throughput and enable you to be part of your customers' purchase and invoice automation initiatives. As an individual or a smaller company, you will have the ability to transact with the many of the largest companies in the world. There are features and concepts like dynamic discount management, where you are able to gain better insight into the deployment of cash flow. For example, with dynamic discount management in SAP Ariba Discount Professional, you can negotiate early payments through the SAP Ariba Network and avoid taking on external capital to bridge the payment cycles. This in turn enables you to accelerate and buttress your internal investments, thanks to the visibility into cash flow opportunities. The SAP Ariba Network will provide you, as a customer or supplier, with this and many other commercial opportunities, such as participating in sourcing events, contract management life cycles, transacting purchase orders, shipment notifications, invoices and payment statutes.

In the following sections, we will discuss the processes for onboarding suppliers using the SAP Ariba Network, the enablement process required to add suppliers into the SAP Ariba Network in bulk, and how to self-register and become a supplier on the sales side of the SAP Ariba Network.

7.1.1 Onboarding Suppliers

Onboarding suppliers is a customer-oriented initiative, and can be done through an assisted or self-service method. If your company has a large number of suppliers, the recommended onboarding procedure is to use the SAP Ariba Network methodology outlined in this section which details the set of activities that need to be followed. The SAP Ariba Network itself keeps all of you information in one place for easy access, in order to better support the supplier enablement process, and to track and determine where the suppliers are in the enablement process.

First of all, you have to have a required minimal set of permissions to access and perform the supplier enablement activities in your buyer realm.

Permission	Description
Supplier Enablement Program Administrator	This permission includes all the other permissions available for the SAP Ariba Supplier Enablement Automation. Configure SE Automation, upload vendors, start supplier enablement, manage SE tasks, and access the Vendor Data Export reports.
Supplier Enablement Configuration	Allows you to configure supplier invitation letters, tasks ad activities for supplier enablement.

Table 7.1 Permissions Needed for Supplier Enablement

Permission	Description
Supplier Enablement Task Management	Allows you to manage and monitor tasks for supplier enablement and edit vendor details (vendor name, preferred language, email, contact information, address, vendor comments, enablement status)
Supplier Enablement Report Administration	Allows you to access reporting and supplier enablement reports: ▸ Supplier Enablement Task Status ▸ Supplier Enablement Status

Table 7.1 Permissions Needed for Supplier Enablement (Cont.)

After you have assigned the appropriate set of security access displayed in the Table 7.1 to the users administering your SAP Ariba realm, the following lists of activities is what you, as a buyer, have to do to onboard suppliers:

- Assign specific activities to the suppliers
- Evaluate how many suppliers are ready to transact on the SAP Ariba Network
- Identify the suppliers that have not yet taken action on their tasks
- Evaluate overall status of the supplier enablement
- Review preconfigured activities and related tasks
- Configure and customize email notifications sent to supplier
- Setup a supplier information portal with custom specific content
- Upload multiple vendors for supplier enablement
- Group vendors by type of trading document exchange, assign the appropriate predefined activities, and start the enablement
- Gather missing contact information or rectify incorrect contact details online
- Resend failed email or fax trading relationship request letters
- Complete, defer, and track pending tasks
- Review the supplier enablement status
- Rely on system-generated reminders and notifications when a task is overdue
- Access all pending and escalated tasks

7.1.2 Supplier Enablement

Supplier enablement is the process of configuring and enabling an unlimited number of suppliers in the SAP Ariba Network, which enables your organization to transact electronically with those suppliers. The enablement methodology encompasses the design and development of processes, infrastructure and materials necessary to support the enablement, education, testing, and support of suppliers in the SAP Ariba Network. The complete enablement lasts for the life of the contract, and involves SAP Ariba supplier enablement services from an SAP Ariba shared organization designed to execute and support the enablement tasks. The SAP Ariba shared service resources will be deployed based on the project timeline and the execution phases of the program. The key drivers of the deployment are the numbers of countries in scope, the number of languages, the buyer's back office enterprise systems, the type of technical adaptors used and the transaction types:

- Purchase order (SAP ERP to SAP Ariba Network)
- Change order (SAP ERP to SAP Ariba Network)
- Order confirmation/acknowledgement (SAP Ariba Network to SAP ERP)
- Advanced shipping notice (SAP Ariba Network to SAP ERP)
- Invoice (SAP Ariba Network to SAP ERP)
- Invoice status update (SAP ERP to SAP Ariba Network)
- SAP ERP-initiated invoice or CC Invoice (SAP ERP to SAP Ariba Network)
- Payment proposal request (SAP ERP to SAP Ariba Network)
- Pay me now request (SAP Ariba Network to SAP ERP)

The standard method is for buyers to ask their suppliers to join the SAP Ariba Network in order to work together and find mechanisms to work more efficiently and effectively on all the shared aspects of business commerce: from sourcing proposals, contracts, and orders, to invoices and payments, doing so in a way that can save time, reduce error handling, and save money and resources. More than likely, if a supplier is receiving an invoice through the network, they will send the invoice using the same mechanism, and this is the part where the supplier will find more value in the process.

The supplier enablement process, as shown in the Figure 7.1, allows you as a buyer to establish trading relationships with suppliers and configure the necessary information to start transacting electronic documents through the SAP Ariba Network.

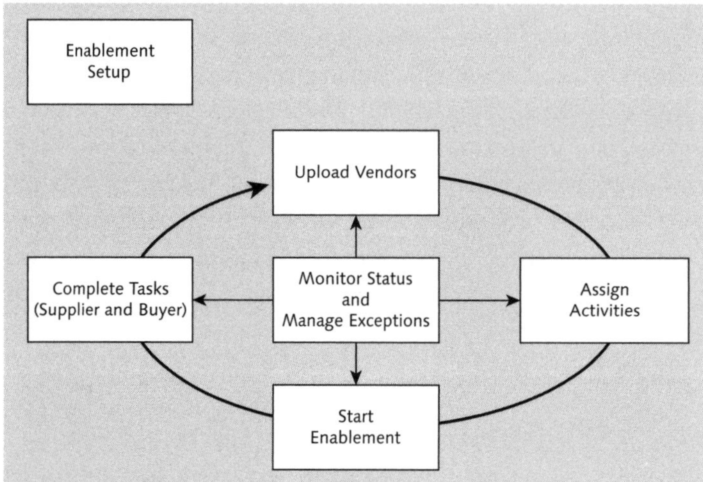

Figure 7.1 Supplier Enablement Process

The SAP Ariba Supplier Enablement Automation process requires three initial steps. First, configure the trading relationship request letter, add your contact information in the contacts screen, and, finally, set up your company's supplier information portal. You can skip the supplier information portal if your company already has a supplier-facing website where you post and communicate instructions to your suppliers.

In the following sections we will cover all the steps necessary for supplier enablement, from configurations and uploading suppliers, to assigning and monitoring tasks, to notifications and reports.

Configurations

The SAP Ariba Supplier Enablement Automation process starts by drafting the trading relationship request letter or quick enablement letter. From the SUPPLIER ENABLEMENT tab, click the CONFIGURE option and the LETTER CONTENT tab as shown in Figure 7.2. From the CONTENT tab you will define the content of the letters to send to the suppliers to be enabled in the SAP Ariba Network.

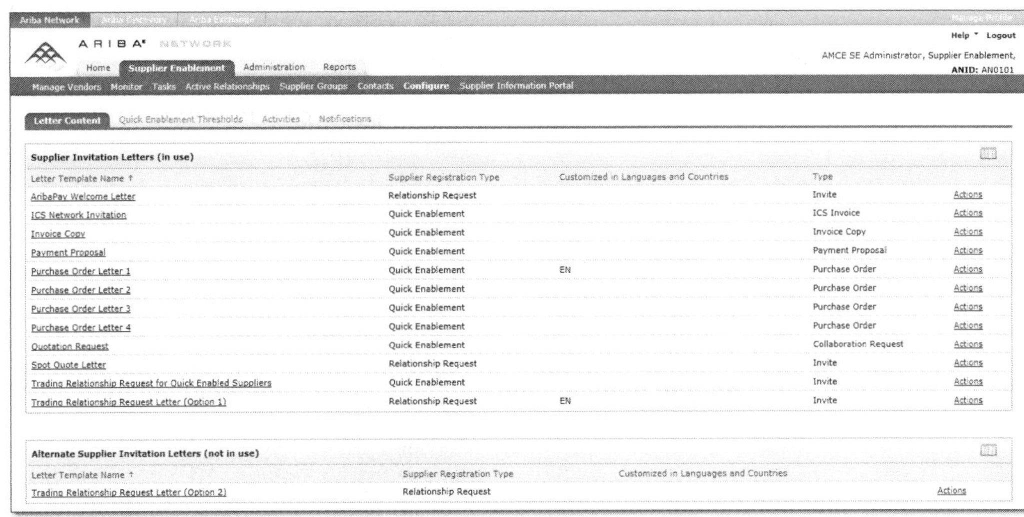

Figure 7.2 Configure Letter Content

When a supplier is invited to join the SAP Ariba Network through quick enablement, or through the SAP Ariba Supplier Enablement Automation process, an invitation letter is sent to them. These letters are called trading relationship request letters and are sent by fax or email. To create or edit a letter, click on the Actions hyperlink associated with the letter you want to modify.

There are different types of trading relationship letters that can be sent to the suppliers. You determine exactly which letter you will need to send based on the business process you are enabling for your organization in the SAP Ariba Network. If you are not sure about which option to choose, you should contact your SAP Ariba customer executive to help you determine how to enact an effective supplier enablement strategy. You can also invite your suppliers to use the SAP Ariba Network by using quick enablement and selecting any of the following: Purchase Order, ICS Invoice (invoices sent from an invoice conversion service provider), Payment Proposal, Request for Quotation, and/or CC Invoice (invoices sent from the SAP Ariba procurement solution or the SAP ERP system).

You have the option of configuring the thresholds for purchase orders and ICS invoice invitations letters sent to quick enabled suppliers. For example, if you set the ICS invoice threshold to five, when SAP Ariba Network receives the fifth invoice from a given supplier, it sends an invitation letter to the supplier. The supplier can use the link in the invitation to register on SAP Ariba Network and view the status of invoices.

After a trading relationship letter is sent to the supplier, your SAP Ariba Network configuration needs to determine the list of tasks you expect the supplier to perform for the business process to be considered fully configured and tested, as displayed in Figure 7.3. For example, to enable the purchase order process, it is recommended to enable the activity PURCHASE ORDER SENT in the SUPPLIER ENABLEMENT ACTIVITIES screen as displayed in Figure 7.3. What this means is that a supplier must complete this task when a purchase order is sent to them via the SAP Ariba Network. This example brings us to another topic: some tasks, like the PURCHASE ORDER SENT, will be automatically completed when the purchase order passes through the SAP Ariba Network, while other tasks will have to be manually completed and closed by the task owner after the requested action has been completed. For example, the manual task BUYING ORGANIZATION IS READY TO SEND ORDERS is required, but can only be completed and closed after you have communicate and coordinated all the required logistics between you and the supplier to send them a purchase order.

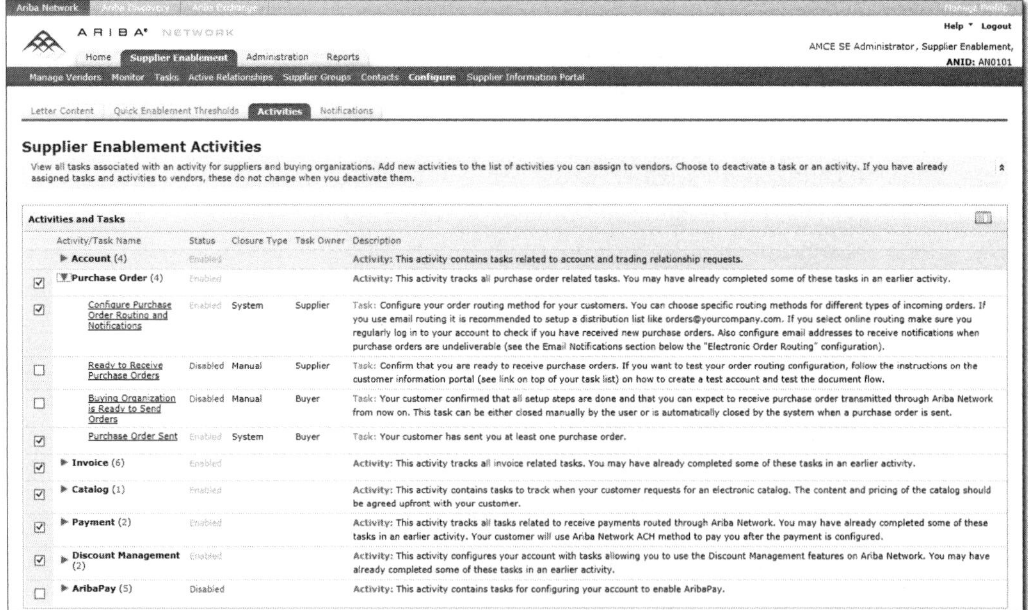

Figure 7.3 Configure Activities/Tasks

You can also choose to send notifications to up to three email addresses if a task is overdue or escalated as displayed in Figure 7.4. If you are enabling a large number of suppliers, you can use the REPORTS tab, or select the TASKS option from the SUPPLIER ENABLEMENT tab, to see all the suppliers with Failed or Overdue statuses.

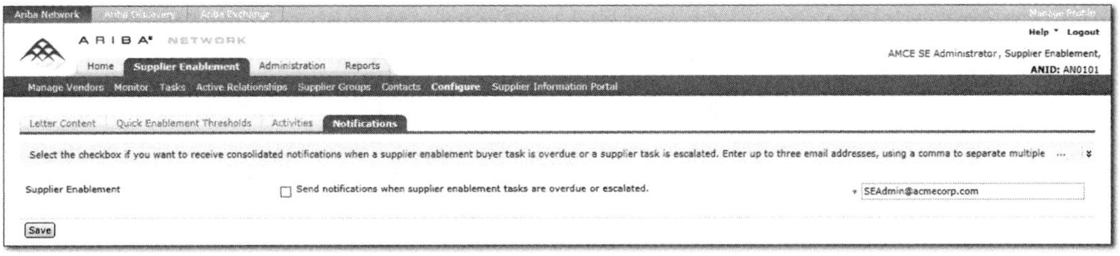

Figure 7.4 Configuration Overdue Notification

The Supplier Information Portal

To allow suppliers easy access to your supplier enablement process, you can create and enable the supplier information portal as shown in Figure 7.5. In the portal, you should upload any PDF, MS Word, Excel or PowerPoint documents that you deem necessary to explain and support your supplier business processes and protocols for transacting with your company via the SAP Ariba Network. For example, you can give suppliers extra information concerning invoices or specific financials processes, or provide the cXML (commerce extensive markup language) or EDI (electronic data interchange) formats necessary to transact with you through the SAP Ariba Network. You can even consider uploading the timeline for the expected testing phase and when the production orders will go out.

The portal is housed in the SAP Ariba Network, and you can access it next to the supplier relationship session. To change its content, it is recommended to send your changes or documents to the SAP Ariba supplier enablement team, and have them make the changes on your behalf (which you can approve before they are published). The portal is accessible by the suppliers, and is for informational purposes only. Suppliers will not need to go through the portal to interact with your organization.

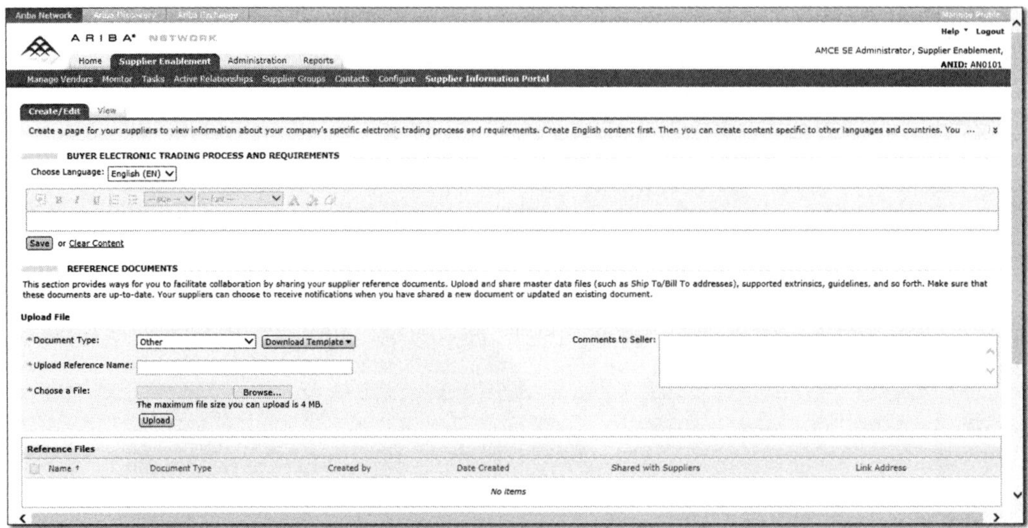

Figure 7.5 Create Supplier Information Portal

Once a supplier receives an invitation to join the SAP Ariba network, a typical question asked by the supplier is "what do I have to do?" Answer: the supplier has to attend supplier summits. Large customers with large supplier bases typically have supplier enablement plans with defined supplier summits.

Tip

The SAP Ariba Network certifications makes the supplier an almost touch-less candidate to start a trading relationship immediately.

Suppliers also have the ability track any new trading relationships with their customers. As a supplier, you must have an SAP Ariba Network supplier account to access the SAP Ariba supplier information portal, or you can use the secure link from the trading relationship request letter. A link to the supplier information portal is available on the following pages:

- Enablement tasks
- Task details
- Customer relationships
- Trading relationship request letter

Upload Suppliers

You can upload a set of new suppliers in the SAP Ariba Network using a CSV or zipped CSV file. The first step is to go to the Manage Vendors section in the Supplier Enablement tab, click on the Upload button, and then Upload Vendors. The Upload Vendors page will appear, and by clicking on Download Template, you will download a copy of the CSV file format you will need to use.

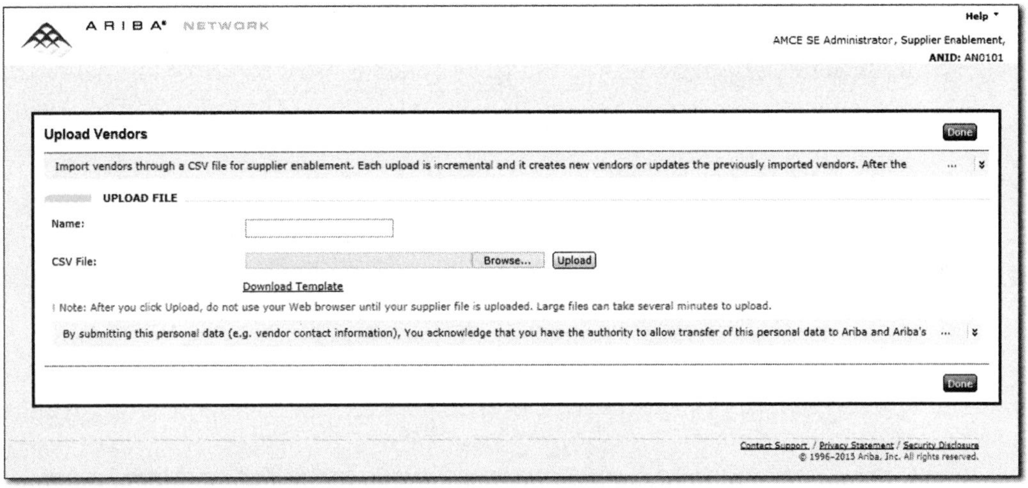

Figure 7.6 Upload Supplier CSV Template

Per Figure 7.6, for uploading suppliers with a CSV file, the following syntax rules apply:

- The file must be saved in a comma-separate values format (CSV file type).
- String values in a CSV file can have commas, but quotes must be used around the string.

The following fields are required in the CSV file:

- Vendor name
- Vendor ID (required only if tax ID is not included in the CSV file)
- Tax ID (required only if vendor ID is not included in the CSV file)
- Vendor city or postal code
- Vendor country code

- Vendor province/state/region (required only if vendor city or vendor postal code is in a U.S. state)
- System ID (required only for multi-ERP buying organizations)
- Buyer ANID (required only for third parties managing supplier enablement on behalf of a buying organization using a provider account

The template also provides basic details on the available fields, and the file must specify the file encoding in the first row.

As a buying organization, you can leave optional fields blank, or just delete the columns you do not use. You can upload up to 100,000 records at a time. Figure 7.7 provides an overview of the upload area.

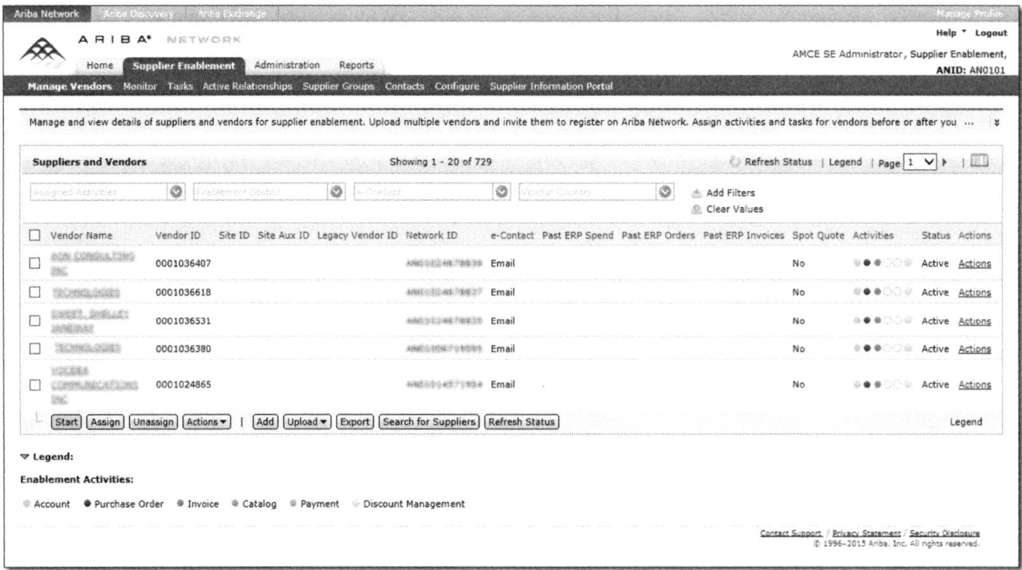

Figure 7.7 Upload Supplier Data

Assign and Monitor Tasks

After the suppliers are loaded, you can assign tasks to them. You will notice that most of the tasks will be automatically assigned by the system based on your previous supplier network configuration activities and tasks that you entered in the screen shown in Figure 7.3.

Figure 7.8 outlines the enablement area for suppliers. Suppliers will appear in the MONITOR tab only in the following cases:

- Case 1: The vendors invited through quick enablement methods (inviting suppliers through purchase orders, payment proposals, carbon copy (CC) invoices, request for quotation (RFQ), or invoices through invoice conversion services) automatically add to the account activity and appear for monitoring in the supplier enablement automation process, under the MONITOR tab.
- Case 2: You can manually add vendors and assign activities. After assigning the vendor, the activity becomes visible in MONITOR tab for tracking.
- Case 3: After completion of the assigned task (task completed) the vendor does not appear in the MONITOR tab, since no tracking activity occurs and the task was completed successfully.

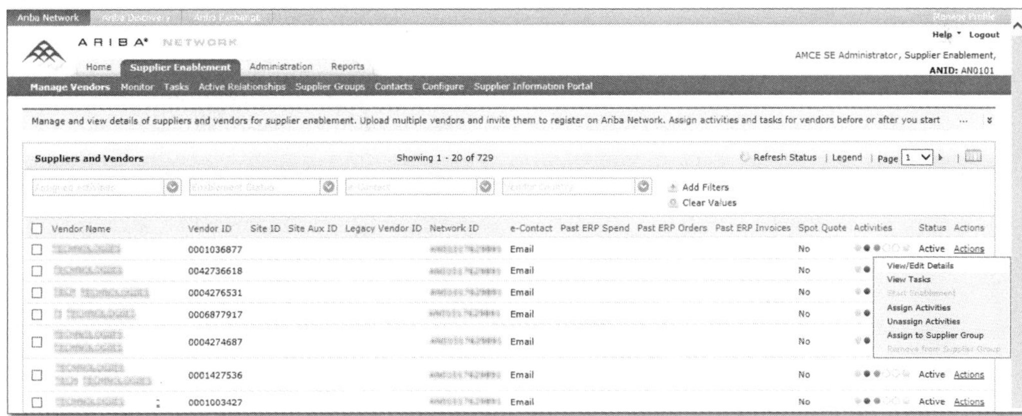

Figure 7.8 Assigning Tasks

The supplier will have a *green status* when their account is active and its tasks are completed on time, even if there are still tasks pending; *yellow status* when there is a task in overdue for completion date; and *red status* when the tasks failed or have been escalated. As seen in Figure 7.9, you can monitor all the tasks for one supplier at once. This is important, as it can help you understand if the process is being held up and if you need to follow up with the supplier.

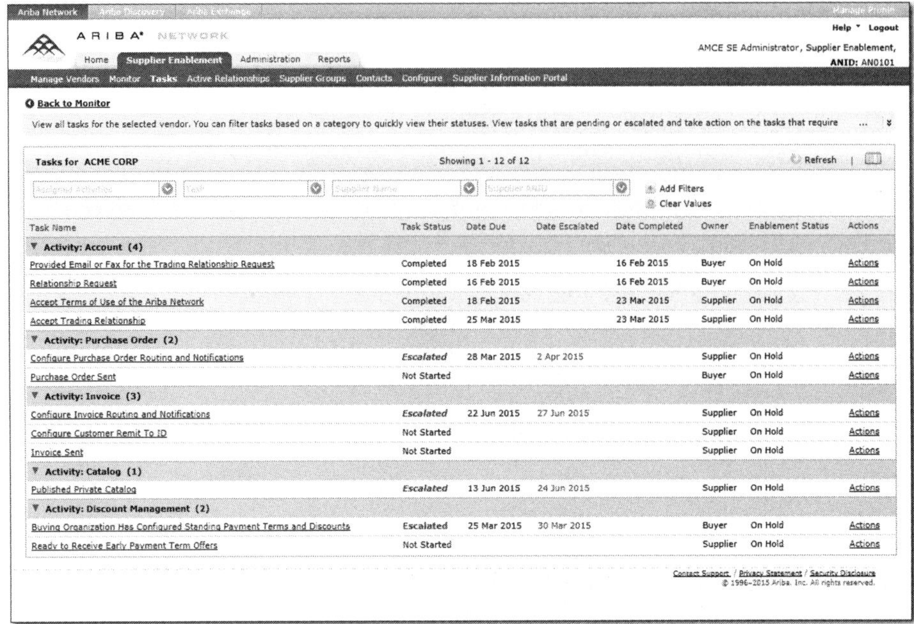

Figure 7.9 Monitor Supplier Tasks

Buyer Tasks

There are also buyer tasks to send a purchase order. If the buyer does not perform specific tasks, then the supplier is unable to complete some of their own tasks. Buyer tasks can be viewed on the TASKS page.

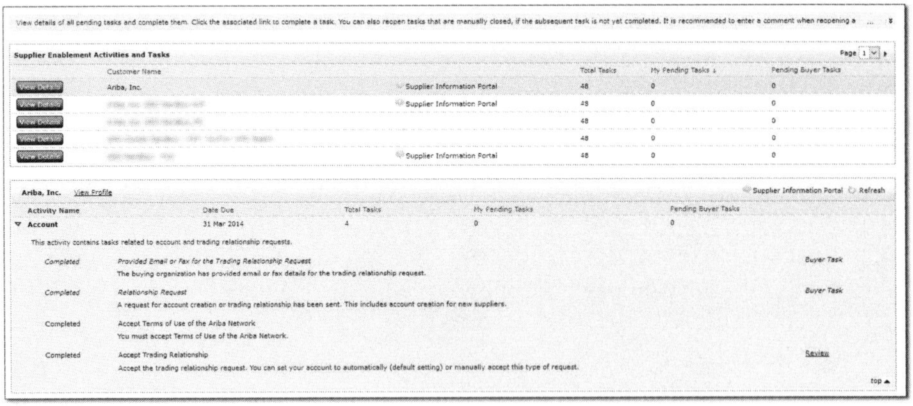

Figure 7.10 Supplier's View

Per Figure 7.10, the number of pending tasks with actions required to complete will be highlighted in red in the SUPPLIER'S VIEW screen.

Monitoring Suppliers

You can track your supplier enablement status for all your vendors by selecting the MONITOR option in the SUPPLIER ENABLEMENT tab. You can view one supplier at a time, or all suppliers at a glance, and retrieve their statuses based on the descriptions depicted at the bottom of the screen. Figure 7.11 shows the monitoring screen.

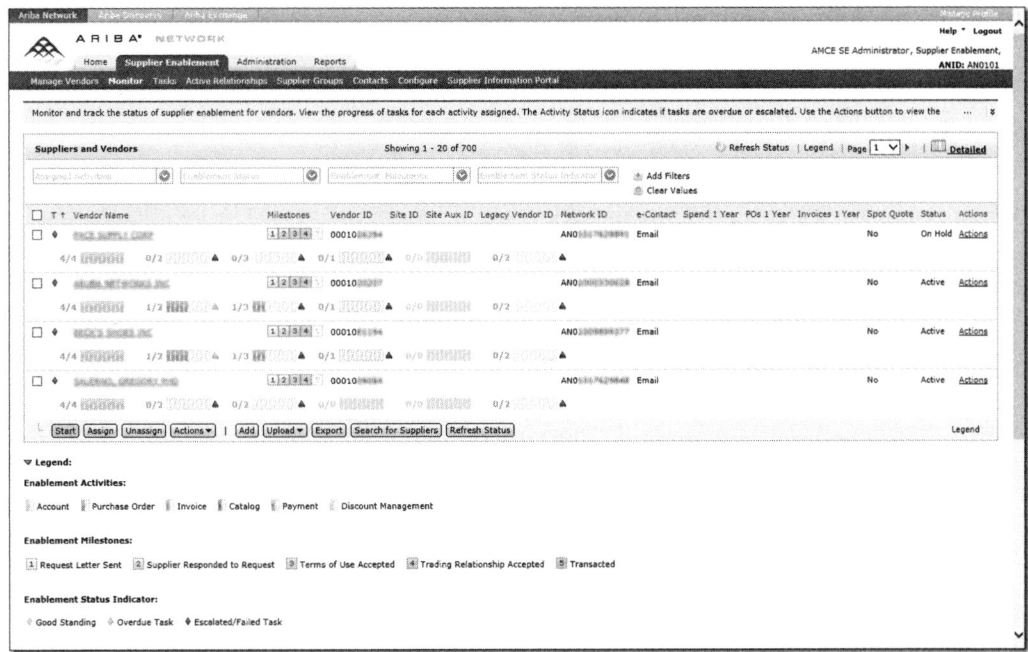

Figure 7.11 Monitor Suppliers

Supplier Enablement Notifications

The buyer will receive notifications when there is a supplier on active supplier enablement status with overdue, escalated, or failed tasks in its profile, and who has not been deferred. To complete your overdue tasks:

- Log in to your SAP Ariba Network buyer account (*http://buyer.ariba.com*).
- Click the SUPPLIER ENABLEMENT tab, and click TASKS.
- Review your task list and complete the overdue and escalated tasks.

System generated reminders will be sent to the supplier account administrator when a task is overdue. Tasks will escalate if the task is not complete after preconfigured timeframes for the task. Reminders can be sent by filtering by PRIVATE SUPPLIERS and clicking SEND INVITATION in the actions pull down menu.

Note that reminders are not sent for failure to accept the Terms of Use.

Supplier Enablement Reports

Three reports are available to provide buyers information regarding supplier enablement. These reports are:

- **Supplier Enablement Status Report**
  This report contains detailed information about suppliers on the SAP Ariba Network assigned to supplier enablement activities. The report includes information on the enablement status, activity status, supplier enablement attributes like wave, supplier address and the relationship status of the supplier. The report also displays information on suppliers with an "On-Hold" status, and the reason provided for this status change.
- **Supplier Enablement Task Status Report**
  This report contains detailed information about supplier task status. This includes information about the supplier status, vendor details, activities, and tasks and their statuses. This report helps when creating aggregated summary reports about tasks and the overall enablement status.
- **Vendor Data Export Report**
  This report contains all vendor profiles. The profile details also include changes made online to the existing/saved data as per Figure 7.12.

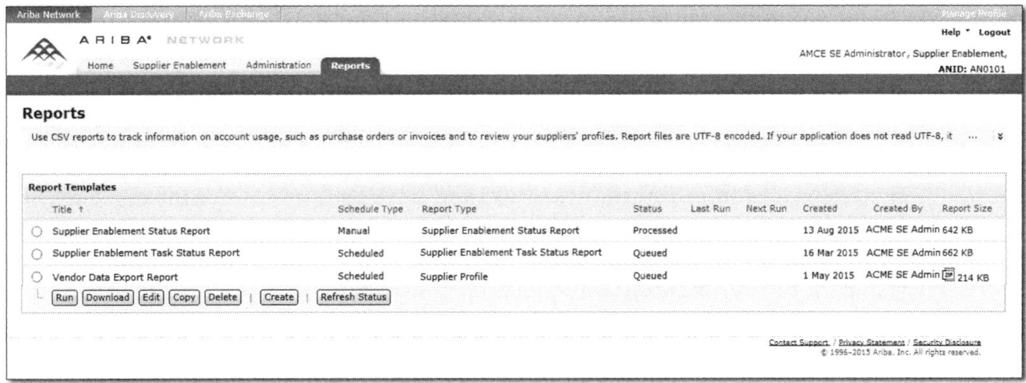

Figure 7.12 Reports

To create a report, log on to your SAP Ariba Network account, click on the REPORTS tab on the HOME dashboard and follow the next steps:

1. Click CREATE.
2. Enter a unique title that helps you and other users easily identify this report from a list.
3. Enter a description.
4. Choose a value from the time zone list.
5. Choose a language.
6. Choose a REPORT TYPE.
7. Click NEXT.
8. Click either MANUAL REPORT or SCHEDULED REPORT. (SAP Ariba Network automatically generates scheduled reports using the frequency that you specify.).

If you choose SCHEDULED REPORT, the SAP Ariba Network refreshes the page and displays the SCHEDULING section. Here, you should:

1. Select a date range.
2. Choose a value from the AUTOMATICALLY RUN list to set the report generation frequency.
3. Enter up to three email addresses, each separated by single comma.
4. SAP Ariba Network sends a notification to these addresses when the report status is "Processed."

5. Click NEXT.
6. Select the parameters for the report.
7. Click SUBMIT.

The SAP Ariba Network saves the created manual report on the REPORTS tab for you to run at your convenience. To run a previously created manual report, follow these instructions:

1. Log on to your account at *http://buyer.ariba.com*.
2. Click the REPORTS tab on the HOME dashboard.
3. You can view and download the report when it has a status of "Processed."
4. To view and download the report, select the report template and click DOWNLOAD.
5. Click on OPEN. Your browser starts Microsoft Excel and displays the report. Save this report. Doing so saves the file to your hard disk.

7.1.3 Supplier Integration

The integration design is something that starts right after the project kickoff with the requirements gathering workbook. Here, SAP Ariba or the consulting partners look to retrieve as much information as possible in order to blueprint what the network-side is going to entail, in order to leverage that information and use it as the road map for building out the guides and configurations. These guides will teach suppliers how to setup their accounts on their network. This includes the EDI and cXML specifications detailing the technical requirement the suppliers will need to use to send you your company's specific required data through the network.

The supplier network ID is an important component, because it is automatically created by SAP Ariba, either when the supplier self-registers or when the supplier information is loaded from SAP ERP. The supplier network ID serves as the conduit between the SAP Ariba Network and SAP ERP. Therefore, to determine the correct approach, the main point is to understand is if SAP ERP will update SAP Ariba, or if SAP Ariba will update SAP ERP: the supplier must have the freedom to update its profile information in the SAP Ariba Network, your company must be able to update the vendor master records in SAP ERP, and both records will need to be aligned.

At this point, is recommended to work with the SAP Ariba supplier enablement lead or the SAP Ariba supplier integration lead to understand the approach and the data flow between all applications before you start preparing any data. Something to keep in mind is that your existing SAP ERP vendor maintenance does not go away, and usually continues to be updated through your existing vendor management process.

The remittance information is another very critical component in most integrations. When the invoicing component is enabled, the remittance becomes a cornerstone and one of the most important components of the invoicing process. All invoices should have banking information, and it is in fact standard for many suppliers to have their banking information on the invoice. Banking information becomes essential to speeding up and streamlining the payment process: having accurate banking information is not only critical, but it will save you a lot of process time. Instead of waiting for an invoice exception to be generated due to an incorrect remittance, you should look ahead and validate the banking information by matching the supplier's banking information with the information you have in SAP ERP, ideally before the invoice arrives in the SAP Ariba Network. Even if all of the information cannot be validated or matched, it is a good approach to validate banking information before an invoice is processed in the SAP Ariba Network.

When SAP Ariba downstream solutions are enabled, the supplier's banking information does not always contain the remittance information, but you can require the supplier to submit a remittance ID to ensure that this information is up-to-date. A remittance ID on the invoice allows you to verify the address and that it returns to the supplier. In order to determine which location to send the payment to, some customers use the vendor ID, the company code, purchasing organization, business unit and several other descriptions to perform a match back in SAP ERP. In this case, SAP Ariba will not have to capture and/or determine the remittance on the network because it will take place through SAP ERP.

The integration part of the deployment is where you connect your SAP ERP system to the SAP Ariba Network using middleware or a communication mechanism that can utilize cXML over standard HTTPs post, single sign on, or a reply response communication. You can be a buyer in the SAP Ariba Network, and the network will allow you to have many supplier relationships. SAP's native integration solutions, as shown in Figure 7.13, include SAP NetWeaver or SAP Business Suite Add-On, which will allow communication to take place via cXML.

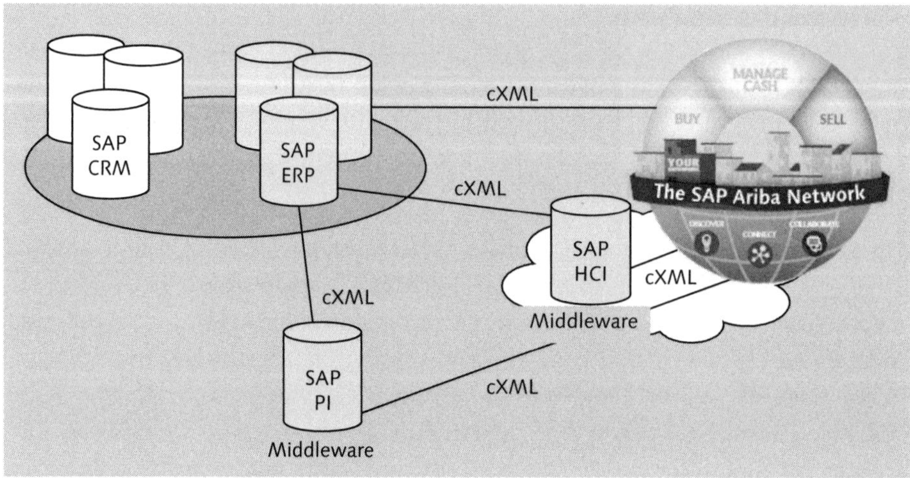

Figure 7.13 SAP Ariba Network Integration for SAP

On the sales side, the supplier can specify how they want to receive transactions via a specific order routing method: cXML, EDI, inbox, fax, email, or using the SAP Ariba Network interface to create manual invoices.

Something important is to determine what, how, and when you want to communicate between SAP ERP and the SAP Ariba Network. All information will be captured during the requirements gathering sessions, utilizing the supplier enablement transactional requirement workbook, where the SAP Ariba team will tell you how the integration works and the different permutations and possible scenarios that can be managed by the integration. The integration team will provide you with the standard mappings for the integrations, have several mapping sessions, and review the cXML, the files and the data.

The integration process will have the following approach:

- Utilize the enablement workbook to document transaction enablement requirements
- Complete requirements gathering questionnaire
- The workbook will be a living document throughout project
- Working sessions/discussions to understand and document transaction enablement and supplier enablement requirements

- Provides opportunity to discuss implications of selecting certain configurations
- Document-specific questions, concerns, and follow-ups
- Gather information needed to build supplier education materials and cXML/EDI technical specifications
- Understand any customization requirements, etc.

The enablement workbook will have the following main sections:

- Project objectives
- Supplier registrations
- Communication/education/support
- Testing
- PO requirements
- Invoice requirements
- Supplier country-based invoice rules
- Extrinsics
- Supplier groups

The more technical your supplier gatherings are, and the more granular you get, the less reworking you will have to do. It is important to always have someone technical from your integration team engaged to help you understand how the two systems communicate, and to start the mapping and documentation. These types of sessions are very technical.

7.1.4 Becoming a Supplier on the Sales Side of the SAP Ariba Network

The SAP Ariba Network delivers the ability for sellers to connect and collaborate electronically with their customers, helping them optimize their business processes and collaborate effectively with their customers. Benefits include:

- **Simplified usability**
  The buyer profile visibility allows for better alignment and status feedback during the spot quote process and improved password reset capability for occasional users.

- **Business collaboration and growth**
  Align with your customers' business requirements better with new extended buyer profiles; enabling of multiple buyer sold-to and bill-to addresses; and comparisons between business configurations of different buyers.
- **Ordering, invoicing, and payment enhancements**
  Start invoice creation by flipping a ship notice or a goods receipt into an invoice. Based on your customer's use of the SAP Ariba Network capabilities, goods scheduling information can now be made available to you in the SAP Ariba Network.

> **Tip**
>
> By obtaining the appropriate SAP Ariba certifications, you can become a more attractive supplier to be part of the customer's supply chain.

- **Globalization**
  New business rules to support tax invoicing requirements in Mexico, Chile, Colombia, Brazil, and France to drive comprehensive compliance.

> **Tip**
>
> The customer can segregate and filter suppliers by location, region, and country. Be sure your information is as up-to-date as possible prior to beginning these steps.

- **Supplier fees**
  Suppliers can start with a free standard supplier subscription and pay fees once the eCommerce business has grown to a certain level, or they can determine the type of SAP Ariba supplier membership program (SMP) suitable for your organization. To determine if you have to pay any fees based on the anticipated transaction level, and to compare the costs to the benefits, the SAP Ariba Network has a seller value calculator (see Figure 7.14).

> **Tip**
>
> It is critical to have your remittance information on-hand, and the best way to accomplish this is by having your SAP Ariba supplier network profile and customer supplemental profile updated.

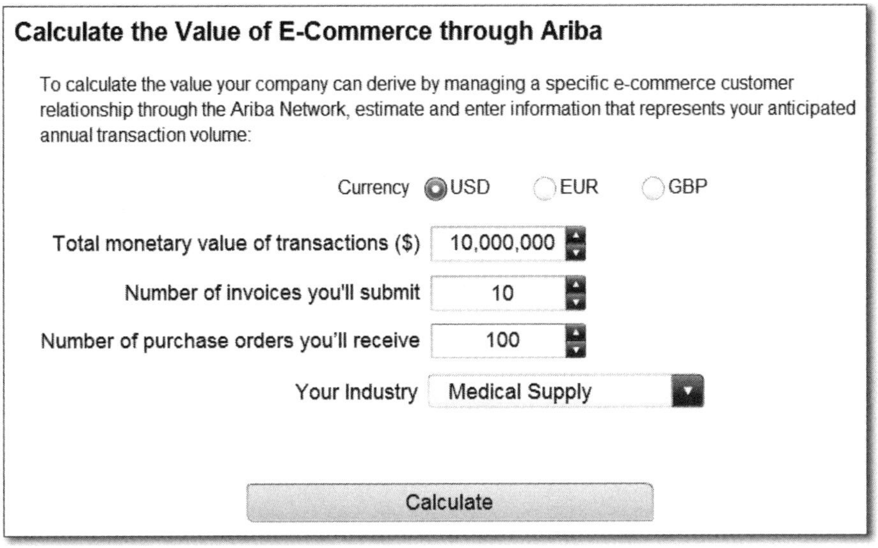

Calculate the Value of E-Commerce through Ariba

To calculate the value your company can derive by managing a specific e-commerce customer relationship through the Ariba Network, estimate and enter information that represents your anticipated annual transaction volume:

Currency USD EUR GBP

Total monetary value of transactions ($) 10,000,000

Number of invoices you'll submit 10

Number of purchase orders you'll receive 100

Your Industry Medical Supply

Calculate

Figure 7.14 Seller Value Calculator

The seller value calculator in Figure 7.15 estimates the benefits of doing business with the customer through the SAP Ariba Network with three components:

1. **Bottom-line benefits for sellers**
   Most of the benefits center on reductions in processing costs. Through automation, you can more efficiently respond to purchase orders and submit invoices minimizing lost and mishandled documents. When you provide a catalog or have electronic transactions with your customer via the SAP Ariba Network, the orders, shipment notifications, confirmations and invoices are more accurate and paid for on time, which helps reduce your days sales outstanding (DSO) and improve your capital position.
2. **Top-line benefits**
   Through network connections and automation, you boost sales by making it easier for customers to routinely buy from you. This helps the customer with compliance and accommodates their eCommerce needs, increasing the likelihood they will stick with you.
3. **Additional benefits**
   Your SAP Ariba subscription includes value-added features designed to give you an even better eCommerce experience. For example, licensing, data services, and sales and marketing activities. Figure 7.15 outlines further benefits.

Supplier costs are made up of two components: a subscription fee and network transaction service fees.

At any point, you can email and discuss your results with an SAP Ariba Network specialist at *commerceassistance@ariba.com*.

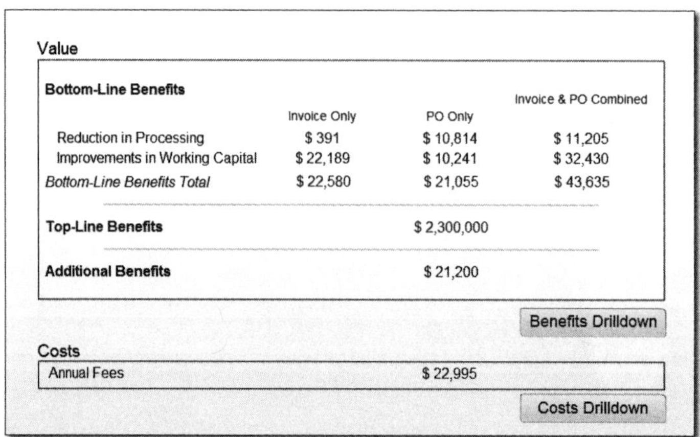

Figure 7.15 Seller Value Calculator Benefits and Cost

To configure an account, you just need to follow a few simple. First, go to *http://supplier.ariba.com*. SAP Ariba P2P also has the remittance update transaction where the SAP ERP can update the SAP Ariba Network and SAP Ariba P2P on the status of scheduled payments. This transaction allows SAP ERP to send the payment details (ACH confirmation, or check details) to the SAP Ariba Network and SAP Ariba P2P, so that suppliers and buyer users can see which payments have been made without having to log into SAP ERP. This transaction also allows you to send updates saying that a payment was cancelled or rejected in SAP ERP.

Other onboarding steps and tools include supplier registration in the SAP Ariba Network and profile updates to allow you to establish a trading relationship with the buyers. Once registered, you can sign in and determine the type of goods and services your company provides.

7.2 Implementing the SAP Ariba Network

To implement the SAP Ariba Supplier Enablement Automation process for a large number of suppliers, you will need the SAP Ariba supplier enablement team. You will also need to be familiar with the SAP Ariba supplier enablement methodology in order to understand the resources, roles, phases and timelines for a successful enablement. It is important to reinforce the concept of supplier enablement and the fact that it is always a function of the business, and not just a single project. Supplier enablement is not an activity that will take a quick couple of months to implement; this is a program that you want to see as ongoing, ensuring your supply chain needs are satisfied and that you are implementing best network practices. As you learn from the process, you will continue improving going forward. Per Figure 7.16, the implementation process breaks down into four chevrons with a couple of interim main phases: strategy, design and build, supplier onboarding, and network growth.

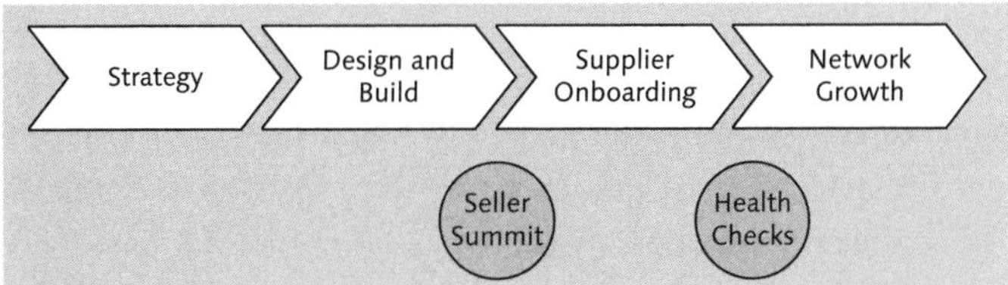

Figure 7.16 Supplier Enablement Four-Phase Process

To implement the SAP Ariba Network you will need the following roles:

- The SAP Ariba supplier network lead
- The catalog enablement lead
- The necessary additional project roles and responsibilities if you are implementing SAP Ariba Invoice Management, SAP Ariba Discount Management, or SAP Ariba Payment Management (see Chapter 5 for more details).

In addition to completing the four main phases shown in Figure 7.16, you will also need to consider the resources necessary for the project, your strategy for change management, and your long-term strategy for supplier enablement.

7.2.1 Strategy

The strategy phase is where you analyze the way things stand right now with your supplier base and company spend data, in order to develop the flight plan and have a final product to move forward with. This phase is where the flight plan and enablement prioritizations will take place. The purpose at this stage is to have obtain visibility and gain the insight on where the spend and the volume resides right now, from the invoice and purchase order standpoint, and which suppliers it would be more beneficial to enable with purchase and invoice automation, or enable with invoice against contracts catalogs on the SAP Ariba P2P or SAP Ariba Procurement Content fronts.

Normally, depending on your supplier universe, a flight plan can have a two to five year enablement wave plan with a clear set of goals. The final timeframe will depend on how fast you want to go; for each of these waves, we will have a projected timing, starting by sending a trading relationship request out to wave one suppliers up to the go-live, when you start transacting with the supplier.

The following are the roles that will support and meet the business goals and objectives.

- **SAP Ariba roles**
  - SAP Ariba will need to understand your customer objectives, conduct an analysis on your customer spend, rationalizing it by commodity and suppliers and develop a supplier flight plan.
  - Recommend and work with you, prioritizing suppliers based on transactional volumes and values, existing SAP Ariba Network suppliers, and different geographical regions.
- **Customer roles**
  - The customer will provide the list of main commodities being procured by the company and the spend data for the analysis.
  - Review and provide feedback on the flight plan.
  - Provide refreshed and current accounts payables transaction data with supplier rationalization and duplicate filtering for strategy analysis to ensure the correct and active suppliers are targeted, and to avoid unproductive efforts.
  - Ensure that the accounts payables transaction data does not include accounts-related information like salaries and benefits.

7.2.2 Design and Build

After the strategy is set in place, we enter the design and build phase. This is where you get into the requirement gathering workshops and start talking about supplier communications and communication plans, which are on the order of events to bring the supplier to a state of being able to transact. The objective of this phase is to develop the processes, infrastructure, and materials necessary to support the enablement, education, testing and support of suppliers. The following are the roles that the SAP Ariba team and the customer will take on in this phase:

- **SAP Ariba roles**
  - Conduct transaction requirements gathering workshops.
  - Support with supplier communication and education materials.
  - Create education portal infrastructure.
  - Assist with buyer network account configuration.
- **Customer roles**
  - Participate in workshops to identify requirements.
  - Appoint an internal team to own the supplier enablement program.
  - Build the compliance message.
  - Validate supplier communications and education materials.
  - Collect supplier data and provide finalized supplier list.
  - Designate SAP Ariba account administrator.
  - SAP Ariba network account configuration.

The supplier information portal infrastructure and the supplier accounts will need to be configured. Once you have signed off on the business requirements, the SAP Ariba team can go ahead and build all of the required materials. Input from the customer during this time ensures the SAP Ariba team has the appropriate counterparts and the right resources working with them. This is not only for supplier enablement, but for all other SAP Ariba solutions currently in motion, in order to ensure that your attention and focus is on areas where it needs to be.

The next step is to build a compliance message. A compliance message is used for your internal stakeholders and customers, as well as external suppliers. Part of the change management, discussed in greater detail in Section 7.2.6, centers on establishing the expectations and usage of the tool. At this point, is important to think about supplier compliance, because you need to set expectations with the supplier for a successful program. It should be an initiative that is pushed through the customer team with the importance of the business factors supporting it. You need the supplier to know that this is a strategic move for both companies, that it is the new direction the business is going in, and that any deviation can decrement the business improvements for both companies. It is critical to have a candid and a gentle means of preparing this message to the suppliers. Normally, a stronger business compliance message directly correlates to a more successful campaign.

It is important to give a clear direction, communication, and expectations. SAP Ariba will provide for communications. It all starts with the requirements gathering on the supplier side: when you are blueprinting the application for the purchase order or invoice automation, or catalogs in SAP Ariba P2P or SAP APC and how the system, as well as the automation part of it, is going to work, you will want to reflect the same thing on the network. The suppliers have access to see what the rules are, and you will also communicate these rules during the supplier summits. Suppliers can also go into their accounts and see what the buyer transaction rules are (for example, are we allowing the sending of a non-PO invoice, etc.). The network side is not as complex as the application side, but the same principles apply.

SAP Ariba follows the same communication and education plan on every deployment, coordinating the critical same high level course of events. The project notification letter is the first message going out to suppliers from the customer team. This is a message for the supplier introducing the customer campaign, letting them know what your business objectives are, and what to expect in the steps ahead. The supplier will receive an email from SAP Ariba with information and instructions. You want to make sure that this email also includes the compliance message. The supplier should be well aware of the program and be ready to receive the letter from SAP Ariba, preventing the dreaded question of "who are you" when a supplier enablement specialist from SAP Ariba calls. The purpose of the project notification is to introduce the initiative more than it is to detail the pricing aspect of it. At this point, you are introducing the supplier to the supplier enablement process, instructing them to follow simple links to understand more about the SAP Ariba process, and your own process.

Both the customer and SAP Ariba and consulting partner teams will host a supplier pre-enablement summit meeting. The summit content is fully customizable to communicate your initiative to your suppliers. The summit's purpose is to align your expectations with the suppliers and present the mutual benefits for both companies. For example, the supplier will be able to speed up payment process by submitting their invoices faster, or eliminating paper and manual errors by sending their documents over the network. Normally the suppliers that are already in the SAP Ariba Network will want you to be in the SAP Ariba Network, as they do not want to support multiple communication methods.

Again, at this point the supplier information portal and education materials will need to be ready. The supplier information portal is an SAP Ariba Network-hosted, customer-managed webpage, specifically dedicated to sharing customer-specific information. It is the primary supplier self-service method for communicating documents and training materials such as the account configuration guide, PO management guide, invoicing guide, EDI guidelines, cXML guidelines, CIF catalog training guide, etc.

All education materials are created after SAP Ariba Network requirements have been gathered. These education materials need to provide links to other documentation (e.g., SAP Ariba standard documentation/help, supplier membership page).

7.2.3 Supplier Onboarding

The objective of the supplier onboarding phase is to enable suppliers on the SAP Ariba Network to transact electronically through three different steps: registration, education, and testing. You will also need to implement health checks with regular project reviews, weekly status calls, process evaluations, and strategy refreshes, along with customer education. The final step during this phase will be supplier deployment.

Registration

During registration, you should determine your communication protocol, and remember that when you receive a purchase order, you are receiving a financially committed document. The following are the roles for this step:

- **SAP Ariba responsibilities**
  - Obtain finalized supplier list from customer in vendor upload file.
  - Upload vendor file to the SAP Ariba Network.
  - Create SAP Ariba Network accounts by sending relationship request letters.
  - Assign supplier enablement tasks.
  - Track supplier registration status/task completion.

  - Provide status reports.
- **Customer responsibilities**
  - Provide finalized list of suppliers with required data in the vendor upload file.
  - Follow-up on supplier escalations for:
    - Invalid supplier data
    - Non-responsive suppliers
    - Non-compliant suppliers

Education

During the education step, the objective is to provide educational materials and communicate business requirements to suppliers. The roles in the step are:

- **SAP Ariba roles**
  - Supplier education materials available (content on supplier portal)
  - Conduct seller summit
  - Record webinars to be posted on portal for supplier viewing
  - Supplier follow-up
- **Customer roles**
  - Participate in supplier education meetings
  - Review and approve supplier education material content
  - Drive compliance messaging with suppliers, as well as within the organization

Testing

The objective of testing is to confirm connectivity and the successful transmission of business documents with a representative subset of suppliers participating in customer testing sessions. The roles during this step are:

- **SAP Ariba roles**
  - Conduct end-to-end testing with a pilot group of suppliers
  - Provide testing support to assist with pilot, integrated, and punchout catalog suppliers testing

- **Customer roles**
  - Determine an end-to-end testing plan
  - Create/validate test transactions to suppliers

Supplier Deployment

During supplier deployment, the following areas are covered;

1. Migration of all production-ready suppliers to the production environment.
2. Communicate go-live to suppliers and internally within the organization. This is a communication to the suppliers that will go out a week or two before the go-live, when the production orders can be expected.
3. Post go-live production monitoring and support.

7.2.4 Network Growth

Once the SAP Ariba solution is live and running, is important to transition to a network growth team to continue with supplier registration, education, and testing. The roles during this step are:

- **SAP Ariba roles**
  - Provide SE customer playbook
  - Continuous supplier registration, education and testing support
  - Strategy refresh support
  - Network utilization assessment
  - Successful business case attainment
  - Monitor suppliers for transactions
  - Report progress and associated actions
- **Customer roles**
  - Continuous involvement in supplier registration, education and testing
  - Maintain revisions of supplier education and communication materials
  - Drive supplier compliance
  - Maintain internal and external change management

7.2.5 Resources

In terms of the human resources for the project, SAP Ariba will normally provide you with a program manager for the solution being deployed, as well as a customer executive. Additionally, you will have the supplier enablement team, which itself will have a supplier enablement lead and a network growth manager working will multiple supplier managers (the supplier integration lead, an electronic supplier integration manager and a catalog knowledge expert) behind the scenes.

Your organization will also require a program sponsor, a finance, procurement and legal subject matter expert to provide ad hoc support, one or two supplier enablement leads, an IT team to work on the integrations, a change management lead, an SAP Ariba Network account administrator, a catalog knowledge expert and a functional team. All the involvement needed from the IT team and change management is variable, depending on the complexity of the rollout plan for the program, the number of countries in scope, the purchase order or invoice automation, and also how employees are there to train. The SAP Ariba Network account administrator and catalog knowledge expert will transition into ad hoc support after the SAP Ariba solution starts going live. The typical timeline for a supplier enablement project is 12–16 weeks from inception to the first wave of onboarding.

7.2.6 Change Management

The planning and execution of several change management activities are need to support the supplier enablement process to increase awareness and to increase the probability of a successful migration path and adoption of the SAP Ariba Network. Supplier enablement requires a considerable initial amount of interaction and communication in support of the implementation of new technology and processes. It is ideal to start planning the change management activities as soon as the scope of the supplier enablement gets determined in the supplier wave plan. The following steps should be taken to ensure a smooth change management for your project:

- Schedule SAP Ariba Network overview for stakeholders to increase awareness of enablement and benefits of the network.
- Ensure executive support of the compliance requirements.

- All divisions/business units signoff on suppliers targeted for enablement.
- Create memo for spend owners with instructions/FAQs to communicate with suppliers in advance of go-live.
- Plan for a solid migration path, which will result in higher compliance from suppliers.
- Ensure that suppliers hear the same message from all company personnel.
- Ensure all stakeholders are aware of what is going on with the project and what is expected from suppliers (buyers, commodity managers, business power users, etc.) IT and supplier enablement plans need to be aligned.
- Plan to reduce delays:
  - Delays related to integration with SAP Enterprise Resource Planning (ERP) are common on SAP Ariba Network projects—proper IT sponsorship will help improve priorities around delays.
  - Aligned project plans also help reduce the impact of IT delays.
  - Be aware that the more integrations needed, the higher the likelihood of IT delays.
- Understand the SAP ERP release schedule to avoid any potential downtime or financial freeze that can affect the enablement activities.
- Be confident that you can answer the following questions:
  - Is the IT work appropriately staffed and scheduled?
  - Are there key dates by which certain milestones need to be completed?
  - Is there a holiday "code freeze" policy that may impact end-of-year enablement efforts?

Supplier education depends on completed requirements and any network customizations; supplier testing depends on technology and test environment availability.

Depending on the approach, allocate a minimum of a part time resource for every 500 suppliers during the data collection time period, which can last for one to three months, depending on the quality of your supplier profile data. The main factors to consider are:

- Supplier profile data does not exist in any one system, and can be found in the contact folders for the procurement buyers. This data is needed from order processing and invoice processing.
- Data collection takes time and effort, which are not always available from understaffed procurement departments. Dedicated resources may be needed. For example, you may need to hire temporary staff.
- Clean supplier data is essential. You will need to clean up vendor record database, DUNS number, confirm supplier contact info (name, address, email, and fax), etc.

Tip

Start early in your efforts to clean up supplier records!

7.2.7 Customer Long-Term Supplier Enablement Program

For your long term supplier enable program, SAP Ariba recommends that you consider the following key elements:

- How will this be supported long term (post-SAP Ariba SOW)?
- What resources are needed to support this process?
- How will roles within our organization change?
- Will there be adequate resource allocation and bandwidth?
- Who will own the program?
- Do we have a sustainable training plan? Do we have program/process experts?
- What is our plan for internal change management and education across departments?
- What is our compliance plan?
- What will the escalation path be for non-compliant suppliers?
- How will we track and manage internal compliance?
- Have we ensured that proper reporting is in place for tracking an end-to-end process?
- Have we created metrics tracking for program success, such as a score card? Have we created an escalation plan for non-compliant suppliers to appropriate staff and define actions needed?

7.3 Summary

In this chapter we introduced you to the SAP Ariba Network—a 21st-century tool for supplier collaboration. SAP Ariba provides options for moving suppliers to an electronic process by leveraging proven methodologies either through a services team to handle the enablement for you or through the self-service tool. These tools empower you to quickly target and enroll suppliers to support your procurement business objectives, ensuring an effective and efficient trading partner collaboration.

This chapter showcases a major analysis area for procurement—Spend Analysis. SAP Ariba Spend Visibility combines supplier data with category and invoice-based spending to build a comprehensive view of your procurement spending.

8 Spend Analysis

The most important strategic area of procurement is analysis. Once the systems to control procurement and underpin all of the processes with data streams are in place, the resulting data streams need to be analyzed. An organization that constantly analyzes its procurement activities will grow smarter with each cycle, create more savings and competitive opportunities, and ultimately increase both bottom and top line revenue: bottom line revenue increases by saving the organization more money, and top line revenue increases by helping identify growth opportunities with a company's key suppliers. To paraphrase Socrates, an unexamined procurement operation is not worth running.

This chapter outlines SAP Ariba Spend Visibility as a solution and shows how to implement it to get a closer look at procurement operations at large and learn where to make changes. Depending on the SAP Ariba solutions you have implemented, you may also run reports on other areas of procurement, such as sourcing events, contracts, purchase orders, requisitions, and suppliers. However, SAP Ariba Spend Visibility, as well SAP Ariba Supplier Information and Performance Management (discussed in Chapter 6 of this book) are the main reporting areas that feature their own focused solution.

8.1 Introduction to SAP Ariba Spend Visibility

SAP Ariba Spend Visibility allows you to extract, classify, and enrich spending data from SAP and other ERP providers, procurement cards, and legacy systems, and then to analyze it using dashboards, risk intelligence, compliance/spend reporting, and benchmarking. There are a couple of different versions and approaches to SAP Ariba Spend Visibility, depending on your data analysis needs and landscape. SAP Ariba Spend Visibility Basic and SAP Ariba Spend Visibility Professional are the two main solutions in this area. In short, Spend Analysis is the general product area, and SAP Ariba Spend Visibility (both Basic and Professional) are the reporting tools that deliver a complete analytics projects, including project management and data enrichment. SAP Ariba Spend Visibility Basic for SAP Spend Performance Management is primarily intended for use with SAP's Spend Performance Management solution and with SAP environments in general, while SAP Ariba Spend Visibility Basic is the non-SAP focused version of this solution. SAP Ariba Spend Visibility Professional is an augmented solution to the Basic versions.

The core functionality of SAP Ariba Spend Visibility Basic for SAP Spend Performance Management includes multiple engines to distill the data into actionable form:

- **Data validation engine**
  SAP Ariba Spend Visibility data file uploading includes automatic data validation, designed to identify formatting errors in the files, as well as reports detailing errors occurring during the data load.
- **Supplier matching engine**
  A supplier engine matches supplier records in your data against SAP Ariba's more than 200-million-record supplier database and enriches validated suppliers for parentage and other information, according to your service level agreement.
- **Rationalization engine**
  A rationalization engine uses learned models, text reading, and linguistic analysis of invoices, general ledgers, and supplier information to rationalize transactions.
- **Business rule engine**
  A business rule engine invokes business rules or mappings specific to your company to categorize transactions.
- **Inference engine**
  An inference engine uses weighted triangulation and multi-vector inference of potential outcomes of classifications to ensure the highest reliability of outcome.

- **Machine learning engine**
  A machine learning engine uses decision trees, classification by example, Bayesian algorithms, and joint field hybrid methods using historically categorized transactions and export refinement to predict classification outcomes.

If you spot commodity classification errors in the data, you can submit those errors via change request workflow for correction. Approved requests are exported and included in the next enrichment cycle. Depending on the service levels defined in the SAP Ariba Spend Visibility deployment description, SAP Ariba will run data enrichment refreshes at given intervals.

Optional features and services include:

- **Custom commodity taxonomies up to six levels**
  This option must be implemented by leveraging SAP Ariba services.
- **Supplier diversity and green reporting**
  This reporting option needs to be enabled by an SAP Ariba representative, and diversity and green data is managed as an SAP Ariba service.
- **Supplier risk and financial data**
  Risk data requires a separate contract with Dun & Bradstreet, an company information provider, which is coordinated with your SAP Ariba representative, whereas your SAP Ariba representative enables financial data directly in SAP Ariba.

SAP Ariba Spend Visibility Professional, on the other hand, includes all of the aforementioned capabilities found in the basic version, as well as a few additional features. One main difference between the Basic and Professional versions of SAP Ariba Spend Visibility is the dashboard, which is exclusively part of the Professional version. This dashboard centralizes the views and reporting in one area, and includes:

- A personal calendar for each user.
- SAP Ariba data, such as to-do lists and document folders, which users can add to their dashboards.
- Company news content. This data can show information from RSS feeds and is configurable by the customer to include news content from their sites.
- Users can create multiple dashboards to cover different areas.

Other differences are found in reporting. SAP Ariba Spend Visibility Professional includes:

- Prepackaged invoice and PO reports.
- Basic supplier financial data.
- Reporting against common commodity benchmark data such as CPI and PPI.
- Custom analytical reporting, including reporting across multiple fact tables and compound reports.
- UNSPSC commodity display in English and up to four different languages.

Each SAP Ariba Spend Visibility subscription includes an SAP Ariba best practice center-managed project, which is, in essence, a coaching engagement that provides recommendations on the technical and functional use of the software. The main difference between Professional and Basic versions is the dashboard provided in Professional, along with augmented reporting services and support included in the Professional version.

8.2 Mining Procurement Operations for Data

In the following sections, we give you an overview of the types of data that SAP Ariba Reporting and Analysis allows you to analyze, the basic facets you should consider focusing your analysis on, and the work areas available for drilling down into data and key reports. Next, we discuss some key reports, along with the areas they can impact. Finally, we cover some key data sources and our options for importing this data into SAP Ariba Spend Visibility.

8.2.1 Data Types

SAP Ariba Spend Visibility provides provide tools that allow you to analyze the following types of data:

- SAP Ariba Spend Visibility invoice and purchase order data. This data may be new, or it may be existing data that has been enriched by SAP Ariba data enrichment with improved supplier and commodity classification.
- SAP Ariba Spend Visibility data also includes common data, such as custom units of measure, currency conversion rates, fiscal hierarchies, taxonomies for commodities and services, diversity certifications, and opportunity search ranges.

- Data from other SAP Ariba spend management solutions such as the SAP Ariba Contract Management, SAP Ariba Sourcing, SAP Ariba Supplier Information Management, and SAP Ariba Supplier Information and Performance Management.
- Custom fact data, which can come from external data sources such as SAP ERP systems, or from SAP Ariba Spend Management solutions.
- Data from other SAP Ariba Spend Management solutions updates through regular, automated data pulls. SAP Ariba Spend Visibility and custom fact data updates through regular data loads.

To make new SAP Ariba Spend Visibility and custom fact data available for reporting and analysis, you perform the following high-level steps:

1. **Acquire data**
   The data may come from data sources such as SAP ERP or other third-party systems, and must be consolidated in data files with the correct format.
2. **Load data**
   After the data is consolidated into data files, designated users add the files to data load operations and schedule those operations to load the data into the data load database schema.
3. **Switch schemas**
   After the data load operation is complete, designated administrative users verify the data and then switch from the data load database schema to the presentation database schema, at which point the data becomes available in reports to all users. Next, an automatic operation that copies the data back from the presentation schema into the data load schema, so that it is ready for the next data load.

8.2.2 SAP Ariba Spend Visibility: Areas for Analysis

Once the data has been loaded and organized, you proceed to analysis. Per Figure 8.1, the main tasks for analysis are: strategic review of categories, direct material order patterns, non-compliant spend (or "maverick" spend), supplier relationship management, and spending by brands. Use these analysis insights can further reduce costs, focus and optimize your supplier base, and understand supplier vulnerabilities and criticalities.

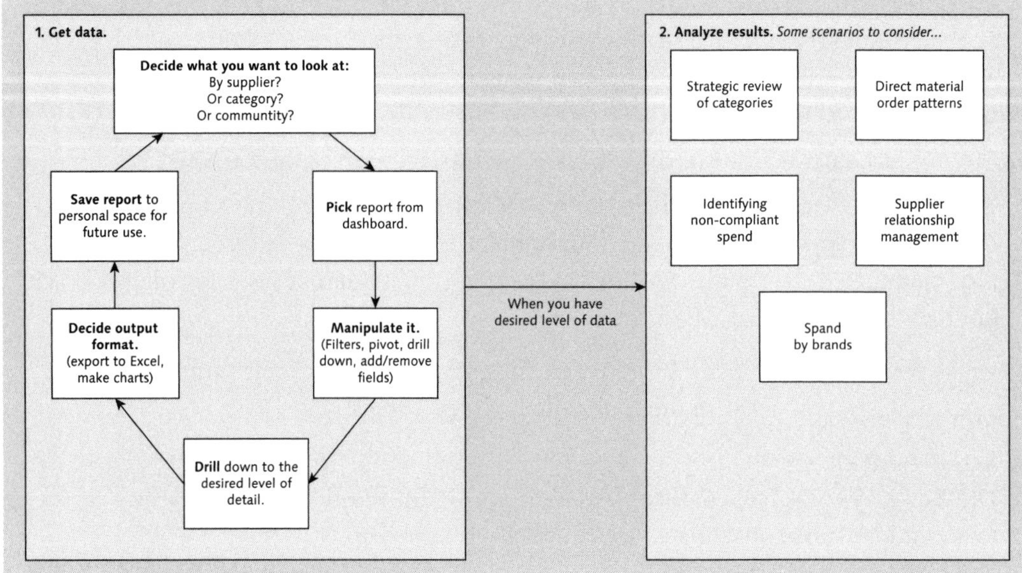

Figure 8.1 SAP Ariba Spend Visibility—Process

Ideally, these insights are funneled back into the SAP Ariba set of solutions (SAP Ariba Sourcing, SAP Ariba P2P, SAP Ariba Invoice Professional, and so forth), to optimize your procurement operations further in system, cycle-by-cycle. For example, if you identify that most non-compliant spend is for items that are not categorized or in the catalogs or contracts available, then adding these to the system and communicating this to the users should significantly improve this area. If you rely on a sole supplier for a key input or category, which puts them in a position to raise prices or impact your supply chain, then efforts should be made to inviting, vetting, and adding similar suppliers to your environment. Similarly, if you have a growing number of suppliers delivering same types of goods and services, standardization and optimization efforts are in order, which help to focus your supply chain on key suppliers, drive up your bargaining power with volume increases, and drive down costs.

8.2.3 Work Areas

SAP Ariba Spend Visibility offers a variety of work areas for drilling down into data and key reports:

- **Ariba SAP Ariba Spend Visibility manager workspace**
  You use the SAP Ariba Spend Visibility manager workspace to manage data related to SAP Ariba Spend Visibility reports. The following authorization groups have access to the manager workspace:
  - Customer administrator (everything except the opportunity search task)
  - SAP Ariba Spend Visibility project manager (everything except the opportunity search task)
  - SAP Ariba Spend Visibility category change request (CCR) reviewer (enrichment change request settings task)
  - SAP Ariba Spend Visibility opportunity analyst (opportunity search task).
- **Source systems**
  A source system represents a distinct data source for your reporting data. Each source system has a source type that defines the format of the data.

  SAP Ariba Spend Visibility project manager group members have access to upload files and load data into all source systems, but members of the SAP Ariba Spend Visibility data file manager group only have access to upload files and load data into their assigned source systems.
- **Import/export star schema**
  You import and export the database star schema in order to synchronize your database with external systems or with the database star schemas in your SAP Ariba solutions.

  Your site has a dedicated database star schema if it includes SAP Ariba Spend Visibility or custom reporting facts.
- **Enrichment data**
  Enrichment data improves commodity and supplier classifications, including a more detailed classification of commodities and services.

  SAP Ariba Spend Visibility project manager group members receive email notifications when users generate enrichment request files, and they can from the site.
- **Data access control**
  Data access rules determine which users are authorized to see specific SAP Ariba Spend Visibility data. You can restrict access to SAP Ariba Spend

Visibility data in reporting facts by writing access control rules based on username or group.

All changes to rules take effect immediately after you import the rules file.

- **Enrichment change request settings**
The feedback loop with SAP Ariba for correcting and adjusting classifications in the data is the enrichment change process. To control access to feedback submission, you use enrichment change request settings to enable or disable enrichment feedback, to manage when newly approved enrichment changes are loaded to the presentation schema, and to manage the current in your site. For example, a user might submit an enrichment change request to correct a report that displays the wrong commodity classification for a particular commodity from a supplier.

  This section also displays all the rules that have been generated by currently submitted enrichment change requests.

- **Manage benchmarking**
SAP Ariba customer support loads benchmarking data to use with your SAP Ariba Spend Visibility reports.

- **Opportunity search**
Opportunity searches are targeted searches, based on commodities, that highlight opportunities for savings, improved efficiency, supplier diversity, and other company goals in your spend data. You can run prepackaged opportunity searches, or create your own opportunity search.

  You use the opportunity search task to configure the accounting date range for opportunity search settings, as outlined in Table 8.1.

Opportunity Search Type	Description
Price variation	Identify areas for savings through more effective choice of suppliers.
Supplier fragmentation	Identify areas for savings through supplier consolidation.
Order fragmentation	Identify inefficient purchasing in your company.
Opportunities for sourcing	Identify commodities for which a large sourcing event might achieve savings.

Table 8.1 Opportunity Search Types

8.2.4 Key Reports and Corresponding Impact Areas

In addition to understanding general spending, there are several reporting areas in SAP Ariba Spend Visibility that can have an immediate impact and return on investment for procurement solutions. Areas like contract awareness, rationalizing pricing across contracts, and understanding supplier ownership structures to consolidate further volume for contract negotiations, all provide relatively quick returns with little required change management or process changes. In essence, you are already working the processes, but "leakage" occurs due to a lack of understanding or visibility in these areas.

Contract Awareness Report

A contract awareness report is built in SAP Ariba Spend Visibility using purchasing price variance data (PPV). You define the variance as where the same supplier billed two different prices for the same item. Another metric is different customer sites purchasing at different prices, which is called purchase price alignment (PPA). Once this data is defined, additional data points, such as supplier optimization cost (SOC), can be calculated, or the savings associated from always buying from the supplier with whom you have the most favorable pricing.

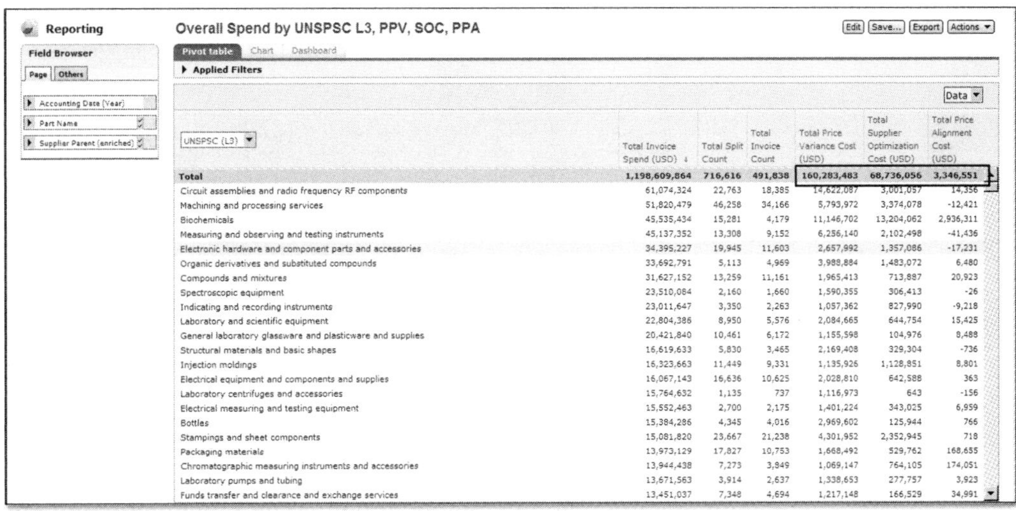

UNSPSC (L3)	Total Invoice Spend (USD) ↓	Total Split Count	Total Invoice Count	Total Price Variance Cost (USD)	Total Supplier Optimization Cost (USD)	Total Price Alignment Cost (USD)
Total	**1,198,609,864**	**716,616**	**491,838**	**160,283,483**	**68,736,056**	**3,346,551**
Circuit assemblies and radio frequency RF components	61,074,324	22,763	18,385	14,622,087	3,001,057	14,356
Machining and processing services	51,820,479	46,258	34,166	5,793,972	3,374,078	-12,421
Biochemicals	45,535,434	15,281	4,179	11,146,702	13,204,062	2,936,311
Measuring and observing and testing instruments	45,137,352	13,308	9,152	6,256,140	2,102,498	-41,436
Electronic hardware and component parts and accessories	34,395,227	19,945	11,603	2,657,992	1,357,086	-17,231
Organic derivatives and substituted compounds	33,692,791	5,113	4,969	3,988,884	1,483,072	6,480
Compounds and mixtures	31,627,152	13,259	11,161	1,965,413	713,887	20,923
Spectroscopic equipment	23,510,084	2,160	1,660	1,590,355	306,413	-26
Indicating and recording instruments	23,011,647	3,350	2,263	1,057,362	827,990	-9,218
Laboratory and scientific equipment	22,804,386	8,950	5,576	2,084,665	644,754	15,425
General laboratory glassware and plasticware and supplies	20,421,840	10,461	6,172	1,155,598	104,976	8,488
Structural materials and basic shapes	16,619,633	5,830	3,465	2,169,408	329,304	-736
Injection moldings	16,323,663	11,449	9,331	1,135,926	1,128,851	8,801
Electrical equipment and components and supplies	16,067,143	16,636	10,625	2,028,810	642,588	363
Laboratory centrifuges and accessories	15,764,632	1,135	737	1,116,973	643	-156
Electrical measuring and testing equipment	15,552,463	2,700	2,175	1,401,224	343,025	6,959
Bottles	15,384,286	4,345	4,016	2,969,602	125,944	766
Stampings and sheet components	15,081,820	23,667	21,238	4,301,952	2,352,945	718
Packaging materials	13,973,129	17,827	10,753	1,668,492	529,762	168,655
Chromatographic measuring instruments and accessories	13,944,438	7,273	3,849	1,069,147	764,105	174,051
Laboratory pumps and tubing	13,671,563	3,914	2,637	1,338,653	277,757	3,923
Funds transfer and clearance and exchange services	13,451,037	7,348	4,694	1,217,148	166,529	34,991

Figure 8.2 SAP Ariba Spend Visibility Contract Awareness Report

In Figure 8.2, the PPV, PPA, and SOC total amounts are circled. Keep in mind that these amounts, if saved, represent immediate additional profitability to a company, and would require significantly more in sales/revenues to realize, depending on the company's net margin. So, if $10 million in savings is realized via these insights in procurement, and the company is working with a 10% net margin, the company would have to sell 100 million more of their products and services to realize this amount.

Supplier Parentage Report

Different types of procurement situations may include this type of opportunity. For example, if you are buying a product category that is supplied by an industry undergoing a lot of mergers and acquisitions activity, you may be unknowingly buying from subsidiaries of the same parent company at different prices and on different contracts. Or, you may be buying off of multiple contracts for the same product for the same supplier, and would thus have an opportunity to consolidate that way. If the suppliers are conglomerates, or if the supplier base in this industry is heavily dominated by a few key players, there may be less opportunity for this type of report to uncover. Also, if the owner of the supplier is an investment entity or conglomerate, this type of contract roll up/consolidation is less fruitful.

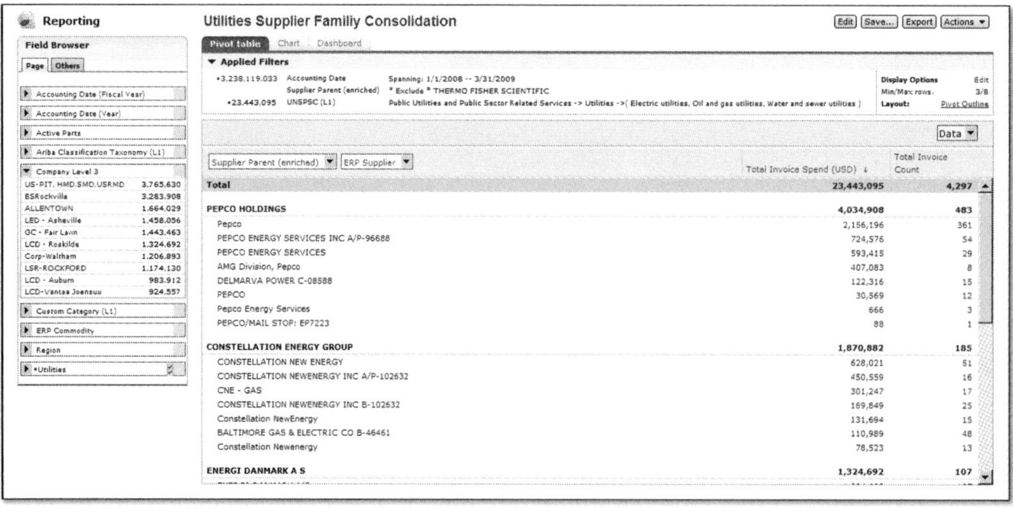

Figure 8.3 Supplier Parentage Report—Utilities

Supplier parentage can be brought to bear on negotiated utilities contracts, as per Figure 8.3 and spend volumes reports. Here, the report shows which utilities share a common parent, as well as your spend volumes and opportunities to consolidate your contracts as parent-to-parent vs. location to subsidiary.

Supplier parentage is also a report where spend volumes and trends come into play—if you are spending higher amounts than before, include this fact in the next negotiation round as leverage and justification for obtaining better pricing and rates. Likewise, understanding which product categories are influenced by price changes in terms of how much your company eventually purchases (price/volume elasticity), and which categories are largely price insensitive, can determine whether you look for external price reductions from your supplier, or for internal measures to curb demand for hat category. If your company's volume of buying in a category is largely driven by price, achieving a price reduction from the supplier will lead to an almost commensurate increase in purchasing, negating the savings effects. Having pricing and category information, as well as historical trend data in the form of volume over time by price, can assist you with understanding whether reducing volume or price leads to the greatest savings. These follow on reports are available in SAP Ariba Spend Visibility as the *Spend Volume* report and the *Spend Variance Analysis Volume vs. Price Effects* report.

Supplier Fragmentation Report

Fragmented markets often represent the best sourcing opportunities, which means, from an economics standpoint, with the correct analysis and understanding of the market, you stand to obtain pricing at, or even below, cost. This is because a fragmented supply market typically encompasses many competitors vying for your business in that product or service category. Conversely, if the market for an item is split neatly between a few large suppliers, your negotiating leverage may be severely reduced. No matter how well laid-out your arguments are, you may still end up paying what the supplier asked for initially, because you do not have much of an alternative. See Figure 8.4 for the Supplier Fragmentation report.

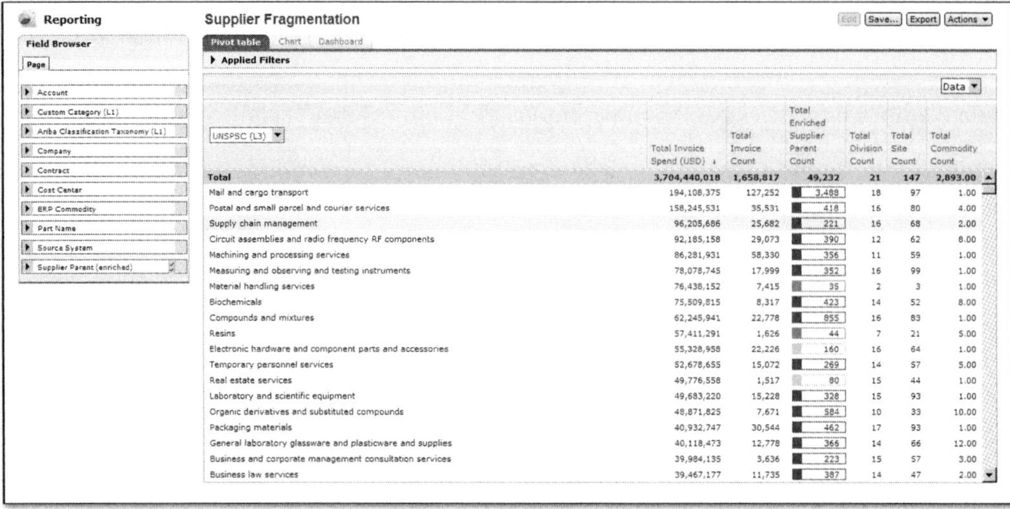

UNSPSC (L3)	Total Invoice Spend (USD)	Total Invoice Count	Total Enriched Supplier Parent Count	Total Division Count	Total Site Count	Total Commodity Count
Total	**3,704,440,018**	**1,658,817**	**49,232**	**21**	**147**	**2,893.00**
Mail and cargo transport	194,108,375	127,252	3,488	18	97	1.00
Postal and small parcel and courier services	158,245,531	35,531	418	16	80	4.00
Supply chain management	96,205,686	25,682	221	16	68	2.00
Circuit assemblies and radio frequency RF components	92,185,158	29,073	390	12	62	8.00
Machining and processing services	86,281,931	58,330	356	11	59	1.00
Measuring and observing and testing instruments	78,078,745	17,999	352	16	99	1.00
Material handling services	76,438,152	7,415	35	2	3	1.00
Biochemicals	75,509,815	8,317	423	14	52	8.00
Compounds and mixtures	62,245,941	22,778	855	16	83	1.00
Resins	57,411,291	1,626	44	7	21	5.00
Electronic hardware and component parts and accessories	55,328,958	22,226	160	16	64	1.00
Temporary personnel services	52,678,655	15,072	269	14	57	5.00
Real estate services	49,776,558	1,517	80	15	44	1.00
Laboratory and scientific equipment	49,683,220	15,228	328	15	93	1.00
Organic derivatives and substituted compounds	48,871,825	7,671	584	10	33	10.00
Packaging materials	40,932,747	30,544	462	17	93	1.00
General laboratory glassware and plasticware and supplies	40,118,473	12,778	366	14	66	12.00
Business and corporate management consultation services	39,984,135	3,636	223	15	57	3.00
Business law services	39,467,177	11,735	387	14	47	2.00

Figure 8.4 SAP Ariba Spend Visibility Supplier Fragmentation Report

Once you account for geographical or other justifications for a larger-than-normal amount of suppliers providing a category, based on Figure 8.5 you next determine whether your sourcing and cost-saving strategies for a particular category had potential from a supplier availability and overall market standpoint.

UNSPSC (L3)	Total Invoice Spend (USD)	Total Invoice Count	Total Enriched Supplier Parent Count	Total Division Count	Total Site Count	Total Commodity Count
Total	**3,704,440,018**	**1,658,817**	**49,232**	**21**	**147**	**2,893.00**
Mail and cargo transport	194,108,375	127,252	3,488	18	97	1.00
Postal and small parcel and courier services	158,245,531	35,531	418	16	80	4.00
Supply chain management	96,205,686	25,682	221	16	68	2.00
Circuit assemblies and radio frequency RF components	92,185,158	29,073	390	12	62	8.00
Machining and processing services	86,281,931	58,330	356	11	59	1.00
Measuring and observing and testing instruments	78,078,745	17,999	352	16	99	1.00
Material handling services	76,438,152	7,415	35	2	3	1.00
Biochemicals	75,509,815	8,317	423	14	52	8.00
Compounds and mixtures	62,245,941	22,778	855	16	83	1.00
Resins	57,411,291	1,626	44	7	21	5.00
Electronic hardware and component parts and accessories	55,328,958	22,226	160	16	64	1.00
Temporary personnel services	52,678,655	15,072	269	14	57	5.00
Real estate services	49,776,558	1,517	80	15	44	1.00
Laboratory and scientific equipment	49,683,220	15,228	328	15	93	1.00
Organic derivatives and substituted compounds	48,871,825	7,671	584	10	33	10.00
Packaging materials	40,932,747	30,544	462	17	93	1.00
General laboratory glassware and plasticware and supplies	40,118,473	12,778	366	14	66	12.00
Business and corporate management consultation services	39,984,135	3,636	223	15	57	3.00
Business law services	39,467,177	11,735	387	14	47	2.00

Figure 8.5 SAP Ariba Spend Visibility Supplier Fragmentation Report

Additional Reports

The *Supplier Footprint* report provides several useful data points with invoicing activity, as well as commodity and site/division count on a supplier, with the goal of facilitating consolidation. Invoicing activity highlights opportunities to streamline ordering with top suppliers, including drill downs by category. Commodity count surfaces niche suppliers, whose spend could potentially be consolidated with a more diverse supplier. Site/division count show how entrenched, or intertwined, a supplier is with your company, as a supplier with relationships with a large number of your company's sites will be more difficult to replace with another.

In the short-term, moving away from a heavily entwined or favored supplier may not be feasible, but understanding from a long-term strategy approach may be the first step in eventually achieving dilution or independence from the relationship. Likewise, the *Spend Concentration* report allows you review categories of spend where you currently have too little competition and too much dependence on one supplier.

Finally, as with demand management, some of the insight gleaned from these reports should drive changes in procurement behaviors in your organization, rather than solely supplier-focused rationalizations. For this, SAP Ariba Spend Visibility provides packaged reports such as *PO vs. Non-PO Spend* (three reports); *Off Contract Spend* by commodity/organization unit/supplier; and *Organizational Analysis* (from source systems).

Understanding multiple aspects of a procurement scenario and finding is necessary to making an informed decision. It would be simple to act with the first report showing that you are overly dependent on a supplier who is underperforming. However, before using this report to justify a host of other actions, it is important to understand (via other reports in SAP Ariba Spend Visibility) just where this supplier fits in, internally at your company, as well as externally in the market. For example, if you do not take into account the supplier's relationship level with your company from a site standpoint, or if you ignore the supplier market make-up for the product being supplied, a sudden "rip and replace" move of the supplier could have negative consequences that outweigh the sought-after savings. Likewise, if you chase a savings target on a commodity via a price reduction with the supplier, without understanding your company's price elasticity to that commodity, achieving a reduction in price could simply lead to more wasteful usage of that commodity and no real savings, due to increased purchasing volumes.

As per Figure 8.6, analysis and cross functional insight is required when leveraging these data points and reports from SAP Ariba's analytics tools to take action. When going after a savings opportunity, it is important to assess not only the opportunity, but also the business impact, supply risk, ease of implementation, and savings potential. To fully understand the savings potential, you need to consider additional historical factors of your spend volumes, supply base concentration, spending concentration with supplier, and savings history, as depicted in Figure 8.7.

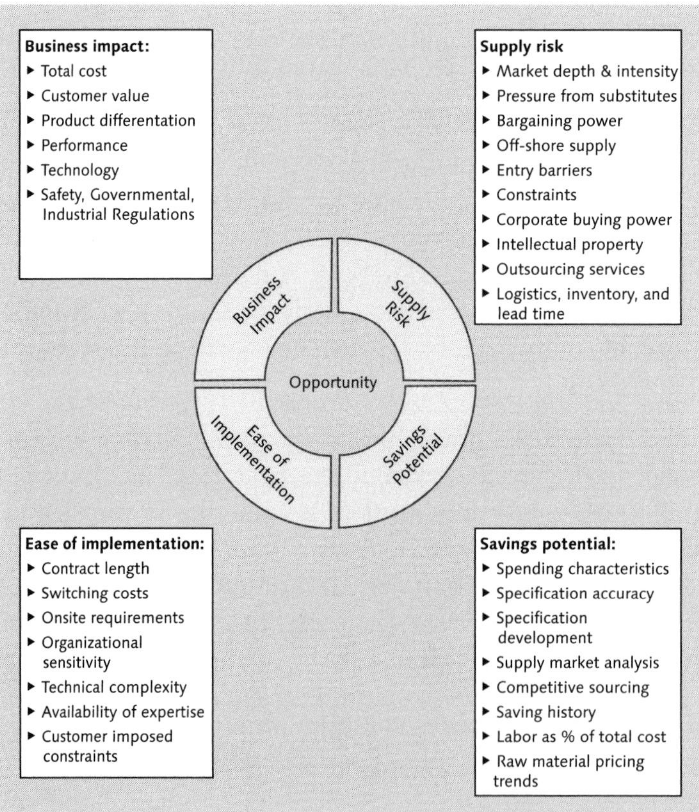

Figure 8.6 SAP Ariba Spend Visibility Insight-Driven Action

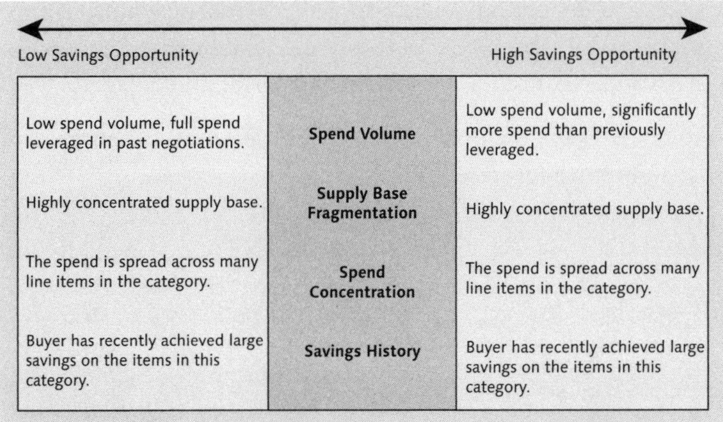

Figure 8.7 Key SAP Ariba Spend Visibility Factors for Sourcing Savings

Insights oftentimes seem obvious once stated, but hidden up until that point. Similarly, if you are not spending a lot of money with a supplier or type of item in the category, it does not make sense to prioritize this area for analysis or savings initiatives. If there is only a couple suppliers in a market, you are dealing with an oligopoly, and oligopolies do not have to negotiate as hard as perfectly competitive markets. Finally, if you have recently secured large savings in a category or with a supplier, the savings opportunities may very well be exhausted for this area at the moment.

Only through measured analysis of these vital areas will you likely achieve the desired results and realization of the actual opportunity estimated from the data. Hasty decision-making based off a one-dimensional report can begin to resemble a game of whack-a-mole, with constant effort only surfacing other problems to replace the targeted one.

8.2.5 Key Data Sources and Options for Importing into SAP Ariba Spend Visibility

SAP Ariba Spend Management and Visibility use the concept of a "source system." This is not necessarily a separate system, but more of a mechanism for segregating data. SAP Ariba Spend Management reporting uses source systems to represent distinct data sources. Each source system has a source type that defines the format of the data that is loaded into it. Users in the SAP Ariba Spend Visibility project manager group can add and delete source systems, and can manage which source systems the users in the SAP Ariba Spend Visibility data file manager group can access in the SAP Ariba administrator SAP Ariba Spend Visibility manager.

Depending on the solutions implemented, your site will use some combination of the following source systems as in Table 8.2.

Source Type	Source System Name	Description
SAP Ariba Spend Management	SAP Ariba Spend Management	Transactional SAP Ariba Contract Management, SAP Ariba Sourcing, SAP Ariba Supplier Information Management, and SAP Ariba Supplier Information and Performance Management data, such as data on projects and tasks. Automated data pulled from these solutions is loaded into this source system. In SAP Ariba Spend Management solutions that do not include SAP Ariba Spend Visibility, you always load custom fact data into the ASM source system.
Global	Default	Global SAP Ariba Contract Management, SAP Ariba Sourcing, SAP Ariba Spend Visibility, SAP Ariba Supplier Information Management, and SAP Ariba Supplier Information and Performance Management data, such as master data. Star schema ZIP files are loaded into this source system.
SAP Ariba Spend Visibility	Defined upon creation of source system	Users in the SAP Ariba Spend Visibility project manager group can create different source systems of type SAP Ariba Spend Visibility for loading SAP Ariba Spend Visibility data files. You can also load custom fact data into an SAP Ariba Spend Visibility source system.

Table 8.2 Source System Types

Source Type	Source System Name	Description
Global	SSP: None	Global, unpartitioned data from SAP Ariba invoice and procurement solutions. Automated data pulls from these solutions are loaded into this source system.
Buyer-Generic	SSP: Generic	Generic format data for SAP Ariba invoice and procurement solutions. Automated data pulls from these solutions are loaded into this source system.
Buyer: SAP	SSP: SAP	SAP format data for SAP Ariba invoice and procurement solutions. Automated data pulls from these solutions are loaded into this source system.
Buyer: Psoft	SSP: Psoft	PeopleSoft format data for SAP Ariba invoice and procurement solutions. Automated data pulls from these solutions are loaded into this source system.

Table 8.2 Source System Types (Cont.)

You can add or delete source systems of the SAP Ariba Spend Visibility source type, but you cannot add or delete ASM, global, or buyer source systems. You can add a single source system at a time, or you can add batches of source systems by uploading a source system CSV file. Source system names cannot be longer than 20 alphanumeric characters or contain spaces.

Custom reporting facts are available in:

- SAP Ariba Contract Management Professional
- SAP Ariba Sourcing Professional
- SAP Ariba Spend Visibility Professional
- SAP Ariba Supplier Information Management
- SAP Ariba Supplier Information and Performance Management

SAP Ariba Spend Management solutions include a set of reporting facts to store data about the basic transactions that users are investigating when they run a report. These facts include invoice, purchase order, contract workspace (procurement), event item summary, and others. SAP Ariba Spend Management automatically loads data into these facts from your solution package at regular intervals. In SAP Ariba Spend Visibility solution packages, SAP Ariba Spend Visibility project managers load external invoice and purchase order data into SAP Ariba Spend Visibility for analytical reporting.

Custom reporting facts are not enabled by default. To enable custom reporting facts, you will need to work with SAP Ariba services. You use custom reporting facts to load other kinds of data from third-party systems into SAP Ariba Spend Management and then run analytical reports to show this data side-by-side with SAP Ariba Spend Management data. You can use custom reporting facts to load:

- Third-party supplier quality data, such as percentage of claims in total freight cost, for use in KPIs in SAP Ariba Supplier Performance Management scorecards.
- Third-party supplier risk data for use in surveys.
- Third-party savings pipeline and tracking data for reporting alongside SAP Ariba Sourcing project data.
- Third-party external contract data for reporting alongside SAP Ariba Spend Visibility invoice and purchase order data.
- Third-party order fulfillment data for reporting alongside SAP Ariba Contract Management workspaces, SAP Ariba Sourcing projects, or SAP Ariba Supplier Performance Management projects.
- Spend forecast data for reporting alongside SAP Ariba Spend Visibility invoice spend data.
- SAP Ariba supplier data in a separate supplier fact for drilling down and filtering supplier data by commodity category, region, minority-owned status, and so on. By default, SAP Ariba stores supplier data in a dimension, which does not allow for this kind of analytical reporting.

As with other aspects of database design, custom reporting facts require careful planning and analysis. After you create a custom fact, it cannot be deleted in the system, and modifications to custom fact data are subject to limitations. For example, you can overwrite existing data with new rows of data that use the same lookup key values as existing data and you also can add new data to the existing data set. However, you cannot delete existing data.

Because of these limitations, custom facts are most suitable for data that is static, or that changes slowly. For example, data from completed rounds of supplier performance evaluations is unlikely to change. You will, however, continue to add to it. Supplier data changes infrequently, and even if your company stops doing business with a supplier, you will want to retain that supplier's record for archival purposes. On the other hand, you are likely to run up against these limitations with large-volume data sets that change rapidly, including procurement documents such as invoices, requisitions, and purchase orders.

There are further limitations to custom facts. Custom facts do not include any default measure fields for common measures such as spend and count, nor do they support currency conversions. You must create all the measure fields you want when you create the custom facts.

If you have enabled the custom fact feature or are implementing SAP Ariba Spend Visibility, you will store data in a dedicated star schema. This star schema uses fact tables to store specific types of records, such as invoices, projects or surveys, and uses dimension tables to store records that are common to most or all facts, such as suppliers and commodities, or regions.

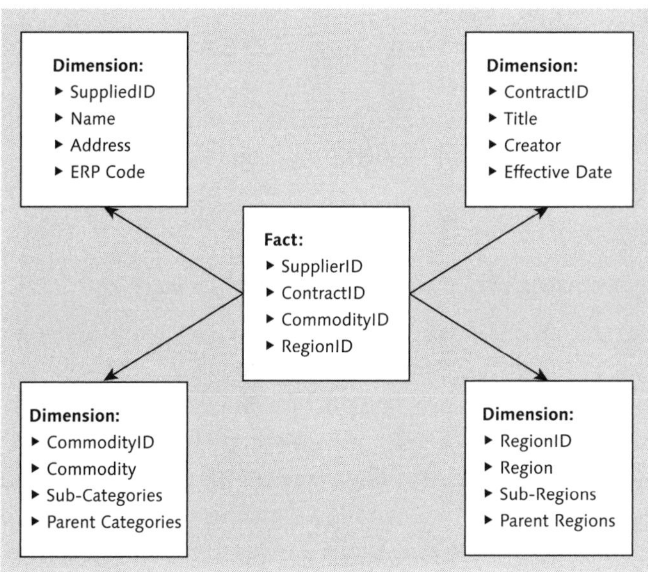

Figure 8.8 SAP Ariba Star Schema Data Model

As depicted in Figure 8.8, dimensions can contain different levels of data, organized in top-down hierarchies that progress from general to specific information. Report queries associate fact and dimension tables so that you can drill down, navigate hierarchy levels, add and remove hierarchy fields, and perform other analytical tasks in reports.

8.3 Implementing SAP Ariba Spend Visibility

The first thing to understand for SAP Ariba Spend Visibility is what constitutes a spending event. Invoices and purchase orders typically form the core of this type of data, but there can be other document types in your organization that also signify a spending event. The next thing to understand and define is where this data is generated and stored.

Project resourcing, phases, and timelines are core focus areas for any implementation. Analytics projects are somewhat more nuanced, however. Analytics oftentimes provide the return on investment for projects, especially procurement projects, where one insight can sometimes pay for the entire implementation. As tantalizing as this may be, analytics projects usually come later in the overall roll-out process of procure-to-pay solutions, as analytics require data, and data needs to be generated before you can report on it. As with the SAP Ariba SIPM implementations outlined in Chapter 6, defining the data set that will underpin these reports is a key effort and ideally should be undertaken prior to project kick-off.

8.3.1 Defining Project Resources, Phases, and Timelines

As outlined in this chapter, spend analysis reports are available in many different SAP Ariba solutions, and provide basic reporting functionality, whereas SAP Ariba Spend Visibility requires an actual project structure and execution. For SAP Ariba Spend Analysis, provided you have defined your project correctly for the applicable SAP Ariba solution, your spend analysis reporting is accessible with the solution and requires little extra set up. The following table depicts the typical phases of a SAP Ariba Spend Visibility project, which applies to both the SAP-centric version and general SAP Ariba Spend Visibility solution.

Phase	Key Activities	Participants—Initial Load of Data	Participants—Data Refreshes
Kickoff	▸ Kickoff meeting including project overview ▸ Data schema training for IT stakeholders	▸ SAP Ariba/Consulting Partner PM ▸ Customer PM (16 hours) ▸ Business Users (8 hours) ▸ Client IT (8 hours) ▸ Client Stakeholders (4 hours)	N/A
Data collection	▸ Write data extraction scripts ▸ Upload iterative data files in SAP Ariba Analysis	▸ SAP Ariba PM ▸ Client PM (20 hours) ▸ Client business users (20 hours combined)	▸ Client IT (2 to 40 hours)
Data validation	▸ SAP Ariba project manager provides feedback on format, contents, enrichment clues, and best practices ▸ Client approves source data for enrichment	▸ ADES	▸ SAP Ariba PM ▸ Client PM (4 hours) ▸ Client business users (4 hours combined)
Data enrichment	▸ Client data exported to ▸ SAP Ariba data enrichment ▸ (ADE) tool ▸ ADES experts analyze and cleanse data	▸ ADES	▸ ADES

Table 8.3 SAP Ariba Spend Visibility Project Phases

Phase	Key Activities	Participants—Initial Load of Data	Participants—Data Refreshes
Supplier enrichment drop	▸ ADES provides supplier enrichment component including supplier parentage for client analysis	▸ ADES	▸ N/A
Deployment	▸ Commodity classifications provided ▸ User training deployment of SAP Ariba analysis to users ▸ Conduct data assessment	▸ SAP Ariba PM ▸ Client PM (8 to 24 hours) ▸ Client power business users (8 hours) ▸ ADES	▸ SAP Ariba PM ▸ Client PM (ongoing) Client power business users ▸ ADES

Table 8.3 SAP Ariba Spend Visibility Project Phases (Cont.)

The following roles, referenced in Table 8.3, are necessary for your SAP Ariba Spend Visibility implementation project:

- **SAP Ariba Data Enrichment Services (ADES)**
  The SAP Ariba Data Enrichment Services team is responsible for all aspects of customer data enrichment for on-demand engagements leveraging SAP Ariba data enrichment technology for supplier enrichment and commodity classifications.
- **SAP Ariba project manager**
  There is both a customer and SAP Ariba and/or consulting partner project manager assigned to a SAP Ariba Spend Visibility project. SAP Ariba Spend Visibility project managers are well-versed in the various aspects of the SAP Ariba Spend Visibility engagement and will assist the customer in:
  - Understanding the overall SAP Ariba Spend Visibility process
  - Mapping their SAP ERP data to the analysis data schema
  - Providing feedback on uploaded source data extracts
  - Identifying the optimal combination of hint fields for enrichment

- Various informational sessions on both analysis and the enrichment process
- Assisting with reviewing enrichment results and refining classifications where appropriate
- Deployment of enriched data to users
- Conducting a data assessment at the completion of the first pass of enrichment

- **Customer project manager**
  The client should assign a project manager to keep all resources focused on the project goals, make key and timely decisions, and to report progress to internal stakeholders, the project sponsor, and/or the steering committee.
- **Customer IT resources—data collection**
  Customer IT staff is required primarily in the data collection phase, as the client's source data is extracted and transformed into the SAP Ariba analysis data schema format.
- **Customer business (procurement) team**
  Obtaining participation and support from subject matter experts (SMEs) on the customer's procurement team, who will eventually be the tool's primary users and beneficiaries, is critical to the success of the project. Throughout the project, these procurement SMEs will have access to increasing levels of data, starting with the raw customer data once it is initially loaded into SAP Ariba Analysis and SAP Ariba Spend Visibility. The first enrichment milestone is available at the mid-way point of the enrichment phase and provides supplier enrichment results including supplier parentage and additional enrichment attributes including diversity, industry codes, and credit ratings. The final stage is at first-pass go-live, when commodity classifications are available and the customer data can be leveraged to achieve numerous pre-defined project objectives, including the identification of sourcing savings opportunities, supplier rationalization activities, and compliance monitoring.
- **Stakeholders**
  Stakeholders are executive-level members of the client organization who sponsor the project and promote buy-in and adoption in order to realize ROI. The customer project manager will normally update stakeholders on progress, issues, and decision making crucial to the completion of the project. Alternatively, stakeholder meetings can be held for such updates.

In the elapsed time between contracting SAP Ariba for a SAP Ariba Spend Visibility engagement and the project kickoff, clients can begin to review the data schema document in order to frame questions for the kickoff. However, it is recommended to delay beginning data extraction work until after kickoff, as key decisions and clarifications will often be made during the kickoff meetings.

It is critical during this time to begin strategizing on how to accomplish data extraction. If not properly planned and resourced, extraction is the greatest risk for delaying the project timeline.

Note

SAP Ariba can offer assistance in your data extraction efforts, so we don't recommend delaying a visibility effort if IT resources are not available to extract data. For more information, ask your SAP Ariba Account Executive.

Finally, several decisions must be made before the client's SAP Ariba Analysis instance can be requested. The client should brainstorm on the following points and be prepared to have an answer for each during the project kickoff. This will allow the SAP Ariba Project Manager to request the development of the new Analysis instance immediately following kickoff. The points you should prepare for are:

- Customer name to appear embedded in URL (20 characters max, lowercase with no spaces)
- Company's fiscal calendar
- The spend currencies which will be available for reporting in Analysis (USD plus four additional currencies, at client's discretion)

Following is a brief summary of each phase of the implementation, per Table 8.3:

- **Project kickoff**
  The project kickoff routinely takes one to two days, depending upon the project size and scope. The kickoff consists of two parts: project overview and data schema training. The SAP Ariba project manager can be onsite or available by teleconference, at the discretion of the client. These two parts break out as follows:

- SAP Ariba Spend Visibility project overview
  The project overview should be attended by all project participants if possible. The discussion will include:
  - An overview of the SAP Ariba Spend Visibility solution and tools
  - A scoping discussion including project resources, data, challenges, and time estimates
  - A high-level overview of the SAP Ariba Spend Visibility process (see Figure 8.1) of this chapter)
  - Data collection talking points
  - An overview of the SAP Ariba data enrichment (ADE) process
  - Next steps
- Analysis data schema
  - The second portion of the kickoff is much more detail-oriented, and consists of the SAP Ariba PM, client IT, and client PM walking through the analysis data schema in a detailed fashion. The objectives of this session are to make key decisions on what spend will be in scope (and out of scope), to map data fields from the client SAP ERP system(s) to the analysis data schema, and to assure the client understands all schema structure and formatting.
  - SAP Ariba Spend Visibility uses a fixed schema designed to enable best practice spend analysis. While all fields are not required, it is in the customer's best interest to populate all available fields. Although the process is flexible to accommodate other formats and SAP Ariba has experience extracting and transforming data from multiple ERPs, customers are far better off building scripts to automate data flows during refreshes and having a structured schema to ensure all useful information is captured. Customers wishing to deviate from the standard SAP Ariba schema should inform SAP Ariba during the sales process in order to ensure scope is adjusted, if necessary.
  - The SAP Ariba Analysis data schema is a series of associated flat-file, csv (comma separated value) tables in a "star-schema" format. The center of the "star" is the client's invoice and PO data. The supporting tables that these tables refer to are the arms of the "star."

- **Data collection**

  Once the data has been extracted in the SAP Ariba Spend Visibility data schema format, the designated individual at the client site will upload the source data files directly into SAP Ariba Analysis. At this time, the SAP Ariba project manager will automatically receive notification.

  IT resources are typically required for data collection to perform the extraction and upload the data files into SAP Ariba Analysis. In the event that assistance is needed extracting data from SAP source systems which are historically the most difficult, SAP Ariba offers an extraction, transformation, and loading (ETL) product, which extracts data from customer source systems, transforms it into the SAP Ariba Analysis loading format, and which can help load the data into SAP Ariba Analysis. The actual product is IBM WebSphere DataStage with their SAP Adapter. SAP Ariba engineering has built "job templates" that are included in the product when purchased through SAP Ariba, and provide a good starting point for customers with SAP sources.

- **Data validation**

  Upon uploading a data file in SAP Ariba Analysis, the user will receive validation messages in various formats depending upon severity. At this time, the SAP Ariba PM will assist by reviewing these validation messages and performing checks on the file formats and content. The un-enriched source data is loaded into Analysis, where it is available for client review and remains available throughout the project. This means that some valuable aspects of the data will be available to the client in the analytic tool within days of the project kickoff, based on being able to aggregate the raw data. Various spend reports should be run at this time to assure that the data appearing in SAP Ariba Analysis matches the data extracted and is consistent with the client's common knowledge of their spend base. Please note that data collection and validation is an iterative cycle. As issues are discovered, data will be re-extracted, loaded, and validated. Once the client is convinced that the data is acceptable to proceed, the client PM will be asked to send a spend approval notice to their designated SAP Ariba project manager. This email is the milestone that completes the data collection/validation phases and moves the project into enrichment.

  Again, obviously this cycle time will vary greatly depending upon the scope of the project. However, SAP Ariba has found the average time to be between two and eight weeks for such an effort, keeping in mind that this depends largely on the client's ability to complete data collection.

- **Data enrichment**
  The first step for SAP Ariba Data Enrichment (ADE) is to perform a data assessment. This provides a more accurate view into the magnitude of work required based on the quantity and quality of the client data. Because the actual quantity and quality of the data often varies significantly from the estimates provided during the sales cycle, there can be a minimal change in the project time estimates at this point—either outwards or inwards. In most cases, the estimate the client receives at kickoff will hold with minimal changes, assuming there are no significant changes in the data. After the data assessment, SAP ADE will run 100% of the client's spend through SAP Ariba's enrichment engines, including those for content, persistence, and supplier matches.

  SAP ADE will provide results and confidence levels on these results based on the data. It is these results that the SAP ADE team will process, update, and approve over the next several weeks for supplier enrichment and parentage, provided at the mid-way point of the enrichment phase, and commodity classifications which are available at first-pass go-live.

  Data enrichment makes up a majority of the project timeline due to the volume of processing, review, and QA required. This is also the phase where the greatest variability exists depending on the scope of the project. Exceptions exist, but in most cases, data enrichment takes between three and ten weeks.

- **Deployment**
  The SAP Ariba PM will work with the client project manager to finalize the customizable dashboard, default reports and user setups as the now-enriched data is deploys for widespread client use in the identification of sourcing savings and analytics. This work is done in the lead time up until deployment. The PM client should allocate two to five days for this work.

  One to two weeks after the first-pass deployment, the SAP Ariba project manager will conduct a spend assessment, which highlights possible opportunities based on the recently available enriched customer data. Note that the data assessment does not include customer input or interviews and is therefore more directional in nature, but does illustrate several examples of how the data can be analyzed for potential action.

A typical SAP Ariba Spend Visibility project runs 17 weeks per Figure 8.9, the project requires involvement from a customer's project manager, business owners, and technical team, especially if third-party systems are involved.

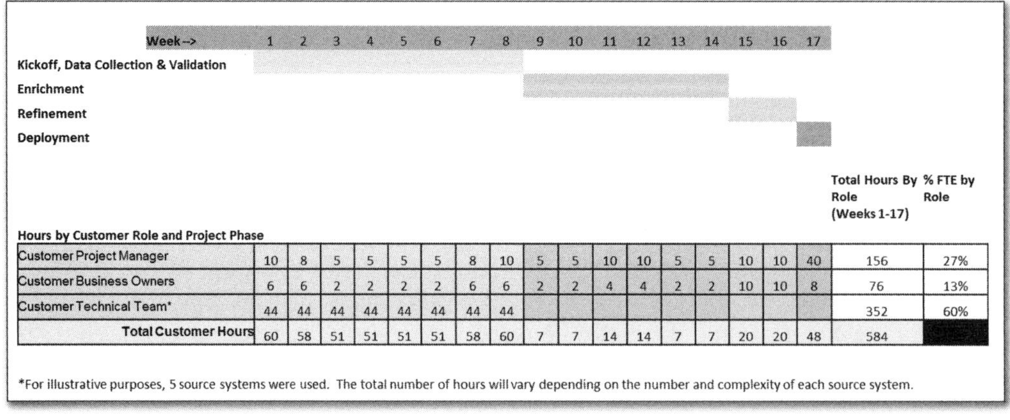

Week-->	1	2	3	4	5	6	7	8	9	10	11	12	13	14	15	16	17
Kickoff, Data Collection & Validation																	
Enrichment																	
Refinement																	
Deployment																	

Hours by Customer Role and Project Phase

	1	2	3	4	5	6	7	8	9	10	11	12	13	14	15	16	17	Total Hours By Role (Weeks 1-17)	% FTE by Role
Customer Project Manager	10	8	5	5	5	5	8	10	5	5	10	10	5	5	10	10	40	156	27%
Customer Business Owners	6	6	2	2	2	2	6	6	2	2	4	4	2	2	10	10	8	76	13%
Customer Technical Team*	44	44	44	44	44	44	44	44										352	60%
Total Customer Hours	60	58	51	51	51	51	58	60	7	7	14	14	7	7	20	20	48	584	

*For illustrative purposes, 5 source systems were used. The total number of hours will vary depending on the number and complexity of each source system.

Typical Activities By Phase

Data Collection and Validation	Enrichment	Refinement	Deployment
Kick-off	Invoice and Supplier Enrichment	Review Results and Provide feedback	Analysis Training
Data schema Training and Mapping	Custom Mapping	Apply feedback	Report Templates, Dashboards
Data Extraction and Validation	Enrichment Training		User Creation
Spend Approval			

Figure 8.9 SAP Ariba Spend Visibility High Level Resource Plan and Timeline

8.3.2 Reporting with Cloud and On-Premise Data Sources

Transactions, especially payment, can be located outside of the SAP Ariba solutions you implement, and this is perfectly okay, as long as you can get to the applicable data in these systems and extract it into SAP Ariba Spend Visibility. SAP Ariba offers a number of ETL tools, the main one being the SAP Ariba Integration Toolkit, and services for making this happen. In addition to adding data from 3rd party systems, SAP Ariba Spend Visibility offers a number of key report settings that can be leveraged to tailor reports to your organization. Some of the fundamental settings are:

- Languages for UNSPSC display: You can set a maximum of four languages in addition to English.
- Fiscal calendar settings: These settings are only available in sites with SAP Ariba Spend Visibility, and determine how invoice and purchase order dates translate into fiscal years in reports, including offset configuration to allow for fiscal years to begin at different times other than the calendar year.

  Custom field hierarchy allows for more tailed fiscal settings, such as a fiscal month beginning several days into a calendar month.

- Custom fields for measure, date, dimension, and string: Steps to enable custom fields are to create the custom fields for your site, load the data to the data load schema, and then load the data to the presentation load schema.
- Customizing field labels: You customize field labels in SAP Ariba Spend Visibility reports by uploading CSV files with field label strings.

Users in the SAP Ariba Spend Visibility project manager group can customize field labels. There are four files available for string customization:

- `aml.analysis.HostedSpendExt.csv` contains flexible field labels.
- `aml.analysis.InvoiceAnalysis.csv` contains strings for field labels in the invoice fact table, such as invoice number and invoice spend.
- `aml.analysis.PurchaseOrderAnalysis.csv` contains strings for field labels in the purchase order fact table, such as PO ID
- `spend.aml.analysis.SpendAnalysis.csv` contains SAP Ariba Spend Visibility-related field labels, such as procurement system and source system.

8.4 Summary

Like SAP Ariba Supplier Information and Performance Management (SIPM), SAP Ariba Spend Visibility came about to address more complex reporting requirements in procurement than the one-dimensional reports available for the various solution areas. SAP Ariba Spend Visibility combines disparate data sources and purchasing documents with actual spend/payment data, to provide the manager and executives with a clear understanding of just where the money is going in procurement. Whether in procurement or politics, following the money is always a good starting point. What is gleaned from SAP Ariba Spend Visibility reporting can then be used to achieve greater savings through targeted initiatives. You should use further analysis with SAP Ariba Spend Visibility to focus on what is important and useful for your organization, using market analysis and reports in the supplier side of the system to identify where the most savings can be achieved with the least amount of effort. As with the other analysis tools in SAP Ariba SIPM, how you interpret and what you do with the insights is just as important as getting to them in the first place.

This chapter explains some of the core integration topics for SAP ERP with SAP Ariba and SAP Fieldglass solutions, providing detailed configuration steps for a sampling of these scenarios.

9 Integrating SAP Ariba and SAP Fieldglass with SAP ERP

Most large enterprises run hybrid models today, in which cloud solutions are integrated with backend, on-premise software implementations such as SAP ERP. SAP Ariba and SAP Fieldglass are no different in this regard, and offer multiple integration points and approaches. This chapter outlines the various tools that are available for integrating SAP Ariba and SAP Fieldglass with on-premise SAP ERP, and outlines how such a project would occur. Non-SAP ERP systems and applications, as well as deep-dive detail, is outside the scope of this book. Every integration project is different, depending on the customizations and the unique customer landscape, as well as the requirements around data and security.

In addition, customers oftentimes have built-out procurement processes on the planned procurement side for their direct procurement in manufacturing operations, which, for example, cannot be easily moved to SAP Ariba due to all of the various linkages to other SAP ERP modules further towards the beginning of the process flows.

Figure 9.1 provides an overview of the integration options as of October 2015, as well as a roadmap for planned integrations to newer products such as SAP S/4HANA. As you can see, SAP Ariba can integrate with SAP ERP via the SAP Business Suite Add-On for PO/IV integration, SAP Process Integration (PI) for the SAP Ariba adapter, and cloud integration toolkits, called "CI-versions 1-x") for solutions such as SAP Ariba P2P and sourcing. SAP Fieldglass can integrate with both SAP ERP Human Capital Management (SAP ERP HCM) and procurement functionality in SAP ERP, leveraging the same CI route as SAP Ariba.

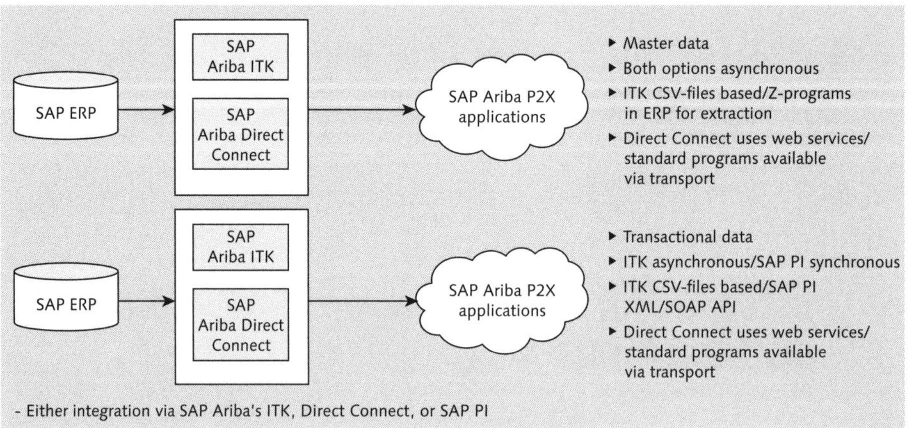

Figure 9.1 SAP ERP to SAP HANA Cloud Integration Overview

The first section in this chapter focuses on the integration of document exchange between an SAP Ariba or SAP Fieldglass system, and an SAP ERP backend environment. This type of integration becomes a requirement when certain parts of the document process flow will remain in the SAP ERP environment. Typically, this is at the front end of the document process or backend of the document process. As SAP Ariba and SAP Fieldglass do not have deep inventory management or accounts payable modules, once the order is fulfilled, these processes and corresponding documents need to revert back to SAP ERP for further management.

For integrating SAP ERP Materials Management (MM) and accounts payable with SAP Ariba Network, the next section outlines the various integration options and approaches. Next, integration options with SAP Ariba Procure-to-Pay and SAP ERP are detailed. Then, SAP Ariba Collaborative Supply Chain integration with SAP ERP and SAP Fieldglass integration topics are covered.

9.1 SAP Ariba Network Purchase Order/Invoice Automation with SAP ERP MM-PUR Integration Options

Customers with built out materials management processes or a SAP Supplier Relationship Management (SRM) classic implementation can opt for integrating these documents with the SAP Ariba Network. The MM purchase order is transmitted from SAP ERP to the SAP Ariba Network, and follow-on documents through to the invoice are exchanged between the two systems.

Integration with procurement document processing on the SAP Ariba Network options include:

- PO and SAP Ariba Invoice Automation
- SAP Ariba Discount Management (optional)
- SAP Ariba Procurement Content (optional)

The diagram in Figure 9.2 details the technical connectivity options for procurement document processing:

- Web service-based connectivity without middleware (direct)
- Web service-based connectivity with SAP HANA Cloud Integration
- Web service-based connectivity with SAP Process Orchestration (SAP PO)
- iDoc-based connectivity with SAP Process Orchestration (SAP PO)

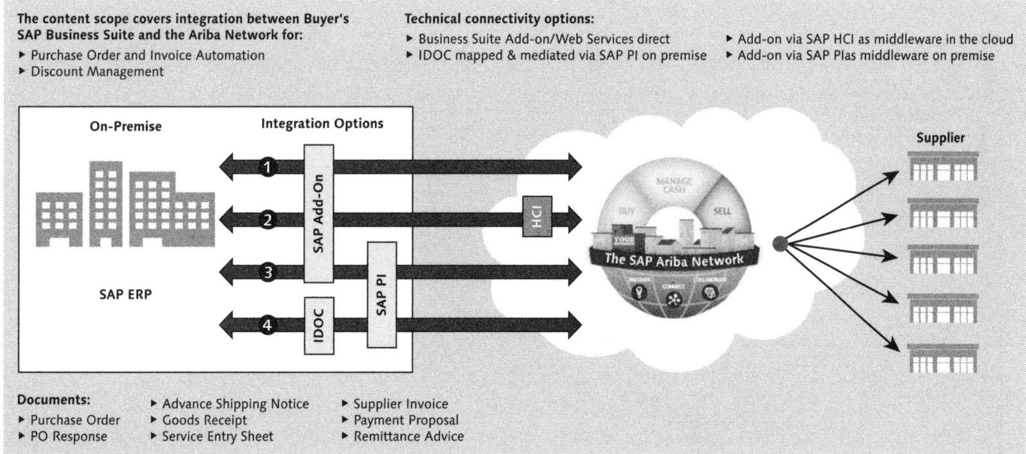

Figure 9.2 System Landscape and Technical Connectivity Options

9.1.1 Integration Options

There are three major integration options for connecting SAP Ariba with SAP ERP:

- SAP Business Suite Add-On direct connection
- SAP Business Suite Add-On Process Orchestration "mediated" integration
- SAP Ariba adapter integration via SAP Process Orchestration

The SAP Business Suite Add-On can be connected directly to the SAP Ariba Network, transmitting and converting documents in SAP Ariba XML format "cXML". The Business Suite Add-On can also leverage a "mediated" approach, either via SAP Process Orchestration (SAP PO) on-premise at the customer, or HCI middleware on the cloud-side in SAP Ariba. The SAP Ariba adapter, built prior to the acquisition of SAP Ariba by SAP, leverages SAP Process Orchestration to convert iDocs into cXML and vice versa.

The Business Suite Add-On is an SAP product that installs on SAP ERP and facilitates the integration and translation of documents into cXML, as well as transmission to and from the SAP Ariba Network. The Business Suite Add-On supports additional middleware and "mediated" approaches, but can also communicate directly with the SAP Ariba Network. Both buyers and suppliers can implement these integrations between SAP ERP and the SAP Ariba Network to enable communications/documents to transmit back and forth.

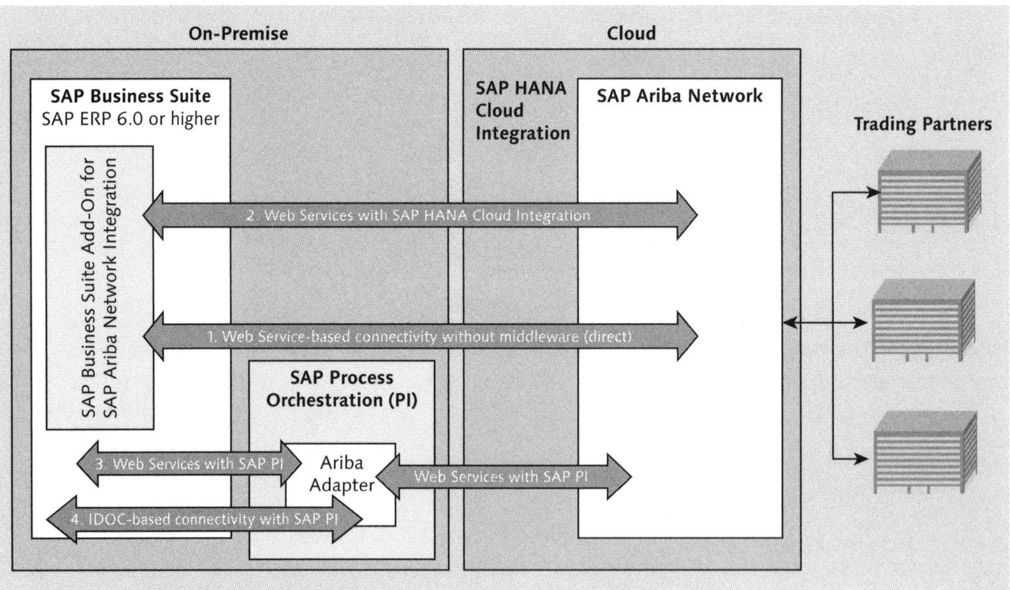

Figure 9.3 System Landscape and Technical Connectivity Options

From a software requirements standpoint, in Figure 9.3, the following is mandatory for SAP ERP if implementing either Business Suite Add-On approach, and depends on selected connectivity technology options for PO and invoice automation:

- For direct connectivity via web service or connectivity via SAP HANA Cloud Integration:
  - SAP ERP 6.0 SP Stack 15 or higher
  - SAP Business Suite Add-On for SAP Ariba Network integration 1.0 SP5
- For connectivity via web service and SAP Process Orchestration (SAP PO):
  - SAP ERP 6.0 SP Stack 15 or higher
  - SAP Business Suite Add-On for SAP Ariba Network integration 1.0 SP5
  - SAP NW 7.3 Process Integration or higher with SAP Ariba Network adapter for SAP Ariba Network integration CI-5 or higher installed. For versions lower than CI-5, the SAP Ariba Integration Tool Kit is required to mediate the connection.
- For connectivity via iDocs and SAP Process Orchestration (SAP PO):
  - SAP Process Integration or higher with SAP Ariba Network Adapter for SAP Ariba Network integration CI-5 or higher installed
  - SAP ERP 6.0 or higher
  - (Optional) SAP Solution Manager

The first step in integrating and automating purchase orders and invoices between SAP ERP and the SAP Ariba Network is choosing which integration option to use. The SAP Business Suite Add-On is the declared go-forward path on SAP's roadmap, so integrations leveraging the Business Suite Add-On should be prioritized over ones using the SAP Ariba adapter. However, there are some instances where the SAP Ariba adapter may still have a temporary advantage in supporting an additional document type, or where the installation of the Business Suite Add-On is not preferred, due to centralized communication requirements via iDocs from SAP ERP (where a middleware has been declared the standard integration approach and iDocs need to be issued from SAP ERP). Even here, it makes sense to evaluate the Business Suite Add-On with SAP Process Orchestration mediation as an option, as no further investment is planned on the SAP Ariba adapter going forward.

If the Business Suite Add-On is selected as the integration path between SAP ERP and the SAP Ariba Network, the next decision point is whether to go direct to the SAP Ariba Network, or to have SAP PI or another middleware mediate the connection. Here, policies, internal IT standards whereby all communication between SAP ERP has to move through a middleware component, or security concerns can play a factor in driving the final decision towards a mediated approach. From a pure cost and simplicity standpoint, the direct connection is the least expensive and least complex.

9.1.2 Solution Implementation Project

This section outlines the key approaches for implementation and should give you an understanding of the project framework for a successful integration of various SAP Ariba and SAP Fieldglass solutions with SAP ERP modules. Each integration project is different, as the systems involved and customizations/requirements can vary significantly from landscape to landscape, from project to project. However, there are main paths to follow on integration, which are outlined in this section.

First, an integration approach needs to be selected. As previously outlined, there are many different options for integrating SAP Ariba, depending on the solution and the requirements, but these center on Business Suite Add-On for PO/IV, and SAP HANA Cloud Integration toolkits for SAP Ariba P2P and other scenarios. Once the integration approach has been selected, the next step is to define the appropriate resources for the project. Here, a project manager, a business process subject matter expert, integration IT expert, and SAP Basis resource are required. If engaging a consulting firm, this can potentially be mirrored resources on both the customer and consulting firm's side.

Rapid-deployment solutions (RDS) are packaged services offered by SAP. These services can be implemented by SAP's delivery organizations, by your consulting partner, or directly by customers themselves. The latest rapid-deployment solution content for these SAP Ariba integration projects can be found at *http://service.sap.com/rds-ariba*. It is highly recommended to peruse this information, as the guides and approaches described within can provide your project with accelerators and templates for success, as well as timelines and expectations. As mentioned, the SAP delivery organizations and their partners can also deliver this RDS turnkey, in conjunction with the customer's resources and involvement.

To download content/software from the SAP Ariba areas shown in Figure 9.4, navigate to *http://connect.ariba.com* and select the DOWNLOAD SOFTWARE tab. The page in Figure 9.5 is where you would download the SAP Ariba adapter, in the event that you selected this approach.

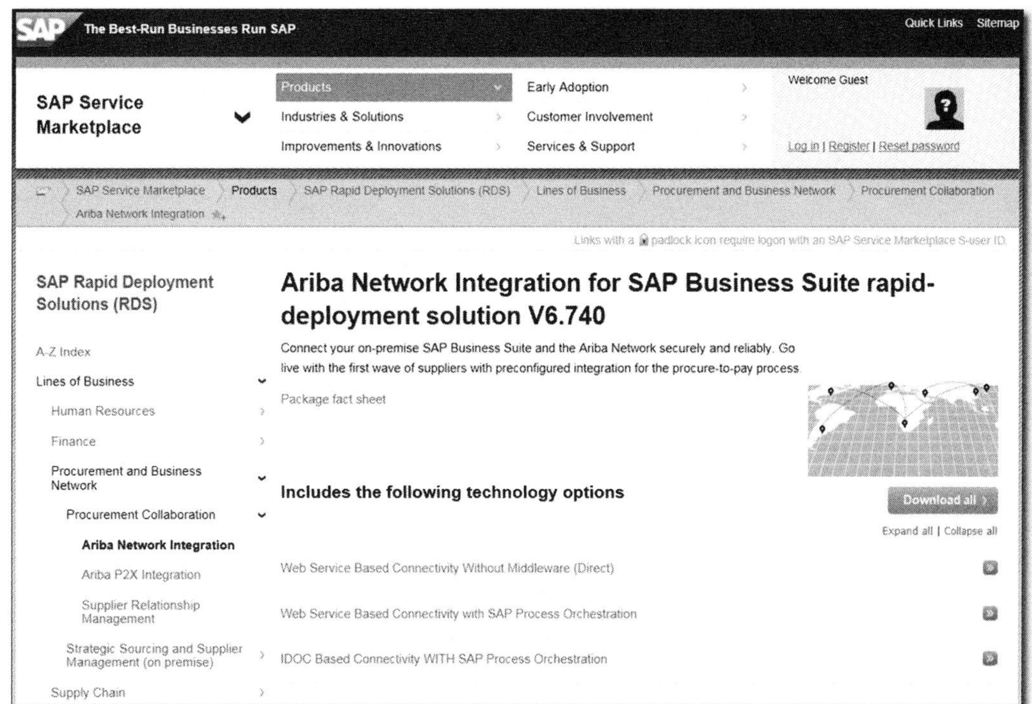

Figure 9.4 SAP Service Marketplace

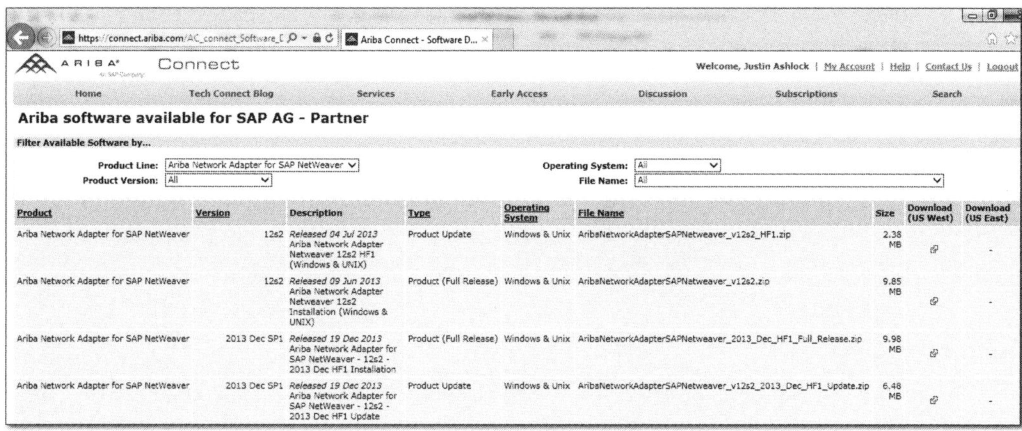

Figure 9.5 SAP Ariba Download Page—SAP PI Adapter for SAP Ariba Network Integration

Once the adapter or SAP Business Suite Add-On is downloaded and installed, additional steps are required in SAP ERP to enable materials management to send and receive documents. What follows are detailed steps for configuring the SAP Business Suite Add-On. You can skip these sections if you are not actively configuring the solution. Prior to configuring a solution, always check online resources (*http://service.sap.com/rds-ariba)* for the latest, most updated versions of these steps.

Business Suite Add-On Configuration Settings

In this section we will cover the SAP Ariba configuration settings, the SAP ERP framework settings, and some application-specific settings.

SAP Ariba Configuration Settings

To configure SAP Ariba, complete the following steps:

1. Go to *http://service.ariba.com* to access the Buyer and Supplier Network.
2. If connecting to the SAP Ariba supplier account for the first time, enter the general settings you received from SAP Ariba or your preferred profile settings, for the demo supplier account.
3. Create a supplier catalog leveraging SAP Ariba-provided spreadsheets (provided by SAP Ariba during the project) with some example items for the catalog.

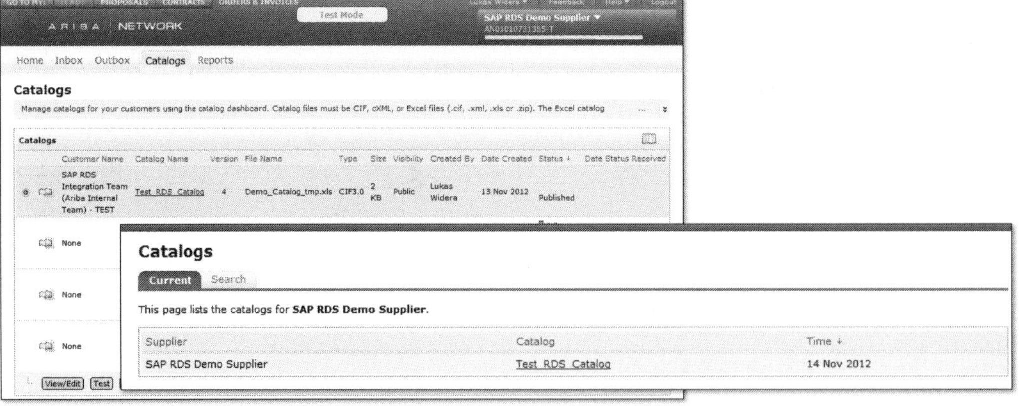

Figure 9.6 SAP Ariba Dummy Supplier Account Settings

4. If connecting to the SAP Ariba buyer account for the first time, enter the general settings for the buyer account in Figure 9.6.
5. Go to the SUPPLIER ENABLEMENT tab and search for (dummy) suppliers with the network ID (login ID). See Figure 9.7.

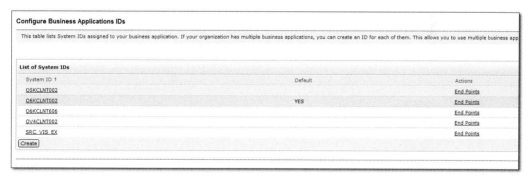

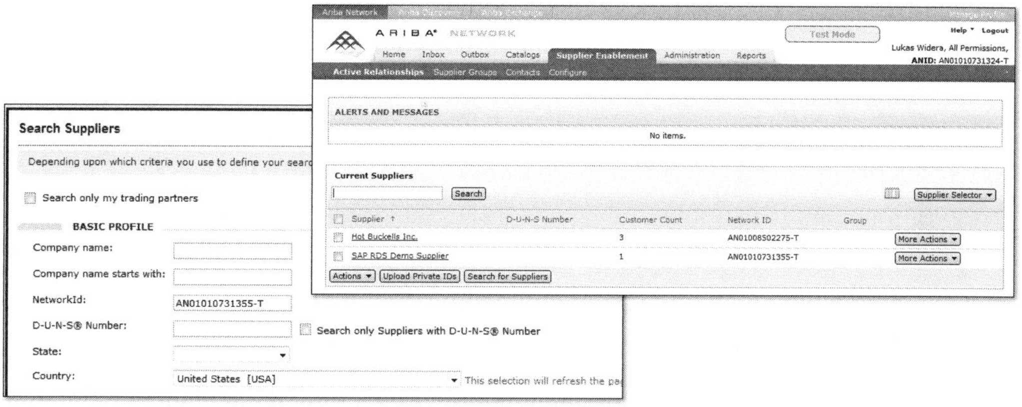

Figure 9.7 SAP Ariba Buyer Account Settings

6. Before leaving the page, subscribe to the supplier catalog.

Next, you'll configure the business application IDs and end points (when the ID will expire) in the ADMINISTRATION/CONFIGURATION area, detailed in Figure 9.8.

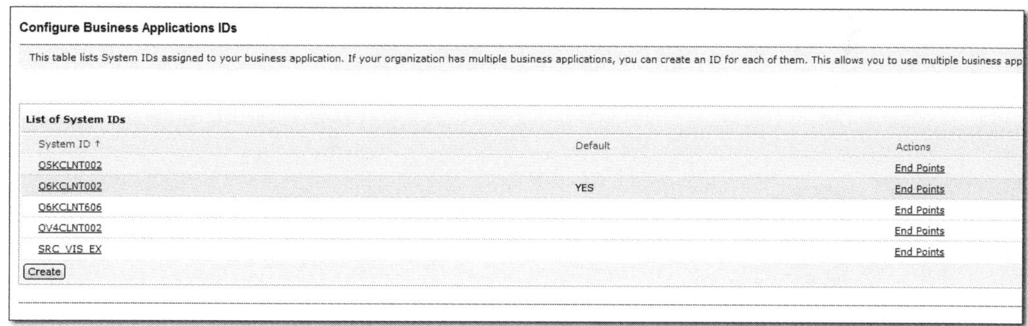

Figure 9.8 SAP Ariba Buyer Account Settings: Configure Business Application IDs

You can also set the configuration for SAP Ariba Discount Management in this area of Figure 9.9.

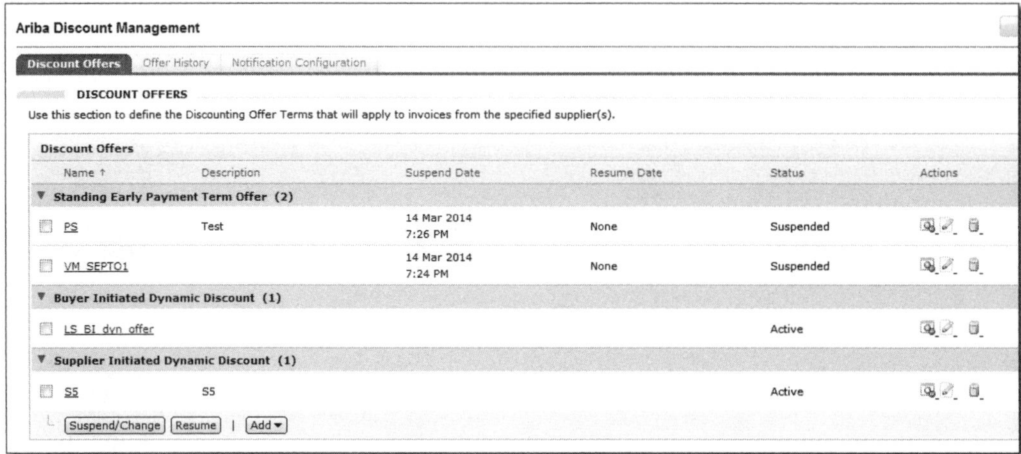

Figure 9.9 SAP Ariba Discount Management

SAP ERP Framework Settings

Once you have configured SAP Ariba, the next step is to configure SAP ERP. Follow these steps:

1. Use Transaction SPRO + [F5] and search for "SAP Business Suite Integration Component for Ariba."
2. Alternatively, use Transaction SIMGH and search for IMG structure [F4] with "Ariba" in the title. Choose SAP BUSINESS SUITE INTEGRATION COMPONENT FOR SAP ARIBA and add it to your favorites. Then, click on the eyeglasses [F7].
3. Next, set the credentials with the SAP Ariba Network in SAP ERP.
4. In the CUSTOMIZING tab, go to FRAMEWORK SETTINGS • DEFINE CREDENTIALS AND END POINTS FOR ARIBA NETWORK (see Figure 9.10).

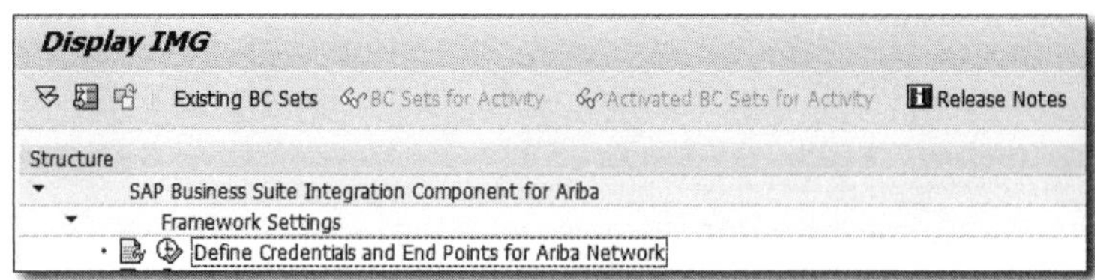

Figure 9.10 Framework Settings—Define Credentials and End Points for the SAP Ariba Network

5. Enter the IDENTITY and PASSWORD for your SAP Ariba account. If it is a test account, mark the field labeled TEST ACCOUNT (see Figure 9.11).

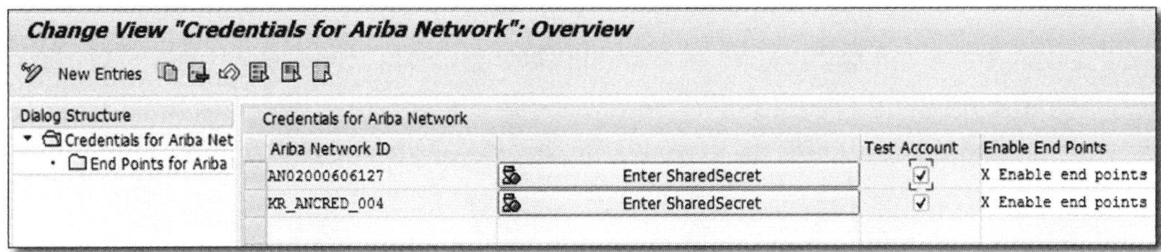

Figure 9.11 Framework Settings—Credentials and End Points for the SAP Ariba Network—Test Account

6. If you need end points, select choose X and maintain your end points (see Figure 9.12).

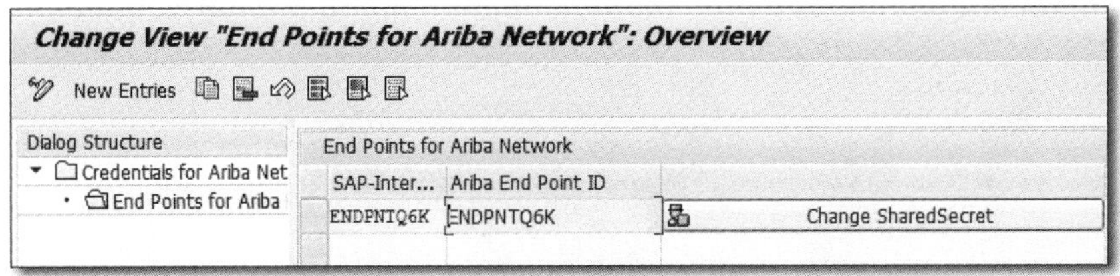

Figure 9.12 Framework Settings—End Points for the SAP Ariba Network

7. In CUSTOMIZING menu, go to FRAMEWORK SETTINGS • DEFINE BASIC MESSAGE SETTINGS.

8. Adjust the cXML message configuration for the business objects as in Figure 9.13.

Change View "cXML Message Configuration": Overview

New Entries

cXML Message Configuration

Application Component...	Object Type	cXML Message Type	Direction	Mapping Version	cXML Version	Send cXMLStatusUpdateReque...
BNS-ARI-SE-ERP	BKPF	CCPAYP	IN Inbound	V001	1.2.024	☑
BNS-ARI-SE-ERP	BKPF	PAYP	OUT Outbound	V001	1.2.024	☐
BNS-ARI-SE-ERP	BKPF	PAYS	OUT Outbound	V001	1.2.024	☐
BNS-ARI-SE-ERP	BUS2012	CONF	IN Inbound	V001	1.2.024	☑
BNS-ARI-SE-ERP	BUS2012	ORDR	OUT Outbound	V001	1.2.024	☐
BNS-ARI-SE-ERP	BUS2015	SHIP	IN Inbound	V001	1.2.024	☑
BNS-ARI-SE-ERP	BUS2081	CCINVC	OUT Outbound	V001	1.2.024	☐
BNS-ARI-SE-ERP	BUS2081	INVC	IN Inbound	V001	1.2.024	☑
BNS-ARI-SE-ERP	BUS2081	STAT	OUT Outbound	V001	1.2.024	☐
BNS-ARI-SE-ERP	FIOPAYAVIS	PAYR	OUT Outbound	V001	1.2.024	☐

Figure 9.13 Framework Settings Basic Message Settings

If you are implementing Business Suite Add-On directly, you will need to complete the following steps. Other approaches (SAP PI-mediated) can skip these steps.

1. In the customizing, go to Framework Settings • Manage and Test Enterprise Services. An SAP NetWeaver Business Client (NWBC) window will open.
2. On the Service Admin tab, click on Web Service Configuration (see Figure 9.14).

Figure 9.14 Manage and Test Enterprise Services

3. Select object type Service Definition, Name contains CXML*, and click Search. Five services will show in the results list.
4. Enter the necessary parameters for all services and click Create Service and use the guided configuration as in Figure 9.15.
5. Once completed, each service will each have a binding/log port.
6. Return to the Configuration Search tab.
7. Select object type Consumer Proxy, Name contains CXML*, and press Search. Nine services will show in the results list.

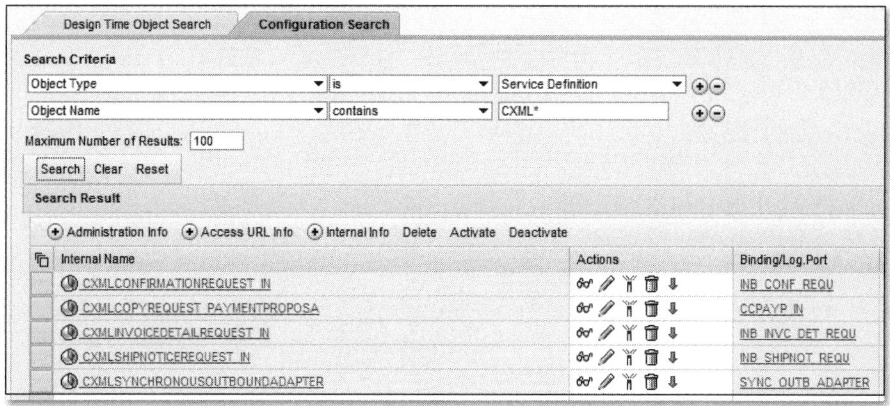

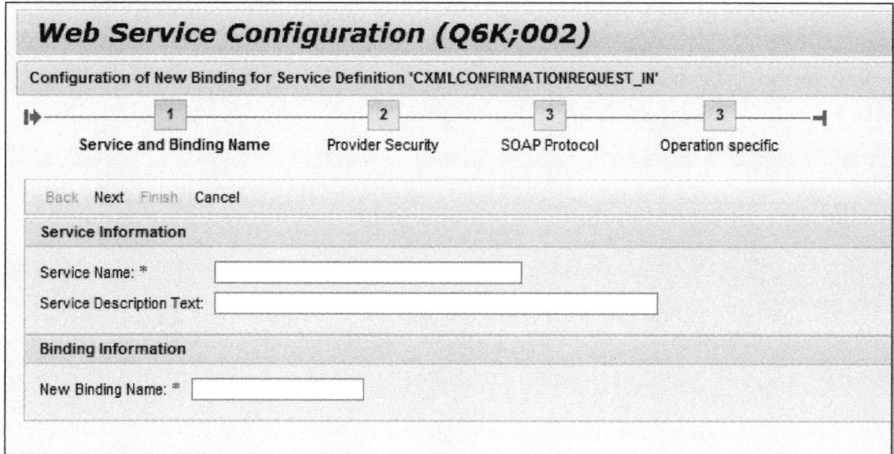

Figure 9.15 Framework Settings Define Inbound Services

8. Enter the necessary parameters for all services and choose CREATE • MANUAL CONFIGURATION and use the guided configuration steps (see Figure 9.16).
9. Once completed, each service will have one binding: only the consumer proxy `CO_ARBFND_PRX_PCAS_OUT` has several bindings/log ports.

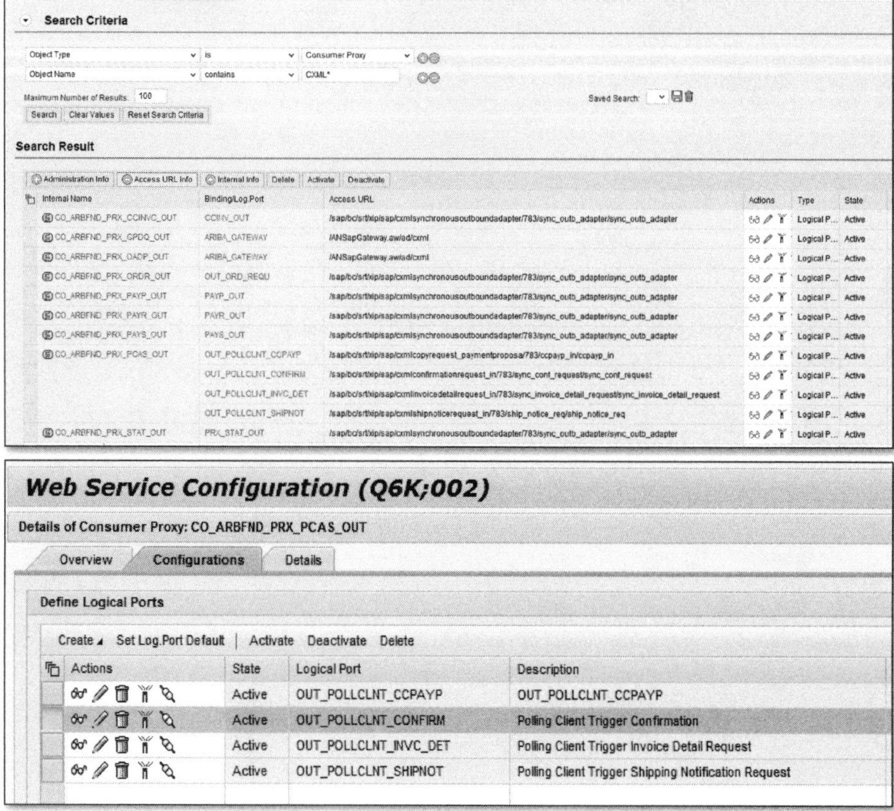

Figure 9.16 Framework Settings Define Outbound Services

Next, you'll need to sort out the certificates for your framework:

1. Go to URL for the SAP Ariba Network at *http://service.ariba.com* and click on the certificate error, or on the padlock.
2. View the certificate, then go to the DETAILS tab and save the certificate.
3. You should now have a .cer file on your PC, as shown in Figure 9.17.
4. In the CUSTOMIZING menu, go to FRAMEWORK SETTINGS • CERTIFICATE MAINTENANCE.
5. Enter the certificate file that you just downloaded.

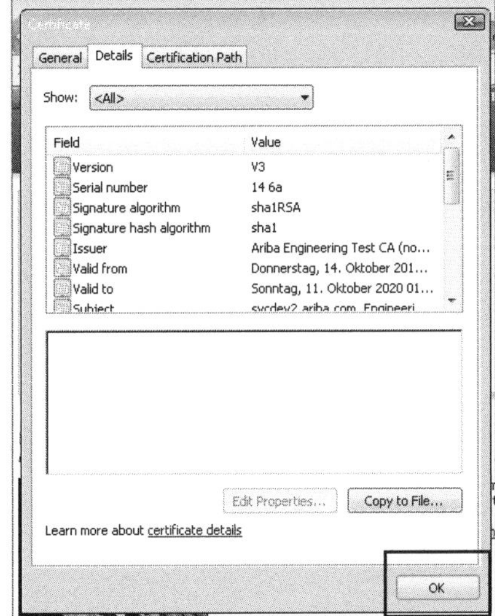

Figure 9.17 Framework Settings Certificate Maintenance

Next, you'll need to enter the framework settings for the polling client:

1. In the CUSTOMIZING menu, go to FRAMEWORK SETTINGS • DEFINE SETTINGS FOR POLLING CLIENT.
2. For your SAP Ariba Network ID, entries need to be created for the following objects as in Figure 9.18 (select NEW ENTRIES to create):
   - CONF
   - SHIP
   - INVC
   - CCPAYP

Change View "Define Settings for Polling Agent": Overview

New Entries

Define Settings for Polling Agent

Ariba Network ID	Logical System	cXML Messa...	SAP-Internal Key...	Max. N...	Logical Port
AN02000606127	Q6KCLNT002	CCPAYP	DPNTQ6K	10	OUT_POLLCLNT_CCPAYP
AN02000606127	Q6KCLNT002	CONF	ENDPNTQ6K	10	OUT_POLLCLNT_CONFIRM
AN02000606127	Q6KCLNT002	INVC	ENDPNTQ6K	10	OUT_POLLCLNT_INVC_DET
AN02000606127	Q6KCLNT002	SHIP	ENDPNTQ6K	10	OUT_POLLCLNT_SHIPNOT

Figure 9.18 Framework Settings Settings for Polling Client

Application-Specific Settings

Our next step will be to create application-specific settings for a number of items.

To set the SAP Ariba Network ID to company code:

1. In customizing, go to Application-Specific Settings • SAP ERP Integration Component for Ariba.
2. Choose Assign Ariba Network ID to Company Code.
3. Assign the relevant company codes to your SAP Ariba Network ID (see Figure 9.19).

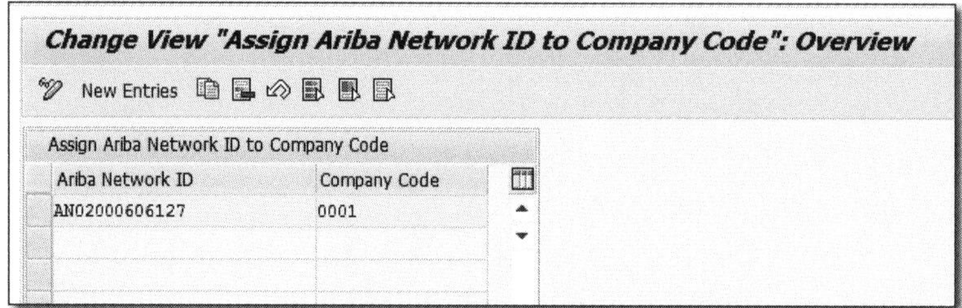

Figure 9.19 Application-Specific Settings SAP Ariba Network ID to Company Code

To enable vendors for SAP Ariba Network:

1. In Customizing, go to Application-Specific Settings • SAP ERP Integration Component for Ariba.
2. Choose Enable Vendors for Ariba Network.
3. For each relevant vendor, an entry needs to be made either with his private ID or his SAP Ariba Network ID.

To define message output control:

1. In CUSTOMIZING, go to APPLICATION-SPECIFIC SETTINGS • SAP ERP INTEGRATION COMPONENT FOR ARIBA.
2. Choose DEFINE MESSAGE OUTPUT CONTROL.
3. In the popup that appears, choose DEFINE CONDITIONS FOR OUTPUT CONTROL (see Figure 9.20).
4. Check/create one message with medium "8 Special function".

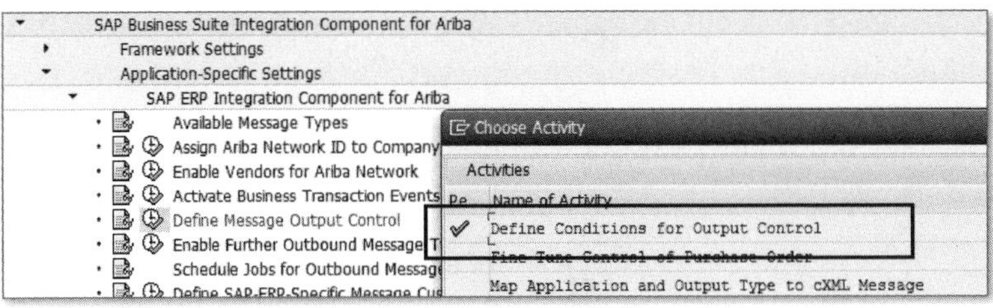

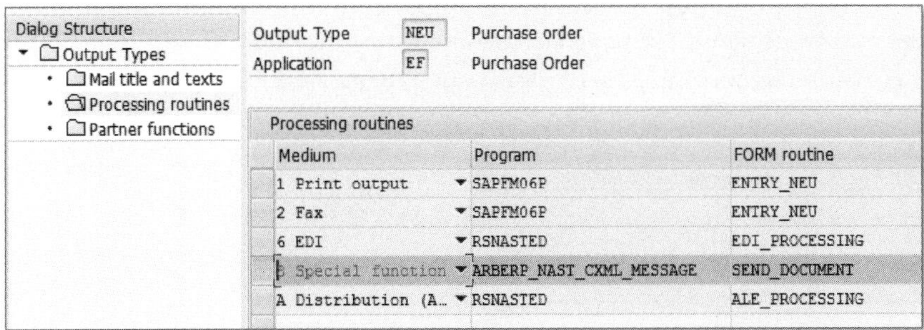

Figure 9.20 Application-Specific Settings Define Message Output Control

5. Go back to the popup.
6. Choose FINE-TUNE CONTROL OF PURCHASE ORDER.
7. Check/create the entries shown in Figure 9.21.
8. Go back to the popup once again.
9. In the popup, choose MAP APPLICATION AND OUTPUT TYPE TO CXML MESSAGE.
10. Create the entry seen in Figure 9.22.

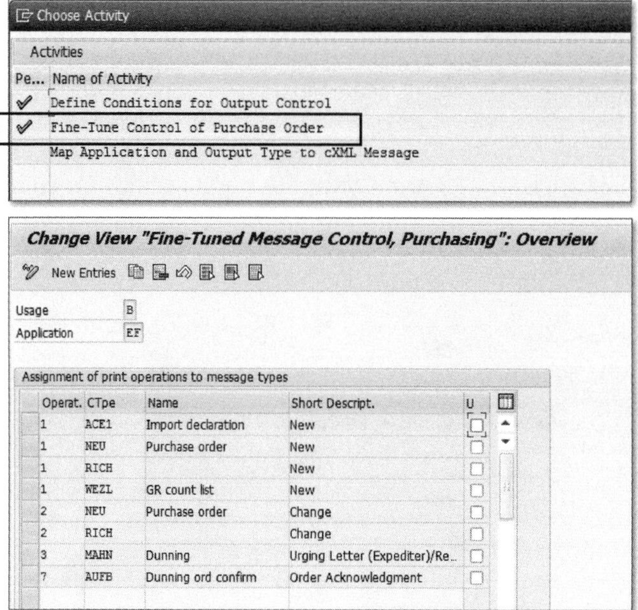

Figure 9.21 Application-Specific Settings Define Message Output Control

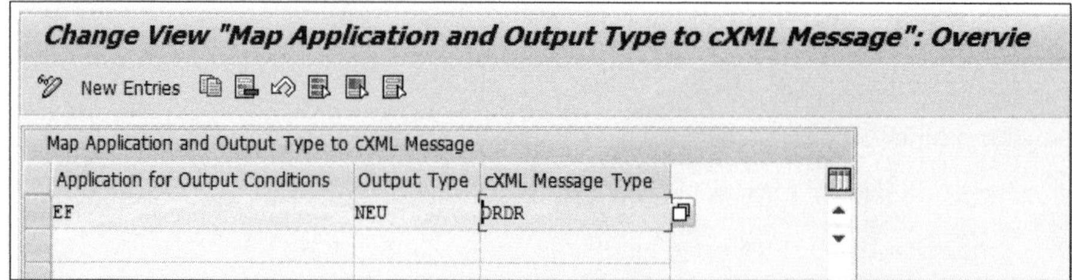

Figure 9.22 Application-Specific Settings Define Message Output Control

11. In Customizing, go to Application-Specific Settings • SAP ERP Integration Component for Ariba.

12. Choose Enable Further Outbound Message Types per Vendor.
13. Create outbound message entries for your vendor, depending on your requirements (what outbound messages need to be exchanged with supplier) in Figure 9.23.

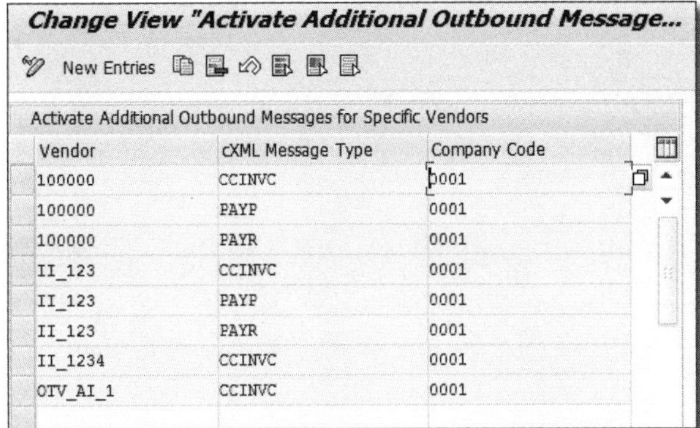
Change View "Activate Additional Outbound Message...

New Entries

Activate Additional Outbound Messages for Specific Vendors

Vendor	cXML Message Type	Company Code
100000	CCINVC	0001
100000	PAYP	0001
100000	PAYR	0001
II_123	CCINVC	0001
II_123	PAYP	0001
II_123	PAYR	0001
II_1234	CCINVC	0001
OTV_AI_1	CCINVC	0001

Figure 9.23 Application-Specific Settings Enable Further Outbound Message Types per Vendor

To define SAP ERP-specific message customizing:

1. In Customizing, go to Application-Specific Settings • SAP ERP Integration Component for Ariba.
2. Choose Define SAP-ERP-Specific Message Customizing.
3. Create the entries in Figure 9.24.

Change View "Define SAP-ERP-Specific Message Customizing": Overview

New Entries

Define SAP-ERP-Specific Message Customizing

Object Type	cXML Messa...	Direction	Attachment Transfer	Attach cXML Message Payload to Business Object
BKPF	CCPAYP	IN Inbound	GOS Generic Object Services	✓
BUS2012	CONF	IN Inbound	GOS Generic Object Services	
BUS2012	ORDR	OUT Outbound	GOS Generic Object Services	
BUS2015	SHIP	IN Inbound	GOS Generic Object Services	✓
BUS2081	CCINVC	OUT Outbound	GOS Generic Object Services	
BUS2081	INVC	IN Inbound	GOS Generic Object Services	✓
FIOPAYAVIS	PAYR	OUT Outbound	GOS Generic Object Services	

Figure 9.24 Application-Specific Settings Define SAP-ERP-Specific Message Customizing

To define mapping settings for shipping notifications:

1. In CUSTOMIZING, go to APPLICATION-SPECIFIC SETTINGS • SAP ERP INTEGRATION COMPONENT FOR ARIBA and expand DEFINE SAP-ERP-SPECIFIC MAPPING SETTINGS.
2. Choose DEFINE MAPPING SETTINGS FOR SHIPPING NOTIFICATIONS.
3. For example, make such entries for your carrier as in Figure 9.25.

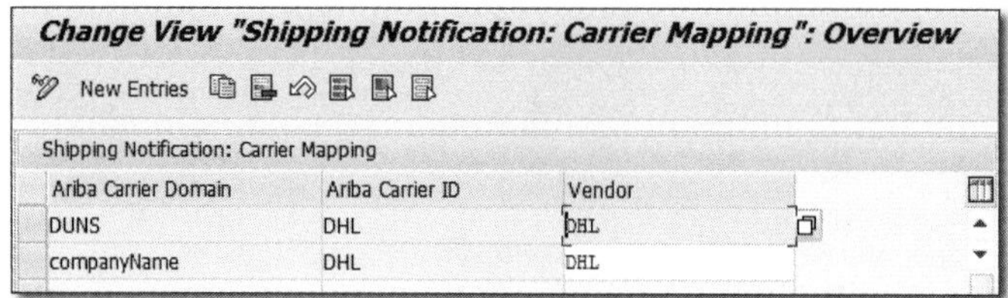

Ariba Carrier Domain	Ariba Carrier ID	Vendor
DUNS	DHL	DHL
companyName	DHL	DHL

Figure 9.25 Application-Specific Settings Define Mapping Settings for Shipping Notifications

To define mapping settings for invoices:

1. In CUSTOMIZING, go to APPLICATION-SPECIFIC SETTINGS • SAP ERP INTEGRATION COMPONENT FOR ARIBA and expand DEFINE SAP-ERP-SPECIFIC MAPPING SETTINGS.
2. Choose DEFINE MAPPING SETTINGS FOR INVOICES.
3. In the popup, select one item at a time and make the following entries (see Figure 9.26 through Figure 9.29).

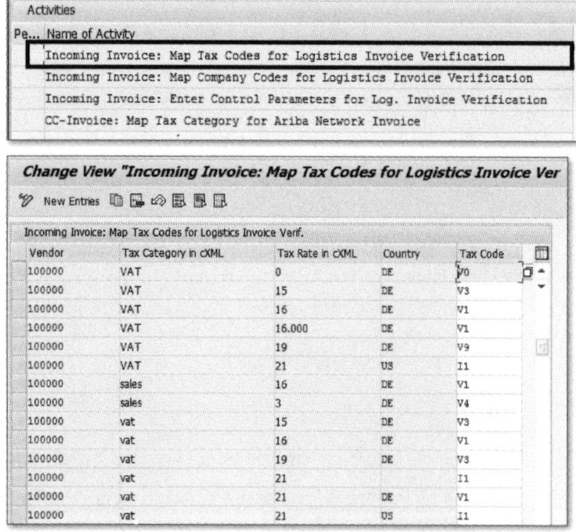

Vendor	Tax Category in cXML	Tax Rate in cXML	Country	Tax Code
100000	VAT	0	DE	V0
100000	VAT	15	DE	V3
100000	VAT	16	DE	V1
100000	VAT	16.000	DE	V1
100000	VAT	19	DE	V9
100000	VAT	21	US	I1
100000	sales	16	DE	V1
100000	sales	3	DE	V4
100000	vat	15	DE	V3
100000	vat	16	DE	V1
100000	vat	19	DE	V3
100000	vat	21		I1
100000	vat	21	DE	V1
100000	vat	21	US	I1

Figure 9.26 Application-Specific Settings Define Mapping Settings for Invoices

To define mapping settings for invoices:

1. Choose Define Mapping Settings for Invoices.
2. In the popup, select one item at a time and make the following entries, as shown in Figure 9.27.

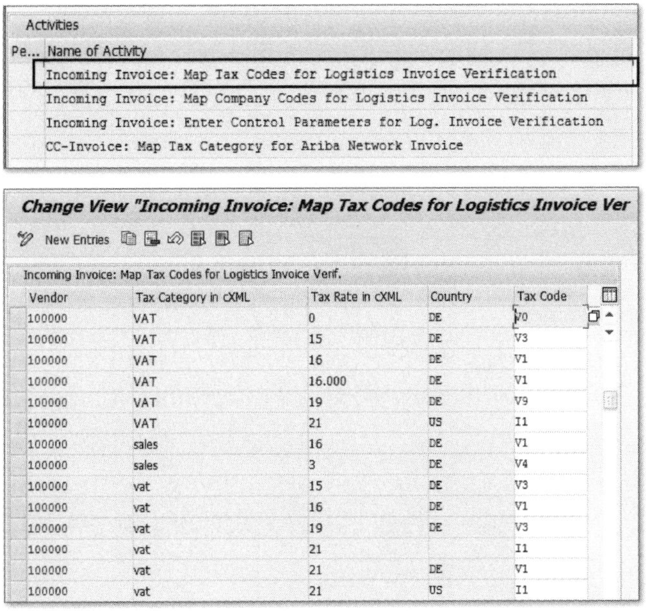

Activities

Pe...	Name of Activity
	Incoming Invoice: Map Tax Codes for Logistics Invoice Verification
	Incoming Invoice: Map Company Codes for Logistics Invoice Verification
	Incoming Invoice: Enter Control Parameters for Log. Invoice Verification
	CC-Invoice: Map Tax Category for Ariba Network Invoice

Change View "Incoming Invoice: Map Tax Codes for Logistics Invoice Ver

New Entries

Incoming Invoice: Map Tax Codes for Logistics Invoice Verif.

Vendor	Tax Category in cXML	Tax Rate in cXML	Country	Tax Code
100000	VAT	0	DE	V0
100000	VAT	15	DE	V3
100000	VAT	16	DE	V1
100000	VAT	16.000	DE	V1
100000	VAT	19	DE	V9
100000	VAT	21	US	I1
100000	sales	16	DE	V1
100000	sales	3	DE	V4
100000	vat	15	DE	V3
100000	vat	16	DE	V1
100000	vat	19	DE	V3
100000	vat	21		I1
100000	vat	21	DE	V1
100000	vat	21	US	I1

Figure 9.27 Application-Specific Settings Define Mapping Settings for Invoices

3. Choose Define Mapping Settings for Invoices.
4. In the popup, select one item at a time and make the following entries, as in Figure 9.28.
5. Choose Define Mapping Settings for Invoices.
6. In the popup, select one item at a time and make the following entries, as shown in Figure 9.29.

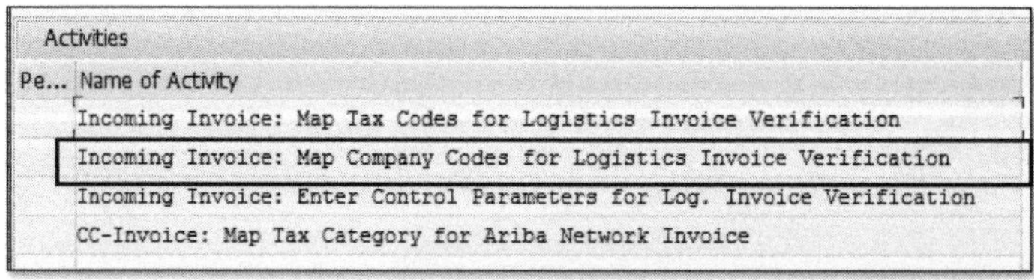

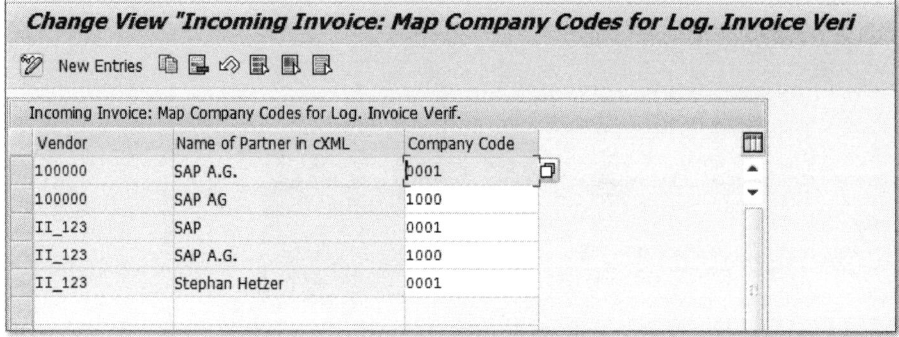

Figure 9.28 Application-Specific Settings Define Mapping Settings for Invoices

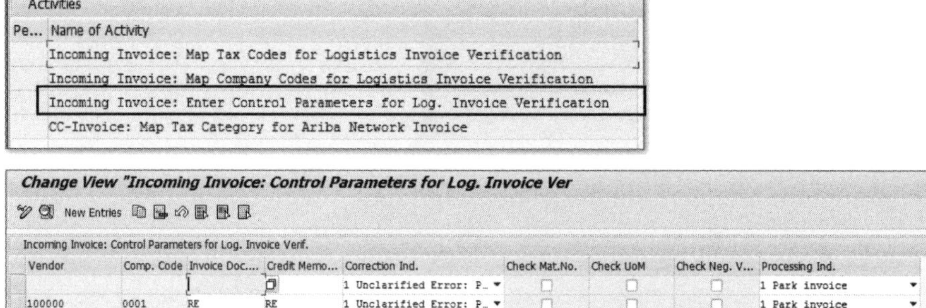

Figure 9.29 Application-Specific Settings Define Mapping Settings for Invoices

7. Choose Define Mapping Settings for Invoices.
8. In the popup, select one item at a time and make the following entries, as in Figure 9.30.

Activities

Pe...	Name of Activity
	Incoming Invoice: Map Tax Codes for Logistics Invoice Verification
	Incoming Invoice: Map Company Codes for Logistics Invoice Verification
	Incoming Invoice: Enter Control Parameters for Log. Invoice Verification
	CC-Invoice: Map Tax Category for Ariba Network Invoice

Change View "Map ERP tax code to cXML tax category": Overview

New Entries

Map ERP tax code to cXML tax category

Vendor	Country	Tax Code	Tax Category in cXML
	US	I0	VAT
	US	I1	VAT
	DE	V0	sales
	DE	V1	VAT
	DE	V2	VAT
	DE	V3	PST
	DE	V8	sales
	DE	V9	PST
100000	DE	SA	asdf

Figure 9.30 Application-Specific Settings Define Mapping Settings for Invoices

To define mapping settings for payments:

1. In the CUSTOMIZING menu, go to APPLICATION-SPECIFIC SETTINGS • SAP ERP INTEGRATION COMPONENT FOR ARIBA and expand DEFINE SAP-ERP-SPECIFIC MAPPING SETTINGS.
2. Choose DEFINE MAPPING SETTINGS FOR PAYMENTS.
3. Create entries for the payment method that you want to use (see Figure 9.31).

Change View "Mapping ERP Payment Method to Ariba Payment Method": Over

New Entries

Mapping ERP Payment Method to Ariba Payment Method

Country	Payment Method	Ariba Payment Method
DE	L	ach
DE	U	ach

Figure 9.31 Application-Specific Settings Define Mapping Settings for Payments

To map texts of SAP ERP and SAP Ariba Network:

1. In the CUSTOMIZING menu, go to APPLICATION-SPECIFIC SETTINGS • SAP ERP INTEGRATION COMPONENT FOR ARIBA.
2. Choose MAP TEXTS OF SAP ERP AND ARIBA NETWORK.
3. In the popup (Figure 9.32 through Figure 9.34), select one item at a time and make the following entries.

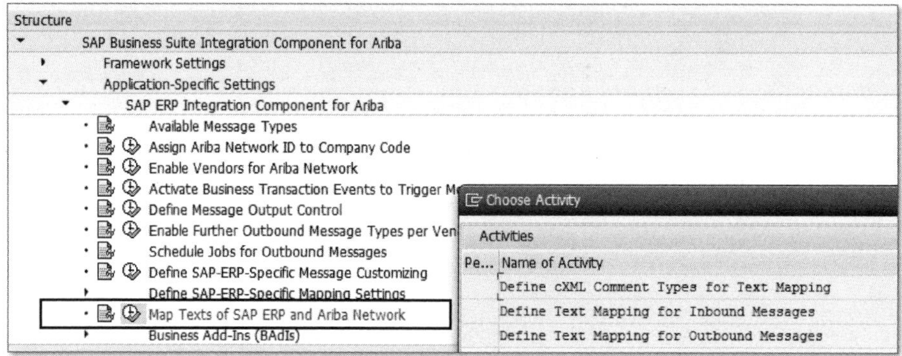

Figure 9.32 Application Specific Settings—Map Texts of SAP ERP to SAP Ariba Network

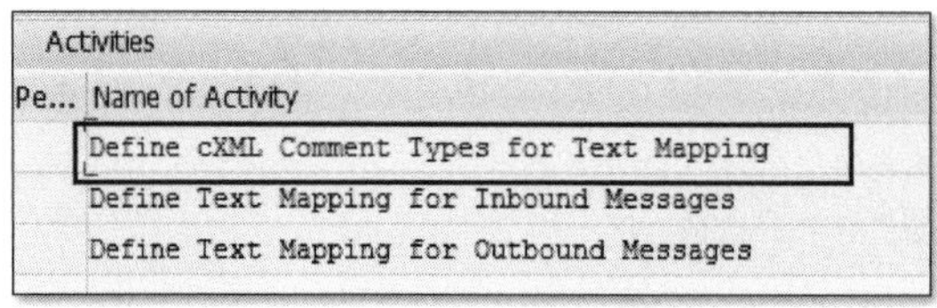

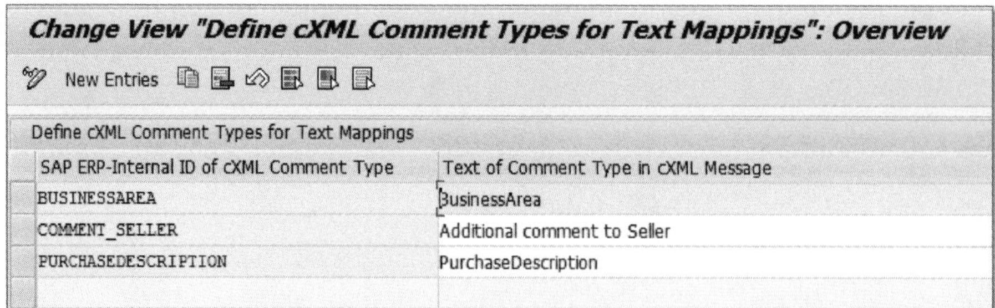

Figure 9.33 Application-Specific Settings—Map Texts of SAP ERP and SAP Ariba Network

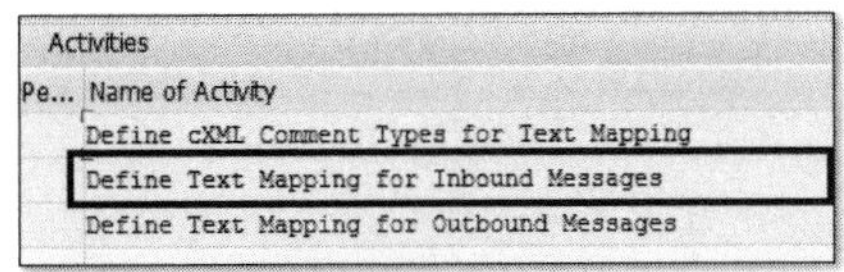

Change View "Define Text Mapping for Inbound Messages": Overview

New Entries

Define Text Mapping for Inbound Messages

cXML Message Type	cXML Element ID	SAP ...	SAP ERP BO Type	SAP ERP BO Node	SAP ERP Text Object	SAP ERP Text ID
CONF	HEADER_COMMENTS	*	BUS2012	HEADER	EKKO	[illegible]5
CONF	ITEM_CONFIRMATION_STATUS_COMMENTS	*	BUS2012	ITEM	EKPO	F04
CONF	ITEM_CONF_STATUS_COMMENTS		BUS2012	ITEM	EKPO	F04
CONF	ITEM_CONF_STATUS_ITEM_IN_COMMENTS	*	BUS2012	ITEM	EKPO	F04
INVC	DETAIL_ORDER_ITEM_COMMENTS		BUS2081	ITEM	DRSEG	SGTXT
INVC	DETAIL_REQUEST_HEADER_COMMENTS		BUS2081	HEADER	RBKP	0001
SHIP	HEADER_COMMENTS	*	BUS2015	HEADER	VBBK	0102

Figure 9.34 Application-Specific Settings—Map Texts of SAP ERP and SAP Ariba Network

4. In the popup in Figure 9.35, select one item at a time and make the following entries.

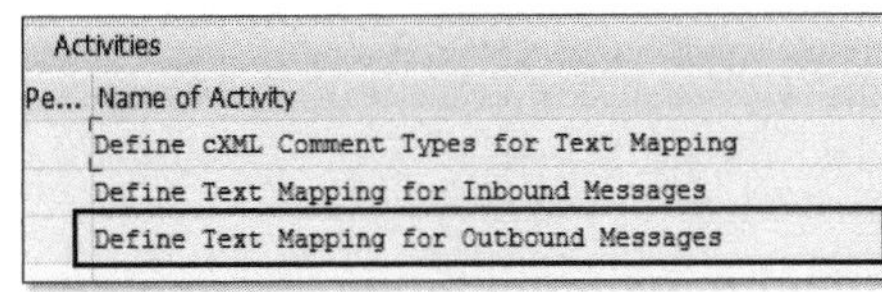

Change View "Define Text Mapping for Outbound Messages": Overview

New Entries

Define Text Mapping for Outbound Messages

SAP ERP BO Type	SAP ERP BO Node	SAP ERP Text Object	SAP ERP Text ID	cXML Message...	cXML Element ID	SAP ERP-Internal ID of cXML Comment T...
BKPF	ITEM	BSEG	SGTXT	PAYP	PAYMENT_PROPOSAL_REQUEST_COMMENTS	COMMENT_SELLER
BUS2012	HEADER	EKKO	F01	ORDR	HEADER_COMMENTS	
BUS2012	HEADER	EKKO	F02	ORDR	HEADER_COMMENTS	
BUS2012	ITEM	EKPO	F01	ORDR	ITEM_OUT_COMMENTS	
BUS2012	ITEM	EKPO	F04	ORDR	ITEM_OUT_COMMENTS	
BUS2081	HEADER	RBKP	0001	CCINVC	DETAIL_REQUEST_HEADER_COMMENTS	COMMENT_SELLER
BUS2081	ITEM	DRSEG	SGTXT	CCINVC	DETAIL_ORDER_ITEM_COMMENTS	COMMENT_SELLER

Figure 9.35 Application-Specific Settings—Map Texts of SAP ERP and SAP Ariba Network

You have now completed the mapping section for set up and can proceed to testing your configuration.

Testing

To test that your settings have been properly entered, you can:

1. Choose the document type or supplier assigned in the message determination for message export (for example, NB). Enter purchase order values.
2. If confirmations are required, open the CONFIRMATIONS tab, select 0001 CONFIRMATIONS FOR CONF. CONTROL and select the ACKNOWL. REQD option.
3. Check your tax code and whether or not the PO is flagged for "Goods Receipt required for Invoice" (GR-Bsd IV-mark).
4. Save the purchase order and note the purchase order number, shown in Figure 9.36.

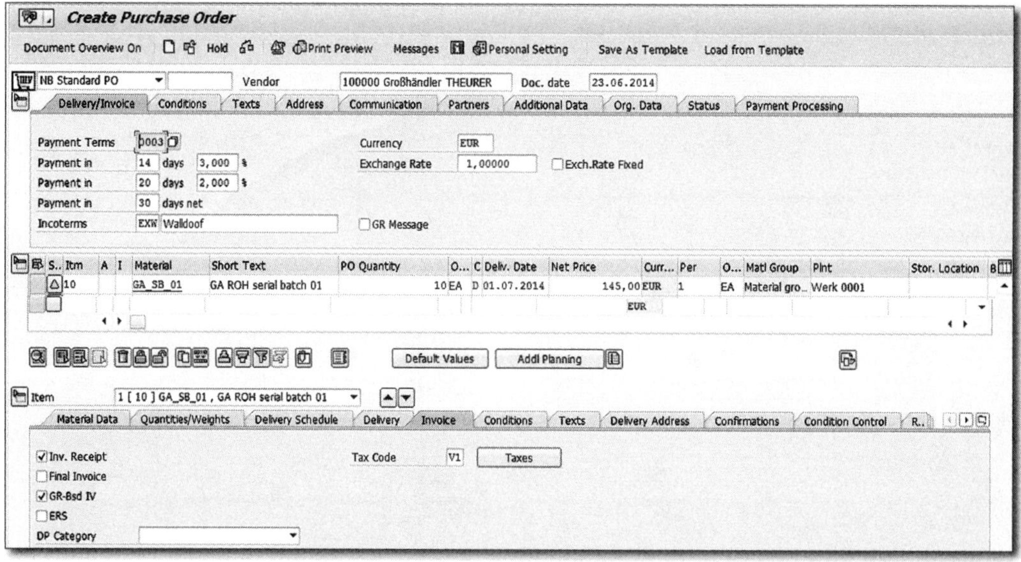

Figure 9.36 Testing Procure-to-Pay Processes—Transaction ME21N

5. If necessary (if you have workflow for purchase order releases enabled), release the purchase order as shown in Figure 9.37.
6. In Transaction ME28, select RELEASE CODE and enter the purchase order number in the DOCUMENT NUMBER field.
7. Choose RUN [F8].
8. Select the line with the newly-created PO and choose RELEASE.

9. Save.

Program Edit Goto System Help

Release (Approve) Purchasing Documents

Release Code			
Release Group		to	
✓ Set Release			
☐ Cancel Release			
✓ Release Prerequisite Fulfilled			
☐ List with Items			
Scope of List	BEST		
Puchasing Document Category	F	to	
Purchasing Organization		to	
Document Number		to	
Document Type		to	
Purchasing Group		to	
Vendor		to	
Supplying Plant		to	
Document Date		to	

Figure 9.37 Testing Procure-to-Pay Processes—Transaction ME28N

If you are mediating the connection to the SAP Ariba Network via Process Orchestration (SAP PO), you can validate whether the transactions were transferred successfully with Transaction SXMB_MONI (see Figure 9.38). In the event that the transfer has gone through, your transfers should appear with green lights and no hard stop error messages.

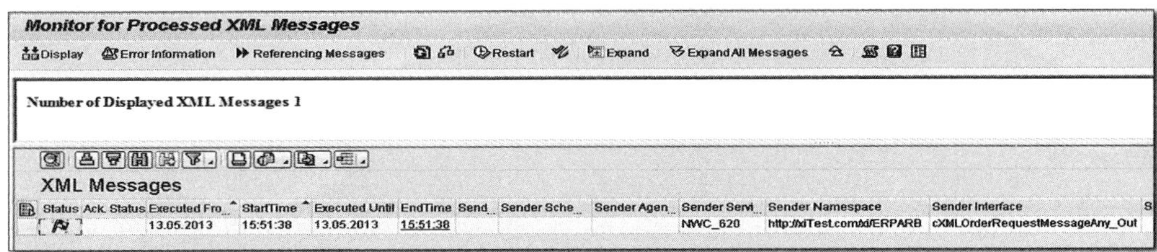

Figure 9.38 Testing Procure-to-Pay Processes—Transaction SXMB_MONI

If you have the direct scenario, whereby SAP ERP communicates directly in cXML with the SAP Ariba Network, Transactions SRT_MONI and SLG1 allow you to verify whether the cXML messages were transferred properly, as shown in Figure 9.39 and Figure 9.40.

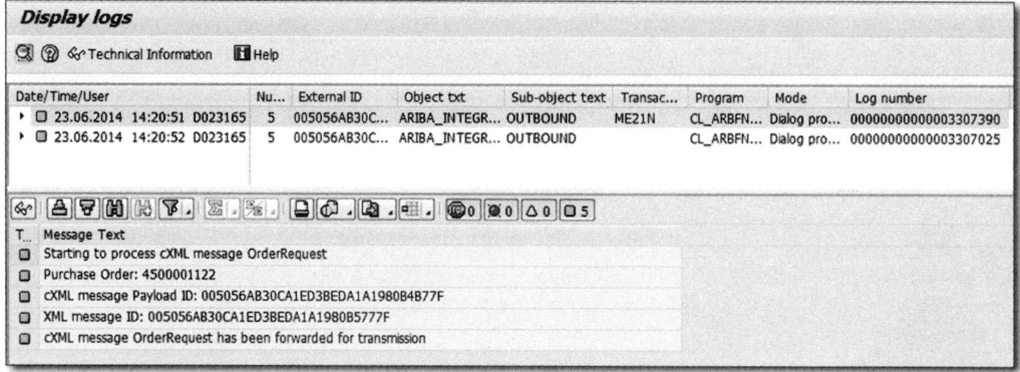

Figure 9.39 Testing Procure-to-Pay Processes—Transaction SLG1

Web Service Utilities: Message Monitor

Re-Select

Action Log | Error Log | Related Messages | Actions | Technical View

Client 002 - Basic View

Nu...	Status	Processing Status	Creation Da...	Creation ...	Execution ...	Executio...	Sender Party	Receiver Interface Name	Erro
4		Delivered	23.06.2014	13:35:32	23.06.2014	13:35:34		cXMLSynchronousOutboundAdapter...	
3		Delivered	23.06.2014	13:33:23	23.06.2014	13:33:24		cXMLSynchronousOutboundAdapter...	
2		Delivered	23.06.2014	13:31:58	23.06.2014	13:32:01		cXMLSynchronousOutboundAdapter...	
1		Delivered	23.06.2014	13:31:54	23.06.2014	13:31:58		cXMLInvoiceDetailRequest_In	

Figure 9.40 Testing Procure-to-Pay Processes—Transaction SLOI

Showing Order Confirmation in SAP ERP

To display the order confirmation in SAP ERP:

1. Enter Transaction ME23N.
2. Choose Other Purchase Order and enter the purchase order number.
3. Select one item from your chosen purchase order and open the Confirmations tab.
4. When the external confirmation from your supplier has been sent, you should see an additional line in the table showing the delivery date, time, quantity, and reference for the chosen item.

To change the purchase order in SAP ERP:

1. Enter Transaction ME22N.
2. Choose Other Purchase Order, enter the previously-created purchase order number, and choose Other Document.
3. Choose Display/Change to edit the selected purchase order.
4. Change the purchase order as required, and choose Save.
5. Select Messages to check whether the change message is triggered. A newly-created message (Medium "8 special-function") should be visible with a green status.
6. Select the newly-created message and choose Processing Log to see a detailed description of the message status in Figure 9.41.

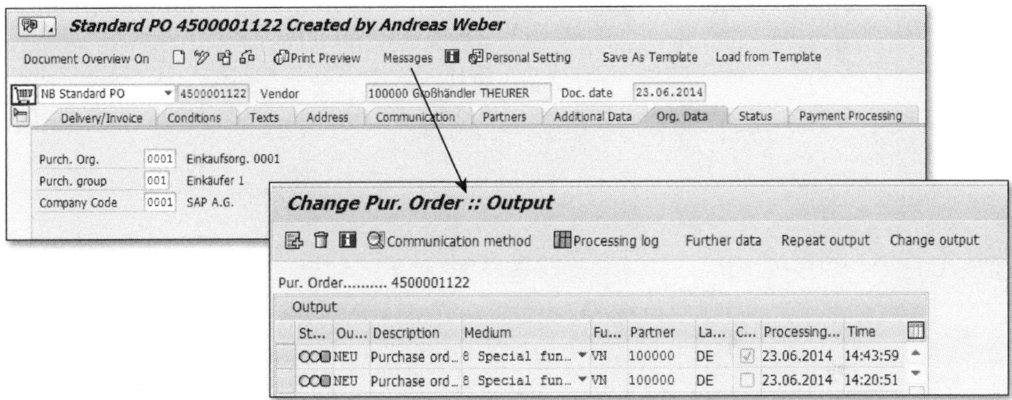

Figure 9.41 Testing Procure to Pay Processes—ME22N: Inbound Delivery

To display the inbound delivery in SAP ERP:

1. Enter Transaction ME23N or VL33N.
2. Choose Other Purchase Order and enter the purchase order number.
3. Choose Other Document to display the purchase order document. Now you can verify the details of your purchase order.
4. Select one item from your chosen purchase order and open the Confirmations tab. When the Confirmation Control is listed as `0001` or `0004 Delivery`, and the external confirmation from your supplier has been sent, you should see an additional line in the table showing the delivery date, time, quantity, and reference for the chosen item.

5. Double click on the Inbound Delivery number.
6. The program brings you to Transaction VL33N (Display Inbound Delivery).

To post a goods receipt in SAP ERP:

1. Enter Transaction MIGO or VL32N.
2. Enter the inbound delivery number, which is found in the created purchase order. Select Post Goods Receipt.
3. Check the system message. It should look like this: "Goods receipt for inbound delivery 180000340 posted (material document 5000000391)".
4. After the post goods receipt, you can see the material document in the PO • Details tab in Purchase Order History, as seen in Figure 9.42.

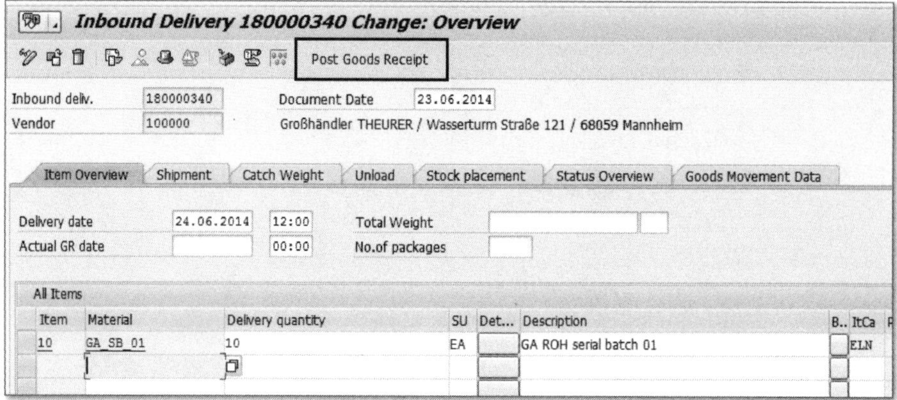

Figure 9.42 Post Goods Receipt—Transaction MIGO or VL32N

To display invoices and FI documents in SAP ERP:

1. Enter Transactions MIR4 and ME23N.
2. In Transaction ME23N, open the Purchase Order History tab, which should appear as soon as a follow-on document to your purchase order has been posted.

3. You should see at least one entry named RE-L in the SH. TEXT column, which is the actual invoice. Note down the number of the invoice and open Transaction MIR4 with this number (and mark ENTRY TYPE SAP ARIBA INVOICE).
4. Alternatively (in Transaction ME23N), simply click on the invoice number.
5. You should see the posted invoice for your purchase order item(s).
6. Click on the follow-on documents icon, and note down the financial document number, as shown in Figure 9.43, Figure 9.44, and Figure 9.45.

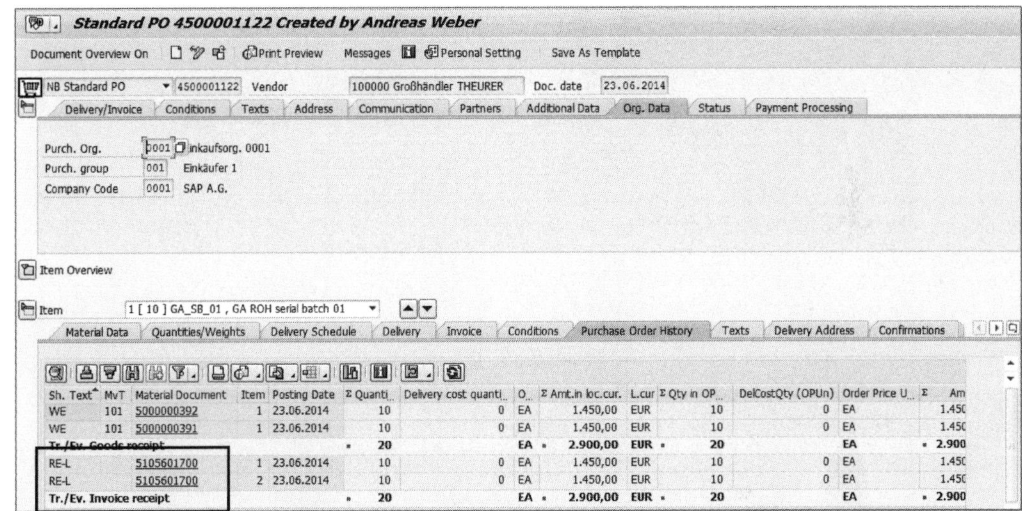

Figure 9.43 Testing Procure-to-Pay Processes—Transaction MIR4 or ME23N

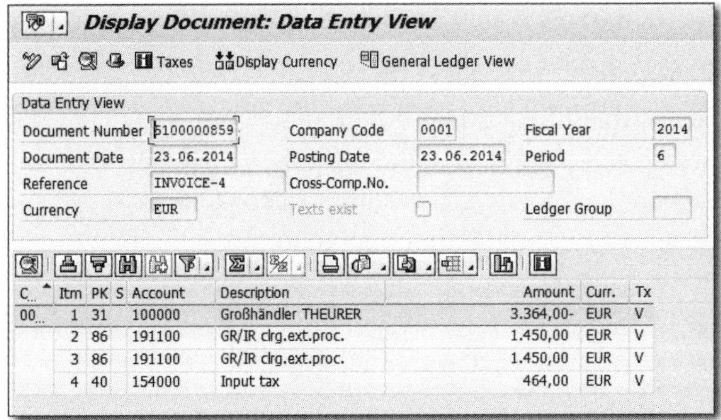

Figure 9.44 Testing Procure-to-Pay Processes—Transaction FB03: Display Details

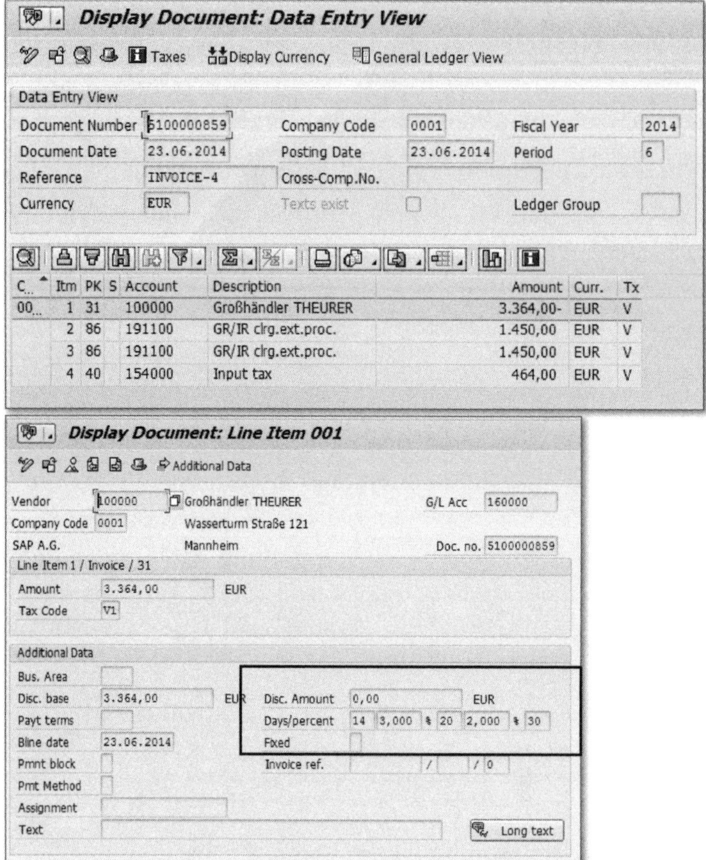

Figure 9.45 Testing Procure-to-Pay Processes—Transaction FB03: Display Details

SAP Ariba Discount Management

SAP Ariba Discount Management is an add-on solution for SAP Ariba Invoicing solutions that was discussed in Chapter 5. Accounts payable can leverage SAP Ariba Discount Management to obtain discounts in exchange for early payment, while suppliers can enhance cash flow without going to factoring options that cost several times more than the discount options provided within the tool. SAP Ariba Discount Management can also be integrated with SAP ERP invoicing/accounts payable scenarios.

If you (the buyer) work with SAP Ariba Discount Management, the supplier receive an early payment offer (see Figure 9.46).

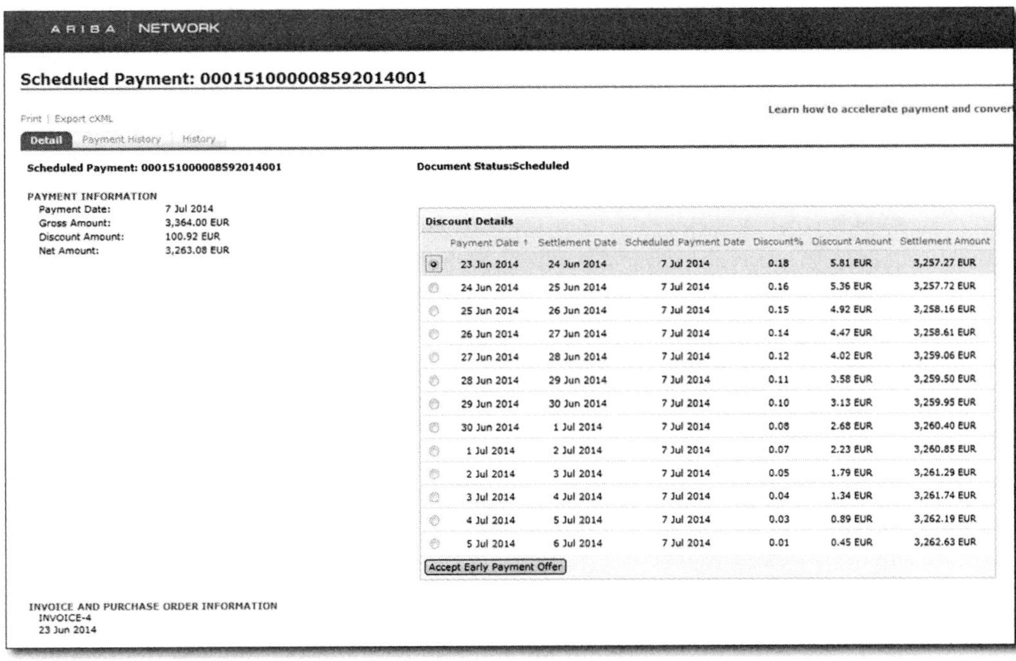
ARIBA NETWORK

Scheduled Payment: 000151000008592014001

Print | Export cXML

Learn how to accelerate payment and conver

Detail | Payment History | History

Scheduled Payment: 000151000008592014001

Document Status:Scheduled

PAYMENT INFORMATION

Payment Date:	7 Jul 2014
Gross Amount:	3,364.00 EUR
Discount Amount:	100.92 EUR
Net Amount:	3,263.08 EUR

Discount Details

Payment Date ↑	Settlement Date	Scheduled Payment Date	Discount%	Discount Amount	Settlement Amount
23 Jun 2014	24 Jun 2014	7 Jul 2014	0.18	5.81 EUR	3,257.27 EUR
24 Jun 2014	25 Jun 2014	7 Jul 2014	0.16	5.36 EUR	3,257.72 EUR
25 Jun 2014	26 Jun 2014	7 Jul 2014	0.15	4.92 EUR	3,258.16 EUR
26 Jun 2014	27 Jun 2014	7 Jul 2014	0.14	4.47 EUR	3,258.61 EUR
27 Jun 2014	28 Jun 2014	7 Jul 2014	0.12	4.02 EUR	3,259.06 EUR
28 Jun 2014	29 Jun 2014	7 Jul 2014	0.11	3.58 EUR	3,259.50 EUR
29 Jun 2014	30 Jun 2014	7 Jul 2014	0.10	3.13 EUR	3,259.95 EUR
30 Jun 2014	1 Jul 2014	7 Jul 2014	0.08	2.68 EUR	3,260.40 EUR
1 Jul 2014	2 Jul 2014	7 Jul 2014	0.07	2.23 EUR	3,260.85 EUR
2 Jul 2014	3 Jul 2014	7 Jul 2014	0.05	1.79 EUR	3,261.29 EUR
3 Jul 2014	4 Jul 2014	7 Jul 2014	0.04	1.34 EUR	3,261.74 EUR
4 Jul 2014	5 Jul 2014	7 Jul 2014	0.03	0.89 EUR	3,262.19 EUR
5 Jul 2014	6 Jul 2014	7 Jul 2014	0.01	0.45 EUR	3,262.63 EUR

Accept Early Payment Offer

INVOICE AND PURCHASE ORDER INFORMATION
INVOICE-4
23 Jun 2014

Figure 9.46 Testing Procure-to-Pay Processes—SAP Ariba Network—Supplier Site DM

After update from the accepted early payment offer, you can see the new discount amount (see Figure 9.47).

Display Document: Line Item 001

Additional Data

Vendor	100000	Großhändler THEURER	G/L Acc	160000
Company Code	0001	Wasserturm Straße 121		
SAP A.G.		Mannheim	Doc. no.	5100000859

Line Item 1 / Invoice / 31

Amount	3.364,00	EUR
Tax Code	V1	

Additional Data

Bus. Area				
Disc. base	3.364,00 EUR		Disc. Amount	106,73 EUR
Payt terms			Days/percent	1 0,000 % 0 0,000 % 0
Bline date	23.06.2014		Fixed	
Pmnt block			Invoice ref.	/ / 0

Figure 9.47 Testing Procure-to-Pay Processes—SAP ERP Transaction FB03 Display Details of FI-Doc

Open Transaction FB03 and fill in your FI document number. Double click on the account number from your vendor to show the supplier and verify the transaction.

Scheduled Payments

After invoicing, the supplier can see a scheduled payment. Rather than calling the helpdesk and consuming the valuable time and resources of your organization providing updates, the suppliers can query here to see when the payment will be made. This section outlines how to schedule a payment and verify the pending payment, as shown in Figure 9.48.

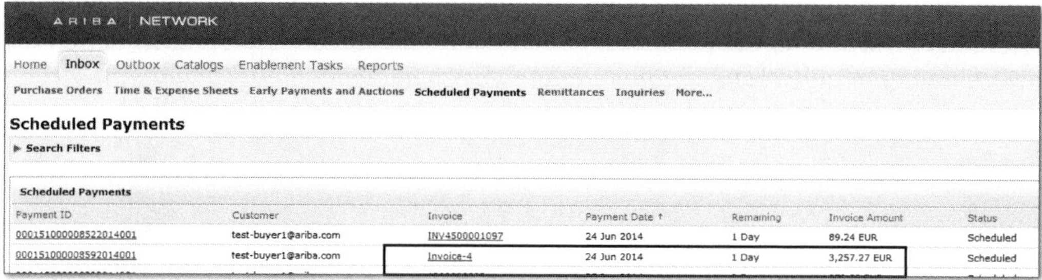

Figure 9.48 Testing Procure-to-Pay Processes—SAP Ariba Network—Supplier Site—Scheduled Payments

1. Next, verify or run payment through SAP ERP: Transaction F110, PAYMENT RUN, as shown in Figure 9.49.

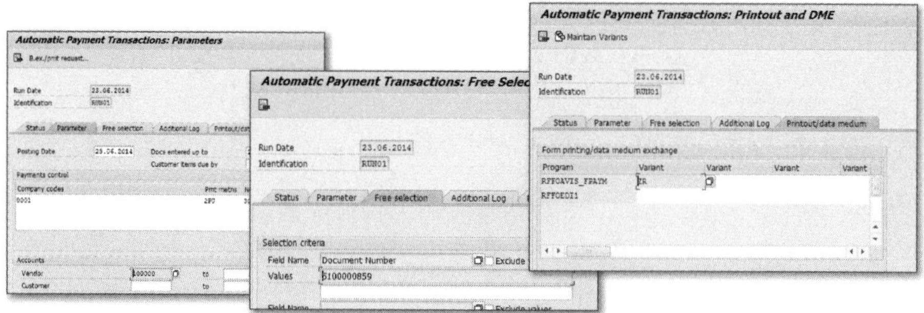

Figure 9.49 Testing Procure-to-Pay Processes—Payment Run Transaction F110

2. Open Transaction F110 and fill in the relevant selection and processing data.

3. Save this payment run.
4. Click on the STATUS tab, schedule a proposal, and then a payment run immediately after that.
5. The PAYMENT RUN LOG will appear (look for the payment advice number), as in Figure 9.50 and Figure 9.51.

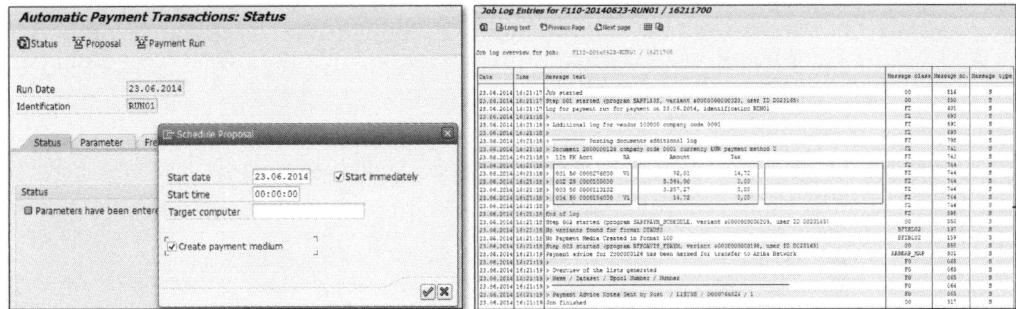

Figure 9.50 Testing Procure-to-Pay Processes—Payment Run Transaction F1102

Figure 9.51 Testing Procure-to-Pay Processes—Remittance Advice

Once payment has been made, it should post to the financial module of SAP ERP, typically in FI/CO areas for SAP. The following steps allow you to verify updates have been made to FI.

1. To display details of the FI documents in SAP ERP, enter Transaction FB03.
2. Open Transaction FB03 and fill in your FI document number.
3. Double click on the account number from your vendor.

Now you can see details, such as discount amount, and days/percent from payment terms, as in Figure 9.52.

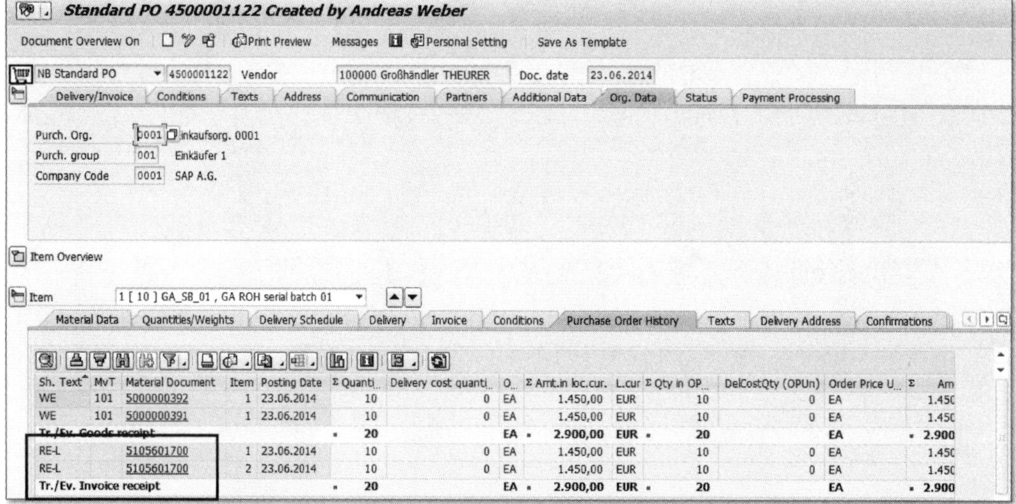

Figure 9.52 Testing Procure-to-Pay Processes—MIR4 ME23N

9.2 SAP Ariba Procure-to-Pay Integration

SAP Ariba P2X (applying both to SAP Ariba P2P and SAP Ariba P2O scenarios) can run as standalone processes in the cloud, but there are also multiple options for integrating SAP Ariba P2X with SAP ERP. Unlike the PO/IV integration with the SAP Ariba Network, where documents are the sole focus of integration, SAP Ariba P2X's focus includes master data exchange between SAP ERP and SAP Ariba P2P. Master data integration areas include suppliers, purchasing organizations, cost elements, and the general ledger (G/L). Document exchange integration between SAP Ariba Procure-to-Pay and SAP ERP includes PO and change PO, goods receipts, invoices, and remittances. As with the SAP Ariba Network integration outlined in the previous section, SAP Ariba P2P integration has several options/paths for enabling integration:

- SAP Ariba P2X integration with SAP ERP via SAP Ariba Integration Toolkit (ITK) for master data and transactional data—this approach involves mediation via the SAP Ariba Integration Toolkit for both master data and transactional data.

  SAP Ariba P2X integration with SAP ERP via ITK for master data and PI for transactional data, and synchronous integration of transactional data using SAP PI. Master data must be integrated using the Integration Toolkit (asynchronous).
- SAP Ariba P2X integration with SAP ERP, with direct connect for master data and ITK for transactional data. SAP Ariba direct connectivity for asynchronous replication of master data. Transactional data integrated with SAP Ariba ITK (asynchronous).
- SAP Ariba P2X integration with SAP ERP, with direct connect for master data and PI for transactional data. SAP Ariba direct connectivity for asynchronous replication of master data; synchronous integration of transactional data with SAP PI.

As with the SAP Ariba Network integration, the SAP Ariba Integration Toolkit (ITK) approach leverages the original approach used pre-acquisition by SAP Ariba to integrate with SAP ERP environments. This means that ITK may provide more short-term functionality and options for integration. However, in the long term, the direct connect and SAP Ariba direct connectivity approaches will receive the majority of the focus at SAP. If your requirements fit in this scenario, it is recommended to use the SAP Ariba direct connectivity approach, given future roadmap considerations.

9.2.1 Solution Implementation Project

This project can be delivered in its various forms in around six weeks. More complex projects requiring the integration of multiple company codes and backend will likely require larger resource allocations or time budgets for delivery. The main consulting resources involved in this are the project manager, and application consultants with knowledge of SAP Ariba and SAP ERP Materials Management (MM) in the SAP ERP environment. On the customer-side, the IT department resources required are as follows: integration support analysts; a project manager counterpart to the consulting PM; and subject matter experts for outlining the master data and document transfers required between the two environments, as well as for the various testing phases.

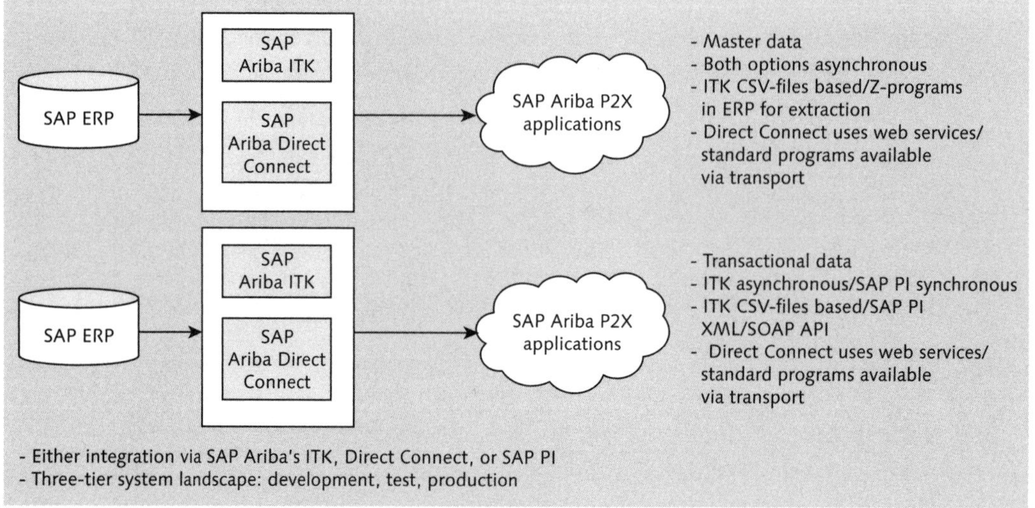

Figure 9.53 P2X Integration System Landscape

SAP Ariba Procure-to-Pay (P2P) is the cloud equivalent of the on-premise SAP SRM. As per Figure 9.53, the solution package runs on SAP Process Orchestration (PO) in the PI scenario, and can be conceived as a library for SAP Process Integration (PI). This library includes integration processes and Java libraries that implement the cXML transport protocol and provide a set of facilities for resolving differences between SAP and Ariba. Alternatively, if SAP PI isn't available, the SAP PI scenario purchasing documents and master data could be exchanged using a web services-based approach via the SAP Ariba data transfer tool, SAP Ariba Direct Connect.

9.2.2 SAP Ariba P2X Solution Package for SAP NetWeaver Building Block ARO

Integrating SAP Ariba P2X with SAP ERP is not supported in the Business Suite Add-On. Instead, you leverage SAP PI with what are called *building blocks* to realize the integration. The SAP Ariba P2X solution package for SAP NetWeaver consists of three components: RO, ARQ, and ARP:

- The SAP Ariba P2X integration basic configuration building block ARO (this section), which illustrates the master data extraction routines and interface objects.
- Building block ARQ: The configuration guide illustrates the deployment and configuration processes of the SAP Ariba adapter integration package in SAP PO, for the SAP PI scenario to exchange transactional procurement data between SAP Ariba P2X and SAP ERP as cXML files, and master data as CSV files. ARQ requires an SAP PI specialist to complete technical steps, and will not be featured at length in this book. If you have SAP PI, and wish to leverage this approach, please access the ARQ building block guide at *http://service.sap.com/rds-ariba*.
- Building block ARP: The configuration guide illustrates the deployment and configuration processes of the SAP Ariba data transfer tool integration package as an alternative to building block ARQ, if SAP PI isn't available. This integration section will focus on direct approaches to connection. For ARO, ARQ, and ARP, please check *http://service.sap.com/rds-ariba*. As with all guides, please check online for the latest updates before embarking on a configuration step.

Figure 9.54 illustrates how this solution package enables the flow of communication between SAP Ariba P2X and your SAP ERP environment. Building blocks ARO and ARQ support option 1, while building blocks 1 and 3 support option 2.

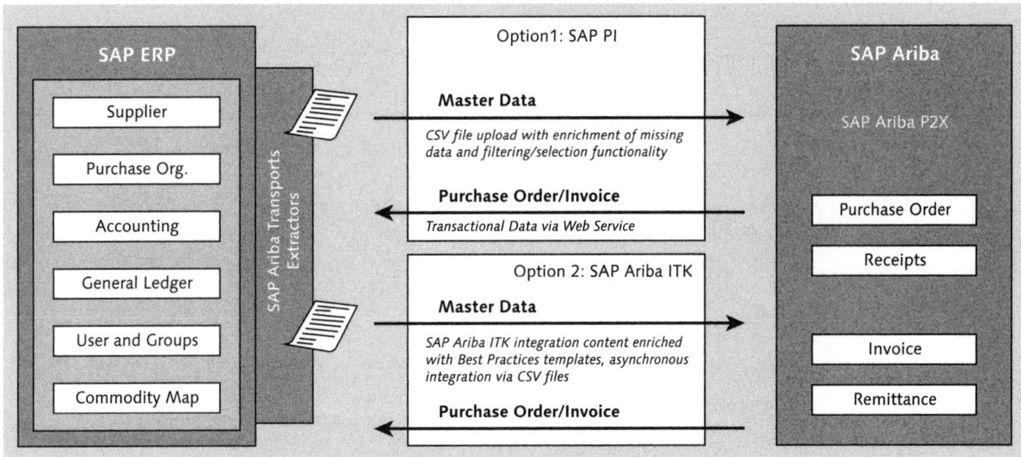

Figure 9.54 P2X Integration System Landscape

The SAP Ariba P2X Solution package for SAP NetWeaver consists of three components:

- Building block 1: The SAP Ariba P2X integration basic configuration building block 1 illustrates the master data extraction routines and interface objects.
- Building block 2: The configuration guide illustrates the deployment and configuration processes of the SAP Ariba adapter integration package in SAP PO for the PI scenario to exchange transactional procurement data between SAP Ariba P2X and SAP ERP as cXML files, and master data as CSV files.
- Building block 3: The configuration guide illustrates the deployment and configuration processes of the SAP Ariba data transfer tool integration package as alternative to building block ARQ if SAP PI isn't available.

Transactional Data Transfer Configuration: Building Block 1

This configuration guide is specific only to the configuration tasks and subsequent integration events for master data extraction in the SAP ERP system and the file based data transfer to SAP Ariba. The transactional data exchange could be performed by either a file-based method, using the SAP Ariba data transfer tool described in configuration guide ARP, or using the web services channel. If you are using the web services channel, the configuration tasks are described in configuration section for building block 3.

You install the SAP Ariba Integration Toolkit by downloading and unpacking it. To begin, please follow these steps:

1. Access *https://connect.ariba.com.* If you do not have a user ID and password for Connect, contact your SAP Ariba account executive.
2. Under QUICK LINKS, click PRODUCT INFO, followed by the name of your solution (such as SAP Ariba Procure-to-Pay).
3. In the ADMINISTRATION TOOLS section, click on SAP TRANSPORTS (SAP ONLY).
4. Click SAVE, and specify a location on your hard drive. The file `Ariba_P2P_SAP_Transports_13s2.zip` downloads to the location you have set.
5. Extract the contents of `Ariba_P2P_SAP_Transports_13s2.zip` to the appropriate locations on your SAP instance.

Readme.txt specifies the order in which you need to install the transports. You can find this readme file is available in the ZIP archive that you download from Connect.

The following transports must be installed if this is the first time you are installing SAP Ariba buyer SAP transports on your SAP system. You must specify the client when importing the transports as they contain both client dependent and independent objects.

- EC6K901534 contains objects for master data pulls and language pulls.
- PECK901479 contains objects for purchase order push.
- PECK901269 contains objects for purchase order change/cancel/PO header status pull.
- N47K902301/N47K902187 contains objects for goods receipts push.
- EC6K901387 contains objects for PO/CPO/change header status.

The following section describes the complete settings for this building block. These settings can be divided into three main groups:

- Prerequisite settings that have to be checked, as well as those which were delivered by SAP (as part of the standard delivery). The term *check* refers to these prerequisite settings.
- Settings defined by the customer (in the customer namespace and customer-specific). The system uses automation to request individual customer settings during the personalization process. These settings can be initial, or reused from existing SAP ERP layers, and are indicated in the text by <your value>.
- Additional settings that need to be covered either by automation or manual configuration (in the customer namespace). The term *create* refers to these additional settings in the text.

Our final task in building block one will be to set up directories to exchange data in SAP ERP using the following commands:

1. **Create processing and error directory**
   Using Transaction SM69, on the External Operating Command screen, create the settings described in Table 9.1.

Field Name	Entry Value
Command Name	ZSSPDIRCREATE
Operating System Command	<your operating system's command to create a new directory>

Table 9.1 Directory Create

The SAP integration function modules use the ZSSPDIRCREATE command to create directories for CSV files. It creates a *processing* directory for CSV files it is in the process of creating (and when done, renames it to *processed*). It also creates an *error* directory. This is where it puts files that encountered a processing error.

The command works as follows:

- It takes the name of the directory to create as input a value for.
- It invokes the command line program, which for Linux is CMD.
- It issues the command to create the directory, which in Linux is the MKDIR command.

You can change ZSSPDIRCREATE to use a different command, depending on your operating system.

2. **Create command to rename a directory**
Using Transaction SM69 on the External Operating Command screen, create the settings detailed in Table 9.2.

Field Name	Entry Value
Command Name	ZSSPREN
Operating System Command	<your operating system's command to rename a new directory>

Table 9.2 Operating System Command

The SAP integration function modules use the ZSSPREN command to rename a directory. For example, it renames the processing directory to processed after the CSV files are written. The command works as follows:

- It takes the name of the directory to rename and the new name as input.
- It invokes the command line program, which for Linux is CMD.
- It issues the command to rename the directory, which in Linux is the mv command.

You can change ZSSPREN to use a different command, depending on your operating system.

3. **Check master data extraction report**
Using Transaction SE38, on the ABAP editor initial screen, create the settings detailed in Table 9.3.

Field Name	Entry Value
Program	/ARBA/MASTER_DATA_EXPORT

Table 9.3 Program Create

On the SAP Ariba screen, create the settings detailed in Table 9.4.

Field Name	Entry Value
Program	/ARBA/MASTER_DATA_EXPORT
Connectivity	<your connectivity ITK or direct connectivity>
Load option	<your load option incremental data load or full load>
Scope of SAP Ariba solution	<procure to pay or procure to order>
Encoding to be used	<your encoding page>
Variant	<your variant>
Partition	<your variant>
Directory path for file download	<your directory on the SAP application server where the export files will be stored>
Organizational data	<choose organizational data to be extracted like plant, company code, purchase organization, plant-purchase organization relation, purchasing group>
Accounting data	<choose accounting data to be extracted like general ledger, internal order, cost center, WBS element, asset>
Cross-application data	<choose application data to be extracted like account category, account category fields, commodity codes, currency conversion, tax codes, payment terms>
Supplier data	<choose parameter if suppliers should be extracted>

Table 9.4 Export Settings

The program /ARBA/MASTER_DATA_EXPORT needs the following parameters: the directory where the CSV files should be written, the encoding, and the data to export as input. You must select a directory that already exists; be sure to use the same directory you specified in the SAP Ariba data transfer tool options file in the SAP PI (which you configure when you transfer master data from SAP). Specify the character encoding to use in the generated CSV files, and use the encoding that corresponds to the data you are supplying from SAP. SAP Ariba supports any of the encodings listed for the Java.io API at *http://java.sun.com/j2se/1.4.2/docs/guide/intl/encoding.doc.html*. To schedule /ARBA/MASTER_DATA_EXPORT to run at regular intervals, save the program input as a variant that you can specify to run as a job. Schedule this program using Transaction SM36.

4. **Check master data extraction files**
   Using Transaction AL11, on the SAP DIRECTORIES screen, navigate to your directory on the SAP application server where the export files will be stored following these steps:
   - On the SAP DIRECTORIES screen, check the following settings:
     - A subdirectory with the file name "processed"
     - The time stamp of the export run
   - On the SAP DIRECTORIES screen navigate to the directory indicated in Table 9.5.

Field Name	Entry Value
File name	<a subdirectory with file named "processed" and time stamp of the export run is created>

Table 9.5 File Name Navigation

On the SAP DIRECTORIES screen, check that for each selected master data a separate CSV file was created. The ARBA/MASTER_DATA_EXPORT program creates a temporary directory called processingyyyymmddhhmmss, where yyyymmddhhmmss is the date and time stamp, indicating when the directory was created. It writes all the requested CSV files into this directory, depending on which data you chose to pull. The processing directory is placed inside the folder you specified as input. When the program ARBA/MASTER_DATA_EXPORT is finished writing the files, it renames the temporary directory to processedyyyymmddhhmmss. This directory is where the SAP PI and the SAP Ariba data transfer tool look for the CSV files. Table 9.6 lists the SAP remote function calls (RFCs) and the CSV files they generate for each data import task.

Task	RFC	CSV File
Export Company Codes	/ARBA/COMPANY_CODE_EXPORT	CompanyCode.csv
Export Plants Data	/ARBA/PLANT_EXPORT	Plant.csv
Export Purchase Organizations	/ARBA/PURCHASE_ORG_EXPORT	PurchaseOrg.csv
Export Purchase Groups	/ARBA/PURCHASE_GROUP_EXPORT	PurchaseGroup.csv
Export Plant To Purchase Organization Mapping	/ARBA/PLANT_PURCHASE_EXPORT	PlantPurchaseOrg-Combo.csv
Export Assets	/ARBA/ASSET_EXPORT	Asset.csv
Export Cost Centers	/ARBA/COST_CENTER_EXPORT	CostCenter.csv
Export General Ledgers	/ARBA/GENERAL_LEDGER_EXPORT	GeneralLedger.csv
Export Internal Order Codes	/ARBA/INTERNAL_ORDER_EXPORT	InternalOrder.csv
Export WBS Elements	/ARBA/WBS_EXPORT	WBSElement.csv
Export Account Categories	/ARBA/ACCOUNT_CATEGORY_EXPORT	AccountCategory.csv
Export Account Category Field Status Combinations	/ARBA/ACCOUNT_FIELD_EXPORT	▶ AccCategoryFieldStatus.csv ▶ Combo.csv
Export Company Code Internal Order Mapping	/ARBA/INTERNAL_ORDER_EXPORT	CompanyCodeIOCombo.csv
Export Company Code WBS Mapping	/ARBA/WBS_EXPORT	CompanyCodeWBSCombo.csv
Export ERP Commodity Codes	/ARBA/MATERIAL_GROUP_EXPORT	ERPCommodityCode.csv
Export Currency Conversion Rates	/ARBA/CURRENCY_CONVERT_EXPORT	CurrencyConversion.csv Rate.csv

Table 9.6 RFC User Generated Files

Task	RFC	CSV File
Export Suppliers	/ARBA/VENDOR_EXPORT	▸ PurchaseOrgSupplierCombo.csv ▸ SupplierConsolidated.csv ▸ SupplierLocationConsolidated.csv ▸ RemittanceLocationConsolidated.csv
Export Tax Codes	/ARBA/TAX_CODE_EXPORT	TaxCode.csv

Table 9.6 RFC User Generated Files (Cont.)

5. **Check master data export settings**
   - Access the SAP Ariba P2P solution core administration: PROCUREMENT • MANAGE • CORE ADMINISTRATION • INTEGRATION CONFIGURATION.
   - Select master data type.
   - Check if the status is ENABLED.

Transactional Data Transfer Configuration: Building Block 2

Building block 2 illustrates the deployment and configuration processes of the SAP Ariba adapter integration package in SAP PO, which will allow the PI scenario to exchange transactional procurement data between SAP Ariba P2X and SAP ERP, as cXML files and master data as CSV files.

The SAP Ariba P2X Solution package for SAP NetWeaver consists of two components:

- The design package, which contains integration processes and interface objects
- Building block 2: the configuration guide (this section) illustrates the deployment and configuration processes of the SAP Ariba P2P integration package in SAP PO for the PI scenario.

Figure 9.55 illustrates how this solution package enables the communication flow between SAP Ariba P2P and your SAP ERP system for the PI scenario.

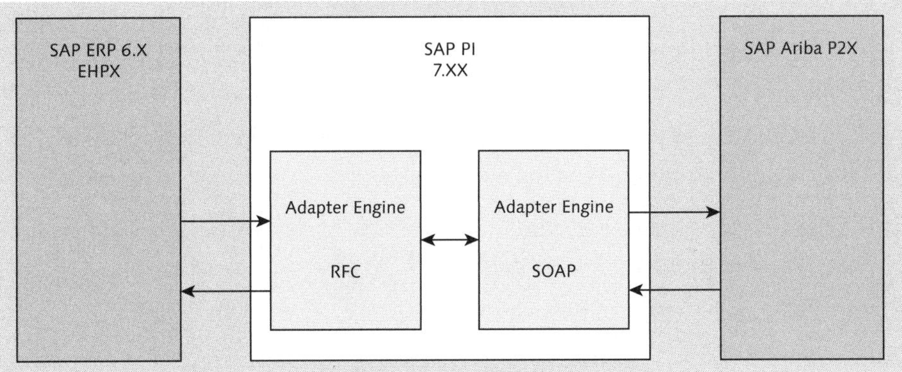

Figure 9.55 P2X Integration via SAP PI with SAP ERP

SAP PO is a platform for process orchestration within SAP NetWeaver. In general, it facilitates cross-system business processes. In particular, it enables different versions of SAP and non-SAP systems from different vendors running on different platforms to communicate with each other.

SAP PI, as part of SAP Process Orchestration, integrates the following components used by the SAP Ariba P2X Solution package for SAP NetWeaver and its modules:

- The business process engine is a runtime component of the SAP PI Integration Server. It processes the integration processes at runtime.
- The integration engine is the central runtime component of the SAP PI Integration Server, and is used for receiving, processing, and forwarding messages.
- The adapter engine is a runtime component of the SAP PI Integration Server. It uses adapters to connect the integration engine to SAP systems (RFC adapter) and external systems.

To check your software requirements, go to *http://connect.ariba.com*, then click on: LOGIN • HOME • PRODUCT SUMMARY • ON-DEMAND • ARIBA PROCURE-TO-PAY • SAP NETWEAVER MAPPING (SAP WEB SERVICE ONLY).

If the SAP Ariba P2P buyer account is configured to use digital certificate authentication, then a valid secure socket layer (SSL) client certificate from one of SAP Ariba P2P's trusted certificate authorities is required.

For the SAP Ariba P2P integration for SAP Business Suite rapid-deployment solution, it is required to import the software components for SAP Basis 7.10 into the enterprise services repository.

After installing the system landscape directory, a task handled by your basis team, you have to perform the following steps:

1. Import the design package containing the transactions supported by the SAP Ariba P2P Adapter for SAP NetWeaver.
2. Configure SAP PI connectivity to the SAP ERP environment.
3. Configure the different transactions in the integration directory by importing the scenarios from the integration repository.
4. Configure the communication channels and the conditions for routing messages, for each supported transaction.
5. Configure the system landscape directory.
6. Import the product and component definitions of SAP Ariba products that will work with SAP PI, as a CIM file.

Transactional Data Transfer Configuration: Building Block 3

Building block 3 illustrates the deployment and configuration processes of the SAP Ariba data transfer tool integration package as an alternative to building block ARQ, if SAP PI is not available.

The SAP Ariba Integration Toolkit allows buying organizations to integrate their SAP ERP systems with an SAP Ariba on-demand solution to exchange master and transactional data via CSV file upload and download.

The SAP Ariba data transfer tool is a command line utility that facilitates data transfer in batch mode between your backend system and your SAP Ariba system. Data is transferred in the form of comma-separated-value (CSV/XLS) files. You can use the SAP Ariba data transfer tool with a scheduler to export transactional data, such as purchase orders, from SAP Ariba to your backend system, or import master data from your backend system to SAP Ariba. You can only import master data as a batch import task.

The SAP Ariba data transfer tool is a simple HTTP client that resides on a system behind your firewall, and which runs on Microsoft Windows or UNIX. You control the SAP Ariba data transfer tool by setting operational parameters in separate options files.

This configuration guide is specific only to the configuration tasks and subsequent integration events for transactional data exchange between SAP Ariba system and the SAP ERP system.

Some prerequisites of the configuration process are:

- You have Java Runtime Environment 1.6 installed.
- You have installed the SAP Ariba data transfer tool by downloading and unpacking it. Before doing so, you must have access to *http://connect.ariba.com.* If you do not have a user ID and a password for SAP Ariba Connect, contact your SAP Ariba account executive.

To download the data transfer tool:

1. Create the installation directory for the SAP Ariba data transfer tool.
2. Go to *http://connect.ariba.com* and log in.
3. In the PRODUCT SUMMARY section, click the PRODUCT INFO page for SAP Ariba Procure-to-Pay.
4. In the ADMINISTRATOR TOOLS section, click ARIBA INTEGRATION TOOLKIT.
5. Click DOWNLOAD and save the `aribaintegrationtoolkit.jar` file to your local system.
6. Extract the contents `aribaintegrationtoolkit.jar` using the following command in the command prompt:
   - `java -jar aribaintegrationtoolkit.jar <your new directory>`

   The command extracts the contents of `aribaintegrationtoolkit.jar` into <your new directory>.

Once you ensure that you meet the prerequisites and download the data transfer tool, you are ready to begin the configuration process. The complete settings for this building block can be divided into three main groups:

- Prerequisite settings that have to be checked, and which were delivered by SAP/SAP Ariba as part of the standard delivery. The term check refers to these prerequisite settings.

- Settings defined by the customer (in the customer namespace and customer-specific). The system uses automation to request individual customer settings during the personalization process. These settings can be initial, or reused from existing SAP ERP layers, and are indicated in the text by <your value>.
- Additional settings that need to be made covered either by automation or manual configuration (in the customer namespace). The term create refers to these additional settings in the text.

Prerequisites Check

Your first step in the configuration process will be to set the shared secret password by following these steps:

1. Navigate to SAP Ariba site: *https://<AribaServer>/Buyer/Main/?realm=<YourSiteID>*.
2. Enter your username and password. Click LOGIN.
3. Click PROCUREMENT.
4. Navigate to MANAGE • CORE ADMINISTRATION.
5. Navigate to INTEGRATION MANAGER • INTEGRATION TOOLKIT SECURITY.
6. Select SHARED SECRET from the pull-down menu.
7. Under SHARED SECRET, enter the <SharedSecret> twice to confirm it, and click SAVE.

Next, you'll need to encrypt the customer key by following these steps:

1. Find the directory containing `java.exe`. (*C:\Program Files\Java\jdk1.6\bin*).
2. Copy the option files you intend to use from *<new directory>\sample-options\DataTransferTool\data-upload*, rename them by removing the sample extension, and then edit them with a text editor. The option file you use for this is not important.
3. Find the `JAVA_HOME` option to the path up to the `bin` directory (see Table 9.7).

Item	Description
<JavaDirectoryPath>	The path to `java.exe` without the `bin` directory.
JAVA_HOME	set `JAVA_HOME=<JavaDirectoryPath>`
JAVA_HOME	set `JAVA_HOME=C:\Program Files\Java\jdk1.6`

Table 9.7 Java Home

4. Open a Microsoft Windows command interpreter. To open a Microsoft Windows command interpreter, click START • RUN, and then type `cmd` and click OK.
5. At the command prompt, change to the directory containing the `encryptcustomerkey` script using, for example, *cd D:\IntegrationToolkit\bin.*
6. Run the script to encrypt the customer key using the following syntax: `encryptcustomerkey.bat <options file><options file>` is the path and name of an options file where you have set the `JAVA_HOME` option. See Table 9.8.

Item	Description
Syntax	`encryptcustomerkey.bat` "*D:\IntegrationToolkit\options\DataTransferTool\data-upload\masterdata.bat*"
<Customer Key>	An alphanumeric string that must be 24 characters in length
Customer Key ·	`TestCustomerKey123456789.`

Table 9.8 Customer Key Syntax

7. When the prompt to enter the key is displayed, enter the customer encryption key to be encrypted. The key must be an alphanumeric string of 24 characters in length. Choose the customer key yourself.
8. The encrypted key is displayed as an output on the command line.
9. Copy the encrypted key from the command line to a .txt file and save the file as `password.txt`.
10. The encrypted key must be the first and only line in the file without any spaces before or after. The path to this file must be passed as the value for the `encryptionKeyPath` parameter in the sample-options file.
11. In the options file, pass the path of the `password.txt` file for the `encryptionKeypath` parameter (see Table 9.9).

Item	Description
encryptionKeyPath	set `encryptionKeyPath=D:\IntegrationToolkit\Password.txt`
<CustomerKeyPath>	The entire path including the .txt file to the encrypted customer key.

Table 9.9 Encryption Key Path

12. Save options file.

After encrypting the customer key, we need to then encrypt the shared secret password that we created in the first step of the configuration. To start:

1. Run the script to encrypt a string using `encryptstring.bat <options file>` where `<options file>` is the path and name of an options file where you have set the `JAVA_HOME` option with the following in syntax: `encryptstring.bat`. For example: *D:\IntegrationToolkit\options\DataTransferTool\data-upload\masterdata.bat.*
2. A prompt to enter the string is displayed. This string is the shared secret that is configured under INTEGRATION TOOLKIT SECURITY in SAP Ariba Administrator.
3. Enter the <SharedSecret> to be encrypted. For example, "Welcome".
4. The encrypted string is displayed as an output on the command line. For example, from "Welcome," we might get `{3DES}xXk8vlgZl6iVmdCJYy/n1w=`.
5. Copy the encrypted string from the command line to a .txt file and save the file as `sharedsecret.txt`. The encrypted string must be the first and only line in the file without any spaces before or after. The path to this file must be passed as the value for the `integrationPasswordKeyPath` parameter in the options file.
6. In the options file pass the path of the sharedsecret.txt file for the `integrationPasswordKeypath` parameter (see Table 9.10).

Item	Description
integrationpasswordKeyPath	set `integrationpasswordKeyPath=D:\IntegrationToolkit\sharedsecret.txt`
<SharedSecretPath>	The entire path including the .txt file to the encrypted shared secret.

Table 9.10 Password Settings

7. Save the options file.

Note

The encrypted string in the examples is prefixed with the string `{3DES}`, indicating the encryption algorithm used is Triple DES. The SAP Ariba data transfer tool uses the entire encrypted string.

Settings Defined by Customer

The next step in our SAP Ariba Procure-to-Pay integration will be to configure the master data uploaded. The main tasks within this step will be to set up directories in which the data will reside and setting rules for the data. First, we'll need to set up a folder structure as in Table 9.11 and Table 9.12.

Item	Description
<topDir>	The path to and including the directory where the various input and output subdirectories must go.
<topDir>	D:\ariba\DataTransferTool\MasterDataUpload

Table 9.11 Directory Settings

Item	Details
topDir	<topDir>
inDir	<topDir>\inDir\
outDir	<topDir>\outDir\
Logs	<topDir>\logs\

Table 9.12 Directory Settings for Logs

Second, we'll need to configure the options file as in the following steps (see Table 9.13).

Item	Description
<Cleanup>	Set value to `1` to clear the *outDir* and *unSent* directories of old files. Set value to `0` to deactivate.
<CleanupTime>	Set numeric value in days for how long to save old files.

Table 9.13 Cleanup Settings

1. Copy `masterdata.bat.sample` from *<new directory>\sample-options\DataTransferTool\data-upload* to a folder of your choice.
2. Rename the .sample file to `masterdata.bat`.
3. Edit the .bat file with a text editor.
4. Set the options listed in Table 9.14.

Items	Description
Site	set `site=<YourSiteId>`
Servicemode	set `servicemode=0`
integrationPasswordKeyPath	set `integrationPasswordKeyPath=<SharedSecretPath>`
encryptionKeyPath	set `encryptionKeyPath=<CustomerKeyPath>`
topDir	set `topDir=<topDir>`
inDir	Set `inDir=%topDir%\InDir`
filterPrefix	set `filterPrefix=processing`
outDir	set `outDir=%topDir%\OutDir`
unsentDir	set `unsentDir=%topDir%\UnSent`
performCleanup	set `performCleanup=<Cleanup>`
cleanupFilesOlderThan	set `cleanupFilesOlderThan=<CleanupTime>`
logDir	set `logDir=%topDir%\logs`
smtpMailServer	set `smtpMailServer=`
fromEmail	set `fromEmail=`
notifyEmail	set `notifyEmail=`
notifyonSuccess	set `notifyonSuccess=0`
notifyonFailure	set `notifyonFailure=0`
notificationSuccessSubject	set `notificationSuccessSubject=AribaFileTransfer Full Master Data Upload: Success`
notificationFailureSubject	set `notificationFailureSubject=AribaFileTransfer Full Master Data Upload: Failed`
JAVA_HOME	set `JAVA_HOME=<JavaDirectoryPath>`

Table 9.14 Bat File Settings

Note

We have disabled e-mail notifications, as they are not necessary for the data transfer to work.

5. Set this option under DO NOT CHANGE: *urlPrefix=https://<AribaServer>/Buyer/fileupload.*
6. Save the options file.

Finally, we need to run the options file. To start:

1. Upload data as follows:
   - Locate your master copy of a CSV file for uploading, such as `address.csv`.
   - As this is a full master data upload, you must have *all* addresses that you need in the file. Any address objects in the SAP Ariba database that do not have a corresponding entry in `address.csv` file are deactivated. This is a "load and delete" operation.
   - Copy address.csv to *<topDir>\inDir\batch0.*
     - The CSV file/files must be in a ZIP file.
     - Any directory that does not begin with the word processing will work
2. Open a Microsoft Windows command interpreter. To open a Microsoft Windows command interpreter, click START • RUN, then type `cmd` and click OK.
3. Enter `cd <new directory>`.
4. Enter `bin\aribafiletransfer<directoryname>\masterdata.bat` where <directoryname> is the directory containing the options file you modified.

The next step in our SAP Ariba Procure-to-Pay integration will be to configure the incremental master data uploaded. First, we'll need to set up a folder structure, much as we did in the previous step for the master data upload, using the information in Table 9.15 and Table 9.16.

Item	Description
<topDir>	The path to and including the directory where the various input and output subdirectories must go.
<topDir>	D:\ariba\DataTransferTool\IncrementalMasterDataUpload

Table 9.15 Directory Creation

Item	Description
topDir	<topDir>
inDir	<topDir>\inDir\
outDir	<topDir>\outDir\
Logs	<topDir>\logs\

Table 9.16 Directory Settings

Second, we'll need to configure the options file, per Table 9.17.

Item	Description
<Cleanup>	Set value to `1` to activate and clear the *outDir* and *unSent* directories of old files. Set value to `0` to deactivate.
<CleanupTime>	Set numeric value in days for how long to save old files.

Table 9.17 Cleanup Settings

The following steps details the settings you need to make for the .bat file:

1. Copy `incremental-masterdata.bat.sample` from *<new directory>\sample-options\DataTransferTool\data-upload* to a folder of your choice.
2. Rename the .sample file `incremental-masterdata.bat`.
3. Edit the .bat file with a text editor.
4. Set the options listed in Table 9.18.

Item	Description
Site	set `site=<YourSiteId>`
Servicemode	set `servicemode=0`
integrationPasswordKeyPath	set `integrationPasswordKeyPath=<SharedSecretPath>`
encryptionKeyPath	set `encryptionKeyPath=<CustomerKeyPath>`
topDir	set `topDir=<topDir>`
inDir	set `inDir=%topDir%\InDir`
filterPrefix	set `filterPrefix=processing`

Table 9.18 Bat File Updates

Item	Description
outDir	set `outDir=%topDir%\OutDir`
performCleanup	set `performCleanup=<Cleanup>`
cleanupFilesOlderThan	set `cleanupFilesOlderThan=<CleanupTime>`
logDir	set `logDir=%topDir%\logs`
smtpMailServer	set `smtpMailServer=`
fromEmail	set `fromEmail=`
notifyEmail	set `notifyEmail=`
notifyonSuccess	set `notifyonSuccess=0`
notifyonFailure	set `notifyonFailure=0`
notificationSuccessSubject	set `notificationSuccessSubject= AribaFileTransfer Incr Master Data Upload: Success`
notificationFailureSubject	set `notificationFailureSubject= AribaFileTransfer Incr Master Data Upload: Failed`
JAVA_HOME	set `JAVA_HOME=<JavaDirectoryPath>`
Site	set `site=<YourSiteId>`
Servicemode	set `servicemode=0`
integrationPasswordKeyPath	set `integrationPasswordKeyPath=<SharedSecret-Path>`

Table 9.18 Bat File Updates (Cont.)

5. Set the following option under Do NOT CHANGE: `urlPrefix=https://<Ariba-Server>/Buyer/fileupload`.
6. Save the options file.

Finally, we will run the options file, following these steps:

1. Locate the master copy of a CSV file for uploading, such as `PurchaseOrderIDImport.csv`. or `<address>.csv`.
2. Copy `<address>.csv` to *<topDir>\inDir\batch0*. Note: Any directory that does not begin with the word "processing" will work.
3. Open a Microsoft Windows command interpreter. To open a Microsoft Windows command interpreter, click START • RUN, and then type `cmd` and click OK.

4. Enter cd <new directory>.
5. Enter bin\aribafiletransfer<directoryname>\transactionaldata.bat where <directoryname> is the directory containing the options file you modified.

The next step in our SAP Ariba Procure-to-Pay integration will be to configure the master data download. Again, we'll start by setting up a folder structure (see Table 9.19 and Table 9.20).

Item	Description
<downloadDir>	The path to and including the directory where the downloaded files will go.
<downloadDir>	C:\ITK_Daten\downloadDir

Table 9.19 Download Directory

Item	Description
downloadDir	<downloadDir>
Logs	<downloadDir>\logs\

Table 9.20 Directory Settings

Next, we'll configure and run the options file using the following settings. The first settings are intended to trigger the export of suppliers after file upload (see Table 9.21).

Item	Description
<event>	The name of the event to trigger on server side after upload, it must be in double quotes.
<event>	"Export Suppliers"

Table 9.21 Export Suppliers

1. Copy masterdata.bat.sample from *<new directory>\sample-options\DataTransferTool\data-download* to a folder of your choice.
2. Rename the .sample file to masterdata.bat.
3. Edit the .bat file with a text editor.
4. Set the options listed in Table 9.22.

Item	Description
Site	set site=<YourSiteId>
Servicemode	set servicemode=0
integrationPasswordKeyPath	set integrationPasswordKeyPath=<SharedSecretPath>
encryptionKeyPath	set encryptionKeyPath=<CustomerKeyPath>
Event	set event=<event>
downloadDir	set downloadDir=<downloadDir>
adapterSource	set adapterSource=All
filePrefix	set filePrefix=Expense
logDir	set logDir=%downloadDir%\logs
smtpMailServer	set smtpMailServer=
fromEmail	set fromEmail=
notifyEmail	set notifyEmail=
notifyonSuccess	set notifyonSuccess=0
notifyonFailure	set notifyonFailure=0
notificationSuccessSubject	set notificationSuccessSubject=AribaFileTransfer Master Data Download: Successful
notificationFailureSubject	set notificationFailureSubject=AribaFileTransfer Master Data Download: Failed
JAVA_HOME	set JAVA_HOME=<JavaDirectoryPath>

Table 9.22 Bat File Settings

5. Set this option under DO NOT CHANGE: urlPrefix=https://<AribaServer>/Buyer/fileupload.
6. Save the options file.
7. Open a Microsoft Windows command interpreter.
8. Enter cd <new directory>.
9. Enter bin\aribafiletransfer<directoryname>\masterdata.bat where <directoryname> is the directory containing the options file you modified.

The next step in our SAP Ariba Procure-to-Pay integration will be to configure the transactional data download for new purchase orders. Again, we'll start by setting up a folder structure using the settings in Table 9.23 and Table 9.24.

First, set up the download directory.

Item	Description
<downloadDir>	The path to and including the directory where the downloaded files will go.
<downloadDir>	C:\ITK_Daten\downloadDir_newPO

Table 9.23 Download Directory

Item	Description
notificationFailureSubject	set `notificationFailureSubject= AribaFileTransfer Master Data Download: Failed`
JAVA_HOME	set `JAVA_HOME=<JavaDirectoryPath>`

Table 9.24 Notification Settings

Next, we'll configure and run the options files, leveraging the following options (see Table 9.25).

Item	Description
<event>	The name of the event to trigger on server side after download, it must be in double quotes.
<event>	"Export Purchase Order"

Table 9.25 Export Purchase Order

1. Copy `transactionaldata.bat.sample` from *<new directory>\sample-options\DataTransferTool\data-download* to a folder of your choice.
2. Rename the .sample file to `transactionaldataNP.bat`.
3. Edit the .bat file with a text editor.
4. Set the options in Table 9.26.

Items	Description
Site	set site=<YourSiteId>
Servicemode	set servicemode=0
integrationPasswordKeyPath	set integrationPasswordKeyPath=<SharedSecretPath>
encryptionKeyPath	set encryptionKeyPath=<CustomerKeyPath>
Event	set event=<"Export Purchase Order">
downloadDir	set downloadDir=C:\ITK_Daten\Transactional-Download\downloadDir_newPOf
timestampFile	set timestampFile=%downloadDir%\POTimeStamp
filePrefix	set filePrefix=PO
logDir	set logDir=%downloadDir%\logs
smtpMailServer	set smtpMailServer=
fromEmail	set fromEmail=
notifyEmail	set notifyEmail=
notifyonSuccess	set notifyonSuccess=0
notifyonFailure	set notifyonFailure=0
notificationSuccessSubject	set notificationSuccessSubject= AribaFileTransfer Transactional Data Download: Successful
notificationFailureSubject	set notificationFailureSubject= AribaFileTransfer Transactional Data Download: Failed
JAVA_HOME	set JAVA_HOME=<JavaDirectoryPath>

Table 9.26 Bat File Settings

5. Set this option under DO NOT CHANGE: `urlPrefix=https://<AribaServer>/Buyer/fileupload`.
6. Save the options file.
7. Open a Microsoft Windows command interpreter.
8. Enter: `cd <new directory>`.
9. Enter `bin\aribafiletransfer<directoryname>\transactionaldataNP.bat` where <directoryname> is the directory containing the options file you modified.

Note

In the options files, you specify your company's site name, partition, authentication information, the location of data to be loaded, and a location to receive the data exported from the SAP Ariba application, along with other options. When you start the SAP Ariba data transfer tool from the command line, it checks for the presence of required values and transfers the data to your site using an HTTPS post. The tool determines whether to use username and password, shared secret, or certificate and sends the correct credential to the service for authentication. The options files also specify whether to send an e-mail notification reporting the status of the data transfer, and also whether to perform a cleanup of old data.

The next step in our SAP Ariba Procure-to-Pay integration will be to configure the transactional data download for changed purchase orders. We'll start by setting up a folder structure as in Table 9.27 and Table 9.28.

Item	Description
<downloadDir>	The path to and including the directory where the downloaded files will go.
<downloadDir>	C:\ITK_Daten\downloadDir_changePO

Table 9.27 Download Directory

Item	Description
downloadDir	<downloadDir>
Logs	<downloadDir>\logs\

Table 9.28 Download Directory

Next, we'll configure and run the options file leveraging the following entries to export POs (see Table 9.29).

Item	Description
<event>	The name of the event to trigger on server side after download, it must be in double quotes.
<event>	"Export Change Purchase Order"

Table 9.29 Export Changed POs

1. Copy transactionaldata.bat.sample from *<new directory>\sample-options\DataTransferTool\data-download* to a folder of your choice.
2. Rename the .sample file to transactionaldataCP.bat.
3. Edit the .bat file with a text editor.
4. Set the options listed in Table 9.30.

Item	Description
Site	set site=<YourSiteId>
Servicemode	set servicemode=0
integrationPasswordKeyPath	set integrationPasswordKeyPath=<SharedSecretPath>
encryptionKeyPath	set encryptionKeyPath=<CustomerKeyPath>
Event	set event=<" Export Purchase Order ">
downloadDir	set downloadDir=C:\ITK_Daten\Transactional-Download\downloadDir_changePO
timestampFile	set timestampFile=%downloadDir%\POTimeStamp
filePrefix	set filePrefix=PO
logDir	set logDir=%downloadDir%\logs
smtpMailServer	set smtpMailServer=
fromEmail	set fromEmail=
notifyEmail	set notifyEmail=
notifyonSuccess	set notifyonSuccess=0
notifyonFailure	set notifyonFailure=0
notificationSuccessSubject	set notificationSuccessSubject=AribaFileTransfer Transactional Data Download: Successful
notificationFailureSubject	set notificationFailureSubject=AribaFileTransfer Transactional Data Download: Failed
JAVA_HOME	set JAVA_HOME=<JavaDirectoryPath>

Table 9.30 Bat File Settings

5. Set this option under DO NOT CHANGE: urlPrefix=https://<AribaServer>/Buyer/fileupload.
6. Save the options file.

7. Open a Microsoft Windows command interpreter.
8. Enter `cd <new directory>`.
9. Enter `bin\aribafiletransfer<directoryname>\transactionaldataCP.bat` where <directoryname> is the directory containing the options file you modified.

The next step in our SAP Ariba Procure-to-Pay integration will be to configure the transactional data download for canceled purchase orders. First, set up a folder structure using the information from Table 9.31 and Table 9.32, as with the previous document types.

Item	Description
<downloadDir>	The path to and including the directory where the downloaded files will go.
<downloadDir>	C:\ITK_Daten\downloadDir_cancelPO

Table 9.31 Download Directory

Item	Description
downloadDir	<downloadDir>
Logs	<downloadDir>\logs\

Table 9.32 Download Logs

Next, we'll configure and run the options file as per Table 9.33.

Item	Description
<event>	The name of the event to trigger on server side after download, it must be in double quotes.
<event>	"Export Cancel Purchase Order"

Table 9.33 Run Options

1. Copy `transactionaldata.bat.sample` from *<new directory>\sample-options\DataTransferTool\data-download* to a folder of your choice.
2. Rename the .sample file to `transactionaldata_cPO.bat`.
3. Edit the .bat file with a text editor.
4. Set the options listed in Table 9.34.

Item	Description
Site	set site=<YourSiteId>
Servicemode	set servicemode=0
integrationPasswordKeyPath	set integrationPasswordKeyPath=<SharedSecretPath>
encryptionKeyPath	set *encryptionKeyPath=<CustomerKeyPath>*
Event	set event=<" Export Cancel Purchase Order ">
downloadDir	set downloadDir=C:\ITK_Daten\Transactional-Download\downloadDir_cancelPO
timestampFile	set timestampFile=%downloadDir%\POTimeStamp
filePrefix	set filePrefix=PO
logDir	set logDir=%downloadDir%\logs
smtpMailServer	set smtpMailServer=
fromEmail	set fromEmail=
notifyEmail	set notifyEmail=0
notifyonSuccess	set notifyonSuccess=0
notifyonFailure	set notifyonFailure=0
notificationSuccessSubject	set notificationSuccessSubject=AribaFileTransfer Transactional Data Download: Successful
notificationFailureSubject	set notificationFailureSubject=AribaFileTransfer Transactional Data Download: Failed
JAVA_HOME	set JAVA_HOME=<JavaDirectoryPath>

Table 9.34 Bat File Settings

5. Set this option under DO NOT CHANGE: `urlPrefix=https://<AribaServer>/Buyer/fileupload`.
6. Save options to the file.
7. Open a Microsoft Windows command interpreter.
8. Enter `cd <new directory>`.
9. Enter `bin\aribafiletransfer<directoryname>\transactionaldataCP.bat` where <directoryname> is the directory containing the options file you modified.

The next step in our SAP Ariba Procure-to-Pay integration will be to configure the transactional data download for good receipt. Again, we'll start by setting up a folder structure as in Table 9.35 and Table 9.36.

Item	Description
<downloadDir>	The path to and including the directory where the downloaded files will go.
<downloadDir>	C:\ITK_Daten\downloadDir_GR

Table 9.35 Download Directory Path

Item	Description
downloadDir	<downloadDir>
Logs	<downloadDir>\logs\

Table 9.36 Download Directory Logs

Next we'll configure and run the options file as in Table 9.37. This is where you export your goods receipts from SAP ERP.

Item	Description
<event>	The name of the event to trigger on server side after download, it must be in double quotes.
<event>	"Export ERP Receipt"

Table 9.37 Options File

1. Copy `transactionaldata.bat.sample` from *<new directory>\sample-options\DataTransferTool\data-download* to a folder of your choice.
2. Rename the .sample file to `transactionaldataGR.bat`.
3. Edit the .bat file with a text editor.
4. Set the options listed in Table 9.38.

Item	Table
Site	set `site=<YourSiteId>`
Servicemode	set `servicemode=0`

Table 9.38 Bat File Settings

Item	Table
integrationPasswordKeyPath	set integrationPasswordKeyPath=<SharedSecretPath>
encryptionKeyPath	set encryptionKeyPath=<CustomerKeyPath>
Event	set event=<"Export ERP Receipt">
downloadDir	set downloadDir=C:\ITK_Daten\Transactional-Download\downloadDir_GR
timestampFile	set timestampFile=%downloadDir%\POTimeStamp
filePrefix	set filePrefix=PO
logDir	set logDir=%downloadDir%\logs
smtpMailServer	set smtpMailServer=
fromEmail	set fromEmail=
notifyEmail	set notifyEmail=
notifyonSuccess	set notifyonSuccess=0
notifyonFailure	set notifyonFailure=0
notificationSuccessSubject	set notificationSuccessSubject= AribaFileTransfer Transactional Data Download: Successful
notificationFailureSubject	set notificationFailureSubject= AribaFileTransfer Transactional Data Download: Failed
JAVA_HOME	set JAVA_HOME=<JavaDirectoryPath>

Table 9.38 Bat File Settings (Cont.)

5. Set this option under DO NOT CHANGE: urlPrefix=https://<AribaServer>/Buyer/fileupload.
6. Save the options file.
7. Open a Microsoft Windows command interpreter.
8. Enter cd <new directory>.
9. Enter bin\aribafiletransfer<directoryname>\transactionaldataGR.bat where <directoryname> is the directory containing the options file you modified.

The next step in our SAP Ariba Procure-to-Pay integration will be to configure the transactional data download for invoices. We'll start by setting up a folder structure as in Table 9.39.

Item	Description
<downloadDir>	The path to and including the directory where the downloaded files will go.
<downloadDir>	C:\ITK_Daten\downloadDir_Inv
downloadDir	<downloadDir>
Logs	<downloadDir>\logs\

Table 9.39 Download Directory Folder

Next we'll configure and run the options file in Table 9.40 to export payment requests.

Item	Description
<event>	The name of the event to trigger on server side after download, it must be in double quotes.
<event>	"Export Payment Requests"

Table 9.40 Export Payment Requests

1. Copy `transactionaldata.bat.sample` from *<new directory>\sample-options\DataTransferTool\data-download* to a folder of your choice.
2. Rename the .sample file to `transactionaldataGR.bat`.
3. Edit the .bat file with a text editor.
4. Set the options listed in Table 9.41.

Item	Description
Site	set `site=<YourSiteId>`
Servicemode	set `servicemode=0`
integrationPasswordKeyPath	set `integrationPasswordKeyPath=<SharedSecretPath>`
encryptionKeyPath	set `encryptionKeyPath=<CustomerKeyPath>`

Table 9.41 Bat File Settings

Item	Description
Event	set event=<" Export Payment Requests ">
downloadDir	set downloadDir=C:\ITK_Daten\Transactional-Download\downloadDir_GR
timestampFile	set timestampFile=%downloadDir%\POTimeStamp
filePrefix	set filePrefix=PO
logDir	set logDir=%downloadDir%\logs
smtpMailServer	set smtpMailServer=
fromEmail	set fromEmail=
notifyEmail	set notifyEmail=
notifyonSuccess	set notifyonSuccess=0
notifyonFailure	set notifyonFailure=0
notificationSuccessSubject	set notificationSuccessSubject= AribaFileTransfer Transactional Data Download: Successful
notificationFailureSubject	set notificationFailureSubject= AribaFileTransfer Transactional Data Download: Failed
JAVA_HOME	set JAVA_HOME=<JavaDirectoryPath>

Table 9.41 Bat File Settings (Cont.)

5. Set this option under Do not change: urlPrefix=https://<AribaServer>/Buyer/fileupload.
6. Save the options file.
7. Open a Microsoft Windows command interpreter.
8. Enter cd <new directory>.
9. Enter bin\aribafiletransfer<directoryname>\transactionaldataGR.bat where <directoryname> is the directory containing the options file you modified.

Verifying Data Exchange

Once you have set up all of the various document types to be exchange between SAP ERP and SAP Ariba, the next step is to verify whether these work.

The following steps will show very quickly whether your integration is up and running or not.

First, you'll check the data exchange by sending data from one system to another. Next, you'll check the master data upload by verifying whether you can transfer master data from one system to another. To begin:

1. Upload the master data to your SAP Ariba system. You will synchronize the SAP Ariba application with your backend system by transferring a snapshot of the master data from your backend system.
2. Check the master data upload.
3. Open a Microsoft Windows command interpreter.
4. Input `masterdata.bat<bin\aribafiletransfer<directoryname>\masterdata.bat>`.
5. Access the SAP Ariba P2P solution core administration: PROCUREMENT • MANAGE • CORE ADMINISTRATION • INTEGRATION MANAGER • DATA IMPORT/EXPORT.
6. Select the master data type.
7. Click the status of the data type.
8. Check if status is completed.
9. Check to see if the client type is equal to the data DataTransferTool—this is to ensure the transfer tool is not set to a client type that does not correspond, which could potentially result in errors.
10. Access the data transfer directory.
11. Check the log file as per Table 9.42.

Item	Description
Logs	<topDir>\logs\
<topDir>\logs	D:\ariba\DataTransferTool\MasterDataUpload\logs

Table 9.42 Data Transfer Directory

Finally, you need to check the transactional data download to ensure that all the previous steps have been properly completed.

Note

An executable program is defined for each file channel integration event. This program can be scheduled to run in the background, listening to CSV data files input from SAP Ariba procurement solutions and exporting them to the SAP database. Transactional data is downloaded into CSV file formats by executing the appropriate transaction integration events. The data transfer tool then picks up these CSV files and moves them into the SAP database.

The custom RFC programs read the data from CSV files on the SAP database, invoke the SAP RFC/BAPI in order to create the data in SAP, and send the response back to SAP Ariba procurement solutions.

1. Open a Microsoft Windows command interpreter.
2. Execute `transactionaldata.bat<bin\aribafiletransfer<directoryname>\transactionaldata.bat>`.
3. Access the data transfer directory (see Figure 9.43).

Item	Description
Logs	<topDir>\<downloadDir>\logs\
<downloadDir\logs\>	C:\ITK_Daten\downloadDir\logs

Table 9.43 Transfer Directory

4. Check the log file.
5. Access the data transfer directory as per Table 9.44.
6. Verify the last download matches your records.

Item	Description
downloadDir	<topDir>\<downloadDir>\<last download>
downloadDir	C:\ITK_Daten\TransactionalDownload\downloadDir\ <Expense?

Table 9.44 Data Transfer Directory—Last Download

7. Check the content of the files `PurchaseOrderDetailExport.csv` and `PurchaseOrderExport.csv`

At this point you should also upload transactional data to your SAP Ariba system by synchronizing the SAP Ariba application with your backend system and transferring transactional data incrementally from your backend system.

9.3 SAP Ariba Collaborative Supply Chain Integration

SAP Ariba Collaborative Supply Chain brings enhanced visibility and efficiency for direct material/merchandise/supply chain collaboration in the SAP Ariba Network. In the past, the SAP Ariba solution platform focused primarily on indirect procurement. Collaborative Supply Chain broadens this focus and the solution capabilities to include direct procurement. Expansion of functionality and integration with the SAP Ariba Network are required in order to achieve this. Direct procurement is driven out of multiple modules, and is typically used to manage and control manufacturing, sales and distribution, production planning, and the ever-present financial aspects.

9.3.1 Supply Network Collaboration

Issuing a PO or conducting a procurement transaction is typically more automated than indirect, as production planning systems and inventory management systems interact during a materials requirements planning run (MRP) to create orders. Once created and processed, these orders are typically transmitted directly to a supplier via a transmission method such as electronic data interchange (EDI), email, or fax. EDI, while efficient once established, is a point-to-point connection that can be expensive to maintain. In order to interact with suppliers, collaboration options typically must be augmented with an in-house portal. Other transmission and collaboration methods do not provide seamless communication options for running the transaction and basing production off lead times, advanced shipping notifications, etc. The SAP Ariba Network in CSC allows you to connect these complex orders and processes, providing a platform-based, one-to-many connection option to direct suppliers. In essence, CSC leverages the SAP Ariba Network to provide additional benefits to EDI and company-maintained supplier portals for direct procurement and complex indirect procurement, at a fraction of the setup and maintenance costs.

Figure 9.56 details how both the buyer and seller are connected via the SAP Ariba Network, leveraging existing user interfaces, processes, and infrastructure, to replace the expensive point-to-point communication and transaction methods of the past. The SAP Supply Network Collaboration integration feature supports five functions of SAP supplier collaboration: forecast, replenishment, work order, inventory, and quality.

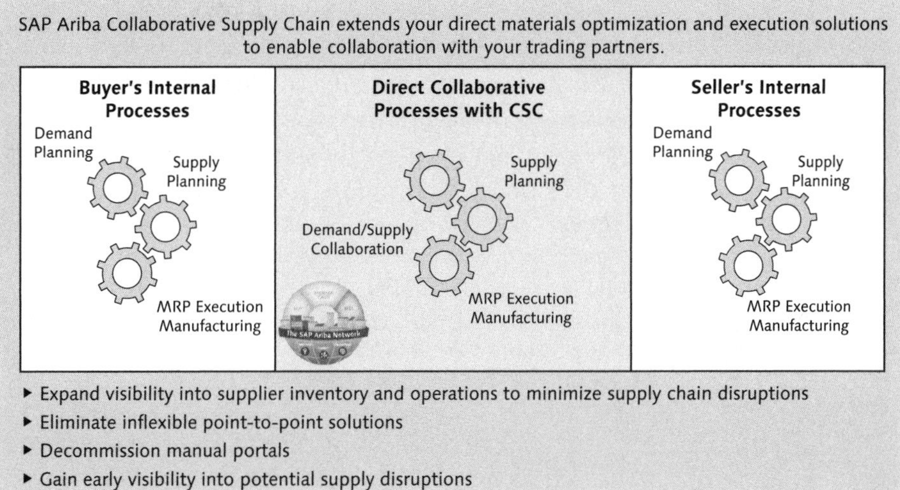

Figure 9.56 SAP Ariba Collaborative Supply Chain Overview

Table 9.45 outlines the functionality added with CSC in order to support the direct procurement processes through the SAP Ariba Network and back.

CSC Function	Description
Forecast	The forecast collaboration component aims to avoid supply shortfalls, and reduces and optimizes supply chain stock levels. It compares and displays the buyer's firm or planned net demands and the supplier's firm or planned receipts. Buyer and supplier have the same view of the planning situation and can quickly obtain a quick overview of critical situations.
Work order	The work order collaboration component provides a consolidated view of the production demands and the current production progress. It offers customers early insight into changes affecting shipping dates and final quantity.

Table 9.45 SCS Functionality

CSC Function	Description
Replenishment	The replenishment collaboration component offers suppliers a value added service by performing the replenishment planning task for their business partners. By increasing visibility into actual consumer demand, as well as customer inventory levels, suppliers can make better decisions on how to distribute goods across various customers, which in turn leads to increased customer service levels, lower transportation costs, reduced inventory, and lower sales cost.
Inventory	The inventory collaboration component ensures greater visibility of the inventory, as well as the supply-and-demand planning situation in a cross-tier environment.
Quality	Suppliers and customers can use the new quality collaboration component to notify each other of quality problems (or other issues with products or subcontracting components) during the manufacturing process, or after delivery, so that the customer or supplier can quickly react to the complaint.

Table 9.45 SCS Functionality (Cont.)

In order to keep documents consistent between the SAP Supply Network Collaboration and the SAP Ariba Network, you must perform the business processes for purchase orders and ship notices through the SAP Ariba Network user interface exclusively, and not through the SAP Supply Network Collaboration application.

Not all functions available in SAP supplier collaboration are supported by SAP Supply Network Collaboration integration. Table 9.46 shows the five functions supported, and their related SAP Supply Network Collaboration (SNC) components and starting screens.

Supply Network Collaboration Integration Function	SAP Supply Network Collaboration Component	SAP Supply Network Collaboration Starting Screen
Forecast	Demand	Order Forecast Monitor
Replenishment	Replenishment	Replenishment VMI Monitor
Work Order	Work Order Collaboration	Work Order List

Table 9.46 Comparison Table—CSC Functions with Supply Network Collaboration

Supply Network Collaboration Integration Function	SAP Supply Network Collaboration Component	SAP Supply Network Collaboration Starting Screen
Inventory	Supply Network Inventory	Supply Network Inventory
Quality	Quality Collaboration	Quality Notification Overview

Table 9.46 Comparison Table—CSC Functions with Supply Network Collaboration (Cont.)

CSC 2.0 includes several updated features and functions crucial to many direct procurement processes.

The improvements in CSC 2.0 center primarily on scheduling agreement releases (SARs), ship notices, and order collaboration. Per Figure 9.57, buyers and suppliers now have access to many direct specific processes and fields that were previously unavailable in the SAP Ariba environment for ship notices, SARs, and order collaboration.

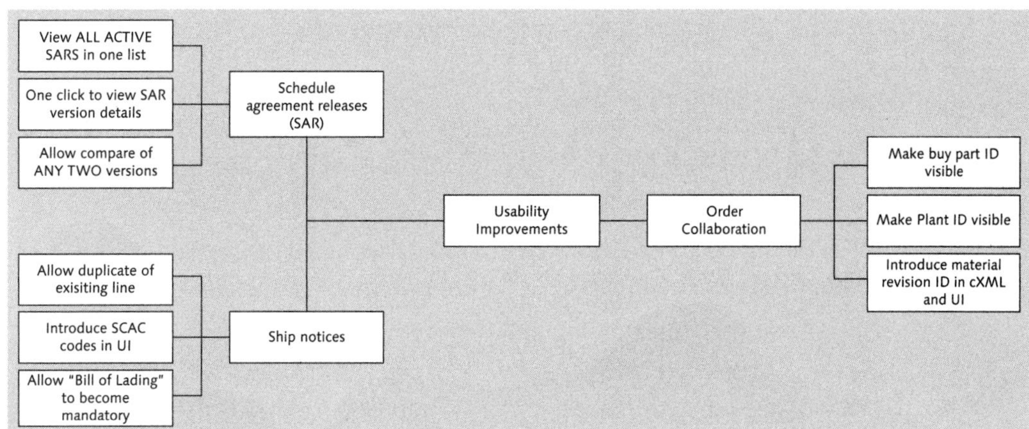

Figure 9.57 CSC 2.0 Improvements

As part of the SCS set up process, suppliers need to be enabled via an adapter in the SAP Ariba cloud integration releases as a prerequisite to support the collaboration processes. This is coordinated via SAP Ariba Supplier Enablement Services. SAP Ariba began providing technical and installation support for the adapters in releases in 2014 for both SAP ERP and Oracle Fusion.

The steps for deploying the SAP Ariba Collaborative Supply Chain extension start with the buyer.

1. The buyer enables the supplier for particular collaborative supply chain features.
2. Fields of data supporting enhanced functionality, such as the ordering of direct materials, are passed from the buyer's SAP ERP system to SAP Ariba Network.
3. Through an enhanced SAP Ariba Network user interface, the enabled supplier makes use of the additional fields and enhanced functionality to collaborate with the buyer on documents such as purchase orders, invoices, and ship notices.

In order to prepare a supplier record in SAP ERP for CSC activities, a relationship flag must be set. This functionality is standard and does not require additional installation or configuration. Once the flag is set, industry-specific functionality can be configured. To complete both these activities, your user role must have "supplier enablement task management" permissions. Buyers do not require further enablement for CSC.

As an administrator, you can disable collaborative supply chain functionality for suppliers. To disable collaborative supply chain or retail-industry functionality for a supplier, do the following:

1. Click the Supplier Enablement tab.
2. Click Active Relationships.
3. Select the suppliers for whom you want to disable collaborative supply chain or retail industry functionality.
4. Click the Actions menu at the bottom of the supplier table and select Enable/Disable Collaborative Supply Chain. Next, perform the following:
   - To disable collaborative supply chain and retail-industry functionality for the selected suppliers, deselect Collaborative Supply Chain.
   - To disable only retail industry functionality for the selected suppliers, deselect Retail Industry fields. Note: the Retail Industry setting enables supplier for Ship Notice Due List.
5. Click OK.

Once a supplier has been appropriately flagged, they can be directed to the Collaborative Supply Chain supplier user interface portal. The CSC supplier UI portal contains all existing SAP Ariba Network supplier functionality, plus Collaborative Supply Chain and industry-specific Collaborative Supply Chain functionality. When suppliers are enabled for Collaborative Supply Chain, they are directed to the Collaborative Supply Chain supplier user interface portal, where they can access the various Collaborative Supply Chain features. Previously, the Collaborative Supply Chain supplier user interface portal was referred to as the Supply Chain Management (SCM) portal. For suppliers, EDI support is provided via Boomi, a Dell integration product. If you require information on EDI support and Boomi, you will need to contact SAP Ariba during the project preparation phase.

Suppliers and buyers often collaborate on the creation of purchase orders, invoices, and ship notices for direct material orders. This collaboration requires the exchange of information specific to direct material orders. These features facilitate the collaboration process by allowing more detailed descriptions of materials being procured. These features also allow the supplier to collaborate through the SAP Ariba Network user interface. This is particularly helpful for suppliers that do not have EDI, cXML, or other integrated business-to-business mechanisms in place.

Direct material fields for order and invoice collaboration facilitate the collaboration process for purchase orders, invoices, and ship notices by allowing more detailed descriptions of materials being procured. This SAP Ariba Network feature is applicable to all supplier users. The buyer's industry type needs to be set as "retail" to enable this functionality. For buyers using external ERP systems, such as SAP ERP, the adapter is required.

The ship notice business rules feature for order confirmation and ship notice rules supports the direct material collaboration process. This SAP Ariba Network feature is applicable to all supplier users.

Direct material includes all items, such as raw materials and parts, required to assemble or manufacture a complete product. A rule may be implemented based on customer and market requirements, or may be driven by individual needs. A rule can be applied to many suppliers, or to a predefined group of suppliers (even if the group only contains one member). Tooltips in the user interface indicate when ship notice rules have been enabled.

The following ship notice rules particularly support collaboration between buyers and suppliers with regard to direct materials:

1. **Require suppliers to provide a unique asset serial number for each purchase order line item on a ship notice.**
   This rule applies within the scope of the order line item. Using the same serial number on any of the ship notice line items for this order line item is not allowed. If validation fails, the error message you receive is "Asset serial numbers for item shipments must be unique."
2. **Require the total count of shipment serial numbers not to exceed the total quantity shipped for line items on ship notices.**
   Within a ship notice item, the number of serial numbers must be less than or equal to the quantity shipped. If validation fails the error message you receive is "The total number of shipment serial numbers exceeds the quantity shipped for the line item."
3. **Require the packing slip ID to be unique on ship notices.**
   Duplicate shipment notice numbers (packing slip IDs) are not allowed. The rule is checked against all ship notice numbers for the particular supplier without a time window restriction. If validation fails the error message you receive is "This packing slip ID has already been used. Please enter a unique ID."

Buyers often want to procure pre-defined quantities of materials in releases received on pre-determined dates. For example, a buyer might order 100 items, but might want them delivered 10 at a time, on a weekly basis. A buyer could therefore send a scheduling agreement release to a supplier.

A scheduling agreement release defines the quantities and dates for the shipments desired for a specific item. The scheduling agreement functionality touches both any supplier for whom you have enabled this functionality, as well as SAP Ariba purchase order automation.

A scheduling agreement release can have multiple schedule lines for any single line in a purchase order or other business document. A single schedule line contains fields for delivery date and time, and for scheduled quantity and unit of measure. Buyers create schedule agreement releases with external ERP systems.

Prior to the CSC 2.0 release, suppliers could view schedule lines, but could not use them in the creation of ship notices through the SAP Ariba Network user interface. With the release of CSC 2.0, scheduling agreement releases become visible in the SAP Ariba Network user interface. Buyers can periodically communicate releases to their suppliers; and suppliers can create ship notices for materials requested through scheduling agreement releases. From the new ITEMS TO SHIP tab, a supplier can create a single ship notice containing items from several purchase orders that all are due by the same date.

It is important to note that scheduling agreement releases do not support order confirmations, or most invoices. You cannot use scheduling agreement release collaboration for invoices, except invoices that have been created as carbon copies by direct material buyers. Also, you cannot use scheduling agreement releases for order confirmations. The processing of non-scheduled items is not affected by scheduling agreement releases. These are not restrictions of CSC 2.0 as much as general restrictions in the scheduling agreement process.

Scheduling agreement release collaboration is disabled by default, but the buyer can enable it following these steps:

1. Log on as a buyer.
2. Click MANAGE PROFILE.
3. On the CONFIGURATION page, click DEFAULT TRANSACTION RULES.
4. Under SCHEDULING AGREEMENT RELEASE SETUP RULES, check the box next to ALLOW SCHEDULING AGREEMENT RELEASE COLLABORATION.

Suppliers view scheduling agreement releases in the list of documents on the ORDERS AND RELEASES tab, and can choose whether to search for only scheduling agreement releases. Suppliers can then create ship notices from scheduling agreement releases.

The cXML 1.2.028 DTD introduced cXML elements and attributes that support scheduling agreement releases as in Table 9.47.

For information about cXML, see the DTD and cXML User's Guide available at *http://www.cxml.org*. Also, see the cXML Solutions Guide on SAP Ariba Network.

cXML Element for Scheduling Release	Description
isSchedulingAgreementRelease	Indicates the type of purchase order is a schedule agreement release. When isSchedulingAgreementRelease is set to yes, orderType must be set to release as-is shown in the following example: <OrderRequestHeader orderDate="2014-05-08T14:37:31-07:00" orderID="SAR301-1-FORECAST" orderVersion="1" orderType="release" agreementID="SA301" type="new">
ReleaseInfo	The OrderRequestHeader element has a new attribute, isSchedulingAgreementRelease that indiReleaseInfo has been added to ItemOut as an optional element. ReleaseInfo stores the details about a release of items or materials.
ScheduleLineReleaseInfo	The element ScheduleLineReleaseInfo, has been added to the ScheduleLine element. ScheduleLineReleaseInfo stores details about a specific release of items or materials for a schedule line. ScheduleLineReleaseInfo contains the following attributes.
AgreementType	The attribute agreementType has been added to the MasterAgreementIDInfo element and MasterAgreementReference element to indicate whether the referenced agreement is a scheduling agreement release. Example for MasterAgreementIDInfo: <MasterAgreementIDInfo agreementID="SA301" agreementType="scheduling_agreement"/>
ShipNoticePortion	ShipNoticePortion now contains the following two new optional elements: MasterAgreementReference and MasterAgreementIDInfo which can contain a reference or an ID, respectively, to the master agreement from which the release is derived. Example: <ShipNoticePortion> <OrderReference orderID="OD1" orderDate= "2014-01-28T11:15:32-08:00"> </OrderReference> <Contact role="buyerCorporate"> </Contact> <ShipNoticeItem quantity="1" line number="1" </ShipNoticeItem> </ShipNoticePortion>

Table 9.47 Elements for Scheduling Agreement Release

Table 9.48 and Table 9.49 summarize additional optional sub-elements and attributes for ReleaseInfo, ScheduleLineReleaseInfo, and ShipNoticePortion.

Type	Name	Description
Sub-Element	ShipNoticeReleaseInfo	References the previous ship notice created from a delivery schedule. This reference is against the previous shipment made for the schedule line in the schedule agreement release.
Sub-Element	UnitofMeasure	Unit of measure for the quantity specified for the schedule line item.
Sub-Element	Extrinsic	Any additional information for the schedule line item.
Attribute	releaseType	A mandatory field. A string value to identify the type of delivery schedule against the schedule agreement release. Possible values: Just in time (JIT) Forecast
Attribute	Forecastcumulative-ReceivedQuantity	A mandatory field. A number value to identify the cumulative quantity of all goods received against the scheduling agreement release over a period up to a certain date.
Attribute	productionGoAheadEndDate	An optional field. Date denoting the end of the production go-ahead period (go-ahead for production).
Attribute	materialGoAheadEndDate	Date denoting the end of the material go-ahead period (go-ahead for purchase of input materials).

Table 9.48 Release Info

The following example shows a ReleaseInfo element:

```
<ReleaseInfo releaseType="forecast" cumulativeReceivedQuantity="0"
productionGoAheadEndDate="2014-06-13T14:37:31-07:00"
materialGoAheadEndDate="2014-11-14T14:37:31-07:00"
<UnitOfMeasure>EA</UnitOfMeasure>
</ReleaseInfo>
```

Type	Name	Description
Attribute	commitmentCode	A string value to identify the type of the delivery. The value can be any of the following: ▸ Firm: Go-ahead for production. Vendor can ship against the schedule line. Customer is responsible for cost of production as well as cost of material procurement. ▸ Tradeoff: Go-ahead for material procurement. Vendor can ship against the schedule line if rule is enabled. Buyer is responsible for cost of material procurement. ▸ Forecast: Informational. Customer can change the schedule line without incurring any liabilities with the vendor.
Attribute	cumulativeSched-uledQuantity	Total quantity to be shipped for a particular line item up through the schedule line.

Table 9.49 Schedule Line Release

Table 9.49 demonstrates direct procurement's use of scheduling agreements. Scheduling agreements allow for a supplier to deliver items based on a pre-determined schedule, with additional orders released at the line level at pre-defined times. This is not typical for indirect procurement, but quite prevalent in direct. The following example shows a ScheduleLineReleaseInfo element:

```
<ScheduleLine quantity="100" requestedDeliveryDate="2014-05-
10T14:37:31-07:00">
<UnitOfMeasure>EA</UnitOfMeasure>
<ScheduleLineReleaseInfo commitmentCode=
"firm" cumulativeScheduledQuantity="100">
<UnitOfMeasure>EA</UnitOfMeasure>
<ScheduleLineReleaseInfo>
</ScheduleLine>
```

Master agreement references are to support releases done on master contracts or agreements. Capturing this field allows for management of amounts outstanding at the master agreement level, and for contract-based direct procurement. For this, there is an optional field available in CSC as per Table 9.50.

Type	Name	Description
Element	MasterAgreementReference	An optional field. Can contain a reference to the master agreement from which the release is derived.
Element	MasterAgreementIDInfo	An optional field. Can contain the ID of the master agreement from which the release is derived.

Table 9.50 Master Agreement

An example of ShipNoticePortion follows.

```
<ShipNoticePortion>
<OrderReference orderID="OD1" orderDate= "2014-01-28T11:15:32-08:00">
</OrderReference>
<Contact role="buyerCorporate">
</Contact>
<ShipNoticeItem quantity="1" line number="1"
</ShipNoticeItem>
</ShipNoticePortion>
```

9.3.2 Contract Manufacturing Collaboration

Large organizations can reduce their costs by transferring the manufacturing, assembly, or processing of parts to third-party contract manufacturers. Contract manufacturers are suppliers who build the parts for these buyers.

With the contract manufacturing collaboration feature, buyers and contract manufacturers can manage the supply of component materials and finished goods through the SAP Ariba Network.

The contract manufacturing collaboration feature includes the following functionalities:

- Buyers can create subcontract purchase orders which can be transmitted to contract manufacturers via SAP Ariba Network.
- Contract manufacturers can view all the data of subcontract purchase orders, including all the component information under the purchase order line item, in the schedule line section.
- Contract manufacturers can confirm orders for finished goods purchased by buyers.

- Buyers can create ship notices for subcontracting components, and can send them to contract manufacturers.
- Contract manufacturers can create receipts for subcontracting components, and can send them to buyers.
- Contract manufacturers can create ship notices for finished goods to be shipped to buyers.
- Contract manufacturers can send component consumption information to buyers for components used to manufacture the finished goods on the subcontract purchase order.

To support these new functionalities, the following types of messages have been enhanced or added for direct materials buyers and contract manufacturers:

- **Subcontracting purchase order**
  A subcontracting purchase order is a purchase order that is sent from a buyer to a contract manufacturer to request the production and delivery of finished goods.

  The subcontracting purchase order has been enhanced to carry not only item level and schedule line level information, but also subcontracting component information. Subcontracting components are the raw materials that are used for manufacturing the finished goods specified at the item level.
- **Component ship notice**
  A component ship notice is a type of ship notice that informs the contract manufacturer of the shipment of subcontracting components.
- **Component receipt**
  A component receipt is a type of goods receipt that informs the buyer of the receipt of subcontracting components. The contract manufacturer can issue the component receipt against one or more component ship notices.
- **Component consumption (backflush) message**
  The ship notice message has been enhanced to include consumption details in a backflush component message. A backflush component consumption message is a type of ship notice request that informs the buyer of the completion of finished goods from subcontracting components. Unlike real-time component consumption reporting, backflush reporting is done only once, at the end of the production process.

- **Component consumption (real-time) message**
  A real-time component consumption message informs the buyer of consumption of components at any phase of the production cycle.
- **Component inventory message**
  A component inventory message has been added to inform suppliers about quantities of components available for manufacturing.
- **CSC limitation**
  If a subcontracting purchase order has been uploaded or downloaded via CSV, a supplier will not see the component level on the downloaded subcontracting purchase order.

In the order collaboration process for direct materials, suppliers typically strive to establish long-term, repeat business with their customers. From the supplier's perspective, a successful business model involves a continual flow of incoming purchase orders from a number of buying customers. The supplier must efficiently process these incoming purchase orders: confirming line items when confirmation is required, creating ship notices, and shipping goods. Also, the supplier must process purchase orders that have been changed. Further, the supplier must not confirm orders for quantities or delivery dates that are not achievable. The process of confirming orders quickly and correctly therefore can be very challenging because of the sheer volume of data and the level of detail required, which is where the items to confirm list comes in.

The items to confirm list feature enables the supplier to efficiently confirm incoming purchase orders across multiple customers. The items to confirm list displays a list of purchase orders that includes information critical for a supplier to accurately confirm many order details simultaneously.

As a buyer, you can enable or disable the visibility of purchase order line items in the items to confirm table. This feature is enabled by default, and to configure it, you should perform the following actions:

1. Click Manage Profile • Default Transaction Rules.
2. Under the heading Order Confirmation and Ship Notice Rules, select or deselect Allow suppliers to send order confirmations on line item level. If deselected, purchase orders between the buyer and the corresponding supplier remain visible, but are not actionable, in that supplier's Items to Confirm table.

3. Select or deselect ALLOW SUPPLIERS TO SEND ORDER CONFIRMATIONS TO THIS ACCOUNT. If disabled, no purchase orders from this buyer will be visible in supplier ITEMS TO CONFIRM TABLES.
4. Click SAVE.

The SAP Ariba Network also supports invoice enhancements for self-billing and scheduling agreement releases for direct materials suppliers. For direct material suppliers and buyers, SAP Ariba Network can automatically transmit self-billing invoices based on data in purchase orders, scheduling agreements, and goods receipts. The buyer creates a self-billing invoice in an external business system and sends it to a supplier over SAP Ariba Network. Suppliers and buyers can deploy self-billing invoices when they have agreed to not require the supplier to manually create invoices for order transactions, but instead to use an automated routine called evaluated receipt settlement (ERS).

ERS determines the invoice amount for ordering transactions from the prices entered in the order, the terms of payment, the tax information, and the delivery quantity entered in the goods receipt.

With the invoice enhancements for self-billing and scheduling agreement releases, suppliers and buyers can employ self-billing invoices for scheduling agreements as well as for purchase orders.

With consignment collaboration deployment, the supplier sends consignments to the buyer, but still retains ownership of the consignments until the buyer pays for the consignments the buyer consumes, through a pre-arranged purchase order method. Consignments stocked in the buyer's warehouses or production facilities are not paid for until they have been used. The transfer of ownership, and often of location, to the buyer at the time of consumption is called a *consignment movement*. SAP Ariba Network Collaborative Supply Chain now provides ways for suppliers to view a list of materials on consignment, for suppliers to create invoices for consignment movements, and for buyers to create self-billing invoices for consignment movements.

The workflow for consignment collaboration is as follows:

1. The buyer creates or changes a consignment purchase order, and sends it, via SAP Ariba Network, to a supplier.
2. The supplier finds a purchase order for a consignment item, clearly differentiated as such in the item category field. The supplier creates a consignment

fill-up order, and sends a consignment purchase order confirmation, via SAP Ariba Network, to the buyer.

3. The supplier creates a ship notice for the consignment purchase order and sends it, via SAP Ariba Network, to the buyer, who receives notice of an inbound delivery.
4. The buyer reports the transfer of materials from consignment to the buyer's own stock, via SAP Ariba Network, to the supplier.
5. The supplier views consignment movements in SAP Ariba Network and can execute either of the following:
6. The buyer executes a consignment settlement, and sends a settlement invoice, via SAP Ariba Network, to the supplier, or the supplier creates an invoice against one or more consignment movements, and sends the invoice, via SAP Ariba Network, to the buyer.

Collaborative Supply Chain represents a broad-based approach towards integrating and supporting direct procurement processes originating in SAP ERP via the SAP Ariba Network. Per Figure 9.58, CSC supports major direct processes, from scheduling agreements to consignment to contract manufacturing. While this solution is relatively new as of 2015, CSC promises to be extend the rich, collaborative functionality of the SAP Ariba Network to SAP ERP direct procurement processes.

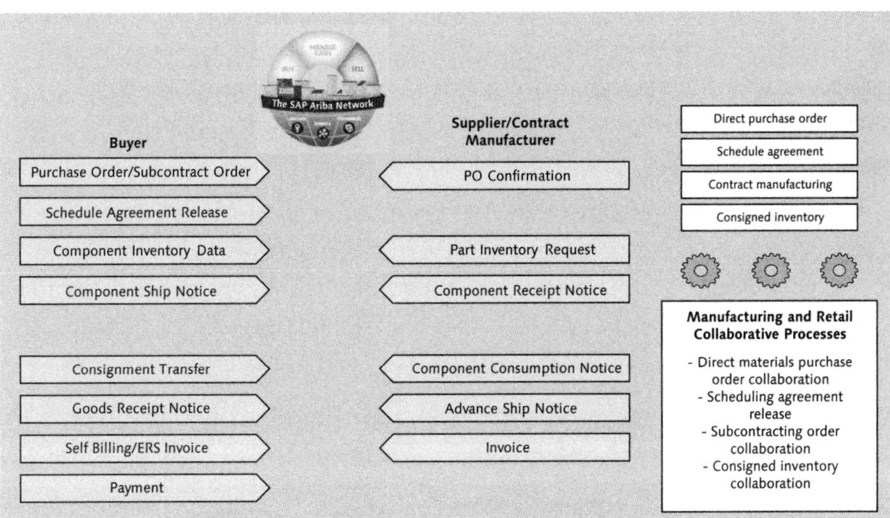

Figure 9.58 CSC Processes

9.4 SAP Fieldglass Integration Points with SAP ERP and HR Systems

Per Figure 9.59, SAP Fieldglass leverages the same integration paths supporting SAP Ariba, which is to say CI-5 through CI-6 integration toolsets.

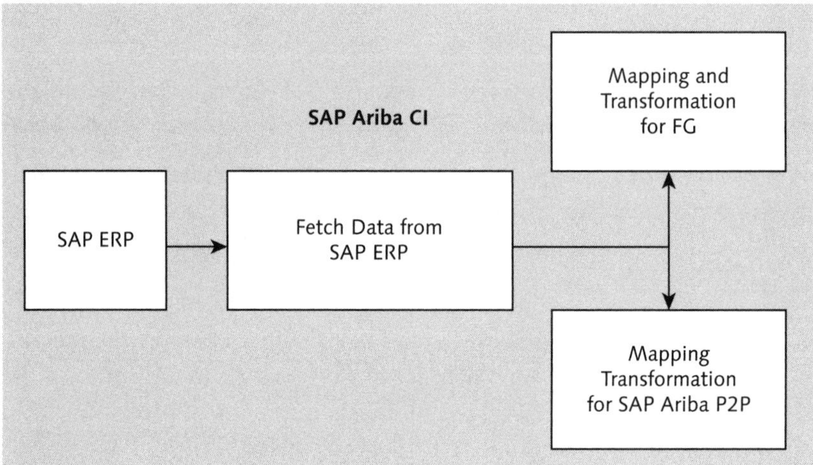

Figure 9.59 Master Data Integration from SAP ERP to SAP Fieldglass—Same CI as SAP Ariba

The SAP Fieldglass platform can be integrated with SAP ERP Human Capital Management (HCM), using standard connectors in CI. This allows transactions in SAP Fieldglass to leverage HR data to further refine the services understanding and accuracy of the system with regards to individual contingent workers. In short, leveraging prepopulated data from HCM further simplifies the ordering process for managers.

In many corporate landscapes, the HR organizational structure (which can be maintained in SAP ERP HCM or another HR management system) is the system of record. This means that the position and job information, which are maintained in the org structure, need to be available in SAP Fieldglass in order to create a requisition. This integration is enabled via standard SAP Fieldglass connectors.

Once the contingent worker is confirmed in SAP Fieldglass, the worker's HR record is interfaced back to SAP ERP HCM. The main focus of HCM is typically to manage internal employees. Customers oftentimes will create a separate group within HCM to delineate contingent workers and this information is accessed from SAP Fieldglass using a standard SAP Fieldglass connector called SAP Fieldglass Worker Download Connector on SAP PI. Pulling this data from HCM allows a customer to understand the number of contingent workers at each site, as well as update worker records in HCM with new activities and transactions generated in SAP Fieldglass. The following Infotypes can be maintained in HCM from SAP Fieldglass-based activities:

- 0000: Actions
- 0001: Organizational Assignment
- 0002: Personal Data
- 0007: Working Time (only for storing the normal work schedule)
- 0016: Contract Details
- 0901: Purchasing Data (with purchasing organization and purchasing group)

Custom fields can also be setup using the SAP Fieldglass Worker Download Connector, as well as supplier-related fields and FI data. After the connector from SAP Fieldglass into SAP ERP HCM is set up, the hiring procedure can bring externals into SAP ERP HCM. Using the same connector, a termination procedure can delimit the infotypes after termination of the contract.

9.4.1 When and Where to Integrate SAP ERP with SAP Ariba

There are several products in the SAP Ariba portfolio which have integration paths to SAP ERP. Guidelines for integration center on document and data exchange. If documents need to be exchanged during operations between SAP ERP and SAP Ariba, additional integration is likely required. These integration options are evolving constantly, and it is always prudent to verify online if there is a new approach or more built out approach for integration. The following are the main schemas for integrating each SAP Ariba solution into SAP ERP. These schemas show with red arrows which integration points are not out-of-the-box today and require further integration development. This integration should be done leveraging SAP Ariba cloud integration (CI-5 or latest adapter available), the SAP Business Suite Add-On (for PO/IV scenario), and other applicable approaches. Table 9.51 outlines the interface mappings for cXML document types.

Process Step	From SAP Application	SAP Ariba cXML Interface
Create Purchase Order	cXMLOrderRequest_Out	MIIn_Async_AddOn_PurchaseOrder_cXML
Change Purchase Order	cXMLOrderRequest_Out	MIIn_Async_AddOn_PurchaseOrder_cXML
Order Response	cXMLConfirmationRequest_In	MIOut_Async_AddOn_OrderConfirmation_cXML
Dispatch Advice (ASN)	cXMLShipNoticeRequest_In	MIOut_Async_AddOn_AdvanceShipNotice_cXML
(Traditional) Invoice (AN initiated)	cXMLInvoiceDetailRequest_In	MIOut_Async_AddOn_Invoice_cXML
Invoice Status	cXMLStatusUpdateRequest_Out	MIAbs_Async_AddOn_InvoiceStatusUpdate_cXML

Table 9.51 cXML Translation Doc Types

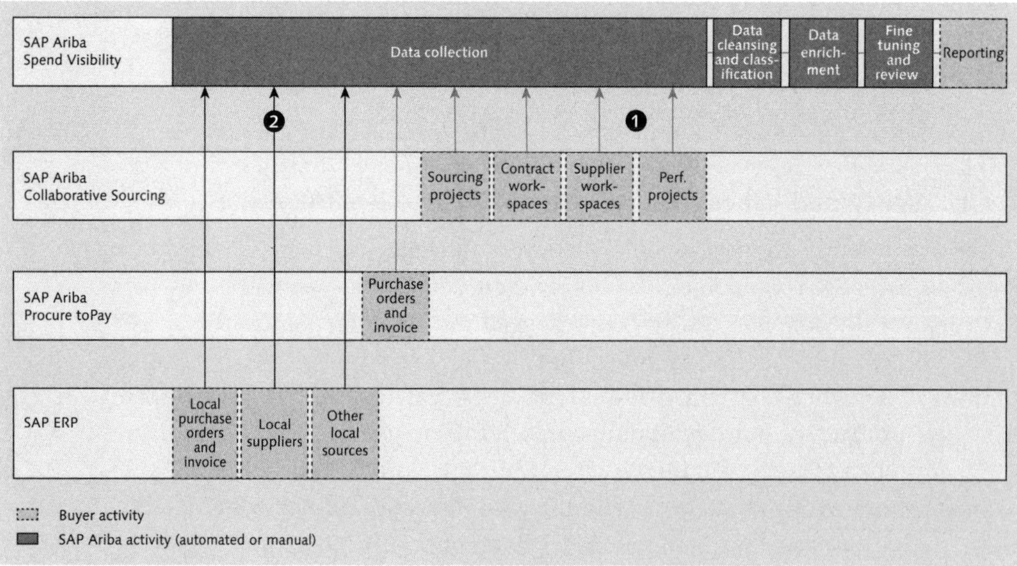

Figure 9.60 SAP Ariba Spend Visibility integrated with SAP ERP

Figure 9.60 has both green ❶ and red arrows ❷. The green arrows are existing, out-of-the-box integrations internal in SAP Ariba, and the red ones need to be established between Spend Visibility and SAP ERP for extraction, transformation, and loading of data from SAP ERP to SAP Ariba.

Figure 9.61 shows SAP ERP pushing a purchase requisition out to the SAP Ariba Sourcing module, the sourcing taking place in SAP Ariba, and the award pushed back to SAP ERP and creating a follow on outline agreement and purchase order in SAP ERP. The red arrows in the figure show the integration points that need to be built.

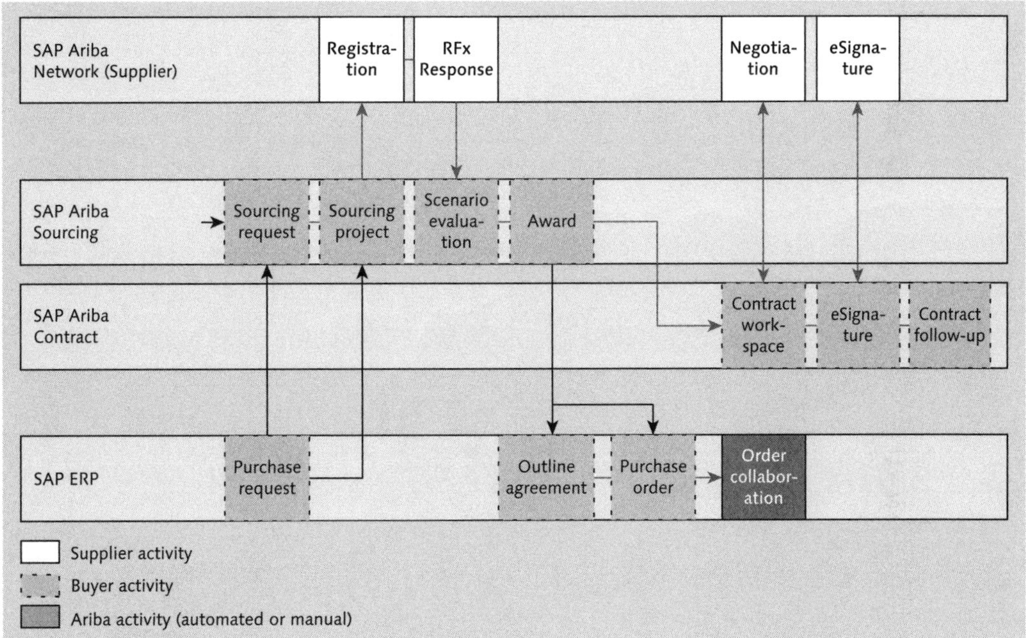

Figure 9.61 SAP Ariba Collaborative Sourcing Integration

Per Figure 9.62, there are no SAP ERP additional integrations required to use SAP Ariba Discovery: provided the SAP Ariba Sourcing integrations are already in place, no further integrations would be required to use SAP Ariba Discovery. This is also the case using qualification steps in this process, as per Figure 9.63.

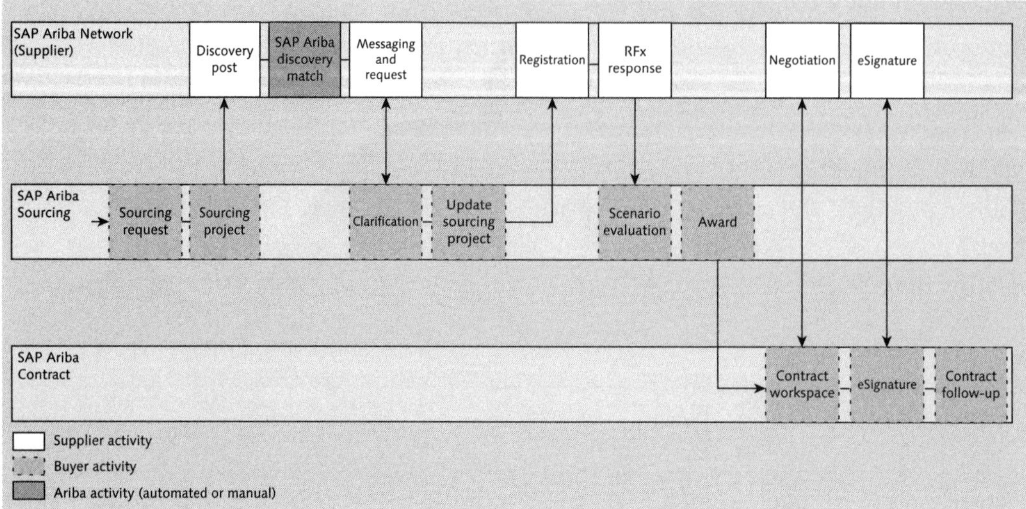

Figure 9.62 SAP Ariba Collaborative Sourcing Using Discovery

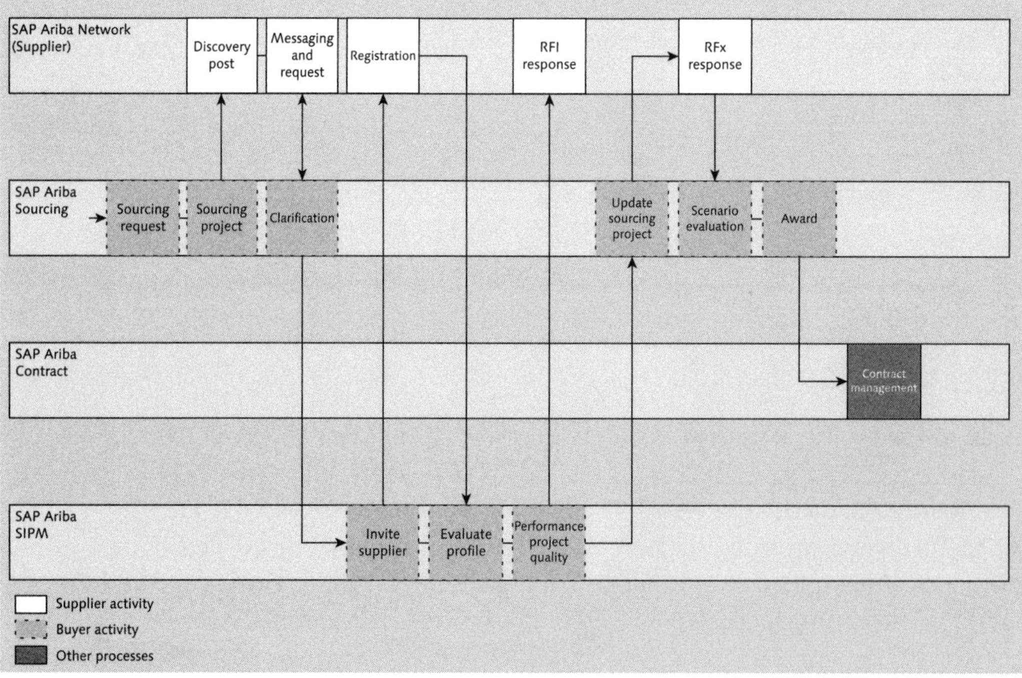

Figure 9.63 SAP Ariba Collaborative Sourcing Using SAP Ariba Discovery and Prequalification Steps

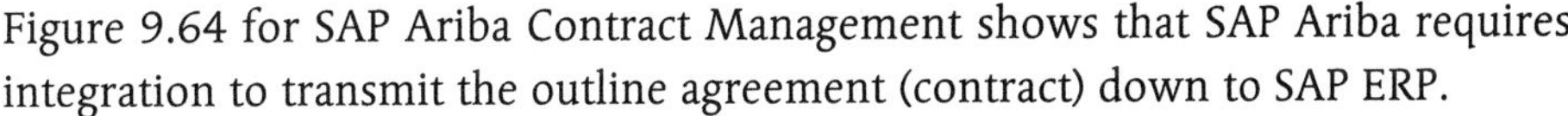

Figure 9.64 for SAP Ariba Contract Management shows that SAP Ariba requires integration to transmit the outline agreement (contract) down to SAP ERP.

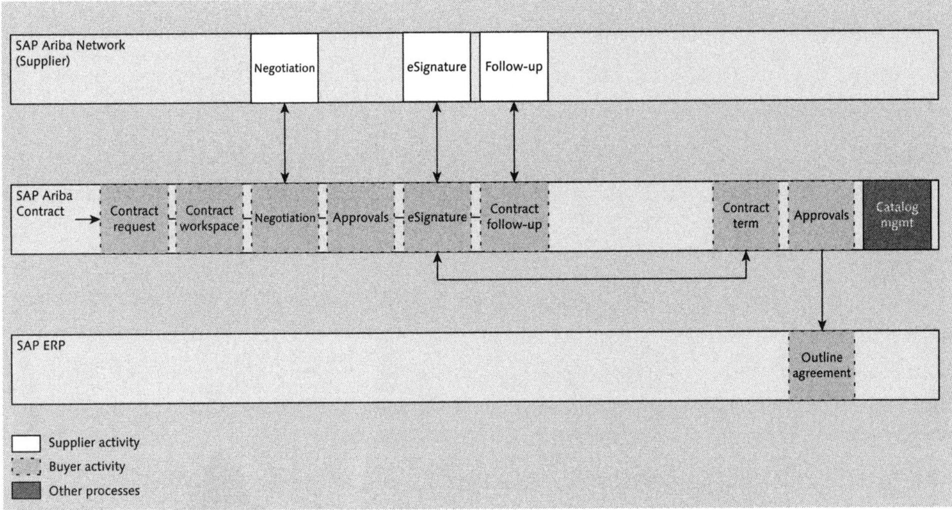

Figure 9.64 SAP Ariba Collaborative Sourcing—SAP Ariba Contract Management

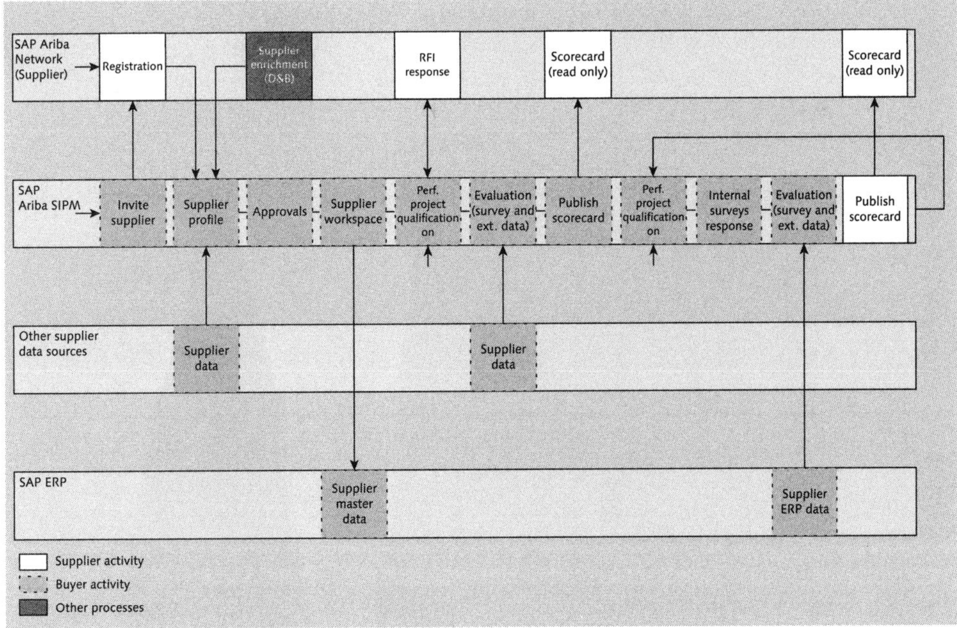

Figure 9.65 SAP Ariba Collaborative Sourcing—SAP Ariba Supplier Management

In Figure 9.65, the supplier master record updates require integration for transfer both to and from SAP ERP.

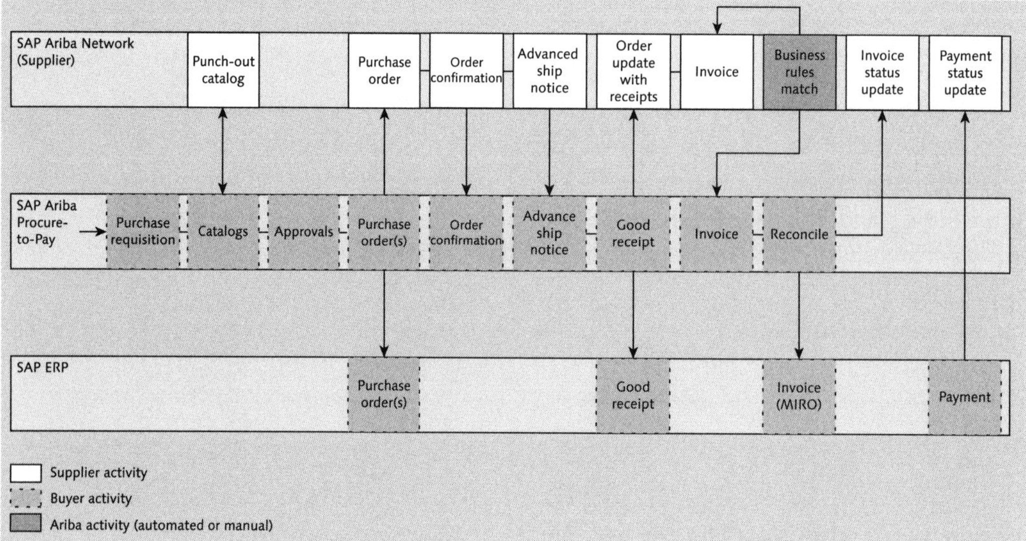

Figure 9.66 SAP Ariba Procure-to-Pay

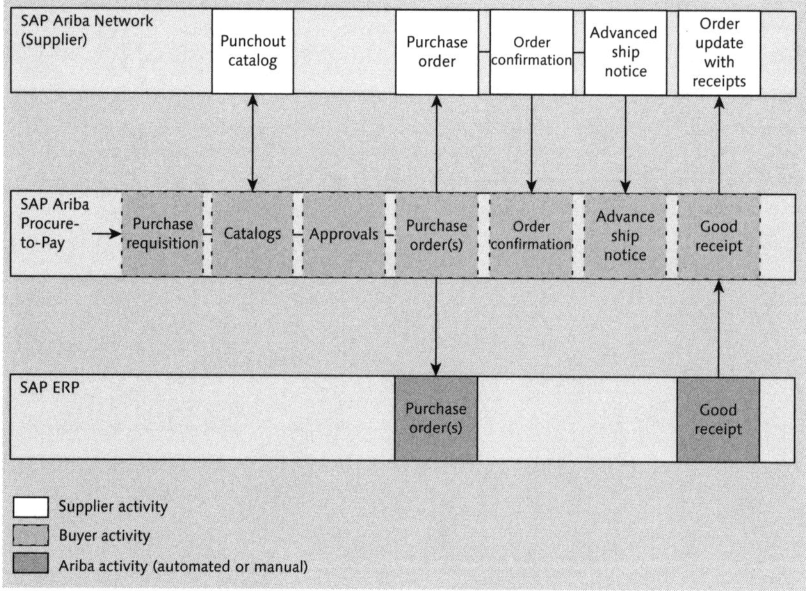

Figure 9.67 SAP Ariba P2O

In Figure 9.66 and Figure 9.67, multiple documents are required for integration: purchase order, goods receipt, and invoice need to be integrated from SAP Ariba P2P down to SAP, and a payment notification path for SAP Ariba P2P needs to be built from SAP ERP up to the SAP Ariba Network. The payment notification is not required for P2O, as payment is completed in SAP ERP.

In this section we reviewed different integration options for combining and augmenting SAP ERP processes with SAP Ariba. Many of these integrations have been built and are relatively turnkey to install and set up. Others are being built and will be standard in the future releases of the solutions. If you are planning on integrating with SAP ERP environments, especially customized ones, it is prudent to assess all of the integration points and identify interfaces as well as gaps with any existing/planned enhancements in either system.

9.5 Summary

This chapter outlined several integration options for pairing SAP's cloud portfolio solutions for procurement with SAP ERP environments. For both SAP Ariba and SAP Fieldglass, many of these integrations are being built and will be standard in future releases. While cloud solutions offer unprecedented savings in maintenance and ease-of-use, data and processes from on-premise ERP systems, such as SAP ERP, are oftentimes core to augmenting and completing processes in SAP Fieldglass and SAP Ariba. For integration, more and more of these linkages are being built and will be native out-of-box for future releases. However, just because it is an SAP cloud solution does not mean that it is completely integrated in all ways with SAP's on-premise solutions. For now, understanding your integration requirements and options for your project are key part for successfully realizing the end-to-end processes in SAP's cloud and on-premise solutions.

This chapter reviews the SAP Ariba and SAP Fieldglass solutions discussed in previous chapters of this book and offers some future predictions for the area of procurement.

10 Conclusion

SAP has invested billions of dollars in its procurement solution portfolio over the years. Over the last five years, with the acquisitions of Ariba and Fieldglass, SAP has invested more in cloud procurement solutions than in all previous years combined. As more transactions move to the cloud, the value of networks and flexible processes integrated with cloud networks will drive accelerated growth and efficiencies. SAP is uniquely positioned for this, having, with the SAP Ariba Network and its $750 billion transaction run rate, the largest business-to-business network of its kind, as well as a recognized leader in vendor management systems in SAP Fieldglass. From an install base standpoint, over 70 percent of transactions worldwide already touch an SAP system at some point during the transaction.

While the technologies supporting procurement transactions, as well as sheer volume of transactions, have evolved dramatically since the inception of computing (especially in the last five years) many of the processes and procurement scenarios have remained largely static. A company still needs to identify demand and then find, vet, and negotiate with suppliers, create contracts and/or purchase order agreements, take receipt of goods/services provided, process the invoice, and analyze performance. On the supplier side, a company needs to find the demand, negotiate terms with potential customers, obtain and fulfil orders and then submit an invoice. The technology underpinning these steps now includes real-time analytics of supplier/spend, automated processing of most orders once submitted, as well as massive networks to facilitate collaboration, document exchange, and new supplier identification.

10.1 Summary

Beginning with SAP Ariba Sourcing, SAP Ariba Discovery, and SAP Ariba Spot Quote, this book reviewed many of the SAP Ariba upstream solutions dedicated to finding and vetting the right supplier or supplier group. In this phase of the procurement cycle, ensuring you have the right partner for the transaction is paramount, both from a quality/delivery perspective, as well as the perennially important price standpoint. Leveraging the power of the SAP Ariba Network with its two-million suppliers and ready channels for posting and bidding, the SAP Ariba Network provides the platform for a successful RFx.

Another key part of SAP Ariba upstream solutions is contracts. SAP Ariba contracts takes the RFx award and turns it into something operational. An RFx award need not result in a verbatim contract or require the creation of new terms and conditions. With clause libraries and negotiation steps, SAP Ariba contracts takes contracts one step further than RFx follow on. With SAP Ariba Contract Management, there is a clause library from which to draw, defined terms and conditions negotiating steps, as well as operationalization of the contracts for procurement via SAP Ariba P2P and SAP APC.

Operational procurement equals SAP Ariba P2X and SAP Fieldglass for SAP cloud. In these areas, you can leverage the upstream sourcing and contract creation efforts into actual consumption. SAP Ariba P2X can integrate at both a system and process level with existing SAP ERP backend systems, allowing for invoice processing to occur in a different system for SAP Ariba P2O, and for the invoice to be processed via SAP Ariba in SAP Ariba P2P. SAP Ariba P2X also leverages a host of SAP Ariba tools to increase effectiveness, such as SAP Ariba Discovery, for identifying and onboarding new suppliers, to SAP Ariba Spot Buy, for obtaining one-off quotes in a straightforward manner during the sourcing of a requisition/shopping cart. SAP Ariba Procurement Content serves as the content repository for all catalog-related activities and items. SAP APC also functions as a basic shopping tool, allowing users to create shopping carts directly in SAP APC and drive the main parts of the shopping process for SAP APC.

SAP Fieldglass's vendor management system orchestrates contingent labor from both a procurement and HR standpoint, managing contract workers during all steps of the contingent labor process, from onboarding and work delivery to offboarding. SAP Fieldglass is a recent addition to the SAP solution portfolio, and follows the same approach as SAP Ariba for cloud integration scenarios, with additional integration points with HR systems. SAP Fieldglass fields its own supplier portal, in which suppliers submit invoices to customers and customers coordinate payments and collaborate on resourcing.

SAP Ariba Supplier Information and Performance Management (SIPM) helps SAP Ariba customers make sense of their supply base from a qualification and onboarding standpoint, and helps ensure ongoing performance analysis based on objective and subjective criteria. Having native integration to the SAP Ariba Network means SIPM can interface with suppliers and drive updates to supplier records in a "one-to-many" manner. Having consulting-driven integration to SAP ERP allows for the transfer of supplier masters to the backend systems. SIPM can essentially front end your supplier management activities, keeping things up-to-date in real time and distributing the relevant updates to backend systems to keep the supplier master in sync.

The SAP Ariba Network plays a significant role in tying the supplier updates together for SAP Ariba SIPM, and the SAP Ariba Network plays a similar role in other process steps of the SAP Ariba solution portfolio. From SAP Ariba P2P processes requiring sourcing via SAP Ariba Discovery, SAP Ariba Spot Buy and SAP Ariba Procurement Content updates managed by the supplier, to RFx and contracting, the SAP Ariba Network is the lynchpin supporting two-million plus suppliers and $750 billion in annual spend.

In addition to analyzing supplier performance in SAP Ariba SIPM, spend performance and visibility requires analysis on the transactional-side of the procurement equation. SAP Ariba Spend Visibility and SAP Ariba Spend Analysis offer a comprehensive suite of reports and analytics engines for understanding how your spending is tracking. The core engines in these solutions include data validation, supplier matching, rationalization, business rule, inference and machine learning. Custom commodity taxonomies, supplier diversity, and supplier risk management are optional add-ons.

A key takeaway from Chapter 8 is that decisions which initially appear straightforward based on a piece of analysis are not always as easy. Macro conditions can impact whether a negotiation proves successful. For example, a consolidated market may prevent significant discounts from being obtained where they otherwise would be. Cleansing data for analysis is also a key step that should be implemented prior to jumping to conclusions on the data. Supplier duplication and incorrect categorization of spend can create blind spots in analysis conducted too quickly.

Some cloud implementations are standalone and if this is your situation, then you could skip the chapter on integration (Chapter 9) of this book. SAP Ariba and SAP Fieldglass require integration when interfacing with SAP ERP environments. While many types of integrations with the SAP Ariba Network now come standard, or planned as such with SAP ERP systems, others require further tuning or outright building. The main packages for integration are cloud integration toolkits (CI-4, CI-5, and CI-6), the SAP Business Suite Add-On, the SAP Ariba Network Adapter, and several point-to-point integrations.

Cloud projects are different from traditional onsite software implementations. They require less of the formality and phase emphasis of an onsite implementation, as the architecture undergirding the application, as well as the application itself, are already in place. This enables businesses to focus faster on the value realization aspects of a project, rather than the technical. SAP Activate is the latest project management methodology for managing cloud projects, and should evolve with the solutions, much like the SAP's ASAP methodology did for on-premise.

A key element of procurement implementations is looking beyond the internal boxes and systems involved and making supplier enablement a core part of the project. Many software-minded projects forget or downplay this area, as supplier enablement is not immediately a must-have for standing up a system. However, once live, without supplier collaboration and participation, a system quickly fails to realize its project benefits for efficiency and automation. Without supplier participation, a procurement system is less than half as effective.

The project methodologies reviewed in this book incorporate a supplier enablement approach for this reason, and any future methodologies for procurement will need to keep this area in focus. With the SAP Ariba Network, the importance of onboarding suppliers becomes core to both the customer and the solution provider, as both the customer and SAP Ariba stand much to gain from having every supplier participating in the network.

10.2 The Future of Procurement Solutions

Over the last several years, procurement technologies have grown in leaps and bounds, while the processes of procurement have remained largely static. Similarly, technology in general evolves at a breakneck pace, while other areas such as adjudication and the legal realm move resoundingly slowly. The distance growing between these two areas creates immense pressures and the conditions for a tectonic-type earthquake when re-alignment does finally occur.

The view of a traditional supplier and customer relationship is also outdated. Customers and suppliers oftentimes interchange their roles during procurement or supply chain processes. Many suppliers are avid customers on the SAP Ariba Network, and leverage the network as a significant channel to move their goods and services.

With real-time analytics now at the heart of many SAP solutions, external as well as internal data can be used to form actionable insights for procurement. These insights are already coming at a velocity that benefits from machine-based responses, in order to act upon the information in time and realize the benefits uncovered in the information. Many of these scenarios already take place today in stock trading and online ad-buying, for example. Systems running complex algorithms make purchasing decisions in an automated fashion. Materials requirements planning (MRP) was a pre-cursor, in a sense, to these sophisticated buying systems. MRP automates the decision process to reorder points and inventory replenishment. The next-level MRP makes some of these re-order point decisions enriched with external market condition data and/or seasonal influences on price and availability.

Mobility and big data also will undoubtedly influence further innovations in procurement systems, as will the need for continued simplifications of processes. As consumers at home expect more and more to have similar user experiences at work, including in their procurement activities, user interfaces and processes will need further adaptation and streamlining to keep up the pace. SAP intends to remain the leader in this evolution in procurement systems, both on-premise and in the cloud. With SAP Ariba and SAP Fieldglass, SAP provides a comprehensive portfolio of cloud solutions for all scenarios in procurement. With the SAP Ariba Network, SAP has a platform with limitless possibilities for growth and further efficiencies.

The Author

Justin Ashlock has spent half of his more than 20-year career in technology at SAP America, serving as the lead consultant for hundreds of global SAP customer projects and engagements in procurement and logistics activities. Justin currently leads a procurement practice for SAP North America, focused on SAP Ariba upstream and downstream solutions, SAP Supplier Relationship Management (SRM), Materials Management (MM), as well as SAP CLM/Sourcing. He holds a Bachelor's Degree from the University of California, Berkeley, and a Master's Degree in Business Administration from the University of Notre Dame.

The Contributors

Rachith Srinivas is a technical consultant at SAP for procurement projects with more than 12 years of business technology experience and more than 8 years of SAP experience. He is also an expert in SAP Ariba cloud solutions such as SAP Ariba Contracts Management, SAP Ariba Sourcing Professional and SAP Ariba SIPM. He is a subject-matter expert in SAP on-premise procurement solutions such as SAP Sourcing/CLM, SAP MM (purchasing), and SAP SRM. He has implemented more than 50 SAP procurement projects, including SAP Ariba upstream implementations. Rachith has a master's degree in computer science and is currently pursuing a master's degree in business administration from the McCombs School of Business at the University of Texas, Austin.

Juan Barrera is a Director of SAP Ariba Consulting Services, responsible for the services delivery organization in the North America Western region, providing consulting to business and procurement leaders worldwide. An engineer based in San Jose, California, he has implemented SAP Ariba solutions on downstream, upstream, on-premise and on-demand. He has sought to identify the best practices in procurement and supply chains in North America, Europe and Asia, leveraging the SAP Ariba solutions. Juan holds a Bachelor's Degree from the Pontificia Universidad Javeriana in Colombia, and he has a lifelong fascination for how technology constantly changes and improves processes and businesses in today's collaborative and innovation-driven economy.

Index

A

D

J

K

L

M

N

O

P

Q

R

S

T

U

V

W

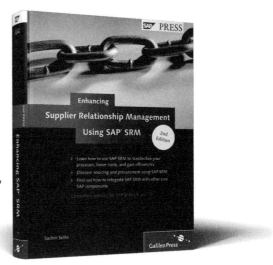

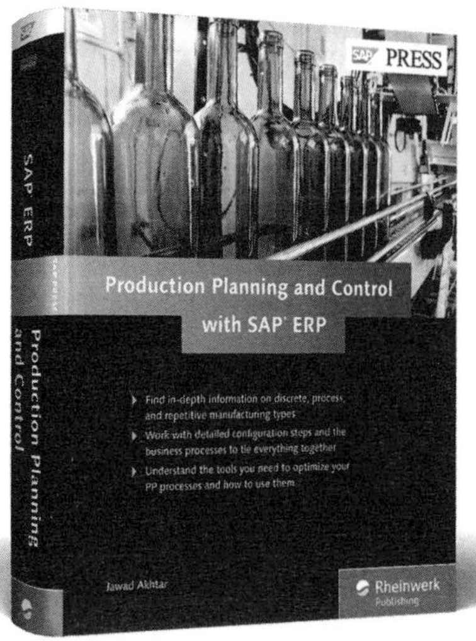

- Find in-depth information on discrete, process, and repetitive manufacturing types
- Work with detailed configuration steps and the business processes to tie everything together
- Understand the tools you need to optimize your PP processes and how to use them

Jawad Akhtar

Production Planning and Control with SAP ERP

Whether your company uses discrete, process, or repetitive manufacturing, this book is here to break down the different production planning processes in SAP ERP. You'll learn the common elements that are used by each process, and then explore the detailed configuration steps for each type of manufacturing approach. You'll increase the effectiveness of your supply chain, and save time and money with the help of expert tips throughout the book.

1040 pages, pub. 09/2013
E-Book: $59.99 | **Print:** $69.95 | **Bundle:** $79.99

www.sap-press.com/3645

www.sap-press.com

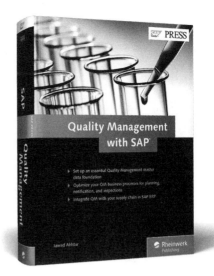

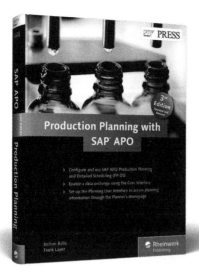